T0326388

Natural Resource Economics

Natural Resource Economics: The Essentials offers a policy-oriented approach to the increasingly influential field of natural resource economics that is based upon a solid foundation of economic theory and empirical research. Students will not only leave the course with a firm understanding of natural resource economics, but they will also be exposed to a number of case studies showing how underlying economic principles provided the foundation for specific natural resource policies. This key text highlights what insights can be derived from the actual experience.

Key features include:

- Extensive coverage of the major issues, including energy, recyclable resources, water policy, land conservation and management, forests, fisheries, other ecosystems, and sustainable development;
- Introductions to the theory and method of natural resource economics, including externalities, experimental and behavioral economics, benefit-cost analysis, and methods for valuing the services provided by the environment;
- Boxed "Examples" and "Debates" throughout the text, which highlight global cases and major talking points.

This second edition provides updated data, new studies, and more international examples. There is a considerable amount of new material, with a deeper focus on climate change. The text is fully supported with end-of-chapter summaries, discussion questions, and self-test exercises in the book, as well as a suite of supplementary digital resources, including multiple-choice questions, simulations, references, slides, and an instructor's manual. It is adapted from the 12th edition of the best-selling *Environmental and Natural Resource Economics* textbook by the same authors.

Tom Tietenberg is the Mitchell Family Professor of Economics Emeritus at Colby College, Maine, USA.

Lynne Lewis is Professor, Department of Agricultural and Resource Economics, Colorado State University, Colorado, USA and Elmer W. Campbell Professor of Economics Emeritus, Department of Economics, Bates College, Maine, USA.

Natural Resource Economics

The Essentials

Second Edition

Tom Tietenberg and Lynne Lewis

Routledge
Taylor & Francis Group

NEW YORK AND LONDON

Designed cover image: Steve Adams / Getty Images

Second edition published 2025
by Routledge
605 Third Avenue, New York, NY 10158

and by Routledge
4 Park Square, Milton Park, Abingdon, Oxon, OX14 4RN

Routledge is an imprint of the Taylor & Francis Group, an informa business

© 2025 Tom Tietenberg and Lynne Lewis

First edition published by Routledge 2020

Library of Congress Cataloging-in-Publication Data
Names: Tietenberg, Thomas H., author. | Lewis, Lynne, author.
Title: Natural resource economics : the essentials / Tom Tietenberg and Lynne Lewis.
Description: 2nd edition. | New York, NY : Routledge, [2025] | Includes bibliographical references and index.
Identifiers: LCCN 2024027204 | ISBN 9781032689098 (hardback) | ISBN 9781032689081 (paperback) | ISBN 9781032689111 (ebook)
Subjects: LCSH: Natural resources. | Natural resources--Government policy. | Environmental economics. | Environmental policy.
Classification: LCC HC85 .T56 2025 | DDC 333.7--dc23/eng/20240625
LC record available at https://lccn.loc.gov/2024027204

ISBN: 978-1-032-68909-8 (hbk)
ISBN: 978-1-032-68908-1 (pbk)
ISBN: 978-1-032-68911-1 (ebk)

DOI: 10.4324/9781032689111

Typeset in Sabon
by SPi Technologies India Pvt Ltd (Straive)

Access the Instructor and Student Resources: www.routledge.com/cw/Tietenberg

Contents in Brief

Contents in Full

Preface

A glance at any newspaper will confirm that environmental and natural resource economics is now a major player in environmental policy. Concepts such as cap-and-trade, renewable portfolio standards, block pricing, renewable energy credits, development impact fees, conservation easements, carbon trading, the commons, congestion pricing, corporate average fuel-economy standards, pay-as-you-throw, debt-for-nature swaps, extended producer responsibility, sprawl, leapfrogging, pollution havens, strategic petroleum reserves, payments for ecosystem services, and sustainable development have moved from the textbook to the legislative hearing room. As the large number of current examples in *Natural Resource Economics: The Essentials* (and its companion book *Environmental Economics: The Essentials*) demonstrates, not only are ideas that were once restricted to academic discussions now part of the policy mix, but they also are making a significant difference as well.

An Overview of the Book

Natural Resource Economics: The Essentials attempts to bring those who are beginning the study of natural resource economics close to the frontiers of knowledge. Although the book is designed to be accessible to students who have completed a two-semester introductory course in economics or a one-semester introductory microeconomics course, it has been used successfully in several institutions in lower-level and upper-level undergraduate courses as well as lower-level graduate courses.

The structure and topical coverage of this book facilitate its use in a variety of contexts. For a survey course in natural resource economics, all chapters are appropriate, although many instructors find that the book contains somewhat more material than can be adequately covered in a quarter or even a semester. This surplus material provides flexibility for the instructor to choose those topics that best fit their course design.

In this edition, we examine many market mechanisms within the context of both theory and practice. Environmental and natural resource economics is a rapidly growing and changing field as many environmental issues become global in nature. In this text, we tackle some of the complex issues that face our globe and explore both the nature of the problems and how economics can provide potential solutions.

This edition retains a strong policy orientation. Although a great deal of theory and empirical evidence is discussed, their inclusion is motivated by the desire to increase understanding of intriguing market situations and policy problems. This explicit integration of research and policy within each chapter avoids a problem frequently encountered in applied economics textbooks—that is, in such texts the theory developed in earlier chapters is often only loosely connected to the rest of the book.

This is an economics book, but it goes beyond economics. Insights from the natural and physical sciences, literature, political science, and other disciplines are scattered liberally throughout the text. In some cases, these references raise outstanding issues that economic analysis can help resolve, while in other cases they affect the structure of the economic analysis or provide a contrasting point of view. They play an important role in overcoming the tendency to accept the material uncritically at a superficial level by highlighting those characteristics that make the economics approach unique.

Intertemporal optimization is introduced using graphical two-period models, and all mathematics, other than simple algebra, is relegated to chapter appendices. Graphs and numerical examples provide an intuitive understanding of the principles suggested by the math and the reasons for their validity. In this edition, we have retained the strengths that are particularly valued by readers, while expanding the number of applications of economic principles, clarifying some of the more difficult arguments, and updating the material to include the very latest global developments.

Interested readers can also find advanced work in the field in journals including *Journal of the Association of Environmental and Resource Economics, Journal of Environmental Economics and Policy, Review of Environmental Economics and Policy, Land Economics, Journal of Environmental Economics and Management, Environmental and Resource Economics, International Review of Environmental and National Resource Economics, Environment and Development Economics, Resource and Energy Economics*, and *Natural Resources Journal*, among others.

A discussion list that involves material covered by this book is ResEcon. It is an academically inclined list focusing on problems related to environmental and natural resource management.

Very useful blog posts and podcasts that deal with issues in environmental economics and their relationship to policy are located at www.env-econ.net, rff.org, and https://www.resources.org/resources-radio.

For additional resources or to see the references for this book, visit the companion website of this text at www.routledge.com/cw/tietenberg. The site includes an online reference section with all the references cited in the book.

Acknowledgments

The most rewarding part of writing this book is that we have met so many thoughtful people. We very much appreciate the faculty and students who pointed out areas of particular strength or areas where coverage could be expanded. Their support has been gratifying and energizing. One can begin to understand the magnitude of our debt to our colleagues by glancing at the several hundred names in the lists of references. Because their research contributions make this an exciting field, full of insights worthy of being shared, our task was easier and a lot more fun than it might otherwise have been.

Working with Routledge has been a terrific experience. We especially want to thank our editors Chloe Herbert and Michelle Gallagher for their continued guidance and careful work with this book. We also thank our terrific copyeditor Andrea Klosterman Harris and production manager Aishwariya Madhana Shankar.

Lynne's most helpful research assistant for this edition was Drew Williams.

Working with all of the fine young scholars who have assisted with this text over the years has made it all the more obvious why teaching is the world's most satisfying profession.

Finally, Tom would like to express publicly his deep appreciation to his wife, Gretchen, his daughter Heidi, and his son Eric for their love and support. Lynne would like to express her gratitude to Jack for his unwavering support, patience, and generosity, and to Chuck Howe for starting her on this journey. This book is for you. She also thanks her many, many Bates College students who used, read, complained about, learned from, and appreciated this book. Thank you.

Tom Tietenberg
Lynne Lewis

PART I

Introduction to the Field of Natural Resource Economics

Chapter 1

Visions of the Future

Introduction

The Self-Extinction Premise

About the time the American colonies won independence, Edward Gibbon completed his monumental *The History of the Decline and Fall of the Roman Empire*. In a particularly poignant passage that opens the last chapter of his opus, he re-creates a scene in which the learned Poggius, a friend, and two servants ascend the Capitoline Hill after the fall of Rome. They are awed by the contrast between what Rome once was and what Rome has become:

> In the time of the poet it was crowned with the golden roofs of a temple; the temple is overthrown, the gold has been pillaged, the wheel of fortune has accomplished her revolution, and the sacred ground is again disfigured with thorns and brambles. . . . The forum of the Roman people, where they assembled to enact their laws and elect their magistrates is now enclosed for the cultivation of potherbs, or thrown open for the reception of swine and buffaloes. The public and private edifices that were founded for eternity lie prostrate, naked, and broken, like the limbs of a mighty giant; and the ruin is the more visible, from the stupendous relics that have survived the injuries of time and fortune.
>
> (Vol. 6, pp. 650–651)

What could cause the demise of such a grand and powerful society? Gibbon weaves a complex thesis to answer this question, suggesting ultimately that the seeds for Rome's destruction were sown by the Empire itself. Although Rome finally succumbed to such external forces as fires and invasions, its vulnerability was based upon internal weakness.

DOI: 10.4324/9781032689111-2

The premise that societies can germinate the seeds of their own destruction has long fascinated scholars.[1] In 1798, Thomas Malthus published his classic *An Essay on the Principle of Population*, in which he foresaw a time when the urge to reproduce would cause population growth to exceed the land's potential to supply sufficient food, resulting in starvation and death. In his view, the most likely response to this crisis would involve rising death rates caused by environmental constraints, rather than a recognition of impending scarcity followed either by innovation or by self-restraint.

Historically, our society has been remarkably robust, having survived wars and shortages, while dramatically increasing living standards and life expectancy. Yet, actual historical examples suggest that a self-extinction vision may in certain contexts sometimes have merit. Example 1.1 examines two specific cases: the Mayan civilization and Easter Island.

EXAMPLE 1.1

A Tale of Two Cultures

The Mayan civilization, a vibrant and highly cultured society that occupied parts of Central America, experienced a collapse. One of the major settlements, Copán, has been studied in sufficient detail to learn why it happened.

After AD 400, the population growth began to bump into an environmental constraint, specifically the agricultural carrying capacity of the land. The growing population depended heavily on a single, locally grown crop—maize—for food. By early in the sixth century, however, the carrying capacity of the most productive local lands was exceeded, and farmers began to depend upon more fragile parts of the ecosystem. Newly acquired climate data show that a two-century period with a favorable climate was followed by a general drying trend lasting four centuries that led to a series of major droughts. Food production failed to keep pace with the increasing population.

By the eighth and ninth centuries, the evidence reveals not only high levels of infant and adolescent mortality but also widespread malnutrition. The royal dynasty, an important source of leadership, collapsed rather abruptly sometime about AD 820–822.

The second case study, Easter Island, shares with this first tale some remarkable similarities to the Malthusian vision. Easter Island lies some 2000 miles off the coast of Chile. Current visitors note that it is distinguished by two features: (1) its enormous statues carved from volcanic rock and (2) a surprisingly sparse vegetation, given the island's favorable climate and conditions. Both the existence of these imposing statues and the fact that they were erected at a considerable distance from the quarry suggest the presence of an advanced civilization, but current observers see no sign of it. What happened? According to scholars, the short answer is that a rising population, coupled with a heavy reliance on wood for housing, canoe building, and statue transportation, decimated the forest (Brander and Taylor, 1998). The loss of the forest contributed to soil erosion, declining soil productivity, and, ultimately, diminished food production. How did the community react to the impending scarcity? Apparently, the social response was war among the remaining island factions over the diminished resources and, ultimately, cannibalism.

We would like to believe not only that in the face of impending scarcity societies would react by changing behavior to adapt to the diminishing resource supplies, but also that this benign response would follow automatically from a recognition of the problem. We even have a cliché to capture this sentiment: "necessity is the mother of invention." These stories suggest, however, nothing is automatic about a problem-solving response. As we shall see as this book unfolds, sometimes societies not only fail to solve the problem, but their reactions can actually intensify it.

Sources: Webster, D., Freter, A., & Golin, N. (2000). *Copan: The Rise and Fall of an Ancient Maya Kingdom*. Fort Worth, TX: Harcourt Brace Publishers; Brander, J. A., & Taylor, M. S. (1998). The simple economics of Easter Island: A Ricardo–Malthus model of renewable resource use. *The American Economic Review*, 88(1), 119–138; Turner, B. L., & Sabloff, J. A. (2012). Classic period collapse of the central Maya lowlands: Insights about human–environment relationships for sustainability. *Proceedings of the National Academy of Sciences*, 109(35), 13908–13914; Pringle, Heather. (November 9, 2012). Climate change had political, human impact on ancient Maya. *Science*, 730–731.

Future Environmental Challenges

Future societies are currently facing challenges arising from resource scarcity and accumulating pollutants. Some even argue that all the challenges combined could possibly pose an existential threat if not dealt with. Many specific examples of these broad categories of problems are discussed in detail in the following chapters, but in this section we can give a flavor of what is to come by illustrating the challenges posed by one pollution problem (climate change), one resource scarcity problem (water accessibility), and the overarching need to assure that any transition associated with meeting the challenges is carried out in a just manner.

The Climate Change Challenge

Energy from the sun drives the earth's weather and climate. Incoming rays heat the earth's surface, radiating heat energy back into space. Atmospheric "greenhouse" gases (methane, carbon dioxide, and other gases) trap some of the outgoing energy.

Without this natural "greenhouse effect," temperatures on the earth would be much lower than they are now and life as we know it would be impossible. It is possible, however, to have too much of a good thing. Problems arise when the concentration of greenhouse gases increases beyond normal levels, thus retaining excessive heat somewhat like a car with its windows closed in the summer.

Since the Industrial Revolution, greenhouse gas emissions have increased, considerably enhancing the heat-trapping capability of the earth's atmosphere. According to the U.S. Global Change Research Program (USGCRP) (2014):

Evidence from the top of the atmosphere to the depths of the oceans, collected by scientists and engineers from around the world, tells an unambiguous story: the planet is warming, and over the last half century, this warming has been driven primarily by human activity—predominantly the burning of fossil fuels.

As the earth warms, the consequences are expected to affect both humans and ecosystems. Humans are susceptible to increased heat, as shown by the thousands of deaths in Europe in the summer of 2022 from the abnormal heat waves. Human health can also be affected by diseases such as Lyme disease, which spread more widely as the earth warms. Rising sea levels (as warmer water expands and previously frozen glaciers melt), coupled with an increase in storm intensity, now force coastal communities to face larger, more economically damaging floods. Ecosystems will be subjected to unaccustomed temperatures; some species will adapt by migrating to new areas, but many others are not expected to be able to react in time. While these processes have already begun, they will intensify throughout the century in the absence of strategies to deal with these threats.

Dealing with the threats posed by climate change will require a coordinated international response. That is a significant challenge to a world system where the nation-state reigns supreme and international organizations are relatively weak. Economics can be very helpful in thinking about both the nature of that challenge and pathways for creating a corrective response.

The Water Accessibility Challenge

Another class of threats is posed by the interaction of a rising demand for resources in the face of a finite supply. Water provides a particularly important example because it is so vital to life.

According to the United Nations, about 40 percent of the world's population lives in areas with moderate-to-high water stress. ("Moderate stress" is defined in the U.N. Assessment of Freshwater Resources as "human consumption of more than 20 percent of all accessible renewable freshwater resources," whereas "severe stress" denotes consumption greater than 40 percent.) By 2025, it is estimated that about two-thirds of the world's population—about 5.5 billion people—will live in areas facing either moderate or severe water stress.

This stress is not uniformly distributed around the globe. For example, in parts of the United States, Mexico, China, and India, groundwater is already being consumed faster than it is being replenished, and aquifer levels are steadily falling. Some rivers, such as the Colorado in the western United States and the Yellow in China, often run dry before they reach the sea. Formerly enormous bodies of water, such as the Aral Sea and Lake Chad, are now a fraction of their once-historic sizes. Glaciers that feed many Asian rivers are shrinking.

The availability of potable water is further limited by human activities that contaminate the remaining supplies. Each day, nearly 1000 children die due to preventable water and sanitation-related diarrheal diseases.

Climate change is expected to intensify both the frequency and duration of droughts, simultaneously increasing the demand for water and reducing its supply. Example 1.2 explores both this interaction between water adequacy and climate change and why it matters.

Some arid areas have compensated for their lack of water by importing it via aqueducts from more richly endowed regions or by building large reservoirs. This solution can, however, promote conflict when the water transfer or the relocation of people living in the area to be flooded by the reservoir produces a political backlash. Additionally, aqueducts and dams may be geologically vulnerable. For example, in California, many of the aqueducts constructed to move water from more water-abundant areas to areas with more scarcity cross or lie on known earthquake-prone fault lines. Further,

EXAMPLE 1.2

Climate Change and Water Accessibility: The Linkage

From a policy analysis point of view, whether these challenges are independent or interdependent matters. If they are linked, their interactions must be considered in the design of any policies created to meet the challenges. Otherwise, the response may be neither efficient nor effective.

On May 3, 2016, the World Bank released a report that documents and analyzes the nature and economic implications of the linkages. It finds that climate change will intensify water scarcity, adding significant new economic impacts and security challenges to the mix. According to the report:

If current water management policies persist, and climate models prove correct, water scarcity will proliferate to regions where it currently does not exist, and will greatly worsen in regions where water is already scarce. Simultaneously, rainfall is projected to become more variable and less predictable, while warmer seas will fuel more violent floods and storm surges. Climate change will increase water-related shocks on top of already demanding trends in water use. Reduced freshwater availability and competition from other uses—such as energy and agriculture—could reduce water availability in cities by as much as two thirds by 2050, compared to 2015 levels.

(vi)

The report concludes:

While adopting policy reforms and investments will be demanding, the costs of inaction are far higher. The future will be thirsty and uncertain, but with the right reforms, governments can help ensure that people and ecosystems are not left vulnerable to the consequences of a world subject to more severe water-related shocks and adverse rainfall trends.

(ix)

Source: World Bank. (2016). *High and Dry: Climate Change, Water, and the Economy*. Washington, D.C.: World Bank. License: Creative Commons Attribution CC BY 3.0 IGO.

the reservoir behind the Three Gorges Dam in China is so vast that the pressure and weight from the stored water have caused tremors and landslides.

The Just Transition Challenge

Meeting the first two challenges as well as others such as threats to biodiversity[2] will require considerable changes in resource allocations. Can policies be devised to assure that the burdens associated with this transition are not borne disproportionally by any group of people, especially the most vulnerable?

For example, economic studies indicate that the damages triggered by a changing climate typically disproportionally affect poor nations more than rich nations (as a percent of their gross domestic product) and poor people more than rich people (as a percent of their income). Additionally, as access to water is diminished, the poor are disproportionately affected.

While we know that the benefits of those transitions (less climate damage and better access to water) will generally support meeting this challenge, how about the costs associated with making the transition? Can and will those costs be distributed fairly as well or will they be regressive?[3]

Individual policies or combinations of policies can be designed to fairly meet both the resource and pollution challenges in both an environmental and economic sense. However, that benign outcome is by no means either automatic or easy to achieve. In the chapters that follow we shall examine the role economics can play in designing approaches that are both efficient and fair.

The Policy Context

As the scale of economic activity has proceeded steadily upward, the scope of environmental problems triggered by that activity has transcended both geographic and generational boundaries. When the environmental problems were smaller in scale, the nation-state used to be a sufficient form of political organization for resolving them, but that is no longer the case. Whereas each generation used to have the luxury of being able to satisfy its own needs without worrying about the needs of generations to come, intergenerational effects are now more prominent. Solving problems such as poverty, climate change, and the loss of biodiversity requires international cooperation. Because unborn future generations cannot speak for themselves, the current generation must speak for them. Current policies must incorporate our obligation to future generations, however difficult or imperfect that incorporation might prove to be.

International cooperation is by no means a foregone conclusion. Global environmental problems can result in very different effects on countries that will sit around the negotiating table. Low-lying countries could be completely submerged by sea level rise, and arid nations could see their marginal agricultural lands succumb to desertification. Other nations may see agricultural productivity rise as warmer climates in traditionally intemperate regions support longer growing seasons.

Countries that unilaterally set out to improve the global environmental situation can run the risk of making their businesses vulnerable to competition from less conscientious nations. Industrialized countries that undertake stringent environmental policies may not suffer much at the national level due to offsetting increases in income and employment in industries that supply renewable, cleaner energy and pollution control equipment. Some specific industries facing stringent environmental regulations, however, may well face higher costs during the transition than their competitors, and can be expected to lose market share accordingly. Declining market share and employment resulting from especially stringent regulations and the threat of outsourced production are powerful influences on both individual and political behavior. The search for solutions must accommodate these concerns.

The market system is remarkably resilient in how it responds to challenges. As we shall see, prices provide incentives not only for the wise use of current resources, but also for promoting innovations that can broaden the menu of future options.

Yet, as we shall also see, market incentives are not always consistent with promoting fair, sustainable outcomes. Currently, many individuals and institutions have a large stake in maintaining the status quo, even when it may pose an existential threat. Fishermen harvesting their catch from an overexploited fishery are loath to reduce harvests, even when the reduction may be necessary to conserve the stock and to return the population to a healthy level. Farmers who depend on fertilizer and pesticide subsidies will give them up reluctantly. Coal companies resist attempts to reduce carbon emissions from coal-fired power plants.

How Will Societies Respond?

The fundamental question is how our society will respond to these challenges. One way to think systematically about this question involves feedback loops.

Positive feedback loops are those in which secondary effects tend to reinforce the basic trend. The process of capital accumulation illustrates one positive feedback loop. New investment generates greater output, which, when sold, generates profits. These profits can be used to fund additional new investments. Notice that with positive feedback loops, the process is self-reinforcing.

Positive feedback loops are also involved in climate change. Scientists believe, for example, that the relationship between emissions of methane and climate change may be described as a positive feedback loop. Because methane is a greenhouse gas, increases in methane emissions contribute to climate change. The resulting rise of the planetary temperature, however, triggers the release of extremely large quantities of additional methane that was previously trapped in the permafrost layer of the earth; the resulting larger methane emissions intensify the temperature increases, resulting in the release of more methane—a positive feedback.

Human behavior can also deepen environmental problems through positive feedback loops. When shortages of a commodity are imminent, for example, consumers typically begin to hoard the commodity. Hoarding intensifies the shortage. Similarly, people faced with shortages of food may be forced to eat the seed that is the key to more plentiful food in the future. Situations giving rise to this kind of downward spiral are particularly troublesome.

In contrast, a *negative feedback loop* is self-limiting rather than self-reinforcing. Perhaps the best-known planetary-scale example of a negative feedback loop is provided in a theory advanced by the English scientist James Lovelock. Called the *Gaia hypothesis*, after the Greek concept for Mother Earth, this view of the world suggests that the earth is a living organism with a complex feedback system that seeks an optimal physical and chemical environment. Deviations from this optimal environment trigger natural, nonhuman response mechanisms that restore the balance. In essence, according to the Gaia hypothesis, the planetary environment is characterized by some negative feedback loops and, therefore, is, **within limits**, a self-limiting, stable process.

As we proceed with our investigation, the degree to which our economic and political institutions serve to intensify or to limit emerging environmental problems, while assuring fair treatment, will be a key focus of our analysis.

The Role of Economics

How societies respond to challenges will depend largely on the behavior of humans acting individually or collectively. Economic analysis provides a useful set of tools for anyone interested in understanding and/or modifying human behavior, particularly in the face of scarcity. In many cases, this analysis points out the sources of the market system's resilience as embodied in negative feedback loops. In others, it provides a basis not only for identifying the circumstances where markets fail, but also for clarifying how and why that specific set of circumstances supports degradation. This understanding can then be used as the basis for designing new incentives that restore a sense of harmony in the relationship between the economy and the environment for those cases where the market fails.

Over the years, two different, but related, economic approaches have been devised to address the challenges the future holds. Debate 1.1 explores the similarities and the differences of ecological economics and environmental economics and what they both can bring to the table.

DEBATE 1.1

Ecological Economics versus Environmental Economics

Over several decades or so, the community of scholars dealing with the role of the economy and the environment has settled into two camps: ecological economics (www.isecoeco.org) and environmental economics (www.aere.org). Although they share many similarities, ecological economics is consciously more methodologically pluralist, while environmental economics is based solidly on the standard paradigm of neoclassical economics. While neoclassical economics emphasizes maximizing human welfare and using economic incentives to modify destructive human behavior, ecological economics uses a variety of methodologies, including neoclassical economics, depending upon the purpose of the investigation.

While some observers see the two approaches as competitive (presenting an "either–or" choice), others, including the authors of this text, see them as complementary. Complementarity, of course, does not mean full acceptance. Significant differences exist not only between these two fields, but also within them over such topics as the valuation of environmental resources, the impact of trade on the environment, and the appropriate means for evaluating policy strategies for long-duration problems such as climate change. These differences arise not only over the operative methodologies in each approach, but also over the values that are brought to bear on the analysis.

This book draws from both fields. Although the foundation for the analysis is environmental economics, the chapters draw heavily from ecological economics to critique that view when it is controversial and to complement it with useful insights drawn from outside the neoclassical paradigm, when appropriate. Pragmatism is the reigning criterion. If a particular approach or study helps us to understand environmental challenges and their resolution, it has been included in the text regardless of which field it came from.

The Use of Models

All topics covered in this book will be examined as part of the general focus on satisfying human wants and needs in light of limited environmental and natural resources. Because this subject is complex, it is better understood when broken into manageable portions. Once we master the components in individual chapters, we will be able to coalesce the individual insights into a more complete picture in the concluding chapter.

In economics, as in most other disciplines, we use models to investigate complex subjects such as relationships between the economy and the environment. Models are simplified characterizations of reality. Consider a familiar analogy. Maps, by design, leave out much detail. They are, nonetheless, useful guides to reality. By showing how various locations relate to each other, maps give an overall perspective. Although they cannot capture all unique details of particular locations, maps highlight those characteristics that are crucial for the purpose at hand.

The models in this text are similar. Through simplification, less detail is considered so that the main concepts and the relationships among them become more obvious.

Fortunately, models allow us to rigorously study issues that are interrelated and global in scale. Unfortunately, due to their selectivity, models may yield conclusions that are dead wrong. Details that are omitted may turn out, in retrospect, to be crucial for understanding a particular dimension. Therefore, models are useful abstractions, but the conclusions they yield depend on the structure of the model. As you shall see as you proceed though this book, change the model structure and you are likely to change the conclusions that flow from it. As a result, models should always be viewed with some caution.

Most people's views of the world are based on models, although frequently the assumptions and relationships involved may be implicit, perhaps even subconscious. In economics, the models are explicit; objectives, relationships, and assumptions are clearly specified so that the reader understands exactly how the conclusions are derived. The models are transparent.

The validity and reliability of economic models are tested by examining the degree to which they can explain actual behavior, not only in markets, but in other settings as well. An empirical field known as *econometrics* uses statistical techniques to derive key economic functions. These data-derived functions, such as cost curves or demand functions, can then be used for such diverse purposes as testing hypotheses about the effects of various water policies or forecasting future prices of solar panels.

Examining human behavior in a non-laboratory setting, however, poses special challenges because it is nearly impossible to control completely for all the various factors that influence an outcome beyond those of primary interest. The search for more control over the circumstances that provide the data we use to understand human behavior has given rise to the use of another complementary analytical approach—*experimental economics* (see Example 1.3). Together, econometrics and experimental economics can provide different lenses to help us understand human behavior and its impact on the world around us.

The Road Ahead

Are current societies on a self-destructive path? In part, the answer depends on whether climatic change and human behavior are perceived as a positive or a negative feedback loop. If increasing scarcity results in a behavioral response that involves a positive feedback loop (intensifies the pressure on the environment), pessimism is justified. If, on the other hand, human responses serve to reduce those pressures or could be reformed to reduce those pressures, optimism may be justified.

Not only does environmental and natural resource economics provide a firm basis for understanding the behavioral sources of environmental problems, but it also provides a firm foundation for crafting specific solutions to them. In subsequent chapters, for example, you will be exposed to how economic analysis can be (and has been) used to forge solutions to many diverse environmental challenges. Many of the solutions are quite novel.

Market forces are extremely powerful. Attempts to solve environmental problems that ignore these forces run a high risk of failure. Where normal market forces are compatible with efficient, just, and sustainable outcomes, those outcomes can be supported and reinforced. Where normal market forces prove inefficient, unsustainable, or unfair they can be channeled into new directions that restore compatibility between outcomes and multifaceted objectives. Environmental and natural resource economics provide a specific set of directions for how this compatibility between goals and outcomes can be achieved.

EXAMPLE 1.3

Experimental Economics: Studying Human Behavior in a Laboratory and in the Field

The appeal of experimental economics is based upon its ability to study human behavior in a more controlled setting. During the mid-twentieth century economists began to design controlled laboratory experiments with human subjects. The experimental designs mimic decision situations in a variety of settings. Participants are informed of the rules of the experiment and asked to make choices. By varying the treatments faced by participants in these controlled settings experimenters can study how the treatments affect both choices and collective outcomes.

Consider one policy example of how these methods have been used in resource policy (Cummings et al., 2004). In April 2000, the Georgia legislature passed The Flint River Drought Protection Act, which required the state to hold an auction in drought years to pay some farmers to suspend irrigation. The purpose was to use a market mechanism to identify the farmers who could forgo irrigation at the lowest cost and to fairly compensate them for their reduction in water use. With time running short to implement this act, state policymakers relied upon laboratory experiments designed by a team of economists, using local farmers as participants. The results were used to inform the process of choosing the specific auction design that was used to fulfill the requirements of this act.

To the extent that the results of experiments such as these have proved to be replicable, they have created a deeper understanding about the effectiveness of markets, policies, and institutions. The large and growing literature on experimental economics both in the lab and in the field (OECD, 2017) has already shed light on such widely divergent topics as the effectiveness of alternative policies for controlling pollution and allocating water, how uncertainty affects choices, and how the nature of cooperative agreements affects the sustainability of shared natural resources. Over the years this approach has provided valuable information that can complement what we have learned from observed behavior using econometrics.

Sources: OECD. (2017). *Tackling Environmental Problems with the Help of Behavioural Insights*, Paris: OECD Publishing, https://doi.org/10.1787/9789264273887-en; Cummings, R. G., & Taylor, L. O. (2001/2002). Experimental economics in natural resource and environmental management. In H. Folmer and T. Tietenberg (Eds.), *The International Yearbook of Environmental and Natural Resource Economics*. Cheltenham, U.K.: Edward Elgar, 123–149; Cummings, Ronald G., Holt, Charles A., & Laury, Susan K. (2004). Using laboratory experiments for policymaking: An example from the Georgia irrigation reduction auction. *Journal of Policy Analysis and Management*, 23(2), 341–363.

Some Overarching Questions to Guide Our Investigation

As we look to the future, optimists see a continued prosperity based upon institutional responses that effectively meet all challenges in a timely manner, while pessimists see the current challenges as sufficiently different in scope and scale as to raise doubts about our ability to deal with them fairly and in time.

As we sort through this complex interaction of challenges, potential ways of meeting them, and choices that prove to be efficient, fair, and feasible, some questions to guide our inquiry will prove helpful. These include:

- How does the economic system respond to scarcities? Is the process mainly characterized by positive or negative feedback loops? Do the responses intensify or ameliorate any initial scarcities? Does the answer depend upon the decision context?
- To what extent can the market meet the challenges on its own? To what extent are there sources of market failure that make the market an insufficient or even counterproductive force in meeting environmental challenges?
- What is the role of the political system in correcting these sources of market failure? In what circumstances is government intervention necessary? What forms of government intervention would work best to meet the challenges? Do these forms have enough political support to be enacted?
- What specific roles are appropriate for the executive, legislative, and judicial branches of government? What are the appropriate roles for nongovernmental organizations?
- Many environmental problems are characterized by uncertainty about the severity of the problem and the effectiveness of possible solutions. Can our economic and political institutions respond to this uncertainty in reasonable ways or does uncertainty become a paralyzing force?
- Can the economic and political systems work together to respect our obligations to future generations while assuring that the transition involves fair treatment of the transitional generations as well? Or do our obligations to future generations inevitably conflict with the desire to treat all people, especially the most vulnerable, with fairness?
- Can short- and long-term goals be harmonized? Is sustainable development feasible? If so, how can it be achieved? What does the need for sustainable outcomes imply about the future of economic activity in the industrialized nations? In the less-industrialized nations?

The rest of this book, *Essentials of Natural Resource Economics*, and its companion book (*Essentials of Environmental Economics*), use economic analysis and evidence to suggest answers to these complex questions.

In the following chapters you will study the rich and rewarding field of natural resource economics. The menu of topics is broad and varied. Economics provides a powerful analytical framework for examining the relationships between the environment, on one hand, and the economic and political systems, on the other. The study of economics can assist in identifying circumstances that give rise to environmental problems, discovering behavioral causes of these problems, and using information about the behavioral causes to craft solutions. Each chapter introduces a unique topic in natural resource economics, while the overarching focus on development in an environment characterized by scarcity weaves these topics into a single theme.

We begin by comparing perspectives being brought to bear on these problems by both economists and noneconomists. The way scholars in various disciplines view problems and potential solutions depends on how they organize the available facts, how they interpret those facts, and what kinds of values they apply in translating these interpretations into policy. Before going into a detailed look at environmental problems, we shall compare the ideology of conventional economics to other prevailing ideologies in the natural and social sciences. This comparison not only explains why reasonable people may, upon examining the same set of facts, reach different conclusions, but also it conveys some sense of the strengths and weaknesses of economic analysis as it is applied to environmental and natural resource problems.

We then delve more deeply into the economic approach, highlighting many of the tools used by environmental economists including benefit-cost analysis, cost-effectiveness analysis, and methods available for monetizing nonmarket goods and services. Specific evaluation criteria are defined, and examples are developed to show how these criteria can be applied to current environmental problems.

We then turn to some of the topics traditionally falling within the subfield known as natural resource economics. The topics covered in these chapters include managing ecological resources such as coral reefs, pollinators, wetlands, and endangered species; managing water, a resource that combines renewable and depletable sources; managing spatially fixed resources such as land; managing storable resources such as forest; and managing especially vulnerable renewable resources such as fisheries. We also examine the topic of energy policy and adaption to climate change.

Following this examination of the economic dimensions of the individual environmental and natural resource problems and the successes and failures of policies that have been used and are being used to manage these individual natural resource problems, we return to the big picture. Sustainable development is the international community's overarching plan to ensure that all human beings from present to future generations can enjoy prosperous and fulfilling lives while ensuring that all progress occurs in harmony with nature. Specifically, we examine the evolution of this concept over time and the challenges it faces, as well as the current plans that flow from it and a status report on progress to date in attaining these lofty goals.

Summary

Are our institutions so myopic that they have chosen a path that can only lead to the destruction of society as we now know it? The pessimistic view is based upon the likelihood of exceeding the capacity of the planet to provide and sustain a rising standard of living as the population and the level of economic activity grow if some risk-reducing actions are not taken. The optimistic view sees increased information about the challenges and the expanding array of options to meet them as triggering sufficiently powerful changes in incentives and increases in technological progress to bring further abundance, not deepening scarcity.

As we engage in the process of validating or refuting different components of these visions, we have identified questions that can guide our assessment of what the future holds. Seeking the answers requires that we accumulate a much better understanding about how choices are made in economic and political systems and how those choices affect, and are affected by, the natural environment. We begin that process in Chapter 2, where the economic approach is developed in broad terms and is contrasted with other conventional approaches.

Discussion Questions

1. In his book *The Ultimate Resource*, economist Julian Simon makes the point that calling the resource base "finite" is misleading. To illustrate this point, he uses a yardstick, with its one-inch markings, as an analogy. The distance between two markings is finite—one inch—but an infinite number of points is contained within that finite space. Therefore, in one sense, what lies between the markings is finite, while in another, equally meaningful sense, it is infinite. Is the concept of a finite resource base useful or not? Why or why not?

2. This chapter describes two views of the future. Since the validity of these views cannot be completely tested until the time period of concern has passed (so that predictions can be matched against actual events), how can we ever hope to establish *in advance* which view is better? What criteria might be proposed for evaluating predictions?

3. Positive and negative feedback loops lie at the core of systematic thinking about the future. As you examine the key forces shaping the future, what examples of positive and negative feedback loops can you uncover?

4. Which point of view (optimistic or pessimistic) do you find more compelling? Why? What logic or evidence do you find most supportive of that position?

5. How specifically might the interdependence of the water accessibility and climate change challenges affect the design of policies enacted to meet these challenges? Give some specific examples of how well-designed policies might differ in the interdependence case compared to the independence case.

6. In his book *Thank you for Being Late: An Optimist's Guide to Thriving in the Age of Accelerations*, Thomas L. Friedman documents how the digital revolution is fundamentally changing life as we have known it. How do you think it will change the relationship between humans and the environment? Is this likely to be a force for renewed harmony or intensified disruption? Why? Do you have any specific examples to share that illustrate one outcome or the other?

Self-Test Exercise

1. Does the normal reaction of the price system to a resource shortage provide an example of a positive or a negative feedback loop? Why?

Notes

1 For two rather different takes on the evidence see, for example, J. A. Tainter. (1988). *The Collapse of Complex Societies* (New York: Cambridge University Press) and G. D. Middleton. (2017). *Understanding Collapse: Ancient History and Modern Myths* (New York: Cambridge University Press).
2 Intergovernmental Science-Policy Platform on Biodiversity and Ecosystem Services. (2019). Summary for policymakers of the global assessment report on biodiversity and ecosystem services of the Intergovernmental Science-Policy Platform on Biodiversity and Ecosystem Services. S. Díaz, J. Settele, E. S. Brondízio, H. T. Ngo, M. Guèze, J. Agard, A. Arneth, P. Balvanera, K. A. Brauman, S. H. M. Butchart, K. M. A. Chan, L. A. Garibaldi, K. Ichii, J. Liu, S. M. Subramanian, G. F. Midgley, P. Miloslavich, Z. Molnár, D. Obura, A. Pfaff, S. Polasky, A. Purvis, J. Razzaque, B. Reyers, R. Roy Chowdhury, Y. J. Shin, I. J. Visseren-Hamakers, K. J. Willis, and C. N. Zayas (Eds.). Bonn, Germany: IPBES secretariat. https://doi.org/10.5281/zenodo.3553579.
3 An allocation of costs is said to be regressive if it consumes a larger proportion of their income for lower-income households than for higher-income households.

Further Reading

Banzhaf, S., Ma, L., & Timmins, C. (2019). Environmental justice: The economics of race, place and pollution. *Journal of Economic Perspectives*, *33(1)* (Winter), 185–208. This work provides a thorough review of the environmental justice literature related to the siting of toxic facilities, particularly where it intersects the work of economists

Barrett, S. (May 2016). Collective action to avoid catastrophe: When countries succeed, when they fail, and why? *Global Policy*: Special Issue: Too Big to Handle: Interdisciplinary Perspectives on the Question of Why Societies Ignore Looming Disasters, 45–55. Using the logic of economic game theory and focusing mainly on climate change, this article identifies circumstances that would cause rational players to fail to avoid a catastrophe, even when avoidance is in their collective interest. It also identifies circumstances that would cause rational players to act in concert to avert a catastrophe. (Game theory is the study of the ways in which interacting choices among economic agents can produce cooperative and noncooperative outcomes depending upon the context. We shall explore the insights from this technique later in the book.)

Batabyal, A. A., & Nijkamp, P. (2011). Introduction to research tools in natural resource and environmental economics. In A. A. Batabyal & P. Nijkamp (Eds.), *Research Tools in Natural Resource and Environmental Economics*. Hackensack, N.J.: World Scientific Publishing, 3–26. An introduction to frequently used theoretical, empirical, experimental, and interdisciplinary research tools in natural resource and environmental economics.

Levin, S. A., Anderies, J. M., Adger, N. et al. (2022). Governance in the face of extreme events: Lessons from evolutionary processes for structuring interventions, and the need to go beyond. *Ecosystems*, 25(3), 697–711, https://doi.org/10.1007/s10021-021-00680-2. This paper explores approaches to prevention, mitigation, and adaptation, drawing inspiration from how evolutionary challenges have made biological systems robust and resilient, and from the general theory of complex adaptive systems. It argues that proactive steps that go beyond the norm will be necessary to reduce unacceptable consequences.

Managi, S. (Ed.). (2015). *The Routledge Handbook of Environmental Economics in Asia*. New York: Routledge. An edited collection of essays that illustrates how the principles and methods of environmental economics can be applied to specific environmental and natural resource issues in Asia.

Repetto, R. (Ed.). (2006). *Punctuated Equilibrium and the Dynamics of U.S. Environmental Policy*. New Haven, C.T.: Yale University Press. A sophisticated discussion of how positive and negative feedback mechanisms can interact to produce environmental policy stalemates or breakthroughs.

Segerson, K. (2019). On the role of theory in contemporary environmental and natural resource economics. *Review of Environmental Economics and Policy*, 13(1), 124–129. Examines the relative roles of theoretical and empirical analysis over the past several decades, finding a diminished focus on theoretical analysis and a concurrent increase in an emphasis on empirical analysis. The author calls for retaining a balance between the two.

Spash, C. (2017). *The Routledge Handbook of Ecological Economics*. New York: Routledge. Edited by a leading figure in the field, this handbook provides a current guide to the literature on ecological economics in an informative and easily accessible form.

Stavins, R. (Ed.). (2019). *Economics of the Environment: Selected Readings*, 7th ed. Cheltenham, U.K.: Edward Elgar Publishing Ltd. An excellent set of complementary readings that captures both the power of the discipline and the controversy it provokes.

Additional references and historically significant references are available on this book's Companion Website: www.routledge.com/cw/Tietenberg

Chapter 2

The Economic Approach

Property Rights, Externalities, and Environmental Problems

Introduction

Before examining specific environmental problems and the policy responses to them, it is important that we develop and clarify the economic approach, so that we have some sense of the forest before examining each of the trees. Having a feel for the conceptual framework makes it easier not only to deal with individual cases but also, perhaps more importantly, to see how they fit into a comprehensive approach.

In this chapter, we develop the general economics conceptual framework as it applies to environmental and natural resource problems. We begin by examining the relationship between human actions, as manifested through the economic system, and the environmental consequences of those actions. We then establish criteria for judging the desirability of the outcomes of this relationship. These criteria provide a basis for identifying the nature and severity of environmental problems and a foundation for designing effective policies to deal with them.

Throughout this chapter, the economic point of view is contrasted with alternative points of view. These contrasts bring the economic approach into sharper focus and stimulate deeper and more critical thinking about all possible approaches.

The Human–Environment Relationship

The Economic Approach

Two different types of economic analysis can be applied to increase our understanding of the relationship between the economic system and the environment: *positive* economics attempts to describe *what is*, *what was*, or *what will be*. *Normative* economics, by contrast, deals with what *ought to be*. Disagreements within positive economics

DOI: 10.4324/9781032689111-3

can usually be resolved by an appeal to the facts. Normative disagreements, however, involve value judgments.

Both branches are useful. Suppose, for example, we want to investigate the relationship between trade and the environment. Positive economics could be used to describe the kinds of impacts trade would have on the economy and the environment. It could not, however, provide any guidance on the question of whether trade was desirable. That judgment would have to come from normative economics, a topic we explore in the next section.

The fact that positive analysis does not, by itself, determine the desirability of some policy action does not mean that it is not useful in the policy process. Example 2.1 provides one historical example of the kinds of economic impact analyses that are used in the policy process.

EXAMPLE 2.1

Economic Impacts of Reducing Hazardous Pollutant Emissions from Iron and Steel Foundries

The U.S. Environmental Protection Agency (EPA) was tasked with developing a "maximum achievable control technology standard" to reduce emissions of hazardous air pollutants from iron and steel foundries. As part of the early rule-making process, the EPA conducted an *ex ante* economic impact analysis to assess the potential economic impacts of the proposed rule.

If implemented, the rule would require some iron and steel foundries to implement pollution control methods that would increase the production costs at affected facilities. The interesting question addressed by the analysis is how large those impacts would be.

The impact analysis estimated annual costs for existing sources to be $21.73 million. These cost increases were projected to result in small increases in output prices. Specifically, prices were projected to increase by only 0.1 percent for iron castings and 0.05 percent for steel castings. The impacts of these price increases were expected to be experienced largely by iron foundries using cupola furnaces as well as consumers of iron foundry products. Unaffected domestic foundries and foreign producers of coke were projected to earn slightly higher profits from the rule.

This analysis helped regulators in two ways. First, by showing that the impacts fell under the $100 million threshold that mandates review by the Office of Management and Budget, the analysis eliminated the need for a much more time- and resource-consuming analysis. Second, by showing how small the expected impacts would be, it served to lower the opposition that might have arisen from unfounded fears of much more severe impacts.

Sources: Office of Air Quality Planning and Standards, United States Environmental Protection Agency. (November 2002). *Economic Impact Analysis of Proposed Iron and Steel Foundries*. NESHAP Final Report; National Emissions Standards for Hazardous Air Pollutants for Iron and Steel Foundries. (April 17, 2007). Proposed Rule. *Federal Register*, 72(73), 19150–19164.

A rather different context can arise when the possibilities are more open ended. For example, we might ask how much we should control emissions of greenhouse gases (which contribute to climate change), and how should we achieve that degree of control? Or, we might ask, how much forest of various types should be preserved? Answering these questions requires us to consider the entire range of possible outcomes and to select the best or optimal one. Although that is a much more difficult question to answer than one that asks us only to compare two predefined alternatives, the basic normative analysis framework used in economics is the same in both cases. That framework is explained in the next section.

Economic Efficiency

Static Efficiency

The chief normative economic criterion for choosing among various outcomes occurring at the same point in time is called *static efficiency*, or merely *efficiency*. *Efficiency* is not the only criterion for choosing among outcomes; *equity* is also an important criterion. To start our analysis, however, we will focus on the definition and measurement of efficiency. An allocation of resources is said to satisfy the static efficiency criterion if the economic surplus derived from those resources is maximized by that allocation. Economic surplus, in turn, is the sum of consumer surplus and producer surplus.

Consumer surplus is the value that consumers receive from an allocation minus what it costs them to obtain it. Consumer surplus is measured as the area under the demand curve minus the consumer cost. This is the shaded triangle in Figure 2.1. The cost to the consumer is the area under the price line, bounded from the left by the vertical axis and the right by the quantity of the good. This rectangle, which captures price times quantity, represents consumer expenditure on this quantity of the good.

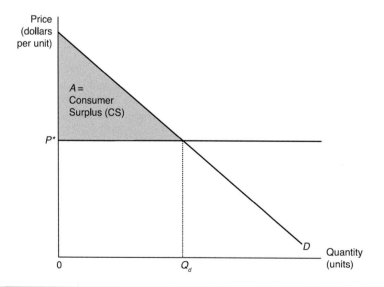

Figure 2.1 The Consumer's Choice.

Why is the area above the price line thought of as a surplus? For each quantity purchased, the corresponding point on the market demand curve represents the amount of money consumers would have been willing to pay for the last unit of the good. The *total willingness to pay* for some quantity of this good—say, three units—is the sum of the willingness to pay for each of the three units. Thus, the total willingness to pay for three units would be measured by the sum of the consumer willingness to pay for the first, second, and third units, respectively. It is now a simple extension to note that the total willingness to pay is the area under the continuous market demand curve to the left of the allocation in question. For example, in Figure 2.1, the total willingness to pay for Q_d units of the commodity is the total area under the demand curve up to Q_d. Thus, it is the shaded triangle of consumer surplus plus the rectangle of cost. Total willingness to pay is the concept we shall use to define the total value consumers would receive from the amount of the good purchased. Thus, the total value consumers would receive is equal to the area under the market demand curve from the origin to the purchased quantity. Consumer surplus is thus the excess of total willingness to pay minus the actual expenditure.

Meanwhile, sellers face a similar choice (see Figure 2.2). Given price P^*, the seller maximizes their own producer surplus by choosing to sell Q_s units. The *producer surplus* is designated by the shaded area B, the area under the price line that lies above the marginal cost curve (supply curve S), bounded from the left by the vertical axis and the right by the quantity of the good. To calculate producer or consumer surplus, notice that as long as the functions are linear (as they are in Figures 1 and 2), each area is represented as a right triangle. Remember that the area of a right triangle is calculated as $1/2 \times$ the base of the triangle $\times$ the height of the triangle. Using this formula, try calculating these areas in the first self-test exercise at the end of this chapter.

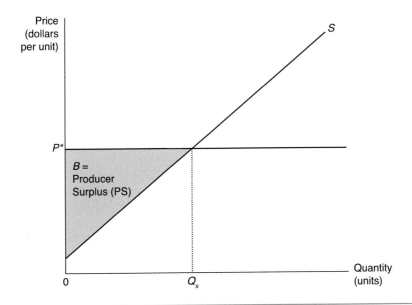

Figure 2.2 **Producer Surplus.**

Property Rights

Property Rights and Efficient Market Allocations

The way producers and consumers use environmental resources depends on the property rights governing those resources. In economics, *property rights* refers to a bundle of entitlements defining the owner's rights, privileges, and limitations for use of the resource. These property rights can be vested with individuals, groups, or the state. By examining such entitlements and how they affect human behavior, we will better understand how environmental problems arise from government and market allocations.

Efficient Property Rights Structures

How can we tell when the pursuit of profits is consistent with efficiency and when it is not?

Let's begin by describing the structure of property rights that could produce efficient allocations in a well-functioning market economy. An efficient structure has three main characteristics:

1. *Exclusivity*—All benefits and costs accrued from owning and using the resources should accrue to the owner, and only to the owner, either directly or indirectly by sale to others.
2. *Transferability*—All property rights should be transferable from one owner to another in a voluntary exchange.
3. *Enforceability*—Property rights should be secure from involuntary seizure or encroachment by others.

An owner of a resource with a well-defined property right (one exhibiting these three characteristics) has a powerful incentive to use that resource efficiently because a decline in the value of that resource represents a personal loss. Farmers who own the land have an incentive to nurture it because the resulting increased production raises income. Similarly, they have an incentive to rotate crops when that raises the productivity of their land.

When well-defined property rights are exchanged, as in a competitive market economy, this exchange facilitates efficiency. We can illustrate this point by examining the incentives consumers and producers face when a system of well-defined property rights is in place for a particular set of objects. Because the seller has the right to prevent the consumer from owning the objects in the absence of payment, the consumer must pay to acquire any of the objects. Given a market price, the consumer decides how much to purchase by choosing the amount that maximizes their individual consumer surplus.

Is this allocation efficient? According to our definition of static efficiency, it is. The economic surplus is maximized by the market allocation and, as seen in Figure 2.3, it is equal to the sum of consumer and producer surpluses (areas $A + B$). Thus, we have not only established a procedure for measuring efficiency, but also a means of describing how the surplus is distributed between consumers and producers.

Efficiency is *not* achieved because consumers and producers are seeking efficiency. They aren't! In a system with well-defined property rights and competitive markets in

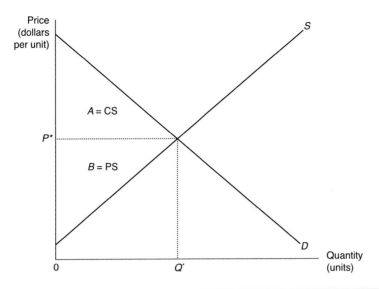

Figure 2.3 Market Equilibrium.

which to sell those rights, producers try to maximize their surplus and consumers try to maximize their surplus. The price system, then, induces those self-interested parties to make choices that also turn out to be efficient from the point of view of society as a whole. In this set of circumstances it channels the energy motivated by self-interest into socially productive paths.

Familiarity may have dulled our appreciation, but it is noteworthy that a system designed to produce a harmonious and congenial outcome could function effectively while allowing consumers and producers so much individual freedom in making choices.

Producer Surplus, Scarcity Rent, and Long-Run Competitive Equilibrium

Since the area under the price line is total revenue, and the area under the marginal cost (or supply) curve is total variable cost, producer surplus is related to profits. In the short run when some costs are fixed, producer surplus is equal to profits plus fixed cost. In the long run when all costs are variable, producer surplus is equal to profits plus rent, the return to scarce inputs owned by the producer. As long as new firms can enter profitable industries without raising the prices of purchased inputs, long-run profits and rent will equal zero.

Scarcity Rent. Most natural resource industries, however, do give rise to rent and, therefore, producer surplus is not eliminated by competition, even with free entry. This producer surplus, which persists even in long-run competitive equilibrium, is called *scarcity rent*.

David Ricardo (1772–1823) was the first economist to recognize the existence of scarcity rent. Ricardo suggested that the price of land was determined by the least fertile marginal unit of land. Since the price had to be sufficiently high to allow the poorer (less productive) land to be brought into production, other, more productive land could be farmed at an economic profit. Competition could not erode that profit because the amount of high-quality land was limited,- and lower prices would serve only to reduce the supply of land below the demand for it. The only way to expand production would be to bring additional, less fertile land (more costly to farm) into production; consequently, additional production does not lower prices, as it would if all land were equally productive.

Externalities as a Source of Market Failure

The Concept Introduced

Exclusivity, one of the chief characteristics of an efficient property rights structure, is frequently violated in practice. One broad class of violations occurs when an economic agent does not bear all of the consequences of their action.

Suppose two firms are located by a river. The first produces steel, while the second, somewhat downstream, operates a resort hotel. Both use the river, although in different ways. The steel firm uses it as a receptacle for its waste, while the hotel uses it to attract customers seeking water recreation. If these two facilities have different owners, an efficient use of the water is not likely to result.

Because the steel plant does not bear the cost of reduced business at the resort resulting from waste being dumped into the river, it is not likely to be very sensitive to that cost in its decision making. As a result, it could be expected to dump an inefficiently large amount of waste into the river.

This situation is called an externality. An *externality* exists whenever the welfare of some agent, typically a firm or household, affects not only their activities, but also activities under the control of some other agent. In this example, the increased waste in the river imposed an external cost on the resort. Since the steel firm did not pay that cost, it was not part of the firm's decision making.

The effect of this external cost on the steel industry is illustrated in Figure 2.4, which shows the market for steel. Steel production produces pollution as well as steel.

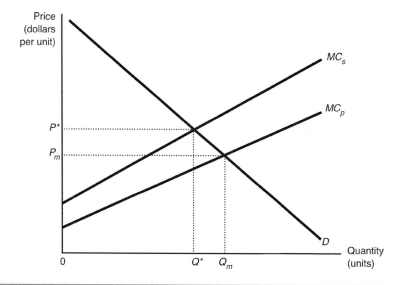

Figure 2.4 The Market for Steel.

The demand for steel is shown by the demand curve D, and the private marginal cost of producing the steel (i.e., exclusive of pollution control and damage) is depicted as MC_p. Because society (including the resort and the steel mill) considers both the cost of pollution and the cost of producing the steel, the social marginal cost function (MC_s) includes both.

If the steel industry faced no outside control on its emission levels, it would seek to produce Q_m. That choice, in a competitive setting, would maximize its private producer surplus. But that is clearly not efficient, since the net benefit is maximized at Q^*, not Q_m. Can you see the loss in net benefits that makes it inefficient? This kind of loss, called a "deadweight loss," arises whenever marginal social costs are not equal to marginal social benefits. In this case, at the profit-maximizing market allocation, marginal social costs are higher than marginal benefits, because the damage caused by the polluter was not borne by the polluter.

With the help of Figure 2.4, we can draw several conclusions about market allocations of commodities causing pollution externalities:

1. The amount of the commodity produced is inefficiently large.
2. Too much pollution is produced.
3. The prices of products responsible for pollution are inefficiently low.
4. As long as the costs remain external to the producer, no incentives to search for ways to reduce pollution per unit of output are introduced by the market.
5. Recycling and reuse of the polluting substances are discouraged because release into the environment is so inefficiently cheap.

The effects of a market imperfection for even one commodity end up affecting several related demands. These include purchases of raw materials, labor, production equipment, building space, and so on. The ultimate effects can be felt through the entire economy.

Types of Externalities

External effects, or externalities, can be positive or negative. Historically, the terms *external cost* (*external diseconomy*) and *external benefit* (*external economy*) have been used to refer, respectively, to circumstances in which the affected party is either damaged or benefited by the externality. Clearly, the water pollution example represents an external cost. As we shall see, other external benefits are not hard to find. Generally, resources conferring external benefits will be undersupplied compared to an efficient supply.

The externalities concept is a broad one, covering a multitude of sources of market failure (Example 2.2 illustrates one).

EXAMPLE 2.2

Shrimp Farming Externalities in Thailand

In the Tha Po village on the coast of Surat Thani Province in Thailand, more than half of the 1100 hectares of mangrove swamps have been cleared for commercial shrimp farms. Although harvesting shrimp is a lucrative undertaking, mangroves also serve as nurseries for fish and as barriers for storms and soil erosion. Following the destruction of the local mangroves, Tha Po villagers experienced a decline in fish catch and suffered storm damage and water pollution. Can market forces be trusted to strike the efficient balance between preservation and development for the remaining mangroves?

Calculations by economists Sathirathai and Barbier (2001) demonstrated that the value of the ecological services that would be lost from further destruction of the mangrove swamps exceeded the value of the shrimp farms that would take their place. Preservation of the remaining mangrove swamps would be the efficient choice.

Would a potential shrimp-farming entrepreneur make the efficient choice? Unfortunately, the answer is no. This study estimated the economic value of mangroves in terms of local use of forest resources, offshore fishery linkages, and coastal protection to be in the range of $27,264–$35,921 per hectare. In contrast, the economic returns to shrimp farming, once they are corrected for input subsidies and for the costs of water pollution, are only $194–$209 per hectare. However, since shrimp farmers are heavily subsidized and do not have to consider the external costs of pollution, their financial returns are typically $7,706.95–$8,336.47 per hectare. In the absence of some sort of regulatory mechanism imposed by collective action that forced these shrimp farmers to bear the extra costs they are causing, converting mangroves to shrimp farming would be the normal, if inefficient, result. The externalities associated with the ecological services provided by the mangroves support a biased decision that results in fewer social net benefits, but greater private net benefits.

Sources: Sathirathai, S., & Barbier, E. B. (April 2001). Valuing mangrove conservation in southern Thailand. *Contemporary Economic Policy*, *19*(2), 109–122; Barbier, E. B., & Cox, M. (2004). An economic analysis of shrimp farm expansion and mangrove conversion in Thailand. *Land Economics*, *80*(3), 389–407.

Alternative Property Right Structures and the Incentives They Create

Private property is, of course, not the only possible way of defining entitlements to resource use. Other possibilities include:

- state-property regimes (the government owns and controls the property);
- common-property regimes (the property is jointly owned and managed by a specified group of co-owners); and
- *res nullius* or open-access regimes (in which no one owns or exercises control over the resources).

Each of these categories creates rather different incentives for resource use.

State-property regimes exist to varying degrees in virtually all countries of the world. Parks and wilderness preserves, for example, are frequently owned and managed by the government. Problems with efficiency can arise in state-property regimes when the incentives of bureaucrats, who implement and/or make the rules for resource use, diverge from the collective interests of society as a whole.

Common-property resources are those shared resources that are managed in common rather than privately. Entitlements to use common-property resources may be formal, protected by specific legal rules, or they may be informal, protected by tradition or custom. Common-property regimes exhibit varying degrees of efficiency and sustainability, depending on the rules that emerge from collective decision making and the degree of compliance they achieve. While some very successful examples of common-property regimes exist, unsuccessful examples are even more common.

One successful example of a common-property regime involves the system of allocating grazing rights in Switzerland. Although agricultural land is normally treated as private property, in Switzerland grazing rights on the Alpine meadows have been treated as common property for centuries. Overgrazing is discouraged by specific rules, enacted by an association of users, which limit livestock use of the meadow. The families included on the membership list of the association were historically stable over time as rights and responsibilities passed from generation to generation. This stability apparently facilitated reciprocity and trust, thereby providing a foundation for continued compliance with the rules.

Unfortunately, that kind of stability may be the exception rather than the rule, particularly in the face of heavy population pressure. The more common situation can be illustrated by the experience of Mawelle, a small fishing village in Sri Lanka. Initially, a complicated but effective rotating system of fishing rights was devised by villagers to assure equitable access to the best spots and best times while protecting the fish stocks. Over time, population pressure and the infusion of outsiders not only raised demand, but also undermined collective cohesion and trust sufficiently that the traditional rules became unenforceable. Not surprisingly, the result was overexploitation of the resource and lower incomes for the participants.

Res nullius property resources, the focus of this section, by definition do not have a process for controlling access to the resource, because no individual or group has the legal power to exercise that control. As a result, it can be exploited on a first-come, first-served basis. *Open-access resources*, as we shall henceforth call them, have given rise to what has become known popularly as the "tragedy of the open-access commons."

The problems created by open-access resources can be illustrated by recalling the fate of the American bison. *Open-accesss, common-pool resources* are shared resources characterized by nonexclusivity and divisibility. *Nonexclusivity* implies that resources can be exploited by anyone, while *divisibility* means that the capture of part of the resource by one group makes that part unavailable to other groups.

In the early history of the United States, bison were plentiful; unrestricted hunting access was not a problem. Frontier people who needed hides or meat could easily get whatever they needed; the aggressiveness of any one hunter did not affect the time and effort expended by other hunters. In the absence of scarcity, efficiency was not threatened by open access.

As the years slipped by, however, the demand for bison increased and scarcity became a factor. As the number of hunters increased, eventually every additional unit of hunting activity increased the amount of additional time and effort required to produce an additional yield of bison.

Consider graphically how various property rights structures (and the resulting level of harvest) affect the economic surplus received by consumers and producers. In this graph that surplus is measured as the difference between the revenues received from the harvest minus the costs associated with producing that harvest. Figure 2.5 compares the revenue and costs for various levels of harvest. In the top panel the revenue is calculated by multiplying, for each level of hunting activity, the (assumed constant)

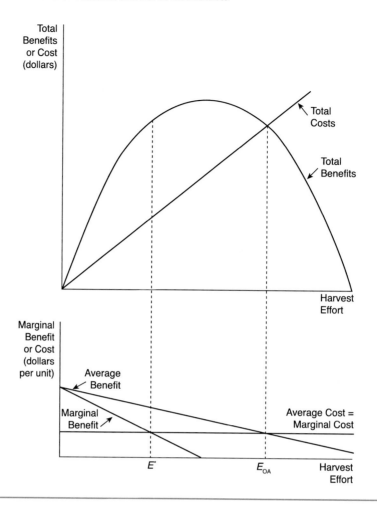

Figure 2.5 Bison Harvesting.

price of bison by the amount harvested. The upward-sloping total cost curve simply reflects the fact that increases in harvest effort result in higher total costs. (Marginal cost is assumed to be constant for this example.)

In terms of the top panel of Figure 2.5, the total surplus associated with any level of effort is measured as the vertical difference between the total revenue (benefits) curve and the total cost curve for that level of harvest.

In the bottom panel the marginal revenue curve is downward sloping (despite the constant price) because as the amount of hunting effort increases, the resulting bison population size decreases. Smaller populations support smaller harvests per unit of effort expended.

The efficient level of hunting activity in this model (E^*) maximizes the surplus. This can be seen graphically in two different ways. First, E^* maximizes the vertical difference between the total cost and total benefit (top panel). Second, in the bottom panel E^* is the level where the marginal revenue, which records the addition to the surplus from an additional unit of effort, crosses the marginal cost curve, which measures the reduction in the surplus due to the additional cost of expending that last unit of effort. These two panels are simply two different (mathematically equivalent) ways to demonstrate the same outcome. (The curves in the bottom panel are derived from the curves in the top panel.)

With all hunters having completely unrestricted access to the bison, the resulting allocation would not be efficient. No individual hunter would have an incentive to protect the surplus by restricting hunting effort. Individual hunters, under this "open access" scenario (without exclusive rights), would exploit the resource until their total benefit equaled total cost, implying a level of effort equal to (E_{OA}). Excessive exploitation of the herd occurs because individual hunters cannot appropriate the surplus, so their additional effort dissipates it. One of the losses from further exploitation that could be avoided by exclusive owners or by effective collective management—the loss of the surplus due to overexploitation—is not available in open-access resources.

Two characteristics of this formulation of the open-access allocation are worth noting: (1) in the presence of sufficient demand, unrestricted access will cause resources to be overexploited; (2) the surplus is dissipated—no one is able to appropriate it, so it is lost.

Why does this happen? Unlimited access destroys the incentive to conserve. A hunter who can preclude others from hunting their herd has an incentive to keep the herd at an efficient level to preserve the surplus. This restraint results in lower costs in the form of less time and effort expended to produce a given yield of bison. On the other hand, a hunter exploiting an open-access resource would not have an incentive to conserve because the potential additional economic surplus derived from self-restraint would, to some extent, be dissipated by other hunters who simply keep harvesting. Thus, unrestricted access to scarce resources promotes an inefficient allocation. As a result of excessive harvest and the loss of habitat as land was converted to farm and pasture, the Great Plains bison herds nearly became extinct (Lueck, 2002).

Public Goods

Public goods, defined as goods that exhibit both consumption indivisibilities and nonexcludability, present a particularly complex category of environmental resources. *Nonexcludability* refers to a circumstance where, once the resource is provided, even those who fail to pay for it cannot be excluded from enjoying the benefits it confers. Consumption is said to be *indivisible* when one person's consumption of a good does not diminish the amount available for others. Several common environmental resources are public goods, including clean air, clean water, and biological diversity.[1]

Biological diversity includes two related concepts: (1) the amount of genetic variability among individuals within a single species and (2) the number of species within a community of organisms. *Genetic diversity*, critical to species survival in the natural world, has also proved to be important in the development of new crops and livestock. It enhances the opportunities for crossbreeding and, thus, the development of new, possibly superior strains. The availability of different strains was the key, for example, in developing a new, disease-resistant barley.

Because of the interdependence of species within ecological communities, any species may have a value to the community far beyond its intrinsic value. Certain species contribute balance and stability to their ecological communities by serving as food sources to other species or holding the population of the species in check.

The richness of diversity within and among species has served as the basis for new sources of food, energy, industrial chemicals, raw materials, and medicines. Yet, considerable evidence suggests that biological diversity is decreasing.

Can we rely solely on the private sector to produce the efficient amount of public goods, such as biological diversity? Unfortunately, the answer is no. Suppose that in response to diminishing biological diversity we decide to take up a collection to provide some means of preserving endangered species. Would the collection be likely to yield sufficient revenue to pay for an efficient level of preservation? The general answer is no. Let's see why.

In Figure 2.6, individual demand curves for preserving biodiversity have been presented for two consumers, A and B. The market demand curve is represented by the

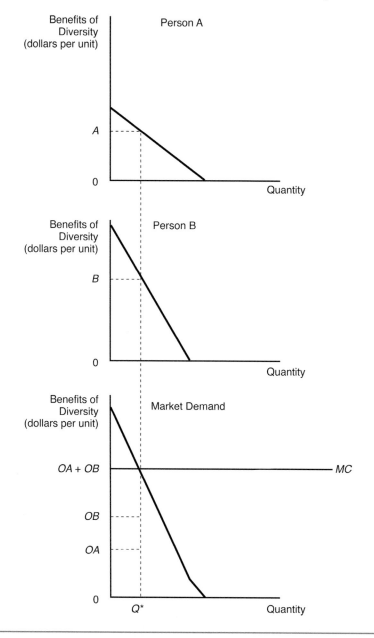

Figure 2.6 The Market for Public Goods.

vertical summation of the two individual demand curves. A vertical summation is necessary because everyone can simultaneously consume the same level of biological diversity. We are, therefore, able to determine the market demand by finding the sum of the amounts of money they would be willing to pay for that level of diversity.

What is the efficient level of diversity? It can be determined by a direct application of our definition of efficiency. The efficient allocation maximizes economic surplus, which is represented geometrically by the portion of the area under the market demand curve that lies above the constant marginal cost curve. The allocation that maximizes economic surplus is Q^*, the allocation where the demand curve crosses the marginal cost curve.

Why would a competitive market not be expected to supply the efficient level of this good? Since the two consumers have very different marginal willingness to pay from the efficient allocation of this good (OA versus OB), the efficient pricing system would require charging a different price to each consumer. Person A would pay OA and person B would pay OB. (Remember consumers tend to choose the level of the good that equates their marginal willingness to pay to the price they face.) Yet the producer would have no basis for figuring out how to differentiate the prices. In the absence of excludability, consumers are not likely to willingly reveal the strength of their preference for this commodity. All consumers have an incentive to understate the strength of their preferences to try to shift more of the cost burden to the other consumers.

Therefore, inefficiency results because each person can become a free rider on the other's contribution. A *free rider* is someone who derives the value from a commodity without paying an efficient amount for its supply. Because of the consumption indivisibility and nonexcludability properties of the public good, consumers receive the value of any biodiversity purchased by other people. When this happens, it tends to diminish incentives to contribute, and the total contributions would not be sufficiently large to finance the efficient amount of the public good; it would be undersupplied. As we shall see, the free-rider problem is also at the heart of why it is so difficult to secure sufficient international cooperation to manage the threats posed by climate change.

The privately supplied amount may not be zero, however. Some diversity would be privately supplied. Indeed, as suggested by Example 2.3, the privately supplied amount may be considerable.

EXAMPLE 2.3

Public Goods Privately Provided: The Nature Conservancy

Can the demand for a public good such as biological diversity be observed in practice? Would the market respond to that demand? Apparently so, according to the existence of organizations such as The Nature Conservancy.

The Nature Conservancy was born of an older organization called the Ecologist Union on September 11, 1950, for the purpose of establishing natural area reserves to aid in the preservation of areas, objects, and fauna and flora that have scientific, educational, or aesthetic significance. This organization purchases, or accepts as donations, land that has some unique ecological or aesthetic significance, to keep it from being used for other purposes. In so doing it preserves many species by preserving their habitat.

From humble beginnings, The Nature Conservancy has been responsible for the preservation of millions of acres of forests, marshes, prairies, mounds, and islands around the world. Additionally, The Nature Conservancy has protected thousands of miles of rivers and operates over 100 marine conservation projects. These areas serve as home to rare and endangered species of wildlife and plants. The Conservancy owns and manages the largest privately owned nature preserve system in the world.

This approach has considerable merit. A private organization can move more rapidly than the public sector. Because it has a limited budget, The Nature Conservancy sets priorities and concentrates on acquiring the most ecologically unique areas. Yet the theory of public goods reminds us that if this were to be the sole approach to the preservation of biological diversity, it would preserve a smaller-than-efficient amount.

Source: The Nature Conservancy, https://www.nature.org/en-us/about-us/who-we-are.

Imperfect Market Structures

Environmental problems can also occur when one of the participants in an exchange of property rights is able to exercise an inordinate amount of power over the outcome. This can occur, for example, when a product is sold by a single seller, or *monopoly*.

It is easy to show that monopolies violate our definition of *efficiency* in the goods market (see Figure 2.7). The efficient allocation would result when *OB is* supplied. This would yield consumer surplus represented by triangle *IGC*, and producer surplus

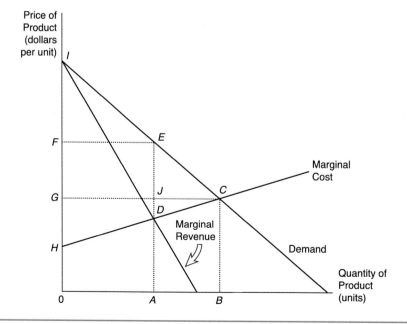

Figure 2.7 Monopoly and Inefficiency.

denoted by triangle *GCH*. The monopoly, however, would produce and sell *OA*, where marginal revenue equals marginal cost, and would charge price *OF*. At this point, although the producer surplus (*HFED*) is maximized, the sum of consumer and producer surplus is clearly not. This choice causes society to lose economic surplus equal to triangle *EDC*.[2] As this shows, monopolies supply an inefficiently small amount of the good.

Imperfect markets, where sellers have market power, clearly play some role in environmental problems. For example, the major oil-exporting countries have formed a cartel, resulting in higher-than-normal prices and lower-than-normal production. A *cartel* is a collusive agreement among producers to restrict production in order to raise prices. This collusive agreement among sellers allows the group to act as a monopolist.

Asymmetric Information

When all parties to a specific situation or transaction have access to the same amount of information about that situation, the information is said to be symmetrically distributed. If, however, one or more parties have more information than the others, the information distribution is said to be asymmetric.

Asymmetric information creates problems for the market when it results in a decision maker knowing too little to make an efficient choice. Suppose, for example, a consumer preferred organic food, but didn't know what food choices were truly organic. Since it would be relatively easy for producers to claim their produce was organically grown, even if it was not, consumers could not accurately distinguish truly organic produce from its fraudulent substitute. Unable to distinguish real organic food from its non-organic substitutes, consumers would be unwilling to pay a higher price for "organic" produce. As a result, both the profits and the output of organic farmers would be inefficiently low. We shall encounter asymmetric information problems in several contexts, including energy, pollution control, toxic substances, and ecosystem services.

Government Failure

Market processes are not the only sources of inefficiency. Political processes are fully as capable of producing inefficient outcomes. As will become clear in the chapters that follow, some environmental problems have arisen from a failure of political, rather than economic, institutions. To complete our study of the ability of institutions to allocate environmental resources, we must understand this source of inefficiency as well.

Government failure shares with market failure the characteristic that improper incentives are the root of the problem. Special interest groups use the political process to engage in what has become known as *rent seeking*. Rent seeking is the use of resources in lobbying and other activities directed at securing legislation that creates more desirable outcomes for the special interest group. Successful rent-seeking activity will typically increase the net benefits going to the special interest group, but it will also frequently lower the surplus to society as a whole. In these instances, it is a classic case of the aggressive pursuit of a larger slice of the pie leading to a smaller pie.

Why don't the losers rise up to protect their interests? One main reason is voter ignorance. It is economically rational for voters to remain at least partially ignorant on many issues simply because of the high cost of keeping fully informed on everything and the low probability that any single vote will be decisive. In addition, it is difficult for diffuse groups of individuals, each of whom is affected only to a small degree, to organize a coherent, unified opposition to an action that will bring large, concentrated benefits to a specific special interest. Successful opposition is, in a sense, a public good, with its attendant tendency for free riding. Opposition to special interests would normally be underfunded, especially when the opposition is dispersed and the special interests are concentrated.

Rent seeking can take many forms. Producers can seek protection via tariffs from competitive pressures brought by imports or can seek price floors to hold prices above their efficient levels. They can seek regulations that raise costs more for their competitors than for them. One example is when the regulatory compliance costs can be afforded by large producers, but not smaller producers. Another example is when organizations seek special subsidies to transfer part of their costs to the general body of taxpayers.

Rent seeking is not the only source of inefficient government policy. Sometimes governments also act without full information and establish policies that turn out to be very inefficient. For example, some time ago, one technological strategy chosen by the government to control motor vehicle pollution involved adding a chemical substance (MTBE) to gasoline. Designed to promote cleaner combustion, this additive subsequently turned out to create a substantial water pollution problem.

These examples provide a direct challenge both to the presumption that more direct intervention by the government automatically leads to greater efficiency and to the presumption that markets are infallible and government interventions should be avoided. Blind faith in one institution or another is no substitute for rational choices that take the specific context into consideration.

These cases illustrate the general economic premise that environmental problems arise because of a divergence between individual and collective objectives. This is a powerful explanatory device because not only does it suggest why these problems arise, but it also suggests how they might be resolved—by realigning individual incentives to make them compatible with collective objectives.

The Pursuit of Efficiency

We have seen that environmental problems can arise when property rights are ill defined, and when these rights are exchanged under something other than competitive conditions. We can now use our definition of efficiency to explore different possible governmental pathways for crafting and implementing remedies. Specifically, we consider judicial remedies, as well as regulation by the legislative and executive branches of government.

Judicial Liability Rules

The court system can respond to environmental conflicts by imposing liability for environmental damages that one party inflicts on another. Oil spills or an accidental release of air or water pollutants causing adverse human health effects are two common examples. Liability (or tort) law involves legal decisions that award compensation for damages to injured parties after the fact. Paid by the responsible party, the amount of the award is designed to correspond to the amount of damage inflicted.

The two main governing doctrines are strict liability and negligence. In a strict liability case, defendants are liable for damages even if they were not negligent or at fault. Typically, courts apply strict liability when abnormally dangerous activities or conditions are involved.

The incentives created by liability law are interesting because early decisions create precedents for later ones. Imagine, for example, how the incentives to prevent oil spills by an oil company are transformed once a precedent has created a legal obligation to clean up after an oil spill and to compensate all parties injured by the spill. It can quickly become evident that once liability is applied, accident prevention can become cheaper than retrospectively dealing with the damage once it has occurred.

The moral of this story is that appropriately designed liability rules can correct inefficiencies by forcing those who cause damage to bear its cost. Internalizing previously external costs causes profit-maximizing decisions to be compatible with efficiency. As we shall see in subsequent chapters, this "internalizing externalities" principle plays a large role in the design of efficient policy in many areas of environmental and natural resource policy.

This judicial approach, however, also has its limitations. Decisions about whether liability should be assessed in a particular case and, if so, how much, rely on a case-by-case determination of the unique circumstances involved. Case-by-case determinations are typically very expensive. Expenses, such as court time, lawyers' fees, and expert witness fees, fall into a category called *transaction costs* by economists. In the present context, these are the administrative costs associated with attempting to reach a fair outcome. Transaction costs in many cases can be quite high. When the number of parties involved in a dispute is large and the circumstances are common, the normal path is to correct the inefficiency by statutes or regulations rather than court decisions.

Legislative and Executive Regulation

Legislative and executive remedies can take several forms. The legislature could set a limit on the amount of pollution emitted over a specific period of time with fines for noncompliance. This regulation might then be backed up with sufficiently large jail sentences or fines to deter potential violators.

Legislatures could also establish rules to permit greater flexibility and yet reduce damage. For example, zoning laws would establish separate areas for steel plants and resorts. This approach assumes that the damage can be substantially reduced by keeping nonconforming uses apart.

They could deny the use of a particular toxic substance (as when lead was removed from gasoline) or require safety equipment (as when seat belts were required on automobiles). In other words, they can regulate outputs, inputs, production processes, emissions, and even the location of production in their attempt to produce an efficient outcome. In subsequent chapters, we shall examine the various options policymakers have at their disposal not only to modify environmentally destructive behavior, but also to promote efficiency.

Victims also have at their disposal other strategies for lowering pollution. They can promote boycotts against corner-cutting producers and dangerous products. Employee victims can turn to strikes or other forms of labor resistance.

Legislation and/or regulation can also help to resolve the asymmetric information problem. In some particularly risky occupations (such as working in nuclear power plants or dealing with toxic substances) employers can be mandated to supply workers with sufficient, crucial, trustworthy information to stay safe. Additionally, the government can require some specialized workers to be licensed, with licenses only awarded to those who can pass rigorous training courses.

Consumers may also face a need for safety information in dealing with potentially dangerous products (such as pesticides). Additionally, they may need information to distinguish organic or fair-trade products from others. For both groups one obvious solution involves providing the necessary information via trustworthy labeling.

One source of encouragement for organic farms has been the demonstrated willingness of consumers to pay a premium for organically grown fruits and vegetables. To allow consumers to discern which products are truly organic, growers need a reliable certification process. Additionally, fear of losing access to important foreign markets, such as the European Union, led to an industry-wide push in the United States for *mandatory* national labeling standards that would provide the foundation for a national uniform seal. (Voluntary U.S. certification programs had proved insufficient to assure access to European markets, since they were highly variable by state.)

In response to these pressures, the Organic Foods Production Act (OFPA) was enacted in the 1990 Farm Bill.[3] Title 21 of that law states the following objectives:

(1) to establish national standards governing the marketing of certain agricultural products as organically produced; (2) to assure consumers that organically produced products meet a consistent standard; and (3) to facilitate interstate commerce in fresh and processed food that is organically produced.

The USDA National Organic Program, established as part of this Act, is responsible for a mandatory certification program for organic production. The Act also established the National Organic Standards Board (NOSB) and charged it with defining the "organic" standards. The rules, which took effect in October 2002, require certification by the USDA for specific labels. Foods labeled as "100 percent organic" must contain only organic ingredients. Foods labeled as "organic" must contain at least 95 percent organic agricultural ingredients, excluding water and salt. Products labeled as "Made with Organic Ingredients" must contain at least 70 percent organic agricultural ingredients.

Certification allows socially conscious consumers to make a difference. As Example 2.4 demonstrates, eco-certification for coffee seems to be one such case.

EXAMPLE 2.4

Can Eco-Certification Make a Difference? Organic Costa Rican Coffee

Environmental problems associated with agricultural production for export in developing countries can be difficult to tackle using conventional regulation because producers are typically so numerous and dispersed, while regulatory agencies are commonly inadequately funded and staffed. In principle, eco-certification of production could circumvent these problems by providing a means for the socially conscious consumer to identify environmentally superior products, thereby providing a basis for paying a price premium for them. These premiums, in principle, would create financial incentives for producers to meet the certification standards.

Does it work in practice? Do socially conscious buyers care enough to actually pay a price premium that is high enough to motivate changes in the way the products are produced? Apparently, for some Costa Rican coffee at least, they are.

One study examined this question for certified organic coffee grown in Turrialba, Costa Rica. This agricultural region in the country's central valley is about 40 miles east of San José, the capital city. This is an interesting case because Costa Rican farmers face significant pressure from the noncertified market to lower their costs, a strategy that can have severe environmental consequences. In contrast, organic production typically not only involves higher labor costs, but the conversion from chemically based production can also reduce yields. Additionally, the costs of initial certification and subsequent annual monitoring and reporting are significant.

The authors found that the organic certification process did improve coffee growers' environmental performance. Specifically, they found that certification significantly reduced the use of pesticides, chemical fertilizers, and herbicides, and increased the use of organic fertilizer. In general, their results also suggest that organic certification has a stronger causal effect on preventing negative practices than on encouraging positive ones. The study notes that this finding is consistent with anecdotal evidence that local inspectors tend to enforce the certification standards prohibiting negative practices more vigorously than the standards requiring positive ones.

Source: Blackman, A., & Naranjo, M. A. (November 2012). Does eco-certification have environmental benefits? Organic coffee in Costa Rica. *Ecological Economics, 83*, 58–66.

Summary

How efficiently producers and consumers use resources depends on the context. Sometimes markets are the major source of degradation. Other times they help to prevent it or are part of the restoration process. One context that explains this difference involves the nature of the entitlements embodied in the property rights governing resource use. When property rights systems are exclusive, transferable, and enforceable, the owner of a resource has a powerful incentive to use that resource efficiently, since the failure to do so results in a personal loss.

Specific circumstances that could lead to inefficient allocations, however, include externalities, improperly defined property rights systems (such as open-access resources and public goods), imperfectly competitive markets (monopoly), and asymmetric information. When these circumstances arise, market allocations typically are not efficient. Even efficient allocations can lead to situations of inequity, however. Paying attention to equity and environmental justice concerns can be an additional part of allocation decisions.

Due to rent-seeking behavior by special interest groups or the less-than-perfect implementation of potentially efficient plans, political systems can produce inefficiencies as well. Voter ignorance on many issues, coupled with the public-good nature of any results of political activity, tends to create situations in which maximizing an industry's private surplus (through lobbying, for example) can be at the expense of a lower economic surplus for the other consumers and producers.

The efficiency criterion can be used not only to assist in the identification of circumstances in which our political and economic institutions lead us astray, but it can also assist in the search for remedies by facilitating the design of approaches that correct these failures. As we proceed through this book, many examples of both successes and failures will be identified. Fortunately, both are useful for providing an experiential basis for improved subsequent choices.

Discussion Questions

1. Recently some new markets have emerged that focus on the sharing of durable goods among a wider circle of users. Examples include Airbnb and Uber. The rise of these sharing markets may well have an impact on the relationship between the economy and the environment.
   a. What are the market niches these firms have found? How is Airbnb different from Hilton? How is Uber different from Hertz or Yellow Cab? Is this a matter mainly of a different type of supply or is the demand side affected as well?
   b. Why now? Markets for personal transportation and temporary housing have been around for a long time. How can these new companies find profitable opportunities in markets that have existed for some time? Is it evidence that the markets are not competitive? Or have the new opportunities been created by some changes in market conditions?
   c. Do you think these new sharing markets are likely on balance to be less harmful or more harmful to the environment than hotels and taxis? Why?

Self-Test Exercises

1. Suppose the state is trying to decide how many miles of a very scenic river it should preserve. There are 100 people in the community, each of whom has an identical inverse demand function given by $P = 10 - 1.0q$, where q is the number of miles preserved and P is the per-mile price they are willing to pay for q miles of preserved river. (a) If the marginal cost of preservation is $500 per mile, how many miles would be preserved in an efficient allocation? (b) How large is the economic surplus?
2. Suppose the market demand function (expressed in dollars) for a normal product is $P = 80 - q$, and the marginal cost (in dollars) of producing it is $MC = 1q$, where P is the price of the product and q is the quantity demanded and/or supplied.
   a. How much would be supplied by a competitive market?
   b. Compute the consumer surplus and producer surplus. Show that their sum is maximized.
   c. Compute the consumer surplus and the producer surplus assuming this same product was supplied by a monopoly. (*Hint*: the marginal revenue curve has twice the slope of the demand curve.)
   d. Show that, when this market is controlled by a monopoly, producer surplus is larger, consumer surplus is smaller, and the sum of the two surpluses is smaller than when the market is controlled by competitive industry.

3. Suppose you were asked to comment on a proposed policy to control oil spills. Since the average cost of an oil spill has been computed as X, the proposed policy would require any firm responsible for a spill immediately to pay the government X. Is this likely to result in the efficient amount of precaution against oil spills? Why or why not?

4. "In environmental liability cases, courts have some discretion regarding the magnitude of compensation polluters should be forced to pay for the environmental incidents they cause. In general, however, the larger the required payments the better." Discuss.

5. Label each of the following propositions as descriptive or normative and defend your choice:
   a. Energy efficiency programs have created jobs.
   b. Money spent on protecting endangered species is wasted.
   c. Fisheries must be privatized to survive.
   d. Raising transport costs lowers suburban land values.
   e. Birth-control programs are counterproductive.

6. Identify whether each of the following resource categories is a public good, a common-pool resource, or neither and defend your answer:
   a. A pod of whales in the ocean to whale hunters.
   b. A pod of whales in the ocean to whale watchers.
   c. The benefits from reductions of greenhouse gas emissions.
   d. Water from a town well that excludes nonresidents.
   e. Bottled water.

Notes

1 Notice that public "bads," such as dirty air and dirty water, are also possible.
2 Producers would lose area JDC compared to the efficient allocation, but they would gain area $FEJG$, which is much larger. Meanwhile, consumers would be worse off, because they lose area $FECJG$. Of these, $FEJG$ is merely a transfer to the monopoly, whereas EJC is a pure loss to society.
3 The European Union has followed a similar, but not identical, policy. See E.U. regulation 889/2008 on rules governing organic production, labeling, and control.

Further Reading

Lueck, D. (2002). The extermination and conservation of the American bison. *Journal of Legal Studies*, 31(S2), s609–s652. A fascinating look at the role property rights played in the fate of the American bison.

Ostrom, E. (1992). Crafting Institutions for Self-Governing Irrigation Systems. San Francisco, C.A.: ICS Press. A classic book by a Nobel Prize laureate that demonstrates that in favorable circumstances common-pool problems can sometimes be solved by voluntary organizations, rather than by a coercive state; among the cases considered are communal tenure in meadows and forests, irrigation communities, and fisheries.

Ostrom, E., Dietz, T., Dolsak, N., Stern, P., Stonich, S., & Weber, E. U. (Eds.). (2002). *The Drama of the Commons*. Washington, D.C.: National Academy Press. A compilation of articles and papers on common-pool resources.

Stavins, R. N. (Ed.). (2019). *Economics of the Environment, Selective Readings*, 7th ed. Northampton, M.A.: Edward Elgar Publishing. A carefully selected collection of readings that would complement this text.

Additional references and historically significant references are available on this book's Companion Website: www.routledge.com/cw/Tietenberg

Chapter 3

Evaluating Trade-Offs

Benefit-Cost Analysis and Other Decision-Making Metrics

Introduction

In the last chapter we noted that economic analysis has both positive and normative dimensions. The normative dimension helps to separate the policies that make sense from those that don't. Since resources are limited, it is not possible to undertake all ventures that might appear desirable, so making choices is inevitable.

Normative analysis can be useful in public policy in several different situations. It might be used, for example, to evaluate the desirability of a proposed new pollution control regulation or a proposal to preserve an area currently scheduled for development. In these cases, the analysis helps to provide guidance on the desirability of a program before that program is put into place. In other contexts, it might be used to evaluate how an already-implemented program has worked out in practice. Here the relevant question is: was this a wise use of resources? In this chapter, we present and demonstrate the use of several decision-making metrics that can assist us in evaluating options.

Normative Criteria for Decision Making

Normative choices can arise in two different contexts. In the first context, we need simply to choose among options that have been predefined, while in the second we try to find the optimal choice among all the possible options.

Evaluating Predefined Options: Benefit-Cost Analysis

If you were asked to evaluate the desirability of some proposed action, you would probably begin by attempting to identify both the gains and the losses from that action. If the gains exceed the losses, then it seems natural to support the action.

DOI: 10.4324/9781032689111-4

That simple framework provides the starting point for the normative approach to evaluating policy choices in economics. Economists suggest that actions have both benefits and costs. If the benefits exceed the costs, then the action is desirable. On the other hand, if the costs exceed the benefits, then the action is not desirable. (Comparing benefits and costs across time will be covered later in this chapter.)

We can formalize this in the following way. Let B be the benefits from a proposed action and C be the costs. Our decision rule would then be

if $B > C$, support the action.

Otherwise, oppose the action.[1]

As long as B and C are positive, a mathematically equivalent formulation would be

if $\dfrac{B}{C} > 1$, support the action.

Otherwise, oppose the action.

So far so good, but how do we measure benefits and costs? In economics, the system of measurement is anthropocentric, which simply means human centered. All benefits and costs are valued in terms of their effects (broadly defined) on humanity. As shall be pointed out later, that does *not* imply (as it might first appear) that ecosystem effects are ignored unless they *directly* affect humans. The fact that large numbers of humans contribute voluntarily to organizations that are dedicated to environmental protection provides ample evidence that humans place a value on environmental preservation that goes well beyond any direct use they might make of it. Nonetheless, the notion that humans are doing the valuing is a controversial point that will be revisited and discussed in Chapters 4 and 5 along with the specific techniques for valuing these effects.

In benefit-cost analysis, benefits are measured simply as the relevant area under the demand curve since the demand curve reflects consumers' willingness to pay. Total costs are measured by the relevant area under the marginal cost curve.

It is important to stress that environmental services have costs even though they are produced without any human input. All costs should be measured as opportunity costs. To firm up this notion of opportunity cost, consider an example. Suppose a particular stretch of river can be used either for white water rafting or to generate electric power. Since the dam that generates the power would flood the rapids, the two uses are incompatible. The opportunity cost of producing power is the forgone net benefit that would have resulted from the white water rafting. The *marginal opportunity cost curve* defines the additional cost of producing another unit of electricity resulting from the associated incremental loss of net benefits due to reduced opportunities for white water rafting.

Since net benefit is defined as the excess of benefits over costs, it follows that net benefit is equal to that portion of the area under the demand curve that lies above the supply curve.

Consider Figure 3.1, which illustrates the net benefits from preserving a stretch of river. Suppose that we are considering preserving a 4-mile stretch of river and that the benefits and costs of that action are reflected in Figure 3.1. Should that stretch be preserved? Why or why not? Hold on to your answer because we will return to this example later.

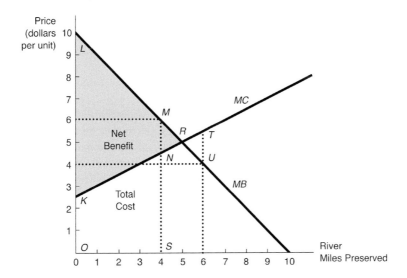

Figure 3.1 The Derivation of Net Benefits.

Finding the Optimal Outcome

In the preceding section, we examined how benefit-cost analysis can be used to evaluate the desirability of specific actions. In this section, we want to examine how this approach can be used to identify "optimal," or best, approaches.

In subsequent chapters, which address individual environmental problems, the normative analysis will proceed in three steps. First, we will identify an optimal outcome. Second, we will attempt to discern the extent to which our institutions produce optimal outcomes and, where divergences occur between actual and optimal outcomes, attempt to uncover the behavioral sources of the problems. Finally, we can use both our knowledge of the nature of the problems and their underlying behavioral causes as a basis for designing appropriate policy solutions. Although applying these three steps to each of the environmental problems must reflect the uniqueness of each situation, the overarching framework used to shape that analysis remains the same.

To provide some illustrations of how this approach is used in practice, consider two examples, one drawn from natural resource economics and another from environmental economics. These are meant to be illustrative and to convey a flavor of the argument; the details are left to upcoming chapters.

Consider the rising number of depleted ocean fisheries. Depleted fisheries, which involve fish populations that have fallen so low as to threaten their viability as commercial fisheries, not only jeopardize oceanic biodiversity, but also pose a threat to both the individuals who make their living from the sea and the communities that depend on fishing to support their local economies.

How would an economist attempt to understand and resolve this problem? The first step would involve defining the optimal stock or the optimal rate of harvest of the fishery. The second step would compare this level with the actual stock and harvest levels. Once this economic framework is applied, not only does it become clear that stocks are much lower than optimal for many fisheries, but also the reason for excessive exploitation becomes clear. Understanding the nature of the problem has led quite naturally to some solutions. Once implemented, these policies have allowed some fisheries to begin the process of renewal. The details of this analysis and the policy implications that flow from it are covered in Chapter 8.

Another problem involves greenhouse gas emissions that are contributing to climate change. As the atmospheric carbon dioxide passes threshold levels (now well over 400 ppm), what can be done?

Economists start by thinking about the "optimal" warming threshold (1.5 degrees Celsius), meaning the level that we do not want to exceed or in this case the maximum warming the planet can sustain without catastrophic damages. The analysis not only reveals that current emissions levels are excessive, but also suggests some specific behavioral sources of the problem. Based upon this understanding, specific economic solutions can be identified and implemented. Communities that have adopted these measures are generally more resilient to climate change impacts.

In the rest of the book, similar analysis is applied to energy, minerals, water, pollution, climate change, and a host of other topics. In each case, the economic analysis helps to point the way toward solutions. To initiate that process, we must begin by defining "optimal."

Relating Optimality to Efficiency

According to the normative choice criterion introduced earlier in this chapter, desirable outcomes are those where the benefits exceed the costs. It is therefore a logical next step to suggest that optimal policies are those that maximize net benefits (benefits minus costs). The concept of *static efficiency*, or merely *efficiency*, was introduced in Chapter 2. An allocation of resources is said to satisfy the static efficiency criterion if the economic surplus from the use of those resources is maximized by that allocation. Notice that the net benefits area to be maximized in an "optimal outcome" for public policy is identical to the "economic surplus" that is maximized in an efficient allocation. Hence, efficient outcomes are also optimal outcomes.

Let's take a moment to show how this concept can be applied. Previously, we asked whether an action that preserved 4 miles of river was worth doing (Figure 3.1). The answer is yes because the net benefits from that action are positive. (Can you see why?)

Static efficiency, however, requires us to ask a rather different question, namely, what is the optimal (or efficient) number of miles to be preserved? We know from the definition that the optimal amount of preservation would maximize net benefits. Does preserving 4 miles maximize net benefits? Is it the efficient outcome?

We can answer that question by establishing whether it is possible to increase the net benefit by preserving more or less of the river. If the net benefit can be increased by preserving more miles, clearly, preserving 4 miles could not have maximized the net benefit and, therefore, could not have been efficient.

Consider what would happen if society were to choose to preserve 5 miles instead of four. Refer back to Figure 3.1. What happens to the net benefit? It increases by area *MNR*. Since we can find another allocation with greater net benefit, 4 miles of preservation could not have been efficient. Could five? Yes. Let's see why.

We know that 5 miles of preservation convey more net benefits than four. If this allocation is efficient, then it must also be true that the net benefit is smaller for levels of preservation higher than five. Notice that the additional cost of preserving the sixth unit (the area under the marginal cost curve) is larger than the additional benefit received from preserving it (the corresponding area under the demand curve).

Therefore, the triangle *RTU* represents the reduction in net benefit that occurs if 6 miles are preserved rather than five.

Since the net benefit is reduced, both by preserving less than 5 miles and by preserving more than five, we conclude that five units is the preservation level that maximizes net benefit (the shaded area). Therefore, from our definition, preserving 5 miles constitutes an efficient or optimal allocation.[2]

One implication of this example, which will be very useful in succeeding chapters, is what we shall call the "first equimarginal principle":

First Equimarginal Principle (the Efficiency Equimarginal Principle): Social net benefits are maximized when the social marginal benefits from an allocation equal the social marginal costs.

The social marginal benefit is the increase in social benefits received from supplying one more unit of the good or service, while social marginal cost is the increase in cost incurred from supplying that additional unit of the good or service.

This criterion helps to minimize wasted resources, but is it fair? The ethical basis for this criterion is derived from a concept called *Pareto optimality*, named after the Italian-born Swiss economist Vilfredo Pareto, who first proposed it around the turn of the twentieth century.

Allocations are said to be Pareto optimal if no other feasible allocation could benefit at least one person without any deleterious effects on some other person.

Allocations that do not satisfy this definition are suboptimal. Suboptimal allocations can always be rearranged so that some people can gain net benefits without the rearrangement causing anyone else to lose net benefits. Therefore, the gainers could use a portion of their gains to compensate the losers sufficiently to ensure they were at least as well off as they were prior to the reallocation.

Efficient allocations are Pareto optimal. Since net benefits are maximized by an efficient allocation, it is not possible to increase the net benefit by rearranging the allocation. Without an increase in the net benefit, it is impossible for the gainers to compensate the losers sufficiently; the gains to the gainers would necessarily be smaller than the losses to the losers.

Inefficient allocations are judged inferior because they do not maximize the size of the pie to be distributed. By failing to maximize net benefit, they are forgoing an opportunity to make some people better off without harming others.

Comparing Benefits and Costs across Time

The analysis we have covered so far is very useful for thinking about actions where time is not an important factor. Yet many of the decisions made now have consequences that persist well into the future. Time is a factor. Exhaustible energy resources, once used, are gone. Biological renewable resources (such as fisheries or forests) can be overharvested, leaving smaller and possibly weaker populations for future generations. Persistent pollutants can accumulate over time. How can we make choices when the benefits and costs occur at different points in time?

Incorporating time into the analysis requires an extension of the concepts we have already developed. This extension provides a way for thinking not only about the magnitude of benefits and costs, but also about their timing. In order to incorporate timing, the decision rule must provide a way to compare net benefits received in different time periods. The concept that allows this comparison is called *present value*. Before introducing this expanded decision rule, we must define present value.

Present value explicitly incorporates the time value of money. A dollar today invested at 10 percent interest yields $1.10 a year from now (the return of the $1 principal plus $0.10 interest). The present value of $1.10 received one year from now is therefore $1, because, given $1 now, you can turn it into $1.10 a year from now by investing it at 10 percent interest. We can find the present value of any amount of money (X) received one year from now by computing $X/(1 + r)$, where r is the appropriate interest rate (10 percent in our preceding example).

What could your dollar earn in 2 years at r percent interest? Because of compound interest, the amount would be $\$1(1 + r)(1 + r) = \$1(1 + r)^2$. It follows then that the present value of X received 2 years from now is $X/(1 + r)^2$. The present value of X received in three years is $X/(1 + r)^3$.

By now the pattern should be clear. The present value of a *one-time* net benefit received n years from now is

$$PV\left(B_n\right) = \frac{B_n}{\left(1+r\right)^n}$$

The present value of a stream of net benefits $\{B_0, \ldots, B_n\}$ received over a period of n years is computed as

$$PV\left(B_0,\ldots,B_n\right) = \sum_{t=0}^{n} \frac{B_t}{\left(1+r\right)^t}$$

where r is the appropriate interest rate and B_0 is the amount of net benefits received immediately. The process of calculating the present value is called *discounting*, and the rate r is referred to as the discount rate. The choice of the discount rate is very important and is addressed later in this chapter.

Note that net benefits (NB) is benefits minus costs, so this equation can also be represented as

$$PVNB = \sum_{t=0}^{n} \frac{B_t - C_t}{\left(1+r\right)^t}$$

The number resulting from a present-value calculation has a straightforward interpretation. Suppose you were investigating an allocation that would yield the following pattern of net benefits on the last day of each of the next 5 years: $3,000, $5,000, $6,000, $10,000, and $12,000. If you use an interest rate of 6 percent $(r = 0.06)$ and the preceding formula, you will discover that this stream has a present value of $29,205.92 (see Table 3.1). Notice how each amount is discounted back the appropriate number of years to the present and then these discounted values are summed.

What does that number mean? If you put $29,205.92 in a savings account earning 6 percent interest and wrote yourself checks, respectively, for $3,000, $5,000, $6,000, $10,000, and $12,000 on the last day of each of the next 5 years, your last check would just restore the account to a $0 balance (see Table 3.2). Thus, you should

Table 3.1 Demonstrating Present Value Calculations

Year	1	2	3	4	5	Sum
Annual Amounts	$3,000	$5,000	$6,000	$10,000	$12,000	$36,000
Present Value ($r = 0.06$)		$2,830.19	$4,449.98	$5,037.72	$7,920.94	$8,967.10 $29,205.92

Table 3.2 Interpreting Present Value Calculations

Year	1	2	3	4	5	6
Balance at Beginning of Year	$29,205.92	$27,958.28	$24,635.77	$20,113.92	$11,320.75	$0.00
Year-End Fund Balance before Payment ($r = 0.06$)	$30,958.28	$29,635.77	$26,113.92	$21,320.75	$12,000.00	
Payment	$3,000	$5,000	$6,000	$10,000	$12,000	

be indifferent about receiving $29,205.92 now or the benefits over 5 years totaling $36,000; given one, you can get the other. Hence, the method is called present value because it translates everything back to its current worth.

It is now possible to show how this analysis can be used to evaluate actions. Calculate the present value of net benefits from the action. If the present value is greater than zero, the action can be supported. Otherwise, it should not be.

Dynamic Efficiency

The static efficiency criterion is very useful for comparing resource allocations when time is not an important factor. How can we think about optimal choices when the benefits and costs occur at different points in time?

The traditional criterion used to find an optimal allocation when time is involved is called *dynamic efficiency*, a generalization of the static efficiency concept already developed. In this generalization, the present-value criterion provides a way for comparing the net benefits received in one period with the net benefits received in another.

An allocation of resources across n time periods satisfies the dynamic efficiency criterion if it maximizes the present value of net benefits that could be received from all the possible ways of allocating those resources over the n periods.[3]

Applying the Concepts

Having now spent some time developing the concepts we need, let's take a moment to examine some actual studies in which they have been used.

Pollution Control

Benefit-cost analysis has been used to assess the desirability of efforts to control pollution. Pollution control certainly confers many benefits, but it also has costs. Do the benefits justify the costs? That was a question the U.S. Congress wanted answered, so in Section 812 of the Clean Air Act Amendments of 1990, it required the U.S. Environmental Protection Agency (EPA) to evaluate the benefits and costs of the U.S. air pollution control policy initially over the 1970–1990 period and subsequently over the 1990–2020 time period (see Example 3.1).

In responding to this congressional mandate, the EPA set out to quantify and monetize the benefits and costs of achieving the emissions reductions required by U.S. policy. Benefits quantified by this study included reduced death rates and lower incidences of chronic bronchitis, lead poisoning, strokes, respiratory diseases, and heart disease as well as the benefits of better visibility, reduced structural damages, and improved agricultural productivity.

We shall return to this study later in the book for a deeper look at how these estimates were derived, but a couple of comments are relevant now. First, despite the fact that this study did not attempt to value all pollution damage to ecosystems that was avoided by this policy, the net benefits are still strongly positive. While presumably the case for controlling pollution would have been even stronger had all such avoided damage been included, the desirability of this form of control is evident even with only a partial consideration of benefits. An inability to monetize all benefits and costs does not necessarily jeopardize the ability to reach sound policy conclusions.

Although these results justify the conclusion that pollution control made economic sense, they do not justify the stronger conclusion that the policy was efficient. To justify that conclusion, the study would have had to show that the present value of net benefits was maximized, not merely positive. In fact, this study did not attempt to calculate the maximum net benefits outcome, and if it had, it would have almost certainly discovered that the policy during this period was not optimal. As we shall see later in the book, the costs of the chosen policy approach were higher than necessary to achieve the desired emissions reductions. With an optimal policy mix, the net benefits would have been even higher.

EXAMPLE 3.1

Does Reducing Pollution Make Economic Sense? Evidence from the Clean Air Act

In its 1997 report to Congress, the U.S. EPA presented the results of its attempt to discover whether the Clean Air Act had produced positive net benefits over the period 1970–1990. The results suggested that the present value of benefits (using a discount rate of 5 percent) was $22.2 trillion, while the costs were

$0.523 trillion. Performing the necessary subtraction reveals that the net benefits were therefore equal to $21.7 trillion. According to this study, U.S. air pollution control policy during this period made very good economic sense.

Soon after the period covered by this analysis, substantive changes were made in the Clean Air Act Amendments of 1990 (the details of those changes are covered in later chapters). Did those additions also make economic sense?

In August of 2010, the EPA issued a report of the benefits and costs of the Clean Air Act from 1990 to 2020. This report suggested that the costs of meeting the 1990 Clean Air Act Amendment requirements were expected to rise to approximately $65 billion per year by 2020 (2006 dollars). Almost half of the compliance costs ($28 billion) would arise from pollution controls placed on cars, trucks, and buses, while another $10 billion would arise from reducing air pollution from electric utilities.

These actions were estimated to cause benefits (from reduced pollution damage) to rise from roughly $800 billion in 2000 to almost $1.3 trillion in 2010, ultimately reaching approximately $2 trillion per year (2006 dollars) by 2020! For persons living in the United States, a cost of approximately $200 per person by 2020 produced approximately a $6,000 gain in benefits per person from the improvement in air quality. Many of the estimated benefits came from reduced risk of early mortality due to exposure to fine particulate matter. Table 3.3 provides a summary of the costs and benefits and includes a calculation of the benefit/cost ratio.

> Table 3.3 **Summary Comparison of Benefits and Costs from the Clean Air Act 1990–2020 (Estimates in Million $2006 Dollars)**

			Annual Estimates	Present Value Estimate
	2000	*2010*	*2020*	*1990–2020*
Monetized Direct Costs:				
Low[1]				
Central	$20,000	$53,000	$65,000	$380,000
High[1]				
Monetized Direct Benefits:				
Low[2]	$90,000	$160,000	$250,000	$1,400,000
Central	$770,000	$1,300,000	$2,000,000	$12,000,000
High[2]	$2,300,000	$3,800,000	$5,700,000	$35,000,000

(Continued)

	2000	2010	Annual Estimates 2020	Present Value Estimate 1990–2020
Net Benefits:				
Low	$70,000	$110,000	$190,000	$1,000,000
Central	$750,000	$1,200,000	$1,900,000	$12,000,000
High	$2,300,000	$3,700,000	$5,600,000	$35,000,000
Benefit/Cost Ratio:				
Low[3]	5/1	3/1	4/1	4/1
Central	39/1	25/1	31/1	32/1
High[3]	115/1	72/1	88/1	92/1

Notes:

1   The cost estimates for this analysis were based on assumptions about future changes in factors such as consumption patterns, input costs, and technological innovation. We recognize that these assumptions introduce significant uncertainty into the cost results; however, the degree of uncertainty or bias associated with many of the key factors cannot be reliably quantified. Thus, we are unable to present specific low and high cost estimates.

2   Low and high benefit estimates are based on primary results and correspond to 5th and 95th percentile results from statistical uncertainty analysis, incorporating uncertainties in physical effects and valuation steps of benefits analysis. Other significant sources of uncertainty not reflected include the value of unquantified or unmonetized benefits that are not captured in the primary estimates and uncertainties in emissions and air quality modeling.

3   The low benefit/cost ratio reflects the ratio of the low benefits estimate to the central costs estimate, while the high ratio reflects the ratio of the high benefits estimate to the central costs estimate. Because we were unable to reliably quantify the uncertainty in cost estimates, we present the low estimate as "less than X" and the high estimate as "more than Y," where X and Y are the low and high benefit/cost ratios, respectively.

Sources: U.S. Environmental Protection Agency. (1997). *The Benefits and Costs of the Clean Air Act, 1970 to 1990*. Washington, D.C.: Environmental Protection Agency, Table 18, p. 56; U.S. Environmental Protection Agency Office of Air and Radiation, *The Benefits and Costs of the Clean Air Act, 1990 to 2020—Summary Report, 8/16/2010*. Full report available at www.epa.gov/clean-air-act-overview/benefits-and-costs-clean-air-act-1990-2010-first-prospective-study (Accessed January 14, 2023).

Estimating Benefits of Carbon Dioxide Emission Reductions

Benefit-cost analysis is frequently complicated by the estimation of benefits and costs that are difficult to quantify. (Chapter 4 takes up the topic of nonmarket valuation in detail.) One such case is the benefit of reductions in carbon emissions.

Since 1981 the U.S. government has required benefit-cost analysis for every economically significant regulation. Executive Order 12866 in 1993 requires government agencies "to assess both the costs and the benefits of the intended regulation and, recognizing that some costs and benefits are difficult to quantify, propose or adopt a regulation only upon a reasoned determination that the benefits of the intended regulation justify its costs."[4]

In applying this Executive Order to carbon policies, calculating the control costs is straightforward, but what about the benefits? The benefits are the avoided damages resulting from the policy. Agencies estimate the marginal value of the avoided damages using a metric called the "social cost of carbon." The social cost of carbon is the estimated present value (in dollars) of the marginal cost of future damages from one additional ton of carbon dioxide emitted. Since the social cost of carbon is a present value calculation, both the timing of the emission reduction and the discount rate play an important role.[5]

In 2022, a long-awaited study that attempts to provide guidance on a new social cost of carbon was published in the journal *Nature* recommending a social cost of carbon of $185 at a 2 percent discount rate (Rennert et al., 2022). Shortly thereafter, the EPA released a proposed rule changing the social cost of carbon to $190 at a 2 percent discount rate. Let's see how we got here.

The Interagency Working Group on Social Cost of Carbon presented the first set of estimates for the social cost of carbon in 2010 and continued through 2016. This group combined the results from three integrated assessment models (IAMs): DICE, FUND, and PAGE. These simple climate models were used to map emissions changes onto temperature changes, and temperature changes into a damage function. The resulting social cost of carbon numbers were used not only to compare the costs and benefits of policies to control carbon emissions directly, but also indirectly such as in the appliances that save energy (Example 3.2).

EXAMPLE 3.2

Using the Social Cost of Capital: The DOE Microwave Oven Rule

In 2013, the Department of Energy (DOE) announced new rules for energy efficiency for microwave ovens in standby mode. By improving the energy efficiency of these ovens, this rule would reduce carbon emissions. In the regulatory impact analysis associated with this rule, it was necessary to value the reduced damages from this lower level of emissions. The social cost of carbon (SCC) was used to provide this information.

Using the 2010 social cost of carbon produced a present value of net benefits for the microwave oven rule over the next 30 years of $4.2 billion. Since this value is positive, it means that implementing this rule would increase efficiency.

Using the revised 2013 number would increase the present value of net benefits, but by how much? According to the DOE, using the 2013 instead of the 2010 social cost of carbon increased the present value of net benefits to $4.6 billion. In this case, the net benefits were large enough both before and after the new SCC estimates to justify implementing the rule, but it is certainly possible that in other cases these new estimates would justify rules that prior to the revision would not have been justified.

DOE noted that due to the increased energy efficiency of the appliances subject to these rules (and the resulting lower energy costs for purchasers), the present value of savings to consumers was estimated to be $3.4 billion over the next 30 years (DOE, 2013), an amount that is larger than the costs. In this case the rules represented a win for both microwave consumers and the planet.

Sources: http://energy.gov/articles/new-energy-efficiency-standards-microwave-ovens-save-consumers-
energy-bills; *Technical Update of the Social Cost of Carbon for Regulatory Impact Analysis—Under
Executive Order 12866*, https://obamawhitehouse.archives.gov/sites/default/files/omb/inforeg/
scc-tsd-final-july-2015.pdf.

Table 3.4 2016 Revised Social Cost of CO_2, 2015–2050 (in 2007 dollars per metric ton of CO_2)

| | | | Discount | Rates |
Year	5% Avg	3% Avg	2.5% Avg	3% 95th
2015	$11	$36	$56	$105
2020	$12	$42	$62	$123
2025	$14	$46	$68	$138
2030	$16	$50	$73	$152
2035	$18	$55	$78	$168
2040	$21	$60	$84	$183
2045	$23	$64	$89	$197
2050	$26	$69	$95	$212

Source: https://19january2017snapshot.epa.gov/climatechange/social-cost-carbon_html (Accessed May 15, 2017).

In 2013, these early estimates were revised upward, with the estimate for the social cost of carbon increasing from $22 to approximately $37 per ton of carbon (using a discount rate of 3 percent). In 2016, they were revised (upward) again. Table 3.4 illustrates the 2016 revised social cost of carbon (in 2020 dollars per metric ton of CO_2) using 2.5, 3, and 5 percent discount rates for selected years. The fourth column presents the extreme case (95th percentile) using a 3 percent discount rate. Notice the importance of the discount rate in determining what value is used. (Can you explain why?)

In 2017, with the election of President Donald Trump, everything changed. Soon after taking office President Trump signed an Executive Order that called on agencies to disband the Interagency Working Group on Social Cost of Greenhouse Gases and to change the basis for the calculation of the social cost of carbon. They made two significant changes. First, they decided to only count domestic damages. Second, they raised the discount rate. Both factors reduced the social cost of carbon by more than 90%! The SCC was now $1–7/ton.

In 2020, the new Biden administration quickly reversed that order and undertook a comprehensive update to the social cost of carbon. In September of 2022, a group of researchers published a new study in the journal *Nature* that recommends the social cost of carbon be revised to $185/ton (at a 2 percent discount rate), three times higher than the current $51. They also recommend the use of a 2 percent discount rate.[6] Shortly thereafter, the EPA released a proposal to change the social cost of carbon to $190 using a 2 percent discount rate (Example 3.3). Those new rates, finalized in December 2023, are illustrated in Table 3.5.

EXAMPLE 3.3

Revisiting the Social Cost of Carbon: Just How High Should It Be?

On President Biden's first day in office, he signed an Executive Order that reestablished the Interagency Working Group on the Social Cost of Greenhouse Gases and charged them with publishing an "interim Social Cost of Carbon within 30 days (along with a Social Cost of Methane and a Social Cost of Nitrous Oxide); and new estimates of the Social Costs of Greenhouse gases sometime in 2022."

Whereas the Trump administration had changed the SCC from about $50/ton to a range of just $1–7/ton, the new administration's interim value of the social cost of carbon was $51/metric ton of carbon at a 3 percent discount rate and $76/ton at a 2.5 percent discount rate. This action basically restored the SCC number to what it had been under the Obama administration.

What we do know is that the climate models in the original IAMs are flawed. The models did not at the time include all the important physical, ecological, and economic impacts of climate change recognized in the climate change literature because of a lack of precise information on the nature of damages and because the science incorporated into these models naturally lags the most recent research.

To be specific, some damage categories such as agriculture had not yet been included and low probability but high damage events (tipping points) are not adequately treated. Both tend to understate the SCC estimates. Moore et al. (2017) show that simply including the impacts to agriculture raises the SCC to about $200/ton. Updating damages in just this one sector would double the SCC. Further, Dietz et al. (2021) find that even the simplest incorporation of tipping points raises the SCC at least 25 percent to $65. Even that correction understates damages from the more extreme climate changes. And important ecosystem services requiring nonmarket valuation are neglected.

Including an emphasis on equity can also raise the SCC, reflecting the reality that the impacts of climate change will be felt by some more than others (Wagner et al., 2021). And as we have seen, the discount rate might be the most contentious and influential piece of this discussion as it strongly impacts the final number. How should damages be discounted to the present? Should we be using a constant exponential discount rate? Many economists think we should not. Potential catastrophic risk favors a lower or declining rate. And real rates have been lower than 3 percent for a number of years. Some countries have already adopted lower rates, including Germany, the Netherlands, Norway, and the United Kingdom (Wagner et al., 2021).

What do other countries use to estimate the damages from a ton of carbon emitted (or the benefits of preventing that ton of carbon from being emitted)? Germany, in 2020, proposed two values: €195 (U.S.$235) and €680 (U.S.$820). In December 2020, New York State raised their social cost of carbon to $125.

In 2022, a large group of researchers from many institutions published a long-awaited study that attempted to provide guidance on a new social cost of carbon. They recommend a social cost of carbon of $185 at a 2 percent discount rate. Much of the increase comes from damages to just two sectors, agriculture and heat-related mortality, and of course the lower discount rate. Their model is available on open source software for others to use. While some sectors are still missing (the value of biodiversity loss and damages from ocean acidification), this study represents a great start in getting it right and provides guidance to the Biden administration.

Later that same year, the EPA released new guidance on the social cost of carbon. The proposed estimates of the social cost of carbon are $120, $190, or $340 per metric ton of CO_2 using discount rates of 2.5 percent, 2.0 percent, and 1.5 percent respectively (Table 3.5). In that same document they also propose new estimates for the social cost of other greenhouse gases as well (methane and nitrous oxide). The social cost of methane, for example, rises to $1,600 per metric ton of methane at a 2 percent discount rate.

These higher numbers significantly increase the benefits of reducing greenhouse gas emissions. Recall that prevented damages are benefits, thus supporting more stringent climate policy. These estimates were adopted by the U.S. EPA in December 2023 and were immediately utilized in a ruling on methane pollution from oil and natural gas wells.[7]

Sources: Moore, F. C., Baldos, U., Hertel, T. et al. (2017). New science of climate change impacts on agriculture implies higher social cost of carbon. *Nature Communications*, 8, 1607. https://doi.org/10.1038/s41467-017-01792-x; Dietz, S., Rising, J., Stoerk, T., and Wagner, G. (August 2021). Economic impacts of tipping points in the climate system. *Proceedings of the National Academy of Sciences*, 118(34), e2103081118; doi: 10.1073/pnas.2103081118; EPA.gov/environmental-economics/scghg; Wagner, G., Anthoff, D., Cropper, M., Dietz, S., Gillingham, K. T., Groom, B., ... & Stock, J. H. (2021). Eight priorities for calculating the social cost of carbon. *Nature*, 590(7847), 548–550.

Issues in Benefit Estimation

The analyst charged with the responsibility for performing a benefit-cost analysis encounters many decision points requiring judgment. If we are to understand benefit-cost analysis, the nature of these judgments must be clear in our minds.

Primary versus Secondary Effects. Environmental projects usually trigger both primary and secondary consequences. For example, the primary effect of cleaning a lake will be an increase in recreational uses of the lake. This primary effect will cause a

Table 3.5 Estimates of the Social Costs of Greenhouse Gases 2020–2080

SC-GHG and Near-term Ramsey Discount Rate

Emission Year	$SC\text{-}CO_2$ (2020 dollars per metric ton of CO_2)			$SC\text{-}CH_4$ (2020 dollars per metric ton of CH_4)			$SC\text{-}N_2O$ (2020 dollars per metric ton of N_2O)		
	Near-term rate			Near-term rate			Near-term rate		
	2.5%	2.0%	1.5%	2.5%	2.0%	1.5%	2.5%	2.0%	1.5%
2020	120	190	340	1,300	1,600	2,300	35,000	54,000	87,000
2030	140	230	380	1,900	2,400	3,200	45,000	66,000	100,000
2040	170	270	430	2,700	3,300	4,200	55,000	79,000	120,000
2050	200	310	480	3,500	4,200	5,300	66,000	93,000	140,000
2060	230	350	530	4,300	5,100	6,300	76,000	110,000	150,000
2070	260	380	570	5,000	5,900	7,200	85,000	120,000	170,000
2080	280	410	600	5,800	6,800	8,200	95,000	130,000	180,000

Values of SC-CO₂, SC-CH₄ and SC-N₂O are rounded to two significant figures. The annual unrounded estimates are available in Appendix A.5 and at: https://www.epa.gov/environmental-economics/scghg. Source: https://www.epa.gov/environmental-economics/scghg. Accessed December 27, 2023.

further ripple effect on services provided to the increased number of users of the lake. Are these secondary benefits to be counted?

The answer depends upon the employment conditions in the surrounding area. If this increase in demand results in employment of previously unused resources, such as labor, the value of the increased employment should be counted. If, on the other hand, the increase in demand is met by a shift in previously employed resources from one use to another, it is a different story. In general, secondary employment benefits should be counted in high unemployment areas or when the particular skills demanded are underemployed at the time the project is commenced. They should not be counted when the project simply results in a rearrangement of productively employed resources.

Accounting Stance. The accounting stance refers to the geographic scale or scope at which the benefits are measured. Scale matters because in a benefit-cost analysis only the benefits or costs affecting that specific geographic area are counted. Suppose, for example, that the federal government picks up many of the costs, but the benefits are received by only one region. Even if the benefit-cost analysis shows this to be a great project for the region, that will not necessarily be the case for the nation as a whole. Once the national costs are factored in, the national project benefits may not exceed the national project costs. Debate 3.1 examines this issue in relation to the social cost of carbon.

Aggregation. Related to accounting stance are challenges of aggregation. Estimates of benefits and costs must be aggregated in order to derive total benefits and total costs. How many people benefit and how many people incur costs are very important in any aggregation, but, additionally, *how* they benefit might impact that aggregation. Suppose, for example, those living closer to the project receive more benefits per household than those living farther away. In this case these differences should be accounted for.

With and Without Principle. The "with and without" principle states that only those benefits that would result from the project should be counted, ignoring those that would have accrued anyway. Mistakenly including benefits that would have accrued anyway would overstate the benefits of the program.

Tangible versus Intangible Benefits. *Tangible benefits* are those that can reasonably be assigned a monetary value. *Intangible benefits* are those that cannot be assigned a monetary value, either because data are not available or reliable enough or because it is not clear how to measure the value even with data.[8] Quantification of intangible benefits is the primary topic of the next chapter.

DEBATE 3.1

What Is the Proper Geographic Scope for the Social Cost of Carbon?

The social cost of carbon is an estimate of the economic damages associated with a small increase in carbon dioxide (CO_2) emissions, conventionally 1 metric ton, in a given year. Any reduction in these damages resulting from a proposed regulation is used to estimate the climate benefits of U.S. rulemakings.

Because climate change is a global public good, the efficient damage estimate must include all damages, not just damages to the United States. Some critics argue that, because it is used in U.S. regulatory procedures, it should include only U.S. damages; otherwise it might justify regulations that impose costs on U.S. citizens for the purpose of producing benefits enjoyed by citizens of other countries who do not bear the cost.

Proponents of the global metric point out that the measure is designed to be a means of internalizing a marginal external cost and it cannot do that accurately and efficiently if it leaves out some of the costs. Calculating it only for U.S. damages would create a biased measure that would underestimate the damages and raise the possibility of biased regulatory decisions based upon it.

Furthermore, they argue that the characterization of this measure as allowing benefits created by American citizens to be enjoyed by foreign citizens is a bit misleading. These benefits do not reflect goods and services purchased by U.S. citizens that are enjoyed abroad. Rather, they reflect a reduction in the damages that U.S. citizens would otherwise be imposing on others. American law typically does not allow someone to inflict damage on neighbors simply because they are on the other side of some boundary. Reducing damages imposed on others has a different moral context than spillover benefits.

Some regulatory analysts have now suggested that the "U.S.-only" measure should not replace the existing measure, but complement it. Both should be provided. What do you think?

Source: Dudley, S. E., Fraas, A., Gayer, T., Graham, J., Lutter, R., Shogren, J. F., & Viscusi, W. K. (February 9, 2016). How much will climate change rules benefit Americans? *Forbes*.

How are intangible benefits to be handled? One answer is perfectly clear: they should not be ignored. To ignore intangible benefits is to bias the results. That benefits are intangible does not mean they are unimportant.

Intangible benefits should be quantified to the fullest extent possible. One frequently used technique is to conduct a sensitivity analysis of the estimated benefit values derived from less than perfectly reliable data. We can determine, for example, whether or not the outcome is sensitive, within wide ranges, to the value of this benefit. If not, then very little time has to be spent on the problem. If the outcome is sensitive, the person or persons making the decision bear the ultimate responsibility for weighing the importance of that benefit.

Approaches to Cost Estimation

Estimating costs is generally easier than estimating benefits, but it is not easy. One major problem for both derives from the fact that benefit-cost analysis is forward-looking and thus requires an estimate of what a particular strategy *will* cost, which is much more difficult than tracking down what an existing strategy *does* cost.

Two approaches have been developed to estimate these costs.

The Survey Approach. One way to discover the costs associated with a policy is to ask those who bear the costs, and presumably know the most about them, to reveal the magnitude of the costs to policymakers. Polluters, for example, could be asked to provide control-cost estimates to regulatory bodies. The problem with this approach is the strong incentive not to be truthful. An overestimate of the costs can trigger less stringent regulation; therefore, it is financially advantageous to provide overinflated estimates.

The Engineering Approach. The engineering approach bypasses the source being regulated by using general engineering information to catalog the possible technologies that could be used to meet the objective and to estimate the costs of purchasing and using those technologies. The final step in the engineering approach is to assume that the sources would use technologies that minimize cost. This produces a cost estimate for a "typical" well-informed firm.

The engineering approach has its own problems. These estimates may not approximate the actual cost to any particular firm. Unique circumstances may cause the costs of that firm to be higher, or lower, than estimated; the firm, in short, may not be typical.

The Combined Approach. To circumvent these problems, analysts frequently use a combination of survey and engineering approaches. The survey approach collects information on possible technologies, as well as special circumstances facing the firm. Engineering approaches are used to derive the actual costs of those technologies, given the special circumstances. This combined approach attempts to balance information best supplied by the source with that best derived independently.

In the cases described so far, the costs are relatively easy to quantify and the problem is simply finding a way to acquire the best information. This is not always the case, however. Some costs are not easy to quantify, although economists have developed some ingenious ways to secure monetary estimates even for those costs.

Take, for example, a policy designed to conserve energy by forcing more people to carpool. If the effect of this is simply to increase the average time of travel, how is this cost to be measured?

For some time, transportation analysts have recognized that people value their time, and a large amount of literature has now evolved to provide estimates of how valuable time savings or time increases would be. The basis for this valuation is opportunity cost—how the time might be used if it weren't being consumed in travel. Although the results of these studies depend on the amount of time involved, individual decisions seem to imply that travelers value their travel time at a rate not more than half their wage rates.

The Treatment of Risk

For many environmental problems, it is not possible to state with certainty what consequences a particular policy will have or a particular threat will pose. Outcomes will be affected by circumstances that are not fully known at the time of the assessment.

For example, consider decisions about the best policy designs to control the potential damages from climate change. While scientists agree on most of the potential impacts of climate change, such as sea level rise and species losses, the timing and extent of those losses are not known with certainty. However, the benefits from reducing the threats posed by these damages, and hence the desirability of policies to manage these risks, will depend on their ultimate timing and extent.

Distinguishing Risk and Uncertainty. In attempting to facilitate decision making with choices like these, Frank H. Knight suggested a useful definition in 1921 that distinguished two terms that historically have been treated as synonyms—risk and uncertainty.[9] Risk, he suggested, involves decision-making situations in which all potential outcomes are identified and the respective probabilities of all outcomes are known. Uncertainty, however, he characterized as situations in which either the possible outcomes or the specific probabilities associated with such outcomes are unknown to the decision maker.

This definition of risk not only offers the possibility that some degree of quantification of it is possible, but it also suggests the general form that quantification might take. Benefit-cost analysis grapples with the evaluation of risk in several ways. Suppose we have a range of policy options A, B, C, D and a range of possible outcomes E, F, G for each of these policies depending on how the economy evolves over the future. These outcomes, for example, might depend on whether the demand growth for the resource is low, medium, or high. Thus, if we choose policy A, we might end up with outcomes AE, AF, or AG. Each of the other policies has three possible outcomes as well, yielding a total of 12 possible outcomes.

We could conduct a separate benefit-cost analysis for each of the 12 possible outcomes. Unfortunately, the policy that maximizes net benefits for E may be different from that which maximizes net benefits for F or G. Thus, if we only knew which outcome would prevail, we could select the policy that maximized net benefits; the problem is that we do not. Furthermore, choosing the policy that is best if outcome E prevails may be disastrous if G results instead.

When a dominant policy emerges, this problem is avoided. A *dominant policy* is one that confers the highest net benefits for every outcome. In this case, the existence of risk concerning the future is not relevant for the policy choice. This fortuitous circumstance is exceptional rather than common, but it can occur.

Other options exist even when dominant solutions do not emerge. Suppose, for example, that we were able to assess the likelihood that each of the three possible outcomes would occur. Thus, we might expect outcome E to occur with probability 0.5, F with probability 0.3, and G with probability 0.2. Armed with this information, we can estimate the expected present value of net benefits. The *expected present value of net benefits* for a particular policy is defined as the sum over outcomes of the present value of net benefits for that policy where each outcome is weighted by its probability of occurrence. Symbolically this is expressed as

$$\text{EPVNB}_j = \sum_{i=0}^{I} P_i \text{PVNB}_{ij}, \ j = 1, \dots, J,$$

where

EPVNB_j = expected present value of net benefits for policy j
P_i = probability of the ith outcome occurring
PVNB_{ij} = present value of net benefits for policy j if outcome i prevails
J = number of policies being considered
I = number of outcomes being considered.

The final step is to select the policy with the highest expected present value of net benefits.

This approach has the substantial virtue that it weighs higher probability outcomes more heavily. It also, however, makes a specific assumption about society's preference for risk.

This approach is appropriate if society is risk-neutral. *Risk-neutrality* can be defined most easily by the use of an example. Suppose you were to choose between being given a definite $50 or entering a lottery in which you had a 50 percent chance of winning $100 and a 50 percent chance of winning nothing. (Notice that the expected value of this lottery is $50 = 0.5($100) + 0.5($0).) You would be said to be risk-neutral if you would be indifferent between these two choices. If you view the lottery as more attractive, you would be exhibiting *risk-loving* behavior, while a preference for the definite $50 would suggest *risk-averse* behavior. Accepting the expected present value of net benefits approach as the decision mechanism implies that society is risk-neutral.

Is that a valid assumption? The evidence is mixed. The existence of gambling suggests that at least some members of society are risk-loving, while the existence of insurance suggests that, at least for some risks, others are risk-averse. Since the same people may gamble and own insurance policies, it is likely that the nature of the risk may be important.

Even if individuals were demonstrably risk-averse, this would not be a sufficient condition for the government to forsake risk-neutrality in evaluating public investments. One famous article (Arrow & Lind, 1970) argues that using a risk-neutrality metric in public policy is appropriate since "when the risks of a public investment are publicly borne, the total cost of risk-bearing is insignificant and, therefore, the government should ignore uncertainty in evaluating public investments." The logic behind this result suggests that as the number of risk bearers (and the degree of diversification of risks) increases, the amount of risk borne by any individual diminishes to zero. Are you convinced? Why or why not?

More Complicated Categories of Risk: Systematic and Compound Risks. Recent history has made it clear that not all types of risks are the same. Some risk assessment challenges, such as dealing with climate change and/or a pandemic such as COVID-19, involve more complicated types of risks. How do they affect benefit-cost analysis?

Systematic Risk. For our purposes *systematic risks* can be defined as risks posed when an event causes economic damage to part of the economy that results in secondary damages that spread throughout the entire economic system. First identified in finance, it is also called a *non-diversifiable risk* because it affects the entire portfolio, not just a few assets.

Pandemics such as COVID-19 and climate change provide good examples of systematic risk.[10] Let's illustrate the point with the impacts of an epidemic. If a virus affects only a local area (shutting down local suppliers, for example), a main strategy for ameliorating the economic impact is to import goods (food, medical supplies, etc.) from unaffected regions. When the spread of the virus becomes a pandemic, even imported supplies are affected, so not only can the alternative production facilities be negatively affected, but the total demand for those supplies is much higher as well. COVID-19 had a large effect on global supply chains, which led to deeper and geographically wider shortages of key materials. By limiting normal alternative sources of goods, systematic risks can have fewer options for limiting the damage they cause. Both material shortages and higher prices flowing from those supplies that remain can be included in the benefit-cost analysis and weighted by the likelihood of these occurrences.

Compound Risks. Compound risks are multiple risks that occur simultaneously or sequentially one after another. One example of a compound risk occurred in

2019–2020 when climate-intensified wildfires occurred during a pandemic.[11] In this case climate change intensified the number, geographic scope, and intensity of wildfires, while the simultaneous presence of the COVID-19 outbreak caused the damage to be higher than it would otherwise have been. Consider one illustration of how intensified damage can result from an interaction between these two risks. The main way of reducing the damage from COVID-19 involved having people isolate in their homes, but wildfires forced many people to leave their homes and gather in community shelters. Because of this exodus, the availability of shelters with adequate capacity to offer temporary housing with sufficient physical distancing to protect against the further spread of COVID-19 was severely strained. The total damage caused by the interaction of these two risks was larger than the total damage that would have occurred if the two risks had not interacted (occurred at completely different times, for example).

This example illustrates a more general implication of this kind of compound risk—it makes it more likely that the ability of impact-reducing measures (in this case shelters) can prove insufficient in the presence of a compound risk. Specifically, any risk assessment that treats all risks as independent can underestimate the value of investing in risk-reducing capacity in the presence of compound risks.

Benefit-cost analysis can accommodate compounding risks by having different outcomes that depend on the degree of expected compounding involved. These outcomes can be included by assigning the probabilities of occurrence to each outcome and by capturing the enhanced damage that results when they interact.

Finally, suppose that the best we can do is assign a range of probabilities to the various outcomes. In this case we can run a large number of expected present value calculations—one for each likely combination of probabilities. This will not give us a single answer, but it will give us a lot of information not only about the range of possible outcomes, but also about how those outcomes depend on the levels and ranges of the probabilities. By itself that information is helpful.

There is a movement in national policy in both the courts and the legislature to search for imaginative ways to define acceptable risk. In general, the policy approaches reflect a case-by-case method. We shall see that current policy reflects a high degree of risk-aversion toward a number of environmental problems.

Distribution of Benefits and Costs

Many agencies are now required to consider the distributional impacts of costs and benefits as part of any economic analysis. For example, the U.S. EPA provides guidelines on distributional issues in its "Guidelines for Preparing Economic Analysis." According to the EPA, distributional analysis "assesses changes in social welfare by examining the effects of a regulation across different subpopulations and entities." Distributional analysis can take two forms: *economic impact analysis* and *equity analysis*. Economic impact analysis focuses on a broad characterization of who gains and who loses from a given policy. Equity analysis examines impacts on disadvantaged groups or subpopulations. The latter delves into the normative issue of equity or fairness in the distribution of costs and benefits. That analysis does not need to be normative, however. Positive distributional analyses assess whether and the extent to which a policy benefits or harms particular subgroups of the population (race, gender, income, geographical location, etc.) without a judgment on a "best" solution (Stafford,

2021). Loomis (2011) outlines several approaches for incorporating distribution and equity into benefit-cost analysis. Distributional weights can be helpful for equity consideration (Adler, 2016, for example). Lorenz curves and Gini coefficients are another. Lorenz curves and Gini coefficients are common metrics to measure inequality and as such are useful for policies that have distributional impacts across a gradient like income (Stafford, 2021).

A Lorenz curve is a graphical representation of the distribution of income. It plots the cumulative percentage of income against the cumulative percentage of the population. A 45-degree line would be perfect income equality. The farther away from this line the Lorenz curve is, the more income inequality there is in that economy. The Gini coefficient is related in that it measures the area between the 45-degree line and the Lorenz curve divided by the total area under the line. The Gini coefficient ranges from 0 to 1, with 0 being perfect equality and 1 representing perfect inequality. One way to assess the distributional impact of a proposed solution to a market failure is to compare the Lorenz curve/Gini coefficient from the baseline or status quo to the estimated Lorenz curve/Gini coefficient under the proposed solution (Stafford, 2021).[12]

In November 2023, the Biden-Harris administration issued revisions to Circular A-4, which includes guidance on how to measure the distributional impacts of regulatory decisions as well as providing a methodology for measuring the impacts on welfare using the income elasticity of marginal utility. This measures how much (less) a dollar is worth as your income goes up. Imagine losing $2,000. Does it matter if your income is $1 million verusus $50,000? The income elasticity of marginal utility measures how much more it matters to someone with lower income.[13]

Choosing the Discount Rate

Recall that discounting allows us to compare all costs and benefits in current dollars, regardless of when the benefits accrue or costs are charged. Suppose a project will impose an immediate cost of $4 million (today's dollars), but the $5.5 million in benefits will not be earned until 5 years out. Is this project a good idea? On the surface it might seem like it is, but recall that $5.5 million in 5 years is not the same as $5.5 million today. At a discount rate of 5 percent, the present value of benefits minus the present value of costs is positive. However, at a 10 percent discount rate, this same calculation yields a negative value, since the present value of costs exceeds the benefits. Can you reproduce the calculations that yield these conclusions?

As Example 3.4 indicates, this has been, and continues to be, an important issue. When the public sector uses a discount rate lower than that in the private sector, the public sector will find more projects with longer payoff periods worthy of authorization. And, as we have already seen, the discount rate is a major determinant of the allocation of resources among generations as well.

The discount rate can be defined conceptually as the social opportunity cost of capital. This cost of capital can be divided further into two components: (1) the riskless cost of capital and (2) the risk premium. Traditionally, economists have used long-term interest rates on government bonds as one measure of the cost of capital, adjusted by a risk premium that would depend on the riskiness of the project considered. Unfortunately, the choice of how large an adjustment to make has been left to the discretion of the analysts. This ability to affect the desirability of a particular project or policy by the choice of discount rate led to a situation in which government

EXAMPLE 3.4

The Importance of the Discount Rate

Let's begin with an historical example. For years the United States and Canada had been discussing the possibility of constructing a tidal power project in the Passamaquoddy Bay between Maine and New Brunswick. This project would have heavy initial capital costs, but low operating costs that presumably would hold for a long time into the future. As part of their analysis of the situation, a complete inventory of costs and benefits was completed in 1959.

Using the same benefit and cost figures, Canada concluded that the project should not be built, while the United States concluded that it should. Because these conclusions were based on the same benefit-cost data, the differences can be attributed solely to the use of different discount rates. The United States used 2.5 percent while Canada used 4.125 percent. The higher discount rate makes the initial cost weigh much more heavily in the calculation, leading to the Canadian conclusion that the project would yield a negative net benefit. Since the lower discount rate weighs the lower future operating costs relatively more heavily, Americans saw the net benefit as positive.

In a more recent illustration of why the magnitude of the discount rate matters, on October 30, 2006, economist Nicholas Stern from the London School of Economics issued a report using a discount rate of 0.1 percent that concluded that the benefits of strong, early action on climate change would considerably outweigh the costs. Other economists, such as William Nordhaus of Yale University, who preferred a discount rate around 6 percent, found that optimal economic policies to slow climate change involve only modest rates of emissions reductions in the near term, followed by sharp reductions in the medium and long term.

In this debate, the desirability of strong current action is dependent (at least in part) on the size of the discount rate used in the analysis. Higher discount rates reduce the present value of future benefits from current investments in abatement, implying a smaller marginal benefit. Since the costs associated with those investments are not affected nearly as much by the choice of discount rate (remember that costs occurring in the near future are discounted less), a lower present value of marginal benefit translates into a lower optimal investment in abatement.

Far from being an esoteric subject, the choice of the discount rate is fundamentally important in defining the role of the public sector, the types of projects undertaken, and the allocation of resources across generations.

Sources: Stokey, E., & Zeckhauser, R. (1978). *A Primer for Policy Analysis*. New York: W. W. Norton, 164–165; Mikesell, R. (1977). *The Rate of Discount for Evaluating Public Projects*. Washington, D.C.: The American Enterprise Institute for Public Policy Research, 3–5; the Stern Report: http://webarchive.nationalarchives.gov.uk/20100407011151/; http://www.hm-treasury.gov.uk/sternreview_index.htm; Nordhaus, W. (September 2007). A review of the Stern Review on the economics of climate change. *Journal of Economic Literature*, XLV (3), 686–702.

agencies were using a variety of discount rates to justify programs or projects they supported. One set of hearings conducted by Congress during the 1960s discovered that, at one time, agencies were using discount rates ranging from 0 to 20 percent.

During the early 1970s, the Office of Management and Budget published a circular that required, with some exceptions, all government agencies to use a discount rate of 10 percent in their benefit-cost analysis. A revision issued in 1992 reduced the required discount rate to 7 percent. This circular also included guidelines for benefit-cost analysis and specified that certain rates would change annually. This standardization reduces biases by eliminating the agency's ability to choose a discount rate that justifies a predetermined conclusion. It also allows a project to be considered independently of fluctuations in the true social cost of capital due to cycles in the behavior of the economy. On the other hand, when the social opportunity cost of capital differs from this administratively determined level, the benefit-cost analysis will not, in general, define the efficient allocation. The OMB recommendations of 3 percent or 7 percent when making calculations of net present value stood for many years, yet market rates have not been that high in a long time. Fixed rates can be very inflexible if they change slower than markets. Only most recently have discount rates started to decline for federal analyses. For example, the 2023 discount rate for water resources is now 2.5 percent.

In 2023, a revised circular dropped the 7 percent rate to reflect the current economics literature. The revised circular also recommends a 2 percent discount rate for beneficial investments such as clean energy or semiconductors and for long term analysis.[14]

Example 3.4 highlights a different aspect of the choice of the discount rate for decisions involving long time horizons. It considers the question of whether discount rates should decline over time. Debate 3.2 explores this question.

DEBATE 3.2

Discounting over Long Time Horizons: Should Discount Rates Decline?

As you now recognize, the choice of the discount rate can significantly alter the outcome of a benefit-cost analysis. This effect is exacerbated over long time horizons and can become especially influential in decisions about spending now to mitigate damages from climate change, which may be uncertain in both magnitude and timing. What rate is appropriate? Recent literature and some evidence argue for declining rates of discount over long time horizons. Should a declining rate schedule be utilized? A blue-ribbon panel of experts gathered to debate this and related questions (Arrow et al., 2012).

An unresolved debate in the economics literature revolves around the question of whether discount rates should be positive ("descriptive"), reflecting actual market rates, or normative ("prescriptive"), reflecting ethical considerations. Those who argue for the descriptive approach prefer to use market rates of return since expenditures to mitigate climate change are investment expenditures. Those who argue for the alternative prescriptive approach argue for including judgments about intergenerational equity. These rates are usually lower than those found in actual markets (Griffiths et al., 2012).

In the United States, the Office of Management and Budget (OMB) currently recommends a constant rate of discount for project analysis. The recommendation is to use 3 percent and 7 percent real discount rates in sensitivity analysis (OMB, 2003), with options for lower rates if future generations are impacted. The United Kingdom and France utilize discount rate schedules that decline over time. Is one of these methods better than the other for discounting over long time horizons? If a declining rate is appropriate, how fast should that rate decline?

The blue-ribbon panel agreed that theory provides strong arguments for a "declining certainty-equivalent discount rate" (Arrow et al., 2012, p. 21). Although the empirical literature also supports a rate that is declining over time (especially in the presence of uncertainty about future costs and/or benefits), the results from the empirical literature vary widely depending on the model assumptions and underlying data. If a declining rate schedule were to be adopted in the United States, this group of experts recommended that the EPA's Science Advisory Board be asked to develop criteria that could be used as the common foundation for determining what the schedule should look like.

Sources: Arrow, K., Maureen, J., Cropper, L., Gollier, C., Groom, B., Heal, G. M., et al. (December 2012). How should benefits and costs be discounted in an intergenerational context: The views of an expert panel. *RFF DP 12–53*; Griffiths, C., Kopits, E., Marten, A., Moore, C., Newbold, S., & Wolverton, A. (2012). The social cost of carbon: Valuing carbon reductions in policy analysis. In R. A. de Mooij, M. Keen, & I. W. H. Parry (Eds.). *Fiscal Policy to Mitigate Climate Change: A Guide for Policy Makers*. Washington, D.C.: IMF, 69–87; OMB (Office of Management and Budget). Circular A-4: Regulatory Analysis. Washington, D.C.: Executive Office of the President. www.whitehouse.gov/omb/circulars_a004_a-4.

Divergence of Social and Private Discount Rates

Earlier we concluded that producers, in their attempt to maximize producer surplus, also maximize the present value of net benefits under the "right" conditions, such as the absence of externalities, the presence of properly defined property rights, and the presence of competitive markets within which the property rights can be exchanged.

Now let's consider one more condition. If resources are to be allocated efficiently, firms must use the same rate to discount future net benefits as is appropriate for society at large. If firms were to use a higher rate, they would extract and sell resources faster than would be efficient. Conversely, if firms were to use a lower-than-appropriate discount rate, they would be excessively conservative.

Why might private and social rates differ? As noted earlier, the social opportunity cost of capital can be separated into two components: the risk-free cost of capital and the risk premium. The *risk-free cost of capital* is the rate of return earned when there is absolutely no risk of earning more or less than the expected return. The *risk premium* is an additional cost of capital required to compensate the owners of this capital when the expected and actual returns may differ. Therefore, because of differences in the risk premium, the cost of capital is higher in risky industries than in no-risk industries.

Another difference between private and social discount rates may stem from a difference in social and private risk premiums. If the risk of certain private decisions is different from the risks faced by society as a whole, then the social and private risk premiums may differ. One obvious example is the risk *caused* by the government.

If the firm is afraid its assets will be confiscated by the government, it may choose a higher discount rate to make its profits before nationalization occurs. From the point of view of society—as represented by government—this is not a risk and, therefore, a lower discount rate is appropriate. When private rates exceed social rates, current production is higher than is desirable to maximize the net benefits to society. Both energy production and forestry have been subject to this source of inefficiency.

Another divergence in discount rates may stem from different underlying rates of time preference. Such a divergence in time preferences can cause not only a divergence between private and social discount rates (as when firms have a higher rate of time preference (focus on the present) than the public sector), but even between otherwise similar analyses conducted in two different countries.

Time preferences would be expected to be higher (more weight on the present), for example, in a cash-poor, developing country than in an industrialized country. Since the two benefit-cost analyses in these two countries would be based upon two different discount rates, they might come to quite different conclusions. What is right for the developing country may not be right for the industrialized country and vice versa.

Although private and social discount rates do not always diverge, they may. When those circumstances arise, market decisions are not efficient.

A Critical Appraisal

We have seen that it is sometimes, but not always, difficult to estimate benefits and costs. When this estimation is difficult or unreliable, it limits the value of a benefit-cost analysis. This problem would be particularly disturbing if biases tended to increase or decrease net benefits systematically. Do such biases exist?

In the early 1970s, Robert Haveman (1972) conducted a major study that continues to shed some light on this question. Focusing on Army Corps of Engineers water projects, such as flood control, navigation, and hydroelectric power generation, Haveman compared the *ex ante* (before the fact) estimates of benefits and costs with their *ex post* (after the fact) counterparts. Thus, he was able to address the issues of accuracy and bias. He concluded that:

> In the empirical case studies presented, ex post estimates often showed little relationship to their ex ante counterparts. On the basis of the few cases and the a priori analysis presented here, one could conclude that there is a serious bias incorporated into agency ex ante evaluation procedures, resulting in persistent overstatement of expected benefits. Similarly in the analysis of project construction costs, enormous variance was found among projects in the relationship between estimated and realized costs. Although no persistent bias in estimation was apparent, nearly 50 percent of the projects displayed realized costs that deviated by more than plus or minus 20 percent from ex ante projected costs.

In the cases examined by Haveman, at least, the notion that benefit-cost analysis is purely a scientific exercise was clearly not consistent with the evidence; the biases of the analysts were merely translated into numbers. A later assessment of costs (Harrington et al., 1999) found evidence of both overestimation and underestimation, although overestimation was more common. The authors attributed the overestimation mainly to a failure to anticipate technical innovation.

Does their analysis mean that benefit-cost analysis is fatally flawed? Absolutely not! Valuation methods have improved considerably since the Haveman study, but problems remain. This study does, however, highlight the enduring importance of calculating an accurate value and of including all of the potential benefits and costs (e.g., nonmarket values). As elementary as it might seem, including both the benefits and the costs is necessary. As Example 3.5 illustrates, that is not always the case in practice.

Haveman's analysis also serves to remind us that benefit-cost analysis is not a stand-alone technique. It should be used in conjunction with other available information. Economic analysis including benefit-cost analysis can provide useful information, but it should not be the only determinant for all decisions.

EXAMPLE 3.5

Is the Two for One Rule a Good Way to Manage Regulatory Overreach?

Environmental regulations can be costly, but they also produce economic benefits. Efficiency suggests that regulations whose benefits exceed their costs should be pursued and that is the path followed by previous Executive Orders (EOs) from Presidents Reagan (EO 12291), Clinton (EO 12866), and Obama (EO 13563).

In 2017, the Trump administration abandoned business as usual and issued EO 13771, mandating that for every new regulation issued, two must be thrown out.[15] What does economic analysis and, in particular, benefit-cost analysis have to say about this one-in, two-out prescription?

Executive Order 13771 reads, in part: "(c) ... any new incremental costs associated with new regulations shall, to the extent permitted by law, be offset by the elimination of existing costs associated with at least two prior regulations."

In his attempt to reduce regulatory overreach President Trump's approach seems to suggest that only the costs are important when evaluating current and new regulations. Benefits don't matter. Since most of the current regulations were put into place based on benefits and costs, removing them based solely on costs would be a "blunt instrument"—one that is poorly targeted on making efficient choices.

Economist Robert Shiller further argues that regulation is in the public interest in many areas and "the world is far too complex to make it possible to count up regulations meaningfully and impose a two-for-one rule."

Alan Krupnick, economist at Resources for the Future, points out that even if a "cost-only" approach were justified, it would not be easy to implement. For example, "What is a cost? Is it a projected cost in the rule or actual costs as implemented? Is it present discounted costs or something else to account for cost streams over time? Is it direct costs or do indirect costs (say, to consumers) count? Is it private costs or costs to society?"

Regardless of the answer to those questions, however, benefits do matter. As Krupnick notes, "How do we determine which regulations are ineffective and unnecessary without considering their benefits? The answer is simple—we cannot."

Imagine if we only saved endangered species that cost the least to save, or cleaned up only the least expensive oil spills. Making decisions based solely on costs is misguided economics.

Sources: www.rff.org/research/publications/trump-s-regulatory-reform-process-analytical-hurdles-and-missing-benefits; www.nytimes.com/2017/02/17/upshot/why-trumps-2-for-1-rule-on-regulations-is-no-quick-fix.html; www.env-econ.net/2017/02/two-for-one-too-blunt-an-instrument-for-good-governance.html.

Benefit-cost analysis is also limited in that it does not really address the question of who reaps the benefits and who pays the cost. It is quite possible for a particular course of action to yield high net benefits, but to have the benefits borne by one societal group and the costs borne by another. This scenario serves to illustrate a basic principle—ensuring that a particular policy is efficient provides an important, but not always the sole, basis for public policy. Other aspects, such as who reaps the benefit or bears the burden, are also important considerations. Distributional benefit-cost analysis can help illuminate potential inequities.

In summary, on the positive side, benefit-cost analysis is frequently a very useful part of the policy process. Even when the underlying data are not strictly reliable, the outcomes may not be sensitive to that unreliability. In other circumstances, the data may be reliable enough to give indications of the consequences of broad policy directions, even when they are not reliable enough to fine-tune those policies. Benefit-cost analysis, when done correctly, can provide a useful complement to the other influences on the political process by clarifying what choices yield the highest net benefits to society.

On the negative side, benefit-cost analysis has been attacked as seeming to promise more than can actually be delivered, particularly in the absence of solid benefit information. This concern has triggered two responses. First, regulatory processes have been developed that can be implemented with very little information and yet have desirable economic properties. The recent reforms in air pollution control, which we cover in later chapters, provide some powerful examples.

The second involves techniques that supply useful information to the policy process while acknowledging that some environmental services are difficult to value. The rest of this chapter deals with the two most prominent of these—cost-effectiveness analysis and impact analysis.

Even when benefits are difficult or impossible to quantify, economic analysis has much to offer. Policymakers should know, for example, how much various policy actions will cost and what their impacts on society will be, even if the efficient policy choice cannot be identified with any certainty. Benefit-cost analysis is well-suited for investigating these trade-offs and informing these decisions. However, interpreting and using the results requires understanding the framework and addressing its limitations, including the uncertainties in benefits estimates and evaluating the distribution of impacts across those who are benefiting and those who are not.

Other Decision-Making Metrics

Cost-Effectiveness Analysis

What can be done to guide policy when the requisite valuation for benefit-cost analysis is either unavailable or not sufficiently reliable? Without a good measure of benefits, making an efficient choice is no longer possible.

In such cases, however, it is often possible to set a policy target on some basis other than a strict comparison of benefits and costs. One example is pollution control. What level of pollution should be established as the maximum acceptable level? In many countries, studies of the effects of a particular pollutant on human health have been used as the basis for establishing that pollutant's maximum acceptable concentration. Researchers attempt to find a threshold level below which no damage seems to occur. That threshold is then further lowered to provide a margin of safety and that becomes the pollution target.

Approaches could also be based upon expert opinion. Ecologists, for example, could be enlisted to define the critical numbers of certain species or the specific critical wetlands resources that should be preserved.

Once the policy target is specified, however, economic analysis can have a great deal to say about the cost consequences of choosing a means of achieving that objective. The cost consequences are important not only because eliminating wasteful expenditure is an appropriate goal in its own right, but also to assure that they do not trigger political backlash.

Typically, several means of achieving the specified objective are available; some will be relatively inexpensive, while others turn out to be very expensive. The problems are frequently complicated enough that identifying the cheapest means of achieving an objective cannot be accomplished without a rather detailed analysis of the choices.

Cost-effectiveness analysis frequently involves an *optimization procedure*. An optimization procedure, in this context, is merely a systematic method for finding the lowest-cost means of accomplishing the objective. This procedure does not, in general, produce an efficient allocation because the predetermined objective may not be efficient. All efficient policies are cost-effective, but not all cost-effective policies are efficient.

Earlier in this chapter we introduced the concept of the efficiency equimarginal principle. According to that principle, net benefits are maximized when the marginal benefit is equal to the marginal cost.

A similar, and equally important, equimarginal principle exists for cost-effectiveness:

Second Equimarginal Principle (the Cost-Effectiveness Equimarginal Principle): The least-cost means of achieving an environmental target will have been achieved when the marginal costs of all possible means of achievement are equal.

Suppose we want to achieve a specific emissions reduction across a region, and several possible techniques exist for reducing emissions. How much of the control responsibility should each technique bear? The cost-effectiveness equimarginal principle suggests that the techniques should be used such that the desired reduction is achieved and the cost of achieving the last unit of emissions reduction (in other words, the marginal control cost) should be the same for all sources.

To demonstrate why this principle is valid, suppose that we have an allocation of control responsibility where marginal control costs are much higher for one set of techniques than for another. This cannot be the least-cost allocation since we could lower cost while retaining the same amount of emissions reduction. To be specific, costs could be lowered by allocating more control to the lower marginal cost sources and less to the high marginal cost sources. Since it is possible to find a way to lower cost while holding emissions constant, clearly the initial allocation could not have minimized cost. Once marginal costs are equalized, it becomes impossible to find any lower-cost way of achieving the same degree of emissions reduction; therefore, that allocation must be the allocation that minimizes costs.

In our pollution control example, cost-effectiveness can be used to find the least-cost means of meeting a particular standard and its associated cost. Using this cost as a benchmark case, we can estimate how much costs could be expected to increase from this minimum level if policies that are not cost-effective are implemented. Cost-effectiveness analysis can also be used to determine how much compliance costs can be expected to change if the EPA chooses a more stringent or less stringent standard. In later chapters, we shall examine in detail the current movement toward cost-effective policies, a movement that was triggered in part by studies showing that the cost reductions from reform could be substantial.

Impact Analysis

What can be done when the information needed to perform a benefit-cost analysis or a cost-effectiveness analysis is not available? The analytical technique designed to deal with this problem is called *impact analysis*. An impact analysis, regardless of whether it focuses on economic impact or environmental impact or both, attempts to quantify the consequences of various actions.

In contrast to benefit-cost analysis, a pure impact analysis makes no attempt to convert all these consequences into a one-dimensional measure, such as dollars, to ensure comparability. In contrast to cost-effectiveness analysis, impact analysis does not necessarily attempt to optimize. Impact analysis places a large amount of relatively undigested information at the disposal of the policymaker. It is up to the policymaker to assess the importance of the various predicted consequences and act accordingly.

On January 1, 1970, President Nixon signed the National Environmental Policy Act of 1969. This act, among other things, directed all agencies of the federal government to:

> include in every recommendation or report on proposals for legislation and other major Federal actions significantly affecting the quality of the human environment, a detailed statement by the responsible official on—
>
> i. the environmental impact of the proposed action;
> ii. any adverse environmental effects which cannot be avoided should the proposal be implemented;
> iii. alternatives to the proposed action;
> iv. the relationships between local short-term uses of man's environment and the maintenance and enhancement of long-term productivity; and
> v. any irreversible and irretrievable commitments of resources which would be involved in the proposed action should it be implemented.[16]

This was the beginning of the environmental impact statement, which is now a familiar, if controversial, part of environmental policy making.

Current environmental impact statements are more sophisticated than their early predecessors and may contain a benefit-cost analysis or a cost-effectiveness analysis in addition to other more traditional impact measurements. Historically, however, the tendency has been to issue huge environmental impact statements that are virtually impossible to comprehend in their entirety.

In response, the Council on Environmental Quality, which, by law, administers the environmental impact statement process, has set content standards that are now resulting in shorter, more concise statements. To the extent that they merely quantify consequences, statements can avoid the problem of "hidden value judgments" that sometimes plague benefit-cost analysis, but they do so only by bombarding the policy-makers with masses of noncomparable information.

Summary

Finding a balance in the relationship between humanity and the environment requires many choices. Some basis for making rational choices is absolutely necessary. If not made by design, decisions will be made by default. Benefit-cost analysis is a powerful tool for evaluating trade-offs and informing decision making. Cost-effectiveness analysis and impact analysis offer alternatives to benefit-cost analysis. All of these techniques offer valuable information for decision making and all have shortcomings. Interpreting results requires understanding the framework and its limitations and understanding the distribution of the impacts across different groups in society.

A static efficient allocation is one that maximizes the net benefit over all possible uses of those resources. The dynamic efficiency criterion, which is appropriate when time is an important consideration, is satisfied when the outcome maximizes the present value of net benefits from all possible uses of the resources. Later chapters examine the degree to which our social institutions yield allocations that conform to these criteria.

Because benefit-cost analysis is both very powerful and very controversial, in 1996 a group of economists of quite different political persuasions got together to attempt to reach some consensus on its proper role in environmental decision making. Their conclusion is worth reproducing in its entirety:

Benefit-cost analysis can play an important role in legislative and regulatory policy debates on protecting and improving health, safety, and the natural environment. Although formal benefit-cost analysis should not be viewed as either necessary or sufficient for designing sensible policy, it can provide an exceptionally useful framework for consistently organizing disparate information, and in this way, it can greatly improve the process and, hence, the outcome of policy analysis. If properly done, benefit-cost analysis can be of great help to agencies participating in the development of environmental, health and safety regulations, and it can likewise be useful in evaluating agency decision making and in shaping statutes.[17]

Robinson et al. (2016) emphasize the importance of paying attention to the distributional consequences. "By making the trade-offs between efficiency and distribution more apparent, increased analysis of distributional impacts would help decision makers make more informed decisions.... Good regulatory decisions require such positive distributional analysis as an input to sound normative judgment" (324).

Even when benefits are difficult to calculate, however, economic analysis in the form of cost-effectiveness can be valuable. This technique can establish the least expensive ways to accomplish predetermined policy goals and can assess the extra costs involved when policies other than the least-cost policy are chosen. What it cannot do is answer the question of whether those predetermined policy goals are efficient.

At the other end of the spectrum is impact analysis, which merely identifies and quantifies the impacts of particular policies without any pretence of optimality or even comparability of the information generated. Impact analysis does not guarantee an efficient outcome.

All three of the techniques discussed in this chapter are useful, but none of them can stake a claim as being universally the "best" approach. The nature of the information that is available and its reliability make a difference.

Discussion Questions

1. Is risk-neutrality an appropriate assumption for benefit-cost analysis? Why or why not? Does it seem more appropriate for some environmental problems than others? If so, which ones? If you were evaluating the desirability of locating a hazardous waste incinerator in a particular town, would the Arrow–Lind rationale for risk-neutrality be appropriate? Why or why not?

2. Was the executive order issued by President George W. Bush mandating a heavier use of benefit-cost analysis in regulatory rule making a step toward establishing a more rational regulatory structure, or was it a subversion of the environmental policy process? Why? President Biden has called for modernizing regulatory reform, including how we implement benefit-cost analysis. What changes might be appropriate?

3. The social cost of carbon (SCC) is an important measure of the present value of damages of an additional ton of CO_2 emitted into the atmosphere. Why might the shape of the damage function matter for this calculation?

Self-Test Exercises

1. Suppose a proposed public policy could result in three possible outcomes: (1) present value of net benefits of $4,000,000, (2) present value of net benefits of $1,000,000, or (3) present value of net benefits of –$10,000,000 (i.e., a loss). Suppose society is risk-neutral, and the probabilities of occurrence of each of these three outcomes are, respectively, 0.85, 0.10, and 0.05. Should this policy be pursued or trashed? Why?

2. Suppose you want to remove ten fish of an exotic species that have illegally been introduced to a lake. You have three possible removal methods. Assume that q_1, q_2, and q_3 are, respectively, the amount of fish removed by each method that you choose to use so that the goal will be accomplished by any combination of methods such that $q_1 + q_2 + q_3 = 10$. If the marginal costs of each removal method are,

respectively, $\$10q_1$, $\$5q_2$, and $\$2.5q_3$, how much of each method should you use to achieve the removal cost effectively?

   a. Why isn't an exclusive use of method 3 cost effective?

   b. Suppose that the three marginal costs were constant (not increasing as in the previous case) such that $MC_1 = \$10$, $MC_2 = \$5$, and $MC_3 = \$2.5$. What is the cost-effective outcome in that case?

3. Consider the role of discount rates in problems involving long time horizons such as climate change. Suppose that a particular emissions abatement strategy would result in a $500 billion reduction in damages 50 years into the future. How would the maximum amount spent now to eliminate those damages change if the discount rate is 2 percent, rather than 10 percent?

Notes

1 Actually if $B = C$, it wouldn't make any difference if the action occurs or not; the benefits and costs are a wash.

2 The monetary worth of the net benefit is the sum of two right triangles, and it equals $(1/2)(\$5)(5) + (1/2)(\$2.50)(5)$ or $\$18.75$. Can you see why?

3 The mathematics of dynamic efficiency are presented in the appendix to Chapter 6.

4 Executive Order 12866 of September 30, 1993. Section 1, No. 6. Federal Register, Vol 58, No. 190. October 4, 1993.

5 The Resources for the Future (RFF) explainer on the social cost of carbon details nicely the SCC history and estimates. https://www.rff.org/publications/explainers/social-cost-carbon-101.

6 Rennert, K., Errickson, F., Prest, B. C. et al. (2022). Comprehensive evidence implies a higher social cost of CO2. *Nature*, 610, 687–692. https://doi.org/10.1038/s41586-022-05224-9.

7 https://www.whitehouse.gov/omb/briefing-room/2023/11/09/biden-harris-administration-releases-final-guidance-to-improve-regulatory-analysis/.

8 The division between tangible and intangible benefits changes as our techniques improve. Recreation benefits were, until the advent of the travel-cost model, treated as intangible. The travel-cost model will be discussed in the next chapter.

9 Knight, F. H. (1921). *Risk, Uncertainty and Profit*. University of Illinois at Urbana-Champaign's Academy for Entrepreneurial Leadership Historical Research Reference in Entrepreneurship. Available at SSRN: https://ssrn.com/abstract=1496192.

10 Rizwan, M. S., Ahmad, G., & Ashraf, D. (October 2020). Systemic risk: The impact of COVID-19.
Finance Research Letters, 36, 1018682.
doi: 10.1016/j.frl.2020.101682; Choudry, B. (2020). Climate Change as Systemic Risk. https://papers.ssrn.com/sol3/papers.cfm?abstract_id=3704962 (October 20).

11 Phillips, C. A., Caldas, A., Cleetus, R. et al. (2020). Compound climate risks in the COVID-19 pandemic. *Nature Climate Change*, 10, 586–588. https://doi.org/10.1038/s41558-020-0804-2.

12 Robinson et al. (2016) examine 24 major environmental, health, and safety regulations that were reviewed by the U.S. Office of Management and Budget for which the benefits exceeded the costs and find a lack of distributional analysis in almost all of them. They offer some reasons why this might be the case and suggest solutions.

13 https://www.whitehouse.gov/omb/briefing-room/2023/11/09/biden-harris-administration-releases-final-guidance-to-improve-regulatory-analysis/.

14 https://www.whitehouse.gov/omb/briefing-room/2023/11/09/biden-harris-administration-releases-final-guidance-to-improve-regulatory-analysis/.

15 Executive Order 13371, Reducing Regulation and Controlling Regulatory Cost.

16 83 Stat. 853.

17 From Arrow, K., et al. (1996). Is there a role for benefit-cost analysis in environmental, health and safety regulation? *Science, 272* (April 12), 221–222. Reprinted with permission from AAAS.

Further Reading

"Advancing the Frontiers of Benefit-Cost Analysis: Federal Priorities and Directions for Future Research". December. Updated guidelines on Benefit-Cost Analysis for federal decision making. https://www.whitehouse.gov/ostp/news-updates/2023/12/14/advancing-the-frontiers-of-benefit-cost-analysis-federal-priorities-and-directions-for-future-research/

Boardman, A. E., Greenberg, D. H., Vining, A. R., & Weimer, D. L. (2018). *Cost–Benefit Analysis: Concepts and Practice*, 5th ed. New York: Cambridge University Press. A comprehensive textbook on concepts and methods of benefit-cost analysis.

Canadian Cost-Benefit Analysis Guide: Regulatory Proposals. https://www.canada.ca/en/treasury-board-secretariat/services/reporting-government-spending/what-we-are-doing/canadian-cost-benefit-analysis-guide-regulatory-proposals.html#Toc178397874. Procedures for analytical work of benefit-cost analysis in Canada.

New Zealand. Guide to Social Cost Benefit Analysis. (2015). https://www.treasury.govt.nz/publications/guide/guide-social-cost-benefit-analysis. Procedures for analytical work of benefit-cost analysis in New Zealand.

Norton, B., & Minteer, B. A. (2002). From environmental ethics to environmental public philosophy: Ethicists and economists: 1973–future. In T. Tietenberg & H. Folmer (Eds.), *The International Yearbook of Environmental and Resource Economics: 2002/2003*. Cheltenham, U.K.: Edward Elgar, 373–407. A review of the interaction between environmental ethics and economic valuation.

Prest, B. C., Wingenroth, J., & Rennert, K. (2022). *The social cost of carbon: Reaching a new estimate*. Resources for the Future. https://www.resources.org/archives/the-social-cost-of-carbon-reaching-a-new-estimate/. A blog post that synthesizes the update information on the (currently) proposed Social Cost of Carbon.

Robinson, L. A., Hammitt, J. K., & Zeckhauser, R. J. (2016). Attention to distribution in U.S. regulatory analyses. *Review of Environmental Economics and Policy*, 10(2), 308–328. A useful set of guidelines for performing benefit-cost analysis, paying close attention to distributional impacts.

Shenot, J., Prause, E., & Shipley, J. (November 2022). *Using Benefit-Cost Analysis to Improve Distribution System Investment Decisions: Regulatory Assistance Project Reference Report*. https://www.raponline.org/wp-content/uploads/2022/11/rap-shenot-prause-shipley-using-benefit-cost-analysis-reference-report-2022-november.pdf. Electric utility regulators are paying closer attention than ever before to individual distribution system investment decisions, in part because of the rapid growth in distributed energy resources and the need for new grid modernization investments. This guide was developed to explore how benefit-cost analysis could inform and improve those decisions.

U.S. Environmental Protection Agency. (2010). *Guidelines for Preparing Economic Analyses (Report # EPA 240-R-10-001)*. www.epa.gov/environmental-economics/guidelines-preparing-economic-analyses#download. The procedures prescribed by the U.S. EPA for its analytical work.

U.S. Office of Information and Regulatory Affairs. Numerous useful resources are available on the U.S. Office of Information and Regulatory Affairs "Regulatory Matters" website, including related executive orders, guidance, and reports. https://www.whitehouse.gov/omb/information-regulatory-affairs/regulatory-matters/.

Additional references and historically significant references are available on this book's Companion Website: www.routledge.com/cw/Tietenberg

Chapter 4

Valuing the Environment

Methods

Introduction

Soon after the *Exxon Valdez* oil tanker ran aground on the Bligh Reef in Prince William Sound off the coast of Alaska on March 24, 1989, spilling approximately 11 million gallons of crude oil, the Exxon Corporation (now Exxon Mobil) accepted the liability for the damage caused by the leaking oil. This liability consisted of two parts: (1) the cost of cleaning up the spilled oil and restoring the site insofar as possible, and (2) compensation for the damage caused to the local ecology. Approximately $2.1 billion was spent in cleanup efforts, and Exxon also spent approximately $303 million to compensate fishermen whose livelihoods were greatly damaged for the 5 years following the spill.[1]

Litigation on environmental damages settled with Exxon agreeing to pay $900 million over 10 years. The punitive damages phase of this case began in May 1994. In January 2004, after many rounds of appeals, the U.S. District Court for the State of Alaska awarded punitive damages to the plaintiffs in the amount of $4.5 billion.[2] This amount was later cut almost in half to $2.5 billion and in 2008 the Supreme Court ruled that even those punitive damages were excessive based on maritime law and further argued that the punitive damages should not exceed the $507 million in compensatory damages already paid.[3]

In the spring of 2010, the Deepwater Horizon, a BP well in the Gulf of Mexico, exploded and began spewing an *Exxon Valdez*–sized oil spill every 4 to 5 days. By the time the leaking well was capped in August 2010, an estimated 134 million gallons had been spread through the Gulf of Mexico, almost 20 times greater than the *Exxon Valdez* spill, and the largest maritime spill in U.S. history. In 2016, a settlement was reached calling for total payments of $20.8 billion; $8.8 billion of this was for natural resource damages.[4] This amount is over and above the approximately $30 billion already spent on cleanup and other claims after the spill.[5] How can the economic

DOI: 10.4324/9781032689111-5

damages from oil spills, like these that caused substantial economic and environmental harm, be calculated? Thousands of birds have been found dead in the Gulf since the BP spill, for example. What are they "worth?" Interestingly, the *Exxon Valdez* spill triggered pioneering work focused on providing monetary estimates of environmental damages, setting the stage for what is today considered standard practice for *nonmarket valuation*—the monetization of those goods and services without market prices.

In Chapter 3, we examined the basic concepts economists use to calculate these damages. Yet implementing these concepts is far from a trivial exercise. While the costs of cleanup are fairly transparent, estimating the damage is far more complex. For example, how were the $900 million in damages in the Exxon case and the $20 billion in the BP case determined?

In this chapter, we explore how we can move from the general concepts to the actual estimates of compensation required by the courts. A series of special techniques has been developed to value the benefits from environmental improvement or, conversely, to value the damage done by environmental degradation. Special techniques are necessary because most of the normal valuation techniques that have been used over the years cannot be applied to environmental resources. Benefit-cost analysis requires the monetization of all relevant benefits and costs of a proposed policy or project, not merely those where the values can be derived from market transactions. As such, it is also important to monetize those environmental goods and services that are not traded in any market. Even more difficult to grapple with are those nonmarket benefits associated with values unrelated to use, topics explored ahead.

Why Value the Environment?

While it may prove difficult, if not impossible, to place a completely accurate value on certain environmental amenities, not making the attempt leaves us valuing them by default at $0. Will valuing them at $0 lead us to the best policy decisions? Probably not, but that does not prevent controversy from arising over attempts to replace $0 with a more appropriate value (Debate 4.1).

Many federal agencies depend on benefit-cost analyses for decision making. Ideally, the goal is to choose the most economically desirable projects, given limited budgets. Estimation of benefits and costs is used for such diverse actions as:

- natural resources damage assessments, such as for oil spills (National Oceanic and Atmospheric Administration);
- the designation of critical habitat under the Endangered Species Act (U.S. Fish and Wildlife Service);
- dam relicensing applications (The Federal Energy Regulatory Commission);
- seeking compensation for injuries and damages to public lands and wildlife (National Park Service); and
- estimating the costs and benefits of the Clean Air Act and the Clean Water Act (U.S. EPA).

These analyses, however, frequently fail to incorporate important nonmarket values. If the analysis does not include all the appropriate values, the results will be flawed. Is this exercise worth it?

DEBATE 4.1

Should Humans Place an Economic Value on the Environment?

Arne Naess, the late Norwegian philosopher, used the term *deep ecology* to refer to the view that the nonhuman environment has "intrinsic" value, a value that is independent of human interests. Intrinsic value is contrasted with "instrumental" value, in which the value of the environment is derived from its usefulness in satisfying human wants.

Two issues are raised by the Naess critique: (1) what is the basis for the valuing of the environment? and (2) how is the valuation accomplished? The belief that the environment may have a value that goes beyond its direct usefulness to humans is in fact quite consistent with modern economic valuation techniques. As we shall see in this chapter, economic valuation techniques now include the ability to quantify a wide range of "nonuse" values as well as the more traditional "use" values.

Controversies over how the values are derived are less easily resolved. As described in this chapter, economic valuation is based firmly upon human preferences. Proponents of deep ecology, on the other hand, would argue that allowing humans to determine the value of other species would have no more moral basis than allowing other species to determine the value of humans. Rather, deep ecologists argue, humans should only use environmental resources when necessary for survival; otherwise, nature should be left alone. And, because economic valuation is not helpful in determining survival necessity, deep ecologists argue that it contributes little to environmental management.

Those who oppose all economic valuation face a dilemma: when humans fail to value the environment, it may be assigned a default value of zero in calculations designed to guide policy. A value of zero, however derived, will tend to justify a great deal of environmental degradation that could not be justified with proper economic valuation. Support seems to be growing for the proposition that economic valuation can be a very useful means of demonstrating when environmental degradation is senseless, even when judged from a limited anthropomorphic perspective.

Sources: Costanza, R., et al. (1998). The value of ecosystem services: Putting the issues in perspective. *Ecological Economics, 25*(1), 67–72; Daily, G., & Ellison, K. (2003). *The New Economy of Nature: The Quest to Make Conservation Profitable*. Washington, D.C.: Island Press.

Valuation

While the valuation techniques we shall cover can be applied to both the damage caused by pollution and the services provided by the environment, each context offers its own unique aspects. We begin our investigation of valuation techniques by exposing some of the special challenges posed by the first of those contexts, pollution control.

In the United States, damage estimates are not only used in the design of policies, but, as indicated in the opening paragraphs of this chapter, they have also become important to the courts, who need some basis for deciding the magnitude of liability awards.[6]

The damage caused by pollution can take many different forms. The first, and probably most obvious, is the effect on human health. Polluted air and water can cause disease when ingested. Other forms of damage include loss of enjoyment from outdoor activities and damage to vegetation, animals, and materials.

Assessing the magnitude of this damage requires (1) identifying the affected categories, (2) estimating the physical relationship between the pollutant emissions (including natural sources) and the damage caused to the affected categories, (3) estimating responses by the affected parties toward mitigating some portion of the damage, and (4) placing a monetary value on the unmitigated physical damages. Each step is often difficult to accomplish.

Because the data used to track down causal relationships do not typically come from controlled experiments, identifying the affected categories is a complicated matter. Obviously, we cannot run large numbers of people through controlled experiments. If people were subjected to different levels of some pollutant, such as carbon monoxide, so that we could study the short-term and long-term effects, some might become ill and even die. Ethical concern precludes human experimentation of this type.

This leaves us essentially two choices. We can try to infer the impact on humans from controlled laboratory experiments on animals, or we can do statistical analysis of differences in mortality or disease rates for various human populations living in polluted environments to see the extent to which they are correlated with pollution concentrations. Neither approach is completely acceptable.

Animal experiments are expensive, and the extrapolation from effects on animals to effects on humans is tenuous at best. Many significant exposure effects do not appear for a long time. Ethical concerns also arise with animal experiments.

Statistical studies, on the other hand, deal with human populations exposed to low doses for long periods, but, unfortunately, they have another set of problems— correlation does not imply causation. To illustrate, the fact that death rates are higher in cities with higher pollution levels does not prove that the higher pollution caused the higher death rates. Perhaps those same cities averaged older populations or perhaps they had more smokers. Existing studies have been sophisticated enough to account for many of these other possible influences but, because of the relative paucity of data, they have not been able to cover them all.

The problems discussed so far arise when identifying whether a particular observed effect results from pollution. The next step is to estimate how strong the relationship is between the effect and the pollution concentrations. In other words, it is necessary not only to discover *whether* pollution causes an increased incidence of respiratory disease, but also to estimate *how much* reduction in respiratory illness could be expected from a given reduction in pollution.

The nonexperimental nature of the data makes this a difficult task. It is not uncommon for different researchers analyzing the same data to come to remarkably different conclusions. Diagnostic problems are compounded when the effects are synergistic—that is, when the effect depends, in a nonadditive way, on contributing factors such as the victims' smoking habits or the presence of other harmful substances in the air or water.

Once physical damages have been identified, the next step is to place a monetary value on them. It is not difficult to see how complex an undertaking this is. Think about the difficulties in assigning a value to extending a human life by several years or to the pain, suffering, and grief borne by both a cancer victim and the victim's family.

How can these difficulties be overcome? What valuation techniques are available not only to value pollution damage, but also to value the large number of services that the environment provides?

Types of Values

Economists have decomposed the total economic value conferred by resources into three main components: (1) use value, (2) option value, and (3) nonuse or passive-use values. *Use value* reflects the direct use of the environmental resource. Examples include fish harvested from the sea, timber harvested from the forest, water extracted from a stream for irrigation, even the scenic beauty conferred by a natural vista. If you used one of your senses to experience the resource—sight, sound, touch, taste, or smell—then you have *used* the resource. Pollution can cause a loss of use value, such as when air pollution increases the vulnerability to illness, an oil spill adversely affects a fishery, or smog enshrouds a scenic vista.

Option value reflects the value people place on a future ability to use the environment. It reflects the willingness to pay to preserve the option to use the environment in the future even if one is not currently using it. Whereas use value reflects the value derived from current use, option value reflects the desire to preserve the potential for possible future use. Are you planning to go to Yellowstone National Park next summer? Perhaps not, but would you like to preserve the option to go someday?

Passive-use or *nonconsumptive use values* arise when the resource is not actually consumed in the process of experiencing it. These types of values reflect the common observation that people are more than willing to pay for improving or preserving resources that they will never use. One type of nonuse value is a *bequest value*. Bequest value is the willingness to pay to ensure a resource is available for your children and grandchildren. A second type of nonuse value, a pure nonuse value, is called *existence value*. Existence value is measured by the willingness to pay to ensure that a resource continues to exist in the absence of any interest in future use. The term existence value was coined by economist John Krutilla in his now-famous quote, "There are many persons who obtain satisfaction from mere knowledge that part of wilderness North America remains even though they would be appalled by the prospect of being exposed to it."[7] These values are "independent of any present or future use these people might make of those resources."[8]

When the Bureau of Reclamation began looking at sites for dams near the Grand Canyon, groups such as the Sierra Club rose up in protest of the potential loss of this unique resource. When Glen Canyon was flooded by Lake Powell, even those who never intended to visit recognized this potential loss. Because this value does not derive from either direct use or potential use, it represents a very different category of value.

These categories of value can be combined to produce the total willingness to pay (TWP):

$$TWP = UseValue + OptionValue + NonuseValue$$

Since nonuse or passive-use values are derived from motivations other than personal use, they are obviously less tangible than use values. Total willingness to pay estimated without nonuse values, however, will be less than the minimum amount that would be required to compensate individuals if they are deprived of this environmental asset. Furthermore, estimated nonuse values can be quite large. Therefore, it is not surprising that they are controversial. Indeed, when the U.S. Department of the Interior drew up its regulations on the appropriate procedures for performing natural resource damage assessment, it prohibited the inclusion of nonuse values unless use values for the incident under consideration were zero. A subsequent 1989 decision by the District of Columbia Court of Appeals (880 F. 2nd 432) overruled this decision and allowed nonuse values to be included as long as they could be measured reliably.

Classifying Valuation Methods

Typically, the researcher's goal is to estimate the total willingness to pay for the good or service in question. This is the area under the demand curve up to the quantity consumed (recall discussion from Chapter 2). For a market good, this calculation is relatively straightforward. However, nonmarket goods and services, the focus of this chapter, require the estimation of willingness to pay either through examining behavior, drawing inferences from the demand for related goods, or through responses to surveys. And, as highlighted previously, capturing all components of value is challenging.

This section will provide a brief overview of some of the methods available to estimate these values and will convey some sense of the range of possibilities and how they are related. Subsequent sections will provide more specific information about how they are actually used.

Valuation methods can be separated into two broad categories: stated preference and revealed preference methods. Revealed preference methods are based on actual observable choices that allow resource values to be directly inferred from those choices. For example, in calculating how much local fishermen lost from the oil spill, the revealed preference method might calculate how much the catch declined and the resulting diminished value of the catch. In this case, prices are directly observable, and their use allows the direct calculation of the loss in value. Or, more indirectly, in calculating the value of an occupational environmental risk (such as some exposure to a substance that could pose some health risk), we might examine the differences in wages across industries in which workers take on different levels of risk.

Compare this with the direct stated preference method that can be used when the value is not directly observable, such as the value of preserving a species. Analysts derive this value by using a survey that attempts to elicit the respondents' willingness to pay (their "stated preference") for preserving that species.

Each of these broad categories of methods includes both indirect and direct techniques. The possibilities are presented in Table 4.1. We start with an examination of stated preference survey methods.

Table 4.1 Economic Methods for Measuring Environmental and Resource Values

Methods	Revealed Preference	Stated Preference
Direct	Market Price Simulated Markets	Contingent Valuation
Indirect	Travel-Cost Hedonic Property Models Hedonic Wage Models Avoidance Expenditures	Choice Experiments Conjoint Analysis Attribute-Based Models

Source: Modified and updated by the authors from Mitchell and Carson (1989).

Stated Preference Methods

Stated preference methods use survey techniques to elicit willingness to pay for a marginal improvement or for avoiding a marginal loss. These methods are typically of two types: contingent valuation surveys and choice experiments. *Contingent valuation*, the most direct approach, provides a means of deriving values that cannot be obtained in more traditional ways. The simplest version of this approach merely asks respondents what they would be willing to pay for a change in environmental quality (such as an improvement in wetlands or reduced exposure to pollution) or on preserving the resource in its current state. Typically this question is framed as, "What is the maximum you are willing to pay for the change?" Alternative versions ask a "yes" or "no" question, such as whether the respondent would pay $X to prevent the change or preserve the species. The answers reveal either an upper bound (in the case of a "no" answer) or a lower bound (in the case of a "yes" answer).

Choice experiments, on the other hand, present respondents with a set of options. Each set consists of various levels of attributes or characteristics of the good. One of the characteristics will be the "price" of that bundle of attributes. Each choice set typically includes the status quo bundle, which includes a price of $0 since it represents no change. Respondents choose their preferred option.

Contingent Valuation Method

The contingent valuation survey approach creates a hypothetical market and asks respondents to consider a willingness-to-pay question *contingent* on the existence of this market. Contingent valuation questions come with their own set of challenges. One major concern with the use of the contingent valuation method has been the potential for survey respondents to give biased answers. Six types of potential bias have been the focus of a large amount of research: (1) strategic bias, (2) information bias, (3) starting-point bias, (4) hypothetical bias, (5) payment vehicle bias (protest bids), and (6) the observed discrepancy between willingness to pay (WTP) and willingness to accept (WTA). More recently, the issue of "bots" answering surveys has emerged. The literature is rich with examples of studies aimed at reducing these biases and there are now some well-accepted methods for avoiding them (see for example, Johnston et al., 2017; Haab et al., 2020 for reviews of the literature and state-of-the-art techniques). Well-designed surveys can minimize bias, but it is useful to understand what those biases are and to know what to do when designing a survey.

Strategic bias arises when the respondent intentionally provides a biased answer in order to influence a particular outcome. If a decision to preserve a stretch of river for fishing, for example, depends on whether the survey produces a sufficiently large value for fishing, the respondents who enjoy fishing may be tempted to provide an answer that ensures a high value, rather than the lower value that reflects their true valuation. Another variation on strategic bias is social desirability bias, which occurs when respondents try to present themselves in a favorable light; one common example is when voters claim to have voted when they did not.

Information bias may arise whenever respondents are forced to value attributes with which they have little or no experience. For example, the valuation by a recreationist of a loss in water quality in one body of water may be based on the ease of substituting recreation on another body of water. If the respondent has no experience using the second body of water, the valuation could be based on an entirely false perception. Providing enough information to the respondent has been shown to significantly reduce this bias.

Visual aids have also been shown to reduce uncertainty and unfamiliarity with the good or service being valued, but the nature of the visual aid may affect the response. Labao et al. (2008) found that colored photographs, as opposed to black-and-white photographs, influenced respondent willingness to pay for the Philippine Eagle. The colored photographs resulted in a higher willingness to pay than black-and-white photos. Why? The authors suggest that the higher willingness to pay could be explained by photographs in color simply providing more information or by "enhancing respondents' ability to assimilate information." In any case, the nature of the visual aid seems important for revealing willingness to pay.

Starting-point bias may arise in those survey instruments in which a respondent is asked to check off their WTP from a predefined range of possibilities. How that range is defined by the designer of the survey may affect the resulting answers. A range of $0–$100 may produce a valuation by respondents different from, for example, a range of $10–$100, even if no responses are in the $0–$10 range. Ladenburg and Olsen (2008), in a study of willingness to pay to protect nature areas in Denmark from new highway development, found that the starting-point bias in their choice experiment was gender-specific, with female respondents exhibiting the greatest sensitivity to the starting point. The use of focus groups during the survey design can help to determine the appropriate ranges for payment cards as well as having multiple versions of the survey.

Hypothetical bias (the difference between hypothetical and actual WTP) can enter the picture because the respondent is being confronted by a contrived, rather than an actual, set of choices. Since they will not actually have to pay the estimated value, the respondent may treat the survey casually, providing ill-considered answers. Some analyses of the literature suggest that hypothetical bias has been a persistent problem (List & Gallet, 2001; Murphy et al., 2005; Parsons & Myers, 2016; Penn & Hu, 2018), but can be reduced by ensuring that the payment vehicle is incentive compatible and using language to ensure consequentiality (making sure the respondent believes they will actually have to pay the amount in question). Using a follow-up certainty scale has been shown to be helpful in reducing hypothetical bias. With a certainty scale, respondents can be asked how certain they are they would pay the amount stated.

Ehmke, Lusk, and List (2008) tested whether hypothetical bias depends on location and/or culture. In a study based on student experiments in China, France, Indiana, Kansas, and Niger, they found significant differences in bias across locations. Given that policymakers frequently rely on existing benefits estimates from other locations when making decisions, this finding should not be taken lightly. The strengths and weaknesses of using estimates derived in one setting to infer benefits in another, a technique known as *benefit transfer*, are discussed later.

Increasingly, environmental economists are using these types of experiments to try to determine the severity of some of these biases as well as to learn how to reduce bias. Some of these experiments are conducted in a laboratory setting, such as a computer lab or a classroom designed for this purpose. In one such experiment on voluntary provision of public goods (donations), Landry et al. (2006) found that for door-to-door interviews, an increase in physical attractiveness of the interviewer led to sizable increases in giving. Interestingly, physical attractiveness also led to increases in response rates, particularly by male households. Sometimes called *interviewer bias*, biases like these can be kept small through well-designed and pretested surveys.

Another challenge is in choosing an appropriate payment vehicle. *Payment vehicle bias* can arise when respondents react negatively to the choice of the payment vehicle. The payment vehicle represents how the stated WTP would be collected. Common choices include donations, taxes, or increases to utility bills. If a respondent is averse to taxes or has a negative perception of the agency collecting the (hypothetical) payment, they may state $0 for their willingness to pay. If their true willingness to pay is actually greater than zero, but they are "protesting" the question or payment vehicle, this zero must be excluded from the analysis. Determining which zero bids are valid and which are protests is important. The payment vehicle must be realistic, believable, and neutral in order to reduce payment vehicle bias.

The final source of potential bias addresses observed gaps between two supposedly closely related concepts—willingness to pay and willingness to accept compensation. Respondents to contingent valuation surveys tend to report much higher values when asked for their willingness to accept compensation for a specified loss of some good or service than if asked for their willingness to pay for a specified increase of that same good or service. Economic theory suggests the two should be equivalent. Debate 4.2 explores some of the reasons offered for the difference.

Measuring willingness to pay or willingness to accept in the presence of price changes makes two new concepts relevant—compensating variation and equivalent variation. *Compensating variation* is the amount of money it would take to *compensate* for a price increase in order to make a consumer just as well off as she or he was before the price increase. How much the consumer was "hurt" by the price increase can be measured by the compensating variation. *Equivalent variation*, on the other hand, is the amount of money it would take to make a consumer indifferent (same income) between the money and the price increase. In other words, how much money would they pay to avoid the price increase?

If the compensating variation is greater than zero, that amount represents willingness to pay. If it is negative, it represents willingness to accept. In other words, for increases in environmental quality, compensating variation should be positive (WTP). For decreases in environmental quality, it should be negative (WTA). Equivalent variation is just the opposite—the amount of money the household would need to be given to be just as well off as before the environmental change. Equivalent variation will be positive for increases in environmental quality (WTA) and negative for decreases (WTP). In theory, in the absence of any income effects, these measures (along with consumer surplus) should be equivalent. WTP has tended to be the preferred metric but is not always the most appropriate. Ando (2022) suggests that WTA is likely more appropriate for things like biodiversity, especially since WTP measures are income constrained.

Much experimental work has been done on contingent valuation to determine how serious a problem biases may present and on testing solutions aimed at reducing or eliminating them. One early survey (Carson et al., 1994) uncovered 1672 contingent valuation studies. A more recent one gives annotations for more than 7500 studies in 130 countries (Carson, 2011)! This number is now well over 8000. Are the results from these surveys reliable enough for the policy process? The answer has been a resounding yes.

DEBATE 4.2

Willingness to Pay versus Willingness to Accept: Why So Different?

Many contingent valuation studies have found that respondents tend to report much higher values for questions that ask what compensation the respondent would be willing to accept (WTA) to give something up than for questions that ask for the willingness to pay (WTP) for an incremental improvement in the same good or service. Economic theory suggests that differences between WTP and WTA should be small, but experimental findings both in environmental economics and in other microeconomic studies have found large differences. Why?

Some economists have attributed the discrepancy to a psychological endowment effect; the psychological value of something you own is greater than something you do not. In other words, you would require more compensation to be as well off without it than you would be willing to pay to get that same good, and as such, you would be less willing to give it up (WTA > WTP) (Kahneman, Knetsch, & Thaler, 1990). This is a form of what behavioral economists call loss aversion—the psychological premise that losses are more highly valued than gains.

Others have suggested that the difference may be explainable in terms of the market context. In the absence of good substitutes, large differences between WTA and WTP would be the expected outcome. In the presence of close substitutes, WTP and WTA should not be that different, but the divergence between the two measures should increase as the degree of substitution decreases (Hanemann, 1991; Shogren et al., 1994).

The characteristics of the good may matter as well. In their review of the evidence provided by experimental studies, Horowitz and McConnell (2002) find that for "ordinary goods" the ratio of WTA/

WTP is smaller than the ratio of WTA/WTP for public and nonmarket goods. Their results support the notion that the nature of the property rights involved is not neutral.

The moral context of the valuation may matter as well. Croson et al. (Draft 2005) show that the amount of WTA compensation estimated in a damage case increases with the culpability of the party causing the damage as long as that party is also paying the damages. If, however, a third party is paying, WTA is insensitive to culpability. This difference suggests that the valuation implicitly includes an amount levied in punishment for the party who caused the damage (the valuation becomes the lost value plus a sanction).

It may also be the case that, in dynamic settings, respondents are uncertain about the value of the good. Zhao and Kling (2004) argue that in intertemporal settings, the equivalence of compensating variation/equivalent variation and WTP/WTA breaks down, in part because WTP and WTA have a behavioral component and the timing of a decision will be impacted by the consumer's rate of time preference and willingness to take risks. A buyer or seller, by committing to a purchase or sale, must forgo opportunities for additional information. These "commitment costs" reduce WTP and increase WTA. The larger the commitment costs, the larger is the divergence between the two measures.

Ultimately, the choice of which concept to use in environmental valuation comes down to how the associated property right is allocated. If someone owns the right to the resource, asking how much compensation they would require to give it up is the appropriate question. If the respondent does not have the right, using WTP to estimate the value of acquiring it is the right approach. However, as Horowitz and McConnell point out, since the holders and non-holders of "rights" value them differently, the initial allocation of property rights can have a strong influence on valuation decisions for environmental amenities. Additionally, as Ando et al. (2024) note, using WTP can increase environmental injustice by undervaluing environmental quality when the losses fall largely on marginalized communities since WTP is typically smaller than WTA. And, as Zhao and Kling note, the timing of the decision can also be an important factor.

Finally, as Ando (2022) points out, for goods with no substitutes, like biodiversity, WTA might actually be the preferred measure if we are deciding how much to compensate people for losing a species, for example.

Sources: Ando, A. W. (2022). Equity and cost-effectiveness in valuation and action planning to preserve biodiversity. *Environmental and Resource Economics*, 1–17; Croson, R., Rachlinski, J. J., & Johnston, J. (Draft 2005). Culpability as an explanation of the WTA–WTP discrepancy in contingent valuation; Hanemann, W. M. (1991). Willingness to pay and willingness to accept:

How much can they differ? *American Economic Review, 81*, 635–647; Horowitz, J. K., & McConnell, K. E. (2002). A review of WTA/WTP studies. *Journal of Environmental Economics and Management, 44*, 426–447; Kahneman, D., Knetsch, J., & Thaler, R. (1990). Experimental tests of the endowment effect and the Coase theorem. *Journal of Political Economy, 98*, 1325–1348; Shogren, J. F., Shin, S. Y., Hayes, D. J., & Kliebenstein, J. B. (1994). Resolving differences in willingness to pay and willingness to accept. *American Economic Review, 84*(1), 255–270; Zhao, J., & Kling, C. (2004). Willingness to pay, compensating variation, and the cost of commitment. *Economic Inquiry, 42*(3), 503–517.

Faced with the need to compute damages from oil spills, the National Oceanic and Atmospheric Administration (NOAA) convened a panel of independent economic experts (including two Nobel Prize laureates) to evaluate the use of contingent valuation methods for determining lost passive-use or nonuse values. Their report, issued on January 15, 1993 (58 FR 4602), was cautiously supportive and provided a set of guidelines for survey design and implementation.

Those guidelines have been influential in shaping subsequent studies. For instance, Example 4.1 shares the results of a large contingent valuation survey, designed to estimate the value of preventing future spills. While influential, those guidelines are outdated, and, in 2017, new "contemporary guidelines" were published (Johnston et al., 2017). These guidelines provide best practice recommendations for both contingent valuation and choice experiments using what has been learned in the approximately 8000 stated preference studies published since the NOAA guidelines were first published. The authors offer 23 recommendations, including designing a survey that clearly describes the status quo or baseline scenario, selecting a random sample of the affected population, and choosing an appropriate survey mode.

The new guidelines also recommend pretesting the survey instrument and cite best practices for eliminating or at least reducing the potential biases listed previously. They emphasize the importance of documentation of study design, implementation, analyses, and results. Finally, they give extensive guidance on when to choose contingent valuation over a choice experiment and vice versa. Example 4.2 illustrates how the careful design and implementation of a stated preference survey can result in well-behaved data and reliable willingness to pay estimates.

Choice Experiments

Indirect hypothetical stated preference methods include several attribute-based methods. Attribute-based methods, such as choice experiments, are useful when project options have multiple levels of different attributes. Like contingent valuation, choice experiments are also survey based, but instead of asking respondents to state a willingness to pay, they are asked to choose among alternate bundles of goods. Each bundle has a set of attributes and the levels of each attribute vary across bundles. Since one of the attributes in each bundle is a price measure, willingness to pay can be identified.

Choice experiments have evolved from both contingent valuation and marketing studies. This approach allows the respondent to make a familiar choice (choose a bundle) and allows the researcher to derive marginal willingness to pay for an attribute from that choice.

Consider an example (Walsh et al., 2022) that surveyed New Zealand residents on their preferences and willingness to pay for water quality. The choice experiment included three attributes: the concentration of nutrients in the water, water clarity, and the presence/absence of E. coli. The authors chose these particular attributes based on the responses from focus groups that suggested these were the most salient. They also aligned with New Zealand governmental policies.

Table 4.2 reproduces the attributes and levels and Table 4.3 presents a sample choice set for their experiment.

Each respondent faced three discrete choice questions, where they choose between a status quo option where water quality attributes remain at their current levels versus two different scenarios with water quality improvements. Those improvements came with permanent increases in a respondent's monthly cost of living (the "cost"). "The size of the water quality changes presented to respondents were based on the magnitude of changes in national targets from the National Policy Statement for Freshwater Management ((MFE 2020), p. 64)" (Walsh et al., 2022, p. 6).

Respondents were given a choice set of two alternative management plans and the status quo (no purchase) option (or Outcome A in Table 4.3). Using an internet panel, the researchers received approximately 2000 responses from across New Zealand.

The researchers found that residents are willing to pay for improvements in all three water quality attributes, with magnitudes that are roughly comparable to a recent Auckland referendum vote on a water quality tax. For example, in Auckland the average willingness to pay values (in NZ dollars) were $22.13 for nutrients, $189.75 for clarity, and $22.13 for E. coli. In the referendum, the tax for the average home was $66. They also found that WTP varies with respondent characteristics, including the types of recreation that a user engages in (Walsh et al., 2022).

Choice experiments can be challenging to implement when respondents have little experience or knowledge of the service being valued or when the distinction between inputs and ecological endpoints is unclear. Do people value wetlands themselves (input) or do they value flood control (endpoint)? A common practice in valuation has been to simplify or "map" ecological information into outcomes that respondents have experience with. An early example is the water quality ladder developed

---

Table 4.2 Choice Experiment: Attributes and Levels

Attribute	Metric	North Island	South Island
Nutrients	Change in % of rivers and streams that are acceptable for aquatic life	2, 4, 8	2, 4, 8
Clarity	Change in average visibility (meters)	0.1, 0.4, 0.8	0.1, 0.4, 1
E. Coli	Change in % rivers and streams that are suitable for recreation	1, 5, 7	1, 3, 6
Cost	Permanent increase in monthly cost of living ($NZ)	2, 6, 10, 14, 18, 20	2, 6, 10, 14, 18, 20

Source: Walsh, P. J., Guignet, D. and Booth, P. 'National Water Quality Values in New Zealand: Policy-Relevant Stated Preference Estimates', NCEE Working Paper 22-02. USEPA. May 2022. Reproduced by kind permission of U.S. Environmental Protection Agency.

Table 4.3 Sample Choice Question

	Outcome A	Outcome B	Outcome C
			Outcomes by 2025
Nutrients *Increase in the* **percent of rivers and streams** *with acceptable levels. For example, a change from 25% of rivers and streams to 27% is a change of +2* **percentage points**	No Change	+5 percentage points	+1 percentage points
Water Clarity *Increase in average visibility in rivers and streams*	No Change	+1 metre	+0.5 metre
E.coli *Increase in the* **percent of rivers and streams** *suitable for swimming, wading, and fishing. For example, a change from 32% of rivers and streams to 35% is a change of +3* **percentage points**	No Change	+6 percentage points	+8 percentage points
Permanent Increase in the Cost of Living for Your Household	$0 per month	$6 per month ($72 per year)	$3 per month ($36 per year)
Your Choice	☐	☐	☐
Please select your preferred outcome	Outcome A (No Change)	Outcome B	Outcome C

Source: Walsh, P. J., Guignet, D. and Booth, P. 'National Water Quality Values in New Zealand: Policy-Relevant Stated Preference Estimates', NCEE Working Paper 22-02. USEPA. May 2022. Reproduced by kind permission of US Environmental Protection Agency.

by Resources for the Future, which was used in a national contingent valuation study (Carson & Mitchell, 1993). This ladder translates water quality measures into the categories "boatable," "fishable," and "swimmable." This attempt to make the specific services being valued understandable to respondents answering the surveys actually creates another problem. Since these terms have no precise ecological definition, it becomes unclear how to interpret the resulting willingness to pay measure (Boyd & Krupnick, 2009).

Researchers have tried to overcome this problem by simplifying the scenarios, but many times simplicity is achieved at the expense of ecological precision. Johnston et al. (2012) note some examples where terms like "low," "medium," and "high" are used to characterize levels of biodiversity or water clarity, but those terms have no specific connection to a precise level of biodiversity or water quality. Not only would their assumed meanings likely vary from respondent to respondent, but it is also not clear what the results would actually mean for specific levels of those attributes. Walsh et al. avoid this challenge by using measurable (and salient) changes to water quality and clarity (Tables 4.2 and 4.3).

EXAMPLE 4.1

Leave No Behavioral Trace: Using the Contingent Valuation Method to Measure Passive-Use Values

Until the *Exxon Valdez* tanker spilled 11 million gallons of crude oil into Prince William Sound in Alaska, the calculation of nonuse (or passive-use) values was not a widely researched topic. However, following the 1989 court ruling in *Ohio v. U.S. Department of the Interior* that said lost passive-use values could now be compensated within natural resources damage assessments and the passage of the Oil Pollution Act of 1990, the estimation of nonuse and passive-use values became not only a topic of great debate, but also a rapidly growing research area within the economics community.

One study (Carson et al., 2003) discusses the design, implementation, and results of a large survey designed to estimate the passive-use values related to large oil spills. In particular, the survey asked respondents their willingness to pay to prevent a similar disaster in the future by funding an escort ship program that would help prevent and/or contain a future spill. The survey was conducted for the state of Alaska in preparation for litigation in the case against the *Exxon Valdez*.

The survey followed the recommendations made by the NOAA panel for conducting contingent valuation surveys and for ensuring reliable estimates. It relied upon face-to-face interviews and the sample was drawn from the national population. The study used a binary discrete choice (yes/no) question where the respondent was asked whether they would be willing to pay a specific amount, with the amount varying across four versions of the survey. A one-time increase in taxes was the chosen method of payment. They also avoided potential embedding bias (where respondents may have difficulty valuing multiple goods) by using a survey that valued a single good. The survey contained pictures, maps, and background information to make sure the respondent was familiar with the good they were being asked to value.

Using the survey data, the researchers were able, statistically, to estimate a valuation function by relating the respondent's willingness to pay to respondent characteristics. After multiplying the estimate of the median willingness to pay by the population sampled, they reported aggregate lost passive-use values at $2.8 billion (in 1990 dollars). They point out that this number is a lower bound, not only because willingness to accept compensation would be a more appropriate measure of actual lost passive-use from the spill (see Debate 4.2), but also because their median willingness to pay was less than the mean.

The *Exxon Valdez* spill sparked a debate about the measurement of non-use and passive-use values. Laws put into place after the spill now ensure that passive-use values will be included in natural resource damage assessments. Should other parts of the world follow suit?

Source: Carson, R. T., Mitchell, R. C., Hanemann, M., Kopp, R. J., Presser, S., & Ruud, P. A. (2003). Contingent valuation and lost passive use: Damages from the *Exxon Valdez* oil spill. *Environmental and Resource Economics*, 25, 257–286.

EXAMPLE 4.2

Careful Design in Contingent Valuation: An Example of WTP to Protect Brown Bears

What is the value of an individual brown bear? That is the question economists Leslie Richardson and Lynne Lewis set out to answer in a stated preference survey of live bear cam viewers in Katmai National Park and Preserve, Alaska. The economics literature on the value of individuals has been mostly nonexistent, focusing instead on population-level changes. However, there are many policy and management contexts that require economic value estimates for individual animals. For instance, park and wildlife agencies are charged with protecting some of the world's most iconic species and their habitats for current and future generations. When an animal is illegally killed, there is often a need to estimate the damages (losses) to the public.

In 2019 and 2020, Mike Fitz, interpretations expert with explore.org; environmental economists Lynne Lewis and Leslie Richardson; and Jeffrey Skibins (Human Dimensions of Wildlife Conservation) surveyed viewers of the live brown bear cam at Katmai National Park. As part of that survey Lewis and Richardson designed and implemented a WTP question about the value of individual bears. The survey asked questions about viewing behavior (frequency and location) and about knowledge of the individual bears and ability to identify them. These questions were followed by a series of statements giving respondents information about the brown bears in Katmai National Park. That information was followed by a willingness to pay question. Partial text of that question was:

> There is consideration for setting up a Katmai Bear Preservation Trust Fund. The fund would raise money that would be used specifically to protect bears at the individual level through research and the use of various technologies. For instance, electromagnetic wildlife detectors could be buried under roads to alert drivers of nearby wildlife, thus preventing vehicular collisions on access roads. Other activities would include increased enforcement against poaching, as well as ongoing research activities to minimize threats to bears. If the fund were established, it would prevent the loss of one bear per year, on average.

Would you make a donation of **$X** annually for the next 5 years to the Katmai Bear Preservation Trust Fund? When making this decision, please consider your budget, what you can afford, and other items you may want to spend your money on. Also, remember that many of the bears in Katmai National Park and Preserve are never seen on the webcams or by park visitors.

$X = random draw from 11 different bid amounts ranging from $5 to $500

Richardson and Lewis did a number of things to ensure the least amount of bias in their survey questions and in the resulting data. First, they followed best practice guidelines from Johnson et al. (2017) and Haab et al. (2020). They pretested their survey instrument with several experts in contingent valuation and with park rangers familiar with the site and the bears. They added a provisioning point to the willingness to pay question to reduce hypothetical bias and asked several follow-up questions to better understand consequentiality and protest bids.

Their raw willingness to pay data are presented in Figure 4.1. Notice the downward trajectory—as the bid goes up, the number of respondents who said "Yes" they are willing to pay that amount goes down. This looks remarkably like a downward-sloping demand curve. This is not always the case with willingness to pay data, but can and should be with careful survey design and an adequate sample size.

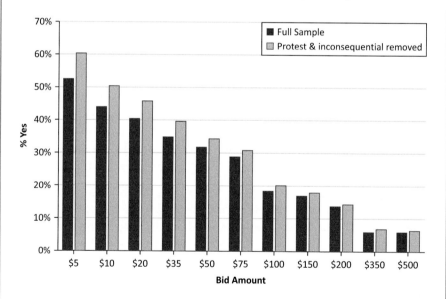

Figure 4.1 **Willingness to Pay to Preserve Individual Brown Bears.**

Source: Richardson, L., & Lewis, L. (March 2022). Getting to know you: Individual animals, wildlife webcams, and willingness to pay for brown bear preservation, *American Journal of Agricultural Economics, 104*(2), 673–692. Have a listen to your textbook author Lynne Lewis talk about the value of brown bears in this 2024 podcast. https://www.resources.org/resources-radio/how-much-is-a-bear-worth-with-lynne-lewis/

In another example, Haefele et al. (2016) present the results of a choice experiment in which they estimated the total economic value of U.S. National Parks (Example 4.3). Including both visitation values and passive-use values for U.S. residents, the total value of U.S. National Parks and Programs more than pays for itself at $92 billion. This estimate is considered a minimum bound since international visitation values were not included.

Sometimes more than one of these techniques may be used simultaneously. In some cases, using multiple techniques is necessary to capture the total economic value; in other cases, it may be used to provide independent estimates of the value being sought as a check on the reliability of the estimate. The ecosystem services chapter, later in this book, will provide several additional examples.

EXAMPLE 4.3

The Value of U.S. National Parks

In 2016, the National Park Service in the United States turned 100 years old. As federal budget deficits loom, there has been some talk of selling off some of these sites. What is the value of the National Park lands, waters, and historic sites? According to the first ever comprehensive estimate, it is, at a minimum, valued at $92 billion.

Haefele et al. (2016) present the results of a survey of American households focused on estimating the total economic value (TEV) of National Parks and Programs. Previous studies have focused on the value of specific National Park or monument sites, but none had attempted to estimate the value of all of these national treasures. The goal was to calculate total economic value, visitation values, and passive-use (or nonuse) values.

Using the population of all U.S. households from which to draw a sample, researchers used a mixed mode approach that utilized both mail and internet surveys with phone call reminders. Two rounds of surveys were implemented between 2013 and 2015.

In the survey, participants were asked whether protecting National Parks was important to them. Nearly 95 percent of the sample said it was, even if they did not visit them. Moreover, 93.5 percent thought it was important to protect trails, parks, and open spaces for current and future generations, whether they use them or not. The language in these questions suggests bequest and passive-use values. Only 6.2 percent thought the United States should sell off some National Parks. The survey also included questions on respondents' political point of view. The sample of respondents leaned to the conservative side of the aisle.

The stated preference survey design was a choice experiment in which respondents chose among bundles that included the size of cuts to programs as well as the percentages of lands sold. Choice experiments typically allow respondents to choose a status quo bundle for which the price is $0. In order to minimize hypothetical bias (respondents stating a higher willingness to pay than they would actually pay), the choice question was followed by reminders to consider their budgets. This "cheap talk" technique has been shown to significantly reduce hypothetical bias.

Respondents were asked their willingness to pay a specific amount of money to pay for the National Park Service Programs. The payment vehicle utilized was an increase in federal income tax for each of the next ten years. As we have discussed in this chapter, protest responses must be omitted from the data since those answers do not represent willingness to pay, instead representing a scenario (usually payment vehicle) protest. Since the payment vehicle chosen was federal income tax, there was some initial concern that protest zeros would be problematic; however, only 7.5 percent of the responses were considered to be protests.

Using econometric analysis, the marginal willingness to pay (or implicit price) for each type of National Park or National Park Service Program was estimated. These values are reproduced in Table 4.4.

These household values were then multiplied by the total number of households in the population to determine the total economic value. In order to present a minimum bound (or very conservative estimate), they assumed that households that did not return a survey were willing to pay $0.

The final tally of $92 billion includes both use values for visitors and passive-use or existence values, $62 billion of which (or two-thirds) is for the National Park Service lands and waters and historic sites, with $30 billion for programs. Of the $62 billion, the authors suggest that approximately half of that value is passive-use value. Of course, these values do not even include the willingness to pay of the millions of international tourists that visit U.S. National Parks each

Table 4.4 Per-Household Total Economic Value (TEV) for the National Park System and NPS Programs

National Parks	Estimated value
Nature-focused National Parks (79,096,632 acres)	$1,113.24
History-focused National Parks (226 sites)	$874.72
Water-focused National Parks (4,818,275 acres)	$977.93
Per-household value for all National Park acres/sites	$2,967.00
NPS Programs: Historic sites and buildings protected each year (2000)	$316.31
Acres transferred to communities each year (2700)	$98.41
National landmarks protected each year (114)	$347.98
Schoolchildren served by NPS educational programs (4.1 million)	$682.62
Per-household value for all NPS programs	$1,445.00

Adapted from Haefele, M., Loomis, J. B., & Bilmes, L. (2016). Total economic valuation of the National Park Service lands and programs: Results of a survey of the American public.

year or those who hold passive-use values for these locations. Thus, the $92 billion TEV also represents "the minimum amount that U.S. households are willing to pay to avoid the loss of the NPS and its programs" (Haelfele et al., 2016, p. 25).

According to one of the authors of the study, Linda Bilmes at Harvard University, the study shows that "Americans value the National Park Service at least 30 times more than the government spends on them." It was a happy 100th birthday indeed.

Sources: Haefele, M., Loomis, J., & Bilmes, L. (June 2016). Total economic valuation of the National Park Service lands and programs: Results of a survey of the American public. Faculty Research Working Paper Series. RWP16-024; Haefele, M., Loomis, J., & Bilmes, L. (2016). Total economic valuation of US National Park Service estimated to be $92 billion: Implications for policy. *The George Wright Forum*, 33(3), 335–345; National Park Foundation Press Release. (June 30, 2016). National Park Foundation announces study determining value of America's National Parks to be $92 billion.

Revealed Preference Methods

Revealed preference methods are "observable" because they involve actual behavior and expenditures and "indirect" because they infer a value rather than estimate it directly. In this chapter, we discuss three revealed preference methods: travel-cost methods, hedonic property value models, and hedonic wage models. We start with the travel-cost methods.

Suppose, for example, a particular sport fishery is being threatened by pollution, and one of the damages caused by that pollution is a reduction in sportfishing. How is this loss to be valued when access to the fishery is free?

Travel-Cost Method. One way to derive this loss is through the *travel-cost* method. The travel-cost method infers the value of a recreational resource (such as a sport fishery, a park, or a wildlife preserve where visitors hunt with a camera) by using information on how much visitors spend in getting to the site to construct a demand curve representing willingness to pay for a "visitor day."

Freeman et al. (2014) identify two variants of this approach. In the first, analysts examine the number of trips visitors make to a site. In the second, analysts examine whether people decide to visit a site and, if so, which site. This second variant includes using a special class of models, known as random utility models, to value quality changes.

The first variant allows the construction of a travel-cost demand function. The value of the flow of services from that site is the area under the estimated demand curve for those services or for access to the site, aggregated over all who visit the site. By estimating a demand curve, individual consumer surplus can be estimated. The area below the demand curve but above the travel cost (price) is the consumer surplus.

The second variant enables an analysis of how specific site characteristics influence choice and, therefore, indirectly how valuable those characteristics are. Knowledge of how the value of each site varies with respect to its characteristics allows the analyst to value how degradation of those characteristics (e.g., from pollution) would lower the value of the site.

Travel-cost models have been used to value National Parks, mountain climbing, recreational fishing, and beaches. They have also been used to value losses from events such as beach closures during oil spills, fish consumption advisories, and the cost of development that has eliminated a recreation area. The methodology for both variants is detailed in Parsons (2003), Freeman et al. (2014), and Champ et al. (2017).

In the random utility model, a person choosing a particular site takes into consideration site characteristics and its price (trip cost). Characteristics affecting the site choice include ease of access and environmental quality. Each site results in a unique level of utility and a person is assumed to choose the site giving the highest level of utility to that person. Welfare losses from an event such as an oil spill can then be measured by the resulting change in utility should the person have to choose an alternate, less desirable site.

Example 4.4 looks at the use of the travel-cost method to estimate the economic impacts of beach closures due to oil spills in Minorca, Spain.

One interesting paradox that arises with travel-cost models is that those who live closest to the site, and may actually visit frequently, will have low travel costs. These users will appear to have a lower value for that site even if their (unmeasured) willingness to pay for the experience is very high. Another challenge in this model is how to incorporate the opportunity cost of time. Usually, this is represented by wages, but that approach is not universally accepted.

Hedonic Property Value and Hedonic Wage Methods. Two other revealed preference methods are the *hedonic property value* and *hedonic wage* methods. They share the characteristic that they use a statistical technique, known as multiple regression analysis, to "tease out" the environmental component of value in a related market. For example, it is possible to discover that, all other things being equal, property values are lower in polluted neighborhoods than in clean neighborhoods. (Property values fall in polluted neighborhoods because they are less desirable places to live.)

EXAMPLE 4.4

Using the Travel-Cost Method to Estimate Recreational Value: Beaches in Minorca, Spain

Minorca, an island in the Mediterranean Sea, is a very popular tourist destination. Minorca's population doubles in the summer months from about 80,000 year-round residents to between 150,000 and 175,000 in the summer. The island's beaches are a major attraction.

Just how valuable are those beaches? To provide an estimate, researchers considered a hypothetical scenario in which an oil spill resulted in closure of certain beaches on the island. The analysis involved using a random utility model based upon survey data to estimate the economic impacts of these closures.

In 2008, 573 face-to-face individual surveys were conducted at 51 different beaches on the island using a discrete choice travel-cost survey. Respondents were asked some typical travel-cost survey questions such as where the trip originated, how they got to the site, how many people they were traveling with and their ages, and some questions to collect socio-economic demographics on the respondents. After being asked about their attitudes toward different beach attributes, they completed a questionnaire on the characteristics of the beach they were visiting. The characteristics included a measure of how urban the area was, the type of sand, how clean the beach was, how crowded it was, whether or not there was a toilet, presence of drink vendors, water temperature, calmness of the water, environmental quality, presence of a lifeguard, the direction the beach faced, and whether or not nudism was present on the beach. Travel costs included the cost of fuel and tolls plus travel time. Travel time varied by mode of transportation—using average walking and average driving speeds.

The random utility model allowed researchers to estimate the impacts on utility of the various beach characteristics identified by the surveys. Those characteristics positively affecting utility included north-facing, presence of a lifeguard, presence of toilets and drink vendors, thin sand, presence of nudism, warm water temperatures, and good environmental quality. Characteristics negatively affecting utility included non-northern beaches, urban beaches, crowding, algae, and calm water.

Because some beach attributes were more highly valued than others, the range of estimates was dramatically affected by the details in the scenario. For example, for a closure affecting beaches on the west coast, the willingness to pay to avoid this loss was .24 euros (2008) per day per person with peak visitation of 25,000 visitors. Aggregating the per-visitor value across visitors produced a daily welfare loss from these closures of 6,000 euros. On the other extreme, a spill forcing closure of the more valuable northern beaches would cause the welfare loss to rise to 1.73 euros per day per person for a total of 43,250 euros during peak visitation.

It is easy to take highly enjoyable recreational sites for granted since they are freely provided by nature. As a result they may not be given their due when resources are allocated for their protection and enhancement. The travel-cost method can help to inform policy not only by demonstrating how truly valuable they are, but also by allowing useful distinctions to be made among various recreation resources.

Source: Pere, R., McConnell, K. E., Giergiczny, M., & Mahieu, P.-A. (2011). Applying the travel-cost method to Minorca beaches: Some policy results. In Jeff Bennett (Ed.), *International Handbook on Non-Market Environmental Valuation*. Cheltenham, U.K.: Edward Elgar, 60–73.

Hedonic property value models use market data (house prices) and then break down the house sales price into its attributes, including the house characteristics (e.g., number of bedrooms, lot size, and features), the neighborhood characteristics (e.g., crime rates, school quality, and so on), and environmental characteristics (e.g., air quality, percentage of open space nearby, distance to a local landfill, etc.). Statistical analysis is then used to estimate a price function from which an analyst can tease out the marginal willingness to pay (MWTP) for any of the attributes of the house; the value of an additional bedroom or bathroom as well as willingness to pay to be near or far from something can be estimated.[9]

Hedonic models allow for the measurement of the marginal willingness to pay for discrete changes in an attribute. Numerous studies have utilized this approach to examine the effect on property value of things such as distance to hazardous waste sites, farm operations, land use, dams and rivers, renewable energy sites, and so forth. This approach has become commonplace with the use of geographic information systems (discussed later). In one recent study, Parsons and Heintzelman (2022) examined hedonic property valuation studies that examined the impact of wind power projects on property values. They looked at 18 studies (ten in Europe and eight in North America) covering 2011–2021. In all of the European studies, wind power projects had a net negative impact on property values. Of the eight in North America, only three had a net negative impact, though the more recent studies showed a more negative impact. Distance matters for the impact; properties closest to the projects experienced the largest impacts.

Hedonic property value models have also been used to examine quasi-experiments such as before and after a dam removal or forest fire and to consider the impact of sea level rise on home values. Bishop et al. (2020) offer contemporary guidelines for hedonic models and the estimation of the marginal willingness to pay for housing attributes, including environmental attributes.

Hedonic wage approaches are similar except that they attempt to isolate the environmental risk component of wages, which serves to isolate the amount of compensation workers require in order to work in risky occupations. It is well known that workers in high-risk occupations demand higher wages in order to be induced to undertake the risks. When the risk is environmental (such as exposure to a toxic substance), the results of the multiple regression analysis can be used to construct a willingness to pay to avoid this kind of environmental risk. Additionally, the compensating wage differential can be used to calculate the value of reduced mortality risk (Evans & Taylor, 2020). Techniques for valuing reductions in life-threatening risks will be discussed later in this chapter.

Benefit Transfer and Meta-Analysis

The NOAA panel report has created an interesting dilemma. Although it legitimized the use of contingent valuation for estimating passive-use (nonconsumptive use) and nonuse values, the panel and the more recently published best practices (Johnston et al., 2017) have also set some rather rigid guidelines that reliable studies should follow. The cost of completing an "acceptable" contingent valuation study could well be so high that they will only be useful for large incidents, those for which the damages are high enough to justify their use. Yet, due to the paucity of other techniques, the failure to use contingent valuation may, by default, result in passive-use values of zero. That is not a very appealing alternative.[10]

One key to resolving the dilemma created by the possible expense of implementing survey best practices may be provided by a technique called benefit transfer. Since original studies are time-consuming and expensive, benefit transfer allows the estimates for the site of interest to be based upon estimates from other sites or from an earlier time period to provide the foundation for a current estimate.

Benefit transfer methods can take one of three forms: value transfers, benefit function transfers, or meta-analysis. Sometimes the actual benefit values derived from point estimates can simply be directly transferred from one context to another, usually adjusted for differences between the study site and the policy site. Function transfer involves using a previously estimated benefit function that relates site characteristics to site values. In this case, the differentiating characteristics of the site of interest are entered into the previously derived benefit function in order to derive newer, more site-specific values (Johnston et al., 2006).

Most recently, meta-analysis has been utilized. *Meta-analysis*, sometimes called the "analysis of analyses," takes empirical estimates from a sample of studies, statistically relates them to the characteristics of the studies, and calculates the degree to which the reported differences can be attributed to differences in location, subject matter, or methodology. For example, meta-analysis has been used with cross sections of contingent valuation studies as a basis for isolating and quantifying the determinants of nonuse value. Once these determinants have been isolated and related to specific policy contexts, it may be possible to transfer estimates from one context to another by finding the value consistent with the new context without incurring the time and expense of conducting new surveys each time.

Benefit transfer methods have been widely used in situations for which financial, time, or data constraints preclude original analysis. Policymakers frequently look to previously published studies for data that could inform a prospective decision. Benefit transfer has the advantage of being quick and inexpensive, but the accuracy of the estimates deteriorates as the new context tends to deviate (either temporally or spatially) the further it is from the context used to derive the estimates. Benefit transfer has not escaped controversy. Johnston and Rosenberger (2010) and Johnston et al. (2015) provide a comprehensive discussion of benefit transfer and outline some of the potential problems with its use, including a lack of studies that are both of sufficiently high quality and policy relevant. Additionally, many of the published studies do not provide enough information on the attributes to allow an assessment of how they might have affected the derived value.

In response to some of these concerns, a valuation inventory database has emerged. The Environmental Valuation Reference Inventory (EVRI) is an online searchable database of over 4000 empirical studies on the economic value of environmental benefits and human health effects. It was specifically developed as a tool for use in benefit transfer.[11]

Benefit transfers are also subject to large errors. A few studies have tested the validity of environmental value transfer across sites. In those that have, the transfer errors have been sizable and wide ranging, sometimes over 100 percent for stated preference survey transfers (Brouwer, 2000, and Rosenberg & Stanley, 2006). Using metadata from 31 empirical studies, Kaul et al. (2013) find a median transfer error of 39 percent. Lewis and Landry (2017) compare original hedonic property value model results to a test of transferring those results via benefit function transfer and find errors ranging from 29 percent to 1000 percent! These results suggest caution with the use of benefit transfer.

Using Geographic Information Systems to Enhance Valuation

Geographic information systems (GIS) are computerized mapping models and analysis tools. A GIS map is made up of layers such that many variables can be visualized simultaneously using overlays. GIS offers a powerful collection of tools for depicting and examining spatial relationships. Most simply, GIS can be used to produce compelling measurements and graphics that communicate the spatial structure of data and analytic results with a force and clarity otherwise impossible. But the technology's real value lies in the potential it brings to ask novel questions and enrich our understanding of social and economic processes by explicitly considering their spatial structure. Models that address environmental externalities have, almost by definition, a strong spatial component.[12]

Fundamentally spatial in nature, use of GIS in hedonic property models is a natural fit. Housing prices vary systematically and predictably from neighborhood to neighborhood. Spatial characteristics, from air quality to the availability of open space, can influence property values of entire neighborhoods; if one house enjoys abundant open space or especially good air quality, it is highly likely that its neighbors do as well.

In a 2008 paper, Lewis, Bohlen, and Wilson used GIS and statistical analysis to evaluate the impacts of dams and dam removal on local property values. In a unique "experiment," they collected data on property sales for 10 years before and after the Edwards Dam on the Kennebec River in Maine was removed (the first federally licensed hydropower dam in the United States to be removed primarily for the purpose of river restoration). They also collected data on property sales approximately 20 miles upstream where two dams were still in place. GIS technology enhanced this study by facilitating the calculation of the distance from each home to both the river and the nearby dams. Lewis et al. (2008) found that homeowners pay a price penalty for living close to a dam. In other words, willingness to pay for identical housing is higher the further away from the dam the house is located. They also found that the penalty near the Edwards Dam site dropped to nearly zero after the dam was removed. Interestingly, the penalty upstream also dropped significantly. While a penalty for homes close to the dams upstream remains, it fell after the downstream dam was removed. Can you think of reasons why?[13]

Example 4.5 shows how the use of GIS can enable hedonic property value models to investigate how the view from a particular piece of property might affect its value.

Averting Expenditures. A final example of an indirect observable method involves examining "averting" or "avoidance" expenditures. Averting expenditures are those designed to reduce the damage caused by pollution by taking some kind of averting or defensive action. Examples include installing indoor air purifiers in response to an influx of polluted air or relying on bottled water as a response to the pollution of local drinking water supplies. Since people would not normally spend more to prevent a problem than would be caused by the problem itself, averting expenditures can provide a lower-bound estimate of the damage caused by pollution. They also cause a disproportionate hardship on poor households that cannot afford such coping expenditures. Dickie (2016) argues that ignoring averting expenditures or behavior may underestimate damages. He offers a simple example using contaminated drinking water. Suppose contaminated drinking water increases waterborne illness by 4 percent. If half the population avoids the contamination by some form of averting action, such as using an alternate source of water, frequency of illness will drop to 2 percent. Only half the population is now exposed, thus reducing damages. However, the avoidance expenses must be included in the damage estimate. If they are not, the damages will be underestimated (Dickie, 2016). Example 4.6 illustrates the impact of coping or averting expenditures on residents of Kathmandu, Nepal.

Challenges

Aggregation. As you have probably figured out by now, nonmarket valuation faces several challenges. One challenge involves the aggregation of estimated values into a total value that can be used in benefit-cost analysis. How large is the relevant population? Do benefits change with distance to the resource in question? Debate 4.3 explores some of these challenging issues.

EXAMPLE 4.5

Using GIS to Inform Hedonic Property Values: Visualizing the Data

GIS offers economists and others powerful tools for analyzing spatial data and spatial relationships. For nonmarket valuation, GIS has proven to be especially helpful in enhancing hedonic property value models by incorporating both the proximity of environmental characteristics and their size or amount. GIS studies have also allowed for the incorporation of variables that reflect nearby types and diversity of land use.

Geo-coding housing transactions assign a latitude and longitude coordinate to each sale. GIS allows other spatial data, such as land use, watercourses, and census data, to be "layered" on top of the map. By drawing a circle of the desired circumference around each house, GIS can help us to calculate the amount of each amenity that is in that circle as well as the density and types of people who live there. Numerous census data are available on variables such as income, age, education, crime rates, and commuting time. GIS also makes it relatively easy to calculate straight-line distances to desired (or undesired) locations, such as parks, lakes, schools, or landfills.

In a 2002 paper entitled "Out of Sight, Out of Mind? Using GIS to Incorporate Visibility in Hedonic Property Value Models," Paterson and Boyle use GIS to measure the extent to which visibility measures affect house prices in Connecticut. In their study, visibility is measured as the percentage of land visible within one kilometer of the property, both in total and broken out for various land use categories. Finally, they add variables that measure the percentage of area in agriculture or in forest or covered by water within one kilometer of each house.

They find that visibility is indeed an important environmental variable in explaining property values, but the nature of the viewshed matters. While simply having a view is not a significant determinant of property values, viewing certain types of land uses is. Proximity to development reduces property values only if the development is visible, for example, suggesting that out of sight really does mean out of mind! They conclude that any analysis that omits variables that reflect nearby environmental conditions can lead to misleading or incorrect conclusions about the impacts of land use on property values. GIS is a powerful tool for helping a researcher include these important variables.

Source: Paterson, R., & Boyle, K. (2002). Out of sight, out of mind? Using GIS to incorporate visibility in hedonic property value models. *Land Economics*, 78(3), 417–425.

Partial Values. Another large challenge for nonmarket valuation is that most studies only capture a portion of the total value of an environmental good or service. For example, ecosystems are bundles of values, but the methods outlined in this chapter are only capable of capturing a portion of the value. Consider an interesting recent example. Chami et al. (2019) estimate the value of a great whale at more than $2 million, and easily over $1 trillion for the current population of great whales. What are these numbers based on? It turns out that by diving deep, whales disturb minerals

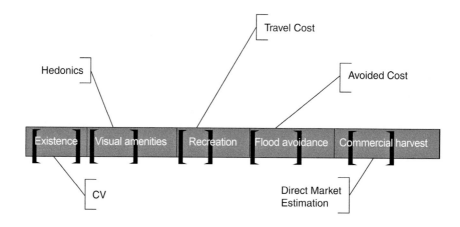

Figure 4.2 Different Methods, Different Experts, Different Data. *Source*: Courtesy of James Boyd, Resources for the Future.

that enhance the growth of phytoplankton. Phytoplankton absorb enormous amounts of carbon dioxide. So while this number seems large and certainly can be used to support whale protection policies, it only represents a partial value of a whale: the value of carbon capture. Other methods covered in this chapter would be used to estimate other values such as whale watching.

Figure 4.2 illustrates the different methods environmental economists use to capture different types of value. Each of these methods relies on different data and, many times, different experts. Rarely is the available time or money sufficient to apply all methods to a particular question.

Debate 4.4 illustrates the challenges and importance of attempts to capture the total economic value by examining a specific case study—polar bears in Canada.

EXAMPLE 4.6

Valuing the Reliability of Water Supplies: Coping Expenditures in Kathmandu Valley, Nepal

Nepal, like many other poor developing countries, experiences chronic shortages of safe drinking water. The Kathmandu Valley is no exception. The National Water Supply Corporation serves 70 percent of the population, but the public water supply is neither reliable nor safe. Shortages are frequent and the water quality is frequently contaminated with fecal coliform and nitrogen-ammonia (Pattanayak et al., 2005).

How much should be invested in improving water quality depends on how valuable clean water is to this population. Quantifying those benefits requires establishing how much residents would be willing to pay for cleaner water. One pathway for quantifying willingness to pay in this context can be found in analyzing how much households spend to cope with the unreliable water supply. It turns out they purchase water from water vendors, collect water from public taps, invest in wells or storage tanks, purchase filtration systems, and/or boil water. All of these coping mechanisms have both a financial cost and a cost associated with the time devoted to coping. Using coping costs as a proxy for willingness to pay can serve as the basis for constructing a lower-bound estimate of the demand curve for water provision in settings where other more direct valuation strategies are simply not practical to implement.

In a survey of 1500 households in five municipalities, researchers found that for households in the Kathmandu Valley, coping or averting behaviors cost the average household about 1 percent of monthly income, most of this attributed to the time spent collecting water. The authors note that these coping costs are almost twice as much as the current monthly bills paid to the water utility.

Some demographic factors were found to have influenced household coping expenditures.

- Wealthier households were found to have higher coping expenditures. As the authors note, this confirms the intuition that relatively rich households have more resources and therefore invest more in water treatment, storage, and purchases.
- More educated respondents also had higher coping costs, perhaps because these households better understood the risks of contaminated water.

If, as suggested by these two findings, the poor face higher financial and educational barriers in their quest for cleaner water, water policy in this region faces an environmental justice issue as well as an efficiency issue.

Even though averting expenditures represent only a lower bound of willingness to pay for water supply, they can provide valuable information for the estimation of benefits of water provision. In addition, these data imply that the common assertion that in poor countries the costs of supplying clean water are so high that they necessarily exceed the benefits received by water users may be a misconception—the value of water in this valley was found to be at least twice the current per-unit charge even when the lower-bound estimating technique was used.

Source: Pattanayak, S. K., Yang, J.-C., Whittington, D., & Bal Kumar, K. C. (2005). Coping with unreliable public water supplies: Averting expenditures by households in Kathmandu, Nepal. *Water Resources Research*, 41(2). doi: 10.1029/2003WR002443.

DEBATE 4.3

Distance Decay in Willingness to Pay: When and How Much Does Location Matter?

One challenge in performing benefit-cost analysis is accurately choosing the "extent of the market." The *extent of the market* refers to **who benefits** from the resource in question. Loomis (1996) argues that not accounting for the full extent of the market (i.e., including every-one who gains some benefit) can lead to **under**estimates of willing-ness to pay and aggregate value.

On the other hand, a more inclusive design might include respond-ents with vastly lower willingness to pay simply because of their loca-tion. For some resources, distant respondents have a lower willingness to pay for their improvement. It seems reasonable to expect, for exam-ple, that the benefits from a reduction in river pollution to an individ-ual household would probably depend on its proximity to the river. Those closest to the river place the highest value on the improvement. In other words, since it seems reasonable to expect that some types of values do experience a "distance decay," in aggregating benefits this deterioration should certainly be taken into account.

Bateman et al. (2006) argue that not accounting for distance decay can lead to **over**estimates of willingness to pay. Those who are further away still benefit and should be counted, but at some kind of decreas-ing rate. Recently, the number of stated preference studies (contin-gent valuation and choice experiments) that focus on distance decay has increased so we have learned more about it.

What do these studies say about the circumstances that give rise to distance decay?

Interestingly, the empirical evidence suggests that both the type of value being measured (use or nonuse value) as well as the type of will-ingness to pay question (compensating versus equivalent variation) matter. Hanley et al. (2003) and Bateman et al. (2006) both find that distance decay does arise for use value, but very little or not at all for nonuse values. If, however, some of the current nonusers become users under the proposed scenario, their valuation would experience some distance decay. This result follows the intuition that if the willing-ness to pay question is framed as a marginal improvement in quality (compensating variation), then some of the nonusers might become users and that possibility would be reflected in their valuations. If the question is framed as equivalent variation (willingness to pay to avoid loss), nonuser valuations experience no distance decay, since they will remain nonusers.

These studies suggest that spatial patterns in nonmarket values have important implications not only for how benefit-cost analysis should be conducted and interpreted but also for how that analysis affects the policy evaluations. Different design choices as to the extent of the market and whether to aggregate across particular political or economic jurisdictions can lead to very different results. As Schaafsma et al. (2012) suggest, these spatial patterns should be taken into account both when drawing samples for willingness to pay surveys, and when aggregating the results.

Sources: Bateman, I., Day, B. H., Georgiou, S., & Lake, I. (September 2006). The aggregation of environmental benefit values: Welfare measures, distance decay and total WTP. Discussion paper; Hanley, N., Schlapfer, F., & Spurgeon, J. (2003). Aggregating the benefits of environmental improvements: Distance-decay functions for use and nonuse values. *Journal of Environmental Management, 68*, 297–304; Loomis, J. B. (1996). How large is the extent of the market for public goods: Evidence from a nationwide contingent valuation survey. *Applied Economics, 28*, 779–782; Schaafsma, M., Brouwer, R., & Rose, J. (2012). Directional heterogeneity in WTP models for environmental valuation. *Ecological Economics, 79*(1), 21–31.

Valuing Human Life

One fascinating public policy area where these various approaches have been applied is in the valuation of human life. Many government programs, from those controlling hazardous pollutants in the workplace or in drinking water, to those improving nuclear power plant safety, are designed to save human life as well as to reduce illness. How resources should be allocated among these programs depends crucially on the value of human life. In order to answer this question, an estimate of the value of that life to society is necessary and federal regulations require such estimates for benefit-cost analysis. How is life to be valued?

DEBATE 4.4

What Is the Value of a Polar Bear?

Because polar bears are such a charismatic species, they have obviously attracted lots of popular support, but exactly how valuable are they? In 2011, the Canadian government issued a report in which it attempted to estimate the different socio-economic values of polar bears in Canada.

They commissioned the study in part to determine the economic impact of adding the polar bear to a list of at-risk species. This study represents one of the few studies to try to estimate the value of polar bears and the only one that tries to do it in a comprehensive fashion.

The authors tried to capture active use values (subsistence and sport hunting, polar bear viewing, and value in scientific research), as well as passive-use values (existence and bequest values). Multiple nonmarket valuation methods were used in this study, including travel-cost (viewing), market prices (hunting), meta-analysis, and benefit transfer (passive-use values). Time and budgetary constraints precluded the use of stated preference methods such as contingent valuation or choice experiments. The summary of their findings is reproduced in Figure 4.3. Note that the direct use values actually comprise a relatively small portion of the total value.

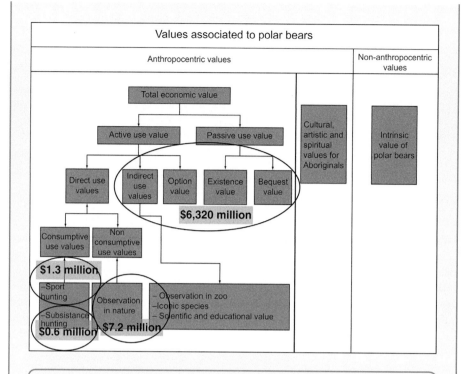

Figure 4.3 Monetary Values Associated with Polar Bears in Canada, by Value Category (Aggregate Amounts for Canada).

Source: ÉcoRessources Consultants, for Environment Canada (2011, 32). https://www.sararegistry.gc.ca/virtual_sara/files/ri_polar_bear_se_ 0911_eng.pdf

An effort to document the value of a species like this produces a value that is no doubt much closer to the truth than the default value of zero, but how close are these numbers to the true value? There are several caveats to consider.

- Consider the calculation for the value of polar bear meat. For this cost, the next best substitute was used, which in this case was beef (for humans) and dog food. One could certainly argue for alternatives.
- Sport values were estimated using the benefit transfer method. Recall the challenges for using benefit transfer, in particular for a unique species like the polar bear. The study closest to this one was conducted in 1989 and focused on big game and grizzly bear hunting. For the polar bear study, the 1989 values were translated

into 2009 dollars. The authors suggest their number might be an underestimate since hunting for a polar bear is such a unique experience. On the other hand, they also acknowledge that the number could just as easily be an overestimate if the charismatic image of the polar bear reduces willingness to pay for hunting.

● Finally, passive-use values were also calculated using benefit transfer. Since no study has been done on the preservation value of the polar bear in Canada, the researchers used a meta-analysis of species at risk (Richardson & Loomis, 2009). While that study calculated a total economic value, for the polar bear study the benefit transfer was specifically designed to capture only preservation value. It was relatively straightforward to remove direct uses (visitors) from the transferred value, but not the indirect use benefits such as scientific value.

Using any of these values as inputs into others creates a potential to double count, a common mistake. In fact, scientific values were calculated separately for the polar bear study as well as being included in the preservation value estimated via benefit transfer. As such, these numbers could overestimate the value.

What would you be willing to pay to protect the polar bear? As we have seen in this chapter, these types of questions are challenging to answer.

Source: ÉcoRessources Consultants. (2011). Evidence of the socio-economic importance of polar bears for Canada. Report for Environment Canada. http://publications.gc.ca/site/archivee-archived.html?url=http://publications.gc.ca/collections/collection_2012/ec/CW66-291-2011-eng.pdf; Richardson, L., & Loomis, J. (2009). Total economic valuation of endangered species: A summary and comparison of the United States and the rest of the world estimates. In K. N. Ninan (Ed.), *Conserving and Valuing Ecosystem Services and Biodiversity: Economic, Institutional and Social Challenges*. London: Earthscan, 25–46.

The simple answer, of course, is that life is priceless, but that turns out to be not very helpful. Because the resources used to prevent loss of life are scarce, choices must be made. The economic approach to valuing lifesaving reductions in environmental risk is to calculate the change in the probability of death resulting from the reduction in environmental risk and to place a value on the change. Thus, it is not life itself that is being valued, but rather a reduction in the probability that some segment of the population could be expected to die earlier than others. This *value of reduced mortality risk (VRMR*[14]) represents an individual's willingness to pay for small changes in mortality risks. It does not represent a willingness to pay to prevent certain death. It is measured as the "marginal rate of substitution between mortality risk and money (i.e., other goods and services)" (Cameron, 2010) and as such is also called *mortality risk valuation*. Debate 4.5 examines the controversy associated with valuing changes in these mortality risks.

DEBATE 4.5

Is Valuing Human Life Immoral?

In 2004, economist Frank Ackerman and lawyer Lisa Heinzerling teamed up to write a book that questions the morality of using benefit-cost analysis to evaluate regulations designed to protect human life. In *Priceless: On Knowing the Price of Everything and the Value of Nothing* (2004), they argue that benefit-cost analysis is immoral because it represents a retreat from the traditional standard that all citizens have an absolute right to be free from harm caused by pollution. When it justifies a regulation that will allow some pollution-induced deaths, benefit-cost analysis violates this absolute right.

Economist Maureen Cropper responds that it would be immoral not to consider the benefits of lifesaving measures. Resources are scarce and they must be allocated so as to produce the greatest good. If all pollution were reduced to zero, even if that were possible, the cost would be extremely high and the resources to cover that cost would have to be diverted from other beneficial uses. Professor Cropper also suggests that it would be immoral to impose costs on people about which they have no say—for example, the costs of additional pollution controls—without at least trying to consider what choices people would make themselves. Like it or not, hard choices must be made.

Cropper also points out that people are always making decisions that recognize a trade-off between the cost of more protection and the health consequences of not taking the protection. Thinking in terms of trade-offs should be a familiar concept. She points out that people drive faster to save time, thereby increasing their risk of dying. They also decide how much money to spend on medicines to lower their risk of disease or they may take jobs that pose morbidity or even mortality risks.

In her response to Ackerman and Heinzerling, Cropper acknowledges that benefit-cost analysis has its flaws and that it should never be the only decision-making guide. Nonetheless, she argues that it does add useful information to the process and throwing that information away could prove to be detrimental to the very people that Ackerman and Heinzerling seek to protect.

Sources: Ackerman, F., & Heinzerling, L. (2004). Priceless: On Knowing the Price of Everything and the Value of Nothing. New York: The New Press; Ackerman, F. (2004). Morality, cost-benefit and the price of life. Environmental Forum, 21(5), 46–47; Cropper, M. (2004). Immoral not to weigh benefits against costs. Environmental Forum, 21(5), 47–48.

It is possible to translate the value derived from this procedure into an "implied value of mortality risk reduction." This is accomplished by dividing the amount each individual is willing to pay for a specific reduction in the probability of death by the probability reduction. Suppose, for example, that a particular environmental policy could be expected to reduce the average concentration of a toxic substance to which 1 million people are exposed. Suppose further that this reduction in exposure could be expected to reduce the risk of death from 1 out of 100,000 to 1 out of 150,000. This implies that the number of expected deaths would fall from 10 to 6.67 in the exposed population as a result of this policy. If each of the 1 million persons exposed is willing to pay $5 for this risk reduction (for a total of $5 million), then the implied value mortality risk reduction or VRMR is approximately $1.5 million ($5 million divided by 3.33). Alternatively, the VRMR can be calculated using the change in WTP divided by the change in risk. For this example, that would be $5 divided by the change in risk of death (1/100,000–1/150,000), or $1.5 million. Thus, the VRMR is capturing the rate of trade-off between money and a very small risk of death.

What actual values have been derived from these methods? One early survey (Viscusi, 1996) of a large number of studies examining reductions in a number of life-threatening risks found that most implied values for human life (in 1986 dollars) were between $3 million and $7 million. This same survey went on to suggest that the most appropriate estimates were probably closer to the $5 million estimate. In other words, all government programs resulting in risk reductions costing less than $5 million per life saved would be justified in benefit-cost terms. Those costing more might or might not be justified, depending on the appropriate value of a life saved in the particular risk context being examined.

In a survey of meta-analyses, Banzhaf (2021) finds the mean VRMRs (also commonly called the Value of Statistical Life or VSL) range from $3.7 million to $12.3 million. After performing a "meta-analysis" of these meta-analyses, Banzhaf finds a central VRMR of $7 million. What about age? Does the value of statistical life change with age? Apparently so. Viscusi (2008) finds an inverted U-shape relationship between VSL and age. Specifically, using the hedonic wage model, they estimate a VSL of $3.7 million for persons aged 18–24, $9.7 million for persons aged 35–44, and $3.4 million for persons aged 55–62. According to their study, VSL rises with age, peaks, and then declines.

What about the value of statistical life across populations or countries with different incomes? Most agencies in the United States use VSLs between $6 million and $10 million.[15] These estimates are based largely on hedonic wage studies that have been conducted in the United States or in other high-income countries.[16] The European Union and OECD countries use values that are much lower. Table 4.5 illustrates the different values across agencies and countries. How might those results be translated into settings featuring populations with lower incomes?

Adjustments for income are typically derived using an estimate of the income elasticity of demand. Recall that income elasticity is the percent change in consumption given a 1 percent change in income. Hammitt and Robinson (2011) note that applying income elasticities derived for countries like the United States might result in nonsensical VSL estimates if blindly applied to lower-income countries. While U.S. agencies typically assume a 0.4 to 0.6 percent change in VSL for a 1 percent change in real income over time, elasticities closer to 1.0 or higher are more realistic for transfers of these values between high- and low-income countries. Using the higher income elasticity number is merited since willingness to pay for mortality risk reduction as a

Table 4.5 Value of Reduced Mortality Risk Applied in Regulatory Analyses

Country or region	Agency or organization	VRMR point estimate (in millions) (original currency and year)[a]	VRMR point estimate (in millions) (2018 US$)[b]	Primary sources for VRMR point estimate
European Union	European Commission[c]	1.09–2.22 (2005€)	1.71–3.56	Stated preference studies
OECD Countries	OECD Commission[d]	1.7–3.1 (2005 US$)	2.24–4.08	Stated preference studies
United States	Environmental Protection Agency[e]	6.3 (2000 US$)	9.38	Primarily hedonic wage studies (21 of 26 studies)
United States	Food and Drug Administration[f]	9.0 (2013 US$)	9.82	Primarily hedonic wage studies (6 of 9 studies)
United States	Department of Transportation and Department of Homeland Security[g]	9.6 (2015 US$)	10.32	Primarily hedonic wage studies

[a] Currency type and year reported in original sources are indicated in parentheses.

[b] All estimates are inflated to 2018 US$ using the U.S. Consumer Price Index.

[c] Estimates obtained from Haswell (2015), which was commissioned by the Directorate General for Environment of the European Commission. VRMR estimates are converted to U.S. dollars using an exchange rate of 0.8125 dollars/euro, the approximate annual average exchange rate in 2005, and then inflated to 2018 US$ using the U.S. Consumer Price Index.

[d] Suggested point estimates are based on a meta-analysis of stated preference studies. Point estimates reported here are the median ($1.7 million) for the quality-screened sample of studies or weighted mean ($3.1 million) of the quality-screened sample. See Organization for Economic Cooperation and Development (2012, p. 127).

[e] Reported in U.S. EPA (2015).

[f] VRMR estimate reported in U.S. Food and Drug Administration (2015). Dollar year of the VRMR estimate is not clearly stated but is reported as 2013 US$ in Robinson and Hammitt (2015), which is the basis for the estimate.

[g] U.S. Department of Transportation (2016).

Source: Evans, M. F., & Taylor, L. O. (August 19, 2020). Using revealed preference methods to estimate the value of reduced mortality risk: Best practice recommendations for the hedonic wage model. Review of Environmental Economics and Policy, 14(2), 282–301.

percentage of income drops at very low incomes; what limited income is available in poorer households is reserved for basic needs.

How are these values used in practice? Regulatory actions that result in lower mortality may be expensive (costs), but these mortality benefits also have significant value. It has been estimated by the U.S. EPA that avoided mortality benefits make up more than 90 percent of the benefits of the Clean Air Act and 60 percent of the benefits of the Clean Power Plan.[17] Similar results have been found for the European Union Clean Air Package. Holland (2014) estimates that reduced mortality makes up 69 percent of the benefits of that rule. A 2021 study published in the journal *Nature* reported that a third of heat-related deaths worldwide (estimated at 9700 deaths per year) can be directly attributed to human-caused climate change. The value of mortality risk reduction can be used to evaluate the costs and benefits of greenhouse gas emissions reductions. These mortality risks should also influence the social cost of carbon that we learned about in the last chapter. Can you see how?

The VRMR has also been used to argue for public health precautions. When COVID-19 made its appearance in early 2020, debates raged about the trade-offs between keeping the economy humming and the cost of lives lost. There was, at the time, fairly widespread consensus among economists and public health experts that lifting the restrictions would impose huge costs in additional lives lost—while providing little lasting benefit to the economy.

How do we balance public health benefits without sacrificing our economy? Example 4.7 explores this question.

EXAMPLE 4.7

Using the Value of Statistical Life to Inform Policy: COVID-19

Economists Michael Greenstone and Vishan Nigam have found that social distancing initiatives and policies in response to the COVID-19 epidemic have substantial economic benefits on the order of $8 trillion.

Long before COVID, however, economists had looked at the impacts of social distancing and other behavioral changes with respect to the 1918 flu pandemic.

Sergio Correia, Stephan Luck, and Emil Verger found that cities that intervened earlier and more aggressively experienced a relative *increase* in real economic activity after the pandemic subsided. Their findings suggest that while pandemics can have substantial economic costs, social distancing and other public health measures can lead to both better economic outcomes **and** lower mortality rates. History suggests that when cities take strong actions at the start of a pandemic and keep mitigation measures in place longer, they tend to do better economically after the crisis has passed. The public framing of the 2020 pandemic as a sterile trade-off between public health and economic productivity was naïve at best.

Policymakers have long used a measure of the value of mortality risk reduction or the "value of statistical life" to measure the costs and benefits that involve trade-offs between public safety and economic cost. These decisions have ranged from seat belt laws to food safety to responses to air pollution regulations and now to responses to COVID-19. And it was *economists* including Kip Viscusi, Laura Taylor, Mary Evans, Cass Sunstein, James Hammitt, Joe Aldy, and others who have worked to develop and update that measure.

The value of statistical life measures what our society is willing to pay to reduce the risk of mortality. It measures the trade-offs we all make between mortality risk and money—car airbags, bike helmets, smoking, risky jobs, and so on.

The novel coronavirus, COVID-19, was new, but the economics framework needed to evaluate policy was not. We study trade-offs! This is familiar territory. The risk valuation framework is central to many policy decisions we already make for health, safety, and environmental concerns.

Viscusi (2020), using the VRMR to monetize COVID-19 deaths, produces a U.S. mortality cost estimate of $1.4 trillion in the first half of 2020. Total global mortality cost through early July 2020 was $3.5 trillion. And those costs are rising. While not without controversy, using our willingness to pay for mortality risk reduction allows government agencies to make decisions about which policies are cost effective. It turns out we are willing to pay a lot to reduce risks of death.

Of course, as economist Lisa Robinson reminds us, "Reducing COVID-19 risks requires making extraordinarily difficult decisions that trade-off saving lives and economic damages. Benefit-cost analysis is well-suited for investigating these trade-offs and informing these decisions. However, interpreting and using the results requires understanding the framework and addressing its limitations, including the uncertainties in the value of mortality risk reductions and the distribution of impacts across those who are advantaged and disadvantaged."

Still—the magnitude of these costs makes it clear—spending trillions of dollars to combat a threat like the COVID-19 pandemic can be a good investment, despite the high cost.

Sources: Correia, S., Luck, S., & Verner, E. (June 5, 2020). Pandemics depress the economy, public health interventions do not: Evidence from the 1918 Flu. SSRN: https://ssrn.com/abstract=3561560 or http://dx.doi.org/10.2139/ssrn.3561560; Greenstone, M., & Nigam, V. (March 30, 2020). Does social distancing matter? University of Chicago, Becker Friedman Institute for Economics Working Paper No. 2020-26. SSRN: https://ssrn.com/abstract=3561244 or http://dx.doi.org/10.2139/ssrn.3561244; Thomson-DeVeaux, A. (March 23, 2020). "What Should the Government Spend to Save a Life?" Economists have done the math. https://fivethirtyeight.com/features/what-should-the-government-spend-to-save-a-life; Robinson, L. (July 1, 2020). On balance: COVID-19 benefit-cost analysis and the value of statistical lives. https://benefitcostanalysis.org/blog/on-balance/2020-07-01-on-balance-covid19-benefitcost-analysis-and-the-value-of-statistical-lives; Viscusi, W. K. (2020). Pricing the global health risks of the COVID-19 pandemic. *Journal of Risk and Uncertainty*, 61(2), 101–128. doi: 10.1007/s11166-020-09337-2; Viscusi, W. K. (March 4, 2021). Economic lessons for COVID-19 pandemic policies. https://doi.org/10.1002/soej.12492; Porter, E., & Tankersley, J. (March 24, 2020). Shutdown spotlights economic cost of saving lives. *New York Times*. https://www.nytimes.com/2020/03/24/business/economy/coronavirus-economy.html.

Damage Assessments: Loss of Ecosystem Services

Another area where the quantification of nonmarket values can play and has played a significant role is in assessing the magnitude of damage to ecosystems caused by human activities.

Oil spills are a case in point. Prior to the catastrophic 2010 Deepwater Horizon spill in the Gulf of Mexico, the Oil Pollution Act of 1990 had established a formal legal framework for determining when an oil spill results in a quantifiable adverse change in a natural resource. Through a process known as the Natural Resources Damage Assessment (NRDA), trustees of the affected ecosystem must attempt to quantify the extent of damages caused by a spill in order to seek compensation from the responsible parties. In 2016, after a six-year study of the impacts, economists estimated the damages to the natural resources from the spill at $17.2 billion.

As a report from the National Research Council notes (NRC, 2013), highlighting the relationship between ecosystem services and the economy can heighten public knowledge of and support for protecting those services. That report advocated incorporating a broader ecosystem services approach to assessing damage from the spill rather than focusing only on provisioning services. By encompassing the wider array of services this broader approach could end up identifying restoration projects that would benefit not only the trustees and direct-use parties, but the larger public as well.

That process of widening the scope of assessment is complex and will ultimately take time. As of 2020, according to its records BP had paid out over $60 billion in cleanup and criminal and civil penalties, but virtually all of that is based upon direct human losses rather than the broader focus suggested by the NRC. One exception, however, involved an oyster reef project in Alabama's Mobile Bay. The restoration project was originally focused on a location that would be convenient for fishermen who lost harvests during the spill, thereby responding directly to their losses. However, the ecosystem services provided by oysters are much greater than their direct value to harvesters. The filtering action of oysters plays an important role not only in removing suspended sediments from the water column but also in cleansing the water of various pollutants. When the broader scope suggested by the NRC was applied, a location that was better suited to supply all these ecosystem services was chosen. In 2016, BP settled for an additional $20.8 billion, $8.8 billion of which will go toward environmental restoration efforts including the restoration of coastal marshes in Louisiana.

Policies to protect ecosystem services are the focus of a later chapter.

Summary: Nonmarket Valuation Today

In this chapter, we have examined the most prominent, but certainly not the only, techniques available to supply policymakers with the information needed to implement efficient policy. Finding the total economic value of the service flows requires estimating three components of value: (1) use value, (2) option value, and (3) nonuse or passive-use values.

Our review of these various techniques included direct observation, contingent valuation, choice experiments, travel cost, hedonic property and wage studies, and averting or defensive expenditures. When time or funding precludes original research, benefit transfer and meta-analysis provide alternate methods for the estimation of values. In January 2011, a panel of experts gathered at the annual meeting of the

American Economic Association to reflect on nonmarket valuation 20 years after the *Exxon Valdez* spill and, unknown to any of them when the panelists were asked to participate, eight months after the *Deepwater Horizon* spill. The panelists had all worked on estimation of damages from the *Exxon Valdez* spill. The consensus among panelists was that while many of the issues with bias had been addressed in the literature, many unanswered questions remain and some areas still need work. While they all agreed that it is "hard to underestimate the powerful need for values" (i.e., some number is definitely better than no number), and we now have in place methods that can be easily utilized by all researchers, they also emphasized several problem areas. First, the value of time in travel-cost models has not been resolved. What is the opportunity cost of time if you are unemployed, for example?

While choice experiments do seem to better represent actual market choices, they do not resolve all of the potential problems with contingent valuation. Some of the issues that arise in contingent valuation, such as the choice of the payment vehicle, also arise with choice experiments. In addition, some new challenges, such as how the sequencing of choices in choice experiments might affect outcomes, arise. The panel highlighted how this area of research has been enhanced by the field of behavioral economics, an emerging research area that combines economics and psychology to examine human behavior. And finally, they suggested that the NOAA panel recommendations be updated to reflect the new body of research. In 2017, a new set of guidelines was published to do just that. The 23 recommendations in those guidelines address these questions regarding stated preference surveys and attempt to synthesize the now large body of research that informs nonmarket valuation (Johnston et al., 2017).

Some of these same experts, along with several others, implemented a nationwide survey following the BP spill to assess what U.S. households would pay to avoid damages from another spill. Using state-of-the-art techniques for stated preference surveys, they found that U.S. households would be willing to pay $17.2 billion to avoid the damages from another spill (Bishop et al., 2017). One author claimed, "this is proof that our natural resources have an immense monetary value to citizens of the United States who visit the Gulf and to those who simply care that this valuable resource is not damaged."

Revealed preference studies also now have their own sets of best practices for implementation. Evans and Taylor (2020) provide clear and thorough guidance on using hedonic wage models to estimate the value of reduced mortality risk. They also recommend best practices for reporting those values. Bishop et al. (2020) provide a detailed description and overview of the hedonic property value model and suggest best practices for hedonic property value models. The appendix of their paper also provides a useful reference for data availability by country for select countries mostly in Europe, North America, and China and Japan.

Discussion Question

1. Certain environmental laws prohibit the EPA from considering the costs of meeting various standards when the levels of the standards are set. Is this a good example of appropriately prioritizing human health or simply an unjustifiable waste of resources? Why?

Self-Test Exercises

1. In Mark A. Cohen, "The Costs and Benefits of Oil Spill Prevention and Enforcement," *Journal of Environmental Economics and Management* Vol. 13 (June 1986), an attempt was made to quantify the marginal benefits and marginal costs of U.S. Coast Guard enforcement activity in the area of oil spill prevention. His analysis suggests (185) that the marginal per-gallon benefit from the current level of enforcement activity is $7.50, while the marginal per-gallon cost is $5.50. Assuming these numbers are correct, would you recommend that the Coast Guard increase, decrease, or hold at the current level their enforcement activity? Why?

2. Professor Kip Viscusi estimated that the cost per life saved by current government risk-reducing programs ranges from $100,000 for unvented space heaters to $72 billion for a proposed standard to reduce occupational exposure to formaldehyde.
   a. Assuming these values to be correct, how might efficiency be enhanced in these two programs?
   b. Should the government strive to equalize the marginal costs per life saved across all lifesaving programs?

3. a. Suppose that hedonic wage studies indicate a willingness to pay $50 per person for a reduction in the risk of a premature death from an environmental hazard of 1/100,000. If the exposed population is 4 million people, what is the implied value of a statistical life?
   b. Suppose that an impending environmental regulation to control that hazard is expected to reduce the risk of premature death from 6/100,000 to 2/100,000 per year in that exposed population of 4 million people. Your boss asks you to tell them what is the maximum this regulation could cost and still have the benefits be at least as large as the costs. What is your answer?

Notes

1 U.S. District Court for the State of Alaska, Case Number A89-0095CV, January 28, 2004.
2 U.S. District Court for the State of Alaska.
3 *Exxon Shipping Company v. Baker*.
4 Bishop, R. C. et al. (2017). Putting a value on injuries to natural assets: The BP oil spill. *Science*, 356(6335), 253–254.
5 In 2017, the United States Department of the Interior released the Deepwater Horizon Response and Restoration Administrative Record, which included an estimate of the total value of damages (see Example 9.4).
6 The rules for determining these damages are defined in Department of Interior regulations. See 40 Code of Federal Regulations 300:72–74.
7 Krutilla, J. V. (1967). Conservation reconsidered. *American Economic Review*, 57(4), 777–786.
8 Krutilla, J. V. (1967). Conservation reconsidered. *American Economic Review*. p. 779.
9 Bishop et al. (2020) offers an accessible description and thorough discussion of the hedonic property value model.
10 Whittington (2002) examines the reasons why so many contingent valuation studies in developing countries are unhelpful. Poorly designed or rapidly implemented surveys could result in costly policy mistakes on topics that are very important in the developing world. The current push for cheaper, quicker studies is risky and researchers need to be very cautious.

11 www.evri.ca/en.
12 For examples see Bateman et al. (2002), who describe the contributions of GIS in incorporating spatial dimensions into economic analysis, including benefit-cost analysis; and Clapp et al. (1997), who discuss the potential contributions GIS can make for urban and real estate economics.
13 Interestingly, after this study was complete, one of the two upstream dams, the Fort Halifax Dam, was removed in July 2008 after years of litigation about its removal.
14 Value of mortality risk reduction has replaced "value of statistical life" or VSL, given the common misperceptions that VSL is the value of a life.
15 See, for example, www.epa.gov/environmental-economics/mortality-risk-valuation.
16 Many labor market estimates of VSL average near $7 million (Viscusi, 2008).
17 Evans and Taylor (2020).

Further Reading

Ando, A., Awokuse, T., Chan, N. W., González-Ramírez, J., Gulati, S., Jacobson, S., Interis, M., Manning, D., Stolper, S. (2024). Environmental and Natural Resource Economics and Systemic Racism. *Review of Environmental Economics and Policy*. A critical evaluation of environmental and resource economics with respect to racial justice and inequality.

Bateman, I. J., Lovett, A. A., & Brainard, J. S. (2005). *Applied Environmental Economics: A GIS Approach to Cost-Benefit Analysis*. Cambridge: Cambridge University Press. Uses GIS to examine land use change and valuation.

Bishop, K. C., Kuminoff, N. V., Banzhaf, H. S., Boyle, K. J., von Gravenitz, K., Pope, J. C., Smith, V. K., & Timmins, C. D. (2020). Best practices for using hedonic property value models to measure willingness to pay for environmental quality. *Review of Environmental Economics and Policy*, 14(2), 260–281. A contemporary set of guidelines and best practices for the appropriate use and interpretation of hedonic property value methods.

Champ, P. A., Boyle, K. J., & Brown, T. C. (2017). *A Primer on Nonmarket Valuation*, 2nd ed. New York: Springer. A thorough overview of nonmarket valuation methods.

Costanza, R., et al. (1998). The value of the world's ecosystem services and natural capital. (Reprinted from *Nature*, 387, 253, 1997.) *Ecological Economics*, 25(1), 3–15. An ambitious, but ultimately flawed, attempt to place an economic value on ecosystem services. This issue of *Ecological Economics* also contains a number of articles that demonstrate some of the flaws.

Evans, M. F., & Taylor, L. O. (2020). Using revealed preference methods to estimate the value of reduced mortality risk: Best practice recommendations for the hedonic wage model. *Review of Environmental Economics and Policy*, 14(2), 282–301. A thorough set of recommendations and guidelines for estimating the value of reduced mortality risk using hedonic wage models.

Freeman, A. Myrick I. I. I., Herriges, J., & Kling, C. (2014). *The Measurement of Environmental and Resource Values*, 3rd ed. Washington, D.C.: Resources for the Future. A comprehensive and analytically rigorous survey of the concepts and methods for environmental valuation.

Haab, T., Lewis, L., & Whitehead, J. (2020). State of the Art of Contingent Valuation. *Oxford Research Encyclopedia of Environmental Science*. doi: 10.1093/acrefore/9780199389414.013.450.

Johnston, R. J., Rolfe, J., Rosenberger, R., & Brouwer, R. (Eds.). (2015). *Benefit Transfer of Environmental and Resource Values. A Guide for Researchers and Practitioners*. Dordrecht, the Netherlands: Springer. This book is a practical guide for the design and use of benefit transfer.

Johnston, R. J., Boye, K. J., Adamowicz, W., Bennett, J., Brouwer, R., Cameron, T. A., Hanemann, W. M., Hanley, N. J., Ryan, M., Scarpa, R., Tourangeau, R., & Vossler, C. A. (2017). Contemporary guidance for stated preference studies. *Journal of the Association of Environmental and Resource Economics*, 4(2). http://dx.doi.org/10.1086/691697. This issue includes an update to the NOAA guidelines for the use of contingent valuation. It also has recommendations for the use of choice experiments.

Mitchell, R. C., & Carson, R. T. (1989). *Using Surveys to Value Public Goods: The Contingent Valuation Method*. Washington, D.C.: Resources for the Future. A comprehensive examination of contingent valuation research with brief summaries of representative studies and recommendations for survey design.

Whitehead, J., Haab, T., & Huang, J. -C. (Eds.). (2011). *Preference Data for Environmental Valuation: Combining Revealed and Stated Approaches*. London: Routledge. A compilation of articles that use more than one valuation method or novel applications of data combinations written by nonmarket valuation economists.

Additional references and historically significant references are available on this book's Companion Website: www.routledge.com/cw/Tietenberg

Chapter 5

Ecosystem Services

Nature's Threatened Bounty

Introduction

In Chapter 4, we learned about the methods available for valuing environmental goods and services and damages to those goods and services. We looked at examples for use values such as recreation, but also for passive/nonuse values. Many of the ecological functions and services are not only supplied by natural processes, but nature charges nothing for their use. Examples of these ecological goods and services include pollination by bees and other pollinators, the aquifer recharge services by wetlands, breathable air, biodiversity, nitrogen fixation in the soil, and climate regulation through carbon sequestration, as well as aesthetic and recreation services. If these services directly benefit at least one person, they are called *ecosystem services*.

In 1997, a team of researchers attempted to place a monetary global value on ecosystem services (Costanza et al., 1997). Basing their estimates on previously published studies and "a few original calculations," they found the (1997) economic value of 17 ecosystem services for 16 biomes to be in the range of U.S.\$16–54 trillion per year, with an average of U.S.\$33 trillion per year (approximately \$61 trillion in 2023 dollars), a number significantly higher than global GDP. This article attracted considerable attention.

However, because the methods they used were controversial, the specific estimated values were controversial as well. In 2014, Costanza and colleagues updated their 1997 estimates. Using the same controversial methods, they suggest that the value of total global ecosystem services in 2011 was \$125 trillion assuming changes to land areas and \$145 trillion assuming no changes to the biomes (\$233 and \$270 trillion in 2023 dollars respectively). These numbers are again much higher than global GDP. They also found that since the earlier study in 1997, losses to ecosystem services due to land use changes were \$4.3–\$20.2 trillion per year. What is not controversial, however, is the fact that ecosystems play a very valuable role in the lives of humans and the loss of those ecosystem services causes significant economic damage.

DOI: 10.4324/9781032689111-6

In 2021, the World Bank released a report, *The Economic Case for Nature*, that shows that a collapse of ecosystem services such as pollination, food from marine sources, and wood from timber harvesting would cause a decline in global GDP by $2.7 trillion in 2030. In low- and middle-income countries those impacts could be as high as 10 percent of GDP.

What role can economic analysis play in assuring that the value provided by these ecosystem services is not only recognized, but also protected from degradation? In this chapter we take up that question, focusing on two specific roles: (1) refining and improving the methods for quantifying the values received from natural services to increase their reliability and to demonstrate their importance, taking care to identify the specific contributions to human welfare; and (2) facilitating the design of private, public, and public–private partnership arrangements as well as incentive mechanisms that can help protect these important components of nature from degradation.

The State of Ecosystem Services

In 2001, U.N. Secretary-General Kofi Annan initiated the Millennium Ecosystem Assessment (MA) with the goal to assess "the consequences of ecosystem change for human well-being and to establish the scientific basis for actions needed to enhance the conservation and sustainable use of ecosystems and their contributions to human well-being."

To examine the connections and the linkages between ecosystems and human well-being, the MA divides ecosystem services into several categories.

- *Provisioning services* provide direct benefits such as water, timber, food, and fiber.
- *Regulating services* include flood control, water quality, disease prevention, and climate.
- *Supporting services* consist of such foundational processes as photosynthesis, nutrient cycling, and soil formation.
- *Cultural services* provide recreational, aesthetic, and spiritual benefits.

In 2005, the MA published four main findings.

- Ecosystems have changed rapidly in the last 50 years—at a rate higher than any other time period. Due to the growing demands on the earth's resources and services, some of these high rates of change are irreversible.
- Many of the changes to ecosystems, while improving the well-being of some humans, have been at the expense of ecosystem health. Fifteen of the 24 ecosystems evaluated are in decline.
- If degradation continues, it will be difficult to achieve many of the U.N. Millennium Development Goals since resources that are vital for certain especially vulnerable groups are being affected.[1] Further degradation not only intensifies current poverty, but it limits options for future generations, thereby creating intergenerational inequity.
- Finally, the MA suggests that reversing the degradation of ecosystems would require significant changes in institutions and policies and it specifically notes that economic instruments can play an important role in this transformation.

Another report, The Economics of Ecosystems and Biodiversity (TEEB), examines the costs of policy inaction on the decline of biodiversity worldwide. It finds that by 2050 under several "business as usual" scenarios, an additional 11 percent of remaining biodiversity could be lost, 40 percent of low-impact agriculture could be converted to intensive agriculture, and 60 percent of coral reefs could be gone (perhaps as early as 2030).

Recognizing the importance of ecosystem services, the Intergovernmental Platform on Biodiversity and Ecosystem Services (IPBES) was established in April 2012 as an independent intergovernmental body open to all member countries of the United Nations. IPBES provides a forum for synthesizing, reviewing, assessing, and critically evaluating relevant information and knowledge generated worldwide on biodiversity and ecosystem services. In 2019, IPBES published an update on the state of ecosystem services. This is the first update since the Millennium Ecosystem Assessment completed in 2005 and the first to be carried out by an intergovernmental body. This assessment is clear that "nature and its vital contributions to people, which together embody biodiversity and ecosystem functions and services, are deteriorating worldwide." Fourteen of the 18 categories of nature that were assessed are deteriorating and 1 million species risk extinction. Nature can be conserved however, and "used" sustainably, but it will require transformative change.

Economic Analysis of Ecosystem Services

Ecosystem services are flows that are generated from stocks of natural assets and that benefit humans. Tropical forests, for example, are assets that can provide carbon sequestration, habitat, watershed protection, and recreation, but also can provide flows of timber. The harvest of flows can either be sustainable or unsustainable.

Economic analysis is helpful both in identifying sources of economic degradation and in evaluating possible approaches to maintain and restore these services. Both of these tasks are enhanced by careful valuation of the flows in question.

One avenue for using these valuations is benefit-cost analysis and the scope for these analyses is wider than you might expect. They are not limited to traditional evaluation of water- or land-use projects. Bandara and Tisdell (2004), for example, use the results of a contingent valuation study on saving the Asian elephant to show that the willingness to pay for the conservation of Asian elephants in Sri Lanka more than compensates for the damage caused by elephants.

Demonstrating the Value of Ecosystem Services

The starting point for economic analysis in reversing ecosystem degradation lies in revealing the economic value forgone by the loss of these services. Quantifying those values, even imperfectly, can make it clear just how much their loss or degradation means.

Many of the services explored in this chapter are nonmarket goods or services, which means that we must use a methodology that does not depend on the availability of market prices to derive their value. As discussed in Chapter 4, two main strategies are available for eliciting these values: revealed preference methods (attributing value by observing or measuring what people spend on goods and services that contain attributes we wish to value) and stated preference methods (using surveys to ascertain willingness to pay). Other methods commonly used for valuing ecosystem services include using adjusted market prices, avoidance costs (or averting expenditures), production function methods, or damage costs avoided.[2] Here we will focus specifically on valuing services that ecosystems provide to humans either directly or indirectly and consider some specific contexts to illustrate both how these techniques can be applied to the valuation of ecosystem services and why the results matter.

The Value of Coral Reefs

Over half a billion people depend on coral reefs for food, storm protection, and income (NOAA, 2019). Coral reefs are an integral part of an extensive and vital landscape of coastal ecosystems. Increasingly they are in jeopardy. One of the specific areas benefited by the new field of ecosystems services research is not only the derivation of better estimates of the value of those ecosystem benefits, but also the identification of the specific sources of that value.

While some of the threat to coral reefs is due to pollution or overfishing, recently coral reef losses have accelerated significantly due to climate change. Specifically, rising water temperatures have induced coral bleaching, and excessive CO_2 dissolution in seawater is causing ocean acidification, which in turn hampers reef regeneration.

What is at stake? Just how valuable are the services provided by coral reefs? And how much do the four different categories of services contribute to the overall value?

One well-known study (TEEB, 2009) provides some relevant estimates to answer these questions by pulling together the existing literature on values of reefs in a global context. Table 5.1, drawn from that study, not only demonstrates that reefs provide valuable ecosystem services, but also divides up the sources of value into the four categories described at the beginning of this chapter.

Note that this study finds that cultural services (particularly tourism and recreation) make the largest contribution to value. The clear implication is that studies that capture only the provisional services from coral reefs seriously underestimate this value.

One use of this type of estimate would be in calculating the reef degradation damages from climate change, a calculation that would be useful in designing climate change policy. Equivalently, the estimates could be used to derive the benefits from reducing that damage via greenhouse gas mitigation policy.

Because the TEEB study aggregates the results from a number of individual studies, it would be helpful to have some sense of what an underlying individual study might look like. What does it include? What methods are used to derive the estimates? What uses are anticipated for these estimates? Example 5.1 provides some insights from one study that help to answer these questions.

For the entire United States, the value of coral reefs has been estimated at $3.4 billion per year, including fisheries, tourism, and coastal protection. Included in this number is $94 million per year in flood damages that coral reefs help protect against. The net economic value of the globe's coral reefs is estimated to be tens of billions of U.S. dollars per year (NOAA, 2019).

Once the value of any local coral reef is recognized and measures to protect that value are considered, the next step is to assess how its future value would be affected by alternative development/conservation plans, as well as how the costs of taking those actions might affect those future values. Benefit-cost analysis can assist in figuring out the economic desirability of various strategies.

Table 5.1 Benefits from Ecosystem Services in Coral Reef Ecosystems

Coral Reefs	Value of Ecosystem Services (in U.S.$/ha/year; 2007 values)		
Ecosystem Service	Average	Maximum	Number of Studies
Provisioning services			
Food	470	3818	22
Raw materials	400	1990	5
Ornamental resources	264	347	3
Regulating services			
Climate regulation	648	648	3
Moderation of extreme events	25,200	34,408	9
Waste treatment/water purification	42	81	2
Biological control	4	7	2
Cultural services			
Aesthetic information/ Amenity	7425	27,484	4
Opportunities for recreation and tourism	79,099	1,063,946	29
Information for cognitive development	2154	6461	4
Total	115,704	1,139,190	83
Supporting services			
Maintenance of genetic diversity	13,541	57,133	7

Note: ha = hectare, a metric unit of area defined as 10,000 square meters.
Source: TEEB. (September 2009). Climate Issues Updated. Table 1, 7.

One study (UNEP, 2018) was commissioned to derive this information for two significant reefs: the Coral Triangle and the Mesoamerican Reef. The Coral Triangle spans six countries, though most of it lies within Indonesian waters. It is one of the most highly biodiverse and ecologically important coral reef regions in the world. It contains 37 percent of all reef fish species and 76 percent of known coral species. Areas of the Mesoamerican Reef lie within Belize, Guatemala, Honduras, and the Yucatan province in Mexico. It is the second-largest reef in the world, with only the Great Barrier Reef being larger. Example 5.1 describes what was learned from that study.

EXAMPLE 5.1

The Value of Protecting Coral Reefs in the Coral Triangle and Mesoamerica

To start, the direct and indirect 2017 total economic returns for both the Coral Triangle and the Mesoamerican Reef systems were calculated, as well as the returns within each of three sources of value categories. Since these categories only reflect use value accruing to the reef systems, they are underestimates. As the results presented in Table 5.2 show, however, even just the economic returns from use values in both systems are large and dominated by the tourism sector, but all sectors are important.

The next questions were how would these economic values be affected in the future depending on whether investments were made to protect the reef values and would the net benefits (after subtracting the cost of the protective steps) be positive? To find out, the economic returns were estimated for both protected and business as usual (unprotected) scenarios between 2017 and 2030 in order to calculate the present value of benefits, costs, and net benefits of protecting the reefs.

First, they find that the protected coral reefs are expected to deliver significantly larger economic benefits across the three measured sectors. Between 2017 and 2030, the estimated increase in economic benefits from protective

Table 5.2 Direct and Indirect Economic Returns from Coral Reefs 2017 in millions (US$)

Sector		Mesoamerican Reef	Coral Triangle
Tourism	Direct	$3,484	$3,113
	Indirect	$871	$3,113
	Total	$4,356	$6,225
Commercial fisheries	Direct	$240	$2,925
	Indirect	$240	$2,925
	Total	$480	$5,850
Coastal development	Direct	$975	$1,323
	Indirect	$837	$1,094
	Total	$1,813	$2,417
All sectors	Direct	$4,700	$7,361
	Indirect	$1,949	$7,132
	Total	**$6,649**	**$14,493**

Source: United Nations Environment Programme. (2018). *The Coral Reef Economy: The Business Case for Investment in the Protection, Preservation and Enhancement of Coral Reef Health.*

investments would total $34.6 billion for the Mesoamerican Reef and $36.7 billion for the Coral Triangle.

They then estimate the net benefits of specific interventions to protect reefs: constructed wetlands, afforestation, vegetative filter strips, and no-take zones (a type of marine protected area). The results for the Mesoamerican Reefs are displayed in Table 5.3 and for the Coral Triangle in Table 5.4.

Table 5.3 Annualized Present Value of Costs, Benefits, and Net-Benefits of Healthy Reef Interventions in Mesoamerica (2017 millions U.S.$)

Intervention			Present Value			Return on Investment (%)
			Costs	Benefit	Net-Benefit	
Int. 3	MSA	Constructed Wetlands	–$8	$22	$14	2.8
Int. 5	MSA	Afforestation	–$7	$25	$18	3.5
Int. 7	MSA	Vegetative Filter Strip	–$5	$24	$20	5.1
Int. 1	MSA	No-Take Zone	–$30	$1,321	$1,291	44.0

Source: United Nations Environment Programme. (2018). *The Coral Reef Economy: The Business Case for Investment in the Protection, Preservation and Enhancement of Coral Reef Health.*

Table 5.4 Annualized Present Value of Costs, Benefits, and Net-Benefits of Healthy Reef Interventions in the Coral Triangle (2017 millions U.S.$)

Intervention			Present Value			Return on Investment (%)
			Costs	Benefit	Net-Benefit	
Int. 4	IDN	Constructed Wetlands	–$193	$134	-$59	0.7
Int. 2	IDN	No-Take Zone	–$212	$453	$240	2.1
Int. 6	IDN	Afforestation	–$61	$206	$145	3.4
Int. 8	IDN	Vegetative Filter Strip	–$183	$1,618	$1,435	8.8

Source: United Nations Environment Programme. (2018). *The Coral Reef Economy: The Business Case for Investment in the Protection, Preservation and Enhancement of Coral Reef Health.* UN Environment, ISU, ICRI, and Trucost. 15–16.

The Mesoamerican Reefs net benefit estimates are positive in present value terms for all protective strategies. The "no-take" scenario has the largest benefit-to-cost ratio by far. Interestingly, for the Coral Triangle, one of the categories (constructed wetlands) actually produces a negative net benefit; the costs exceed the benefits. And for this reef system the vegetative strips intervention results in the largest benefit-to-cost ratio.

These estimates suggest not only that these coral reefs have significant economic value, but also that well-targeted protection strategies produce increases in value well above their cost.

Continued degradation could significantly impact local livelihoods and government revenue in regions with coral reefs and worldwide due to the ecosystem services they provide.

Source: United Nations Environment Programme. (2018).
The Coral Reef Economy: The Business Case for Investment in the Protection, Preservation and Enhancement of Coral Reef Health. https://wedocs.unep.org/20.500.11822/26694

Valuing Supporting Services: Pollination

Ecosystem valuation can also help to raise awareness of extremely valuable, but probably underappreciated, ecosystem services, especially when the continuation of those services is threatened. Pollination services supplied by honeybees and wild bees is one such valuable ecosystem service. Many valuable agricultural crops rely on bees for pollination. Between $235 and $577 billion (U.S.) worth of annual global food production relies on the direct contribution of honeybee pollinators (Lautenbach et al., 2012; Porto et al., 2020).

Some 2 million honeybee hives, or about 90 percent of all the beehives in the United States, were required just for cross-pollination of the $4.7 billion almond crop in California in 2021. That works out to be about one bee per 20 nuts![3] When the almond trees flower, managed honeybee hives are moved by flatbed trucks to the San Joaquin Valley to provide sufficient bees to pollinate the crop.

The benefits from pollination, however, include not only the direct economic impacts of increasing the productivity of agricultural crops but also such nonmarket impacts as aiding in genetic diversity, improving ecosystem resilience, and providing nutrient cycling. Unfortunately, these important ecosystem services may be in jeopardy.

In 2006, the popular press began reporting on what has been called colony collapse disorder, an unexplained disappearance of honeybee colonies. Beekeeper surveys suggest that 33 percent of honeybee colonies in the United States died in the winter of 2010. In 2019 that number rose to 40 percent. While the exact causes are as of yet unknown, multiple causes are likely to blame.

Ratnieks and Carreck (2010) speculate about the economic impact of potential future losses and ask an important question:

> Is the future of U.S. commercial beekeeping going to be based on pollinating a few high-value crops? If so, what will be the wider economic cost arising from crops that have modest yield increases from honey bee pollination? These crops

cannot pay large pollination fees but have hitherto benefited from an abundance of honey bees providing free pollination.

The damage caused by loss of pollination services to other parts of the world could be even higher than in the United States. One study argues that possible future global shortages of pollination services are likely not only to be profound, but to have quite different economic impacts around the globe (Example 5.2).

EXAMPLE 5.2

Valuing Pollination Services: Two Illustrations

Pollinator services valued in the tens of billions of dollars worldwide are disappearing. Declining populations of pollinator insects, including wild bees, risk losses to agricultural production worldwide with disproportionate impacts on developing countries.

Wild bees from a nearby tropical forest provide pollination services to aid Costa Rican coffee production. While this coffee (*C. arabica*) can self-pollinate, pollination from wild bees has been shown to increase coffee productivity from 15 to 50 percent.

One study (Ricketts et al., 2002) examined this relationship and placed an economic value on this particular ecological service. They found that the pollination services from bees living in two specific preserved forest fragments (46 and 111 hectares, respectively) were worth approximately $60,000 per year for one large, nearby Costa Rican coffee farm. As the authors conclude:

> The value of forest in providing crop pollination service alone is … of at least the same order [of magnitude] as major competing land uses, and infinitely greater than that recognized by most governments (i.e., zero).

Although these estimates only partially capture the value of this forest, because they consider only a single farm and a single type of ecological service, they are apparently sufficient, by themselves, to demonstrate the economic value of preserving this particular forest.

Recognizing that this kind of partial analysis, which focuses on an individual case, should be complemented by studies with a more macro focus has encouraged different methodologies with a more global focus. One of these studies, which used a multiregional, computable general equilibrium (CGE) model of agricultural production and trade, examined the global economic impacts of pollinator declines (Bauer & Wing, 2010).

CGE models produce numerical assessments of economy-wide consequences of various events or programs. They include not only the direct effects on the crop sector, but also the indirect, non-crop effects. Using this type of model allows the authors to estimate the impacts of a decline in pollination services in different geographic regions. They also are able to estimate how these impacts are affected by the presence of different local substitutes for pollination services.

The authors find that the annual global losses to the crop sector attributable to a decline in direct pollination services are estimated to be $10.5 billion, but economy-wide losses (non-crop sectors) are estimated to be much larger, namely $334 billion. Clearly, estimates based only on direct services would seriously underestimate the value of pollination services.

They also find that some regions of the world, especially western Africa, are likely to suffer disproportionately. Their enhanced vulnerability is due not only to the larger share that pollinator-dependent crops make up in western Africa's agricultural output, but also to the relatively higher importance of the agriculture sector in the African economy.

Richer countries are not immune. In early 2017, the rusty patched bumble bee (*Bombus affinis*), a key pollinator of blueberries, tomatoes, and wildflowers, became the first bumble bee and the first wild bee of any kind to be listed on the Endangered Species list in the United States. Wild bumble bees are important pollinators of one-third of U.S. crops. Pollination services in the United States have been estimated at $3 billion per year (Gorman, 2017).

Sources: Ricketts, T. H. et al. (August 24, 2002). Economic value of tropical forest to coffee production. *PNAS (Proceedings of the National Academy of Sciences)*, 101(34), 12579–12582; Bauer, D. M., & Wing, I. S. (October 2010). Economic consequences of pollinator declines: A synthesis. *Agricultural and Resource Economics Review*, 39(3), 368–383; Gorman, S. (January 11, 2017). U.S. lists a bumble bee species as endangered for the first time. *Scientific American*.

Valuing Supporting Services: Forests and Coastal Ecosystems

Valuation methods have been used extensively to value forest ecosystem services, coastal and marine ecosystem services, and biodiversity. In his summary of the literature on coastal and marine ecosystem services (CMEs) valuation, Barbier (2012) notes that losses to fishery nurseries, mangroves that provide storm protection, coral reefs that are a rich source of biodiversity, filtering services of wetlands, and sea grasses have now been measured worldwide. Quantifying the benefits of these services can provide an empirical foundation for decision making and for setting priorities.

The TEEB (2009) presents several other examples that demonstrate the numerous and diverse possible sources of benefits. One such example derives the ecosystem benefits from protecting a forest with high biodiversity in Madagascar. Benefits flowing from that resource include medicines (estimated net present value of $1.57 million), erosion control (estimated NPV of $380,000), carbon storage (estimated NPV of $105 million), recreation, and forest products (estimated value of $9.4 million).

This study also notes the complicated scale dimension of ecosystem services by demonstrating how benefits flow from developing countries to a distant city, in this case London. These transboundary benefits include medicines, fish, coffee, flood control, and existence value. Valuing services that simultaneously affect several different scales (local, regional, global) can be challenging, but not including all scales can produce a serious underestimate.

Challenges and Innovation in Ecosystem Valuation

In order for valuations to be useful, their derivations must be based upon consistent methodologies. Consistency is important not only to assure that various valuation projects can be directly compared, but also so that benefit transfers are facilitated. (Recall from Chapter 4 that benefit transfer involves using values from one study site to provide the basis for valuing services at another policy site.)

Achieving this kind of consistency requires precise definitions of the services as well as agreement on how these services contribute to value. It also requires that the valuation procedures avoid double counting.

For nonmarket goods and services these issues are especially challenging. While market goods have well-defined units based on actual purchases, nonmarket goods and services may offer a large variety of attributes, each of which could have value. If different analysts choose different attributes to value, the result will not only be inconsistent valuations, but inconsistent valuations also make policy-relevant benefit transfer impossible (Johnston et al., 2005).

The Millennium Ecosystem Assessment (2005) provides a classification of ecosystem services that has been widely cited, but unfortunately these classifications are vulnerable to double counting. "Water purification" and the "provision of freshwater" are listed as separate services, for example (Balmford et al., 2011; Boyd & Banzhaf, 2007). Double counting can also occur if an ecosystem service provides both an intermediate good and a final good. When both are separately valued and simply added together—a common mistake—the resulting values are inflated. On the other hand, intermediate services cannot simply be ignored since they are one source of the final value (Johnston & Russell, 2011).

Given these challenges, how do nonmarket valuation methods fare in practice? The quest for clean, reliable estimates of the value of ecosystem services is still evolving. For example, Boyd and Krupnick (2009) note in their survey of the stated preference literature that a lack of consistency in definitions is still relatively common. Johnston and Russell (2011) also lament the lack of clarity in definitions of final ecosystem goods and services.

Researchers using stated preference methods are beginning to grapple with this aspect of inconsistency—how to distinguish between intermediate and final goods. The specific challenge for economists using stated preference techniques is to design surveys that identify commodities that are both true to the ecological science and meaningful and understandable to respondents (Boyd & Krupnick, 2009; Johnston et al., 2012). This is no easy undertaking. Recall from Chapter 4, in a survey on water quality in New Zealand, Walsh et al. (2022) avoid this challenge by using measurable (and salient) changes to water quality and clarity (Tables 4.2 and 4.3) rather than scales of low, medium, high or boatable vs. fishable.

For revealed preference methods the challenge of properly treating intermediate and final goods is smaller because those methods typically deal only with final goods; they rarely attempt to measure intermediate ecological inputs (Johnston, 2014). However, revealed preference methods are only available for a subset of ecosystem services, namely those where purchases actually occur. Additionally, with revealed preference methods, even when final goods have been demonstrated to have value, it is sometimes difficult to know the specific underlying source of that value. For example, if a hedonic property value study finds that being near beaches raises land value, which attributes of the beaches are the source of that value? Is it the beach width? The sand quality? Both?

Moore et al. (2011) provide a useful example of how an attribute-based study can bring greater clarity to the question of *what* is being valued. In their study aimed at estimating marginal values of forest protection programs, they utilized a stated preference survey that asked respondents to consider two different types of conservation sites—one with distinct use values like recreation and easy access, and another with high ecological values like a richer biodiversity or providing habitat for endangered species. Identifying and valuing these specific attributes, as opposed to deriving only an overall value for the site, allows for the estimation of the marginal value of each type of service. Note that estimating separate marginal values for specific ecosystem services also facilitates more precise benefit transfers.

One response to the high cost of conducting new site-specific studies for each ecosystem service is to use meta-analysis, the technique (discussed in Chapter 4) that can draw insights from a large number of previously completed studies. This approach has the advantage that not only will the service value be based on a large number of studies, but it can also identify the study characteristics that seem to play a role in the resulting value. Despite the challenges, the role for nonmarket valuation is already clear and numerous studies have highlighted the benefits of protection of one or more ecosystem service in ways that have made for better policy.

Institutional Arrangements and Mechanisms for Protecting Nature's Services

Valuation is only one of the contributions economic analysis can make to the maintenance and protection of important ecosystem services. Another is using economics to help design institutions and policies that can bring economic incentives to bear.

Payments for Environmental Services (PES)

One avenue where economic analysis has been helpful in this regard lies in identifying ways to create institutional arrangements in which the providers of ecosystem services can be compensated for nonmarket services. This would not only create better incentives for maintaining and enhancing those services, but also provide a revenue source that could be used to further that purpose. Around the globe there are 550 active PES programs (Salzman et al., 2018). We highlight just a few examples here to illustrate the scope of these arrangements.

Costa Rica's Pago por Servicios Ambientales (PSA) Program

One of the earliest examples of this approach can be found in Costa Rica. Built upon an existing forestry law, the PSA program includes four specific environmental services provided by forest ecosystems: (1) greenhouse gas emission mitigation; (2) water services for human consumption, irrigation, and energy production; (3) biodiversity conservation; and (4) scenic beauty for recreation and ecotourism. For our purposes in this chapter the water services component is the most interesting and we shall focus on it.

The program started with voluntary agreements involving payments to private landowners from water users in return for conserving certain forested areas that served as recharge or purification areas in the watershed. Bottlers, municipal water supply systems, irrigation water users, and hotels have all chosen to participate in these agreements. Whereas early agreements saw water users paying for a quarter of conservation costs (since water services were only one of four services that the law enumerated as provided by forests), in more recent agreements water users are not only paying the entire cost of conservation, but the administrative costs as well. These agreements typically cover a five-year period.

As the program has matured, a water tariff has been added to finance the payments, effectively transforming one aspect of the program from a voluntary one into a mandatory one. Interestingly the voluntary agreements are still occurring not only because the payments made under these agreements are deducted from the amounts owed under the tariff, but the voluntary agreements give somewhat more control to the signatory over exactly how the payment will be used.

Pagiola (2008) reports that the PSA program has been very popular with landowners (with requests to participate far outstripping available financing) and that recipients had a higher percentage of their forest under conservation than nonrecipients. He also points out, however, that the program does have some specific inefficiencies. In particular, because the PSA program offers a relatively low, undifferentiated, and mostly untargeted payment, it tends to attract participants whose opportunity cost of participation is low or negative. As a result some socially desirable land-use practices are not adopted because the payment being offered is insufficient.

This program also provides a good opportunity to discuss an issue of some importance to these types of programs—economic sustainability. Programs will only be successful over the long term if they create the means to sustain themselves financially after the initial enthusiasm. This can occur either because (1) the incentives created by the program are large enough to cause private benefits to be higher than costs for both payees and recipients, or (2) sufficient required financing is provided by law.

Indeed, some payments for service arrangements (including some in the PSA program) are funded by limited-term grants from international organizations. These are no doubt helpful in setting up the program and providing some initial successes, but many times what happens after these grants run out is not clear. In the case of the PSA water services program, the existence of the tariff coupled with the apparent private landowner interest in participating suggest that the outlook for the economic sustainability of this program seems relatively good.

Other Watershed Payment Programs

Investing in watershed services is a broad category that covers payments for watershed services, water quality trading markets, instream buybacks, and water funds. Salzman et al. (2018) report on the state of watershed payments and find 387 active programs worldwide in 2015. In 2011, $8.17 billion was transacted, though not all payments were in cash. In-kind payments, training programs, or agriculture inputs are also included (Bennett et al., 2013). The most well-known of these programs is the Conservation Reserve Program (CRP) in the United States. The CRP pays farmers to fallow their land with the goal of protecting water quality and preventing topsoil loss. The program also incentivizes farmers to use practices that increase carbon sequestration. In 2023 alone, the U.S. Department of Agriculture paid approximately $1.8 billion to over 677,000 farmers on 23 million acres of land.[4]

In China, the City of Beijing implemented a program of paying farmers to convert land from rice cultivation to dryland farming with a goal of reducing nutrient loads into Miyun Reservoir. Zheng (2013) estimates a benefit-cost ratio of 1.5 for this program, suggesting it has been quite successful.

Quito charges a 1 percent surcharge on monthly water bills, along with monies from beer companies to fund projects aimed at protecting forests and grasslands (Salzman et al., 2018). In Australia, the government has committed $3.1 billion in the Murray–Darling to purchase water entitlements from farmers to ensure instream flows.[5]

Having users pay for services that they previously received for free can serve to produce an efficient outcome by providing both an incentive and revenue to protect those services. Suppose, however, the provider threatens to cut off supplies of those services unless the desired payments are forthcoming. Is this extortion or simply good business? (See Debate 5.1.)

DEBATE 5.1

Paying for Ecosystem Services or Extortion? The Case of Yasuni National Park

Designated a UNESCO Biosphere Reserve in 1989, Yasuni National Park is one of the most biologically diverse places on earth. It is also the location for an estimated 846 million barrels of crude oil, 20 percent of Ecuador's reserves. As a developing country Ecuador was faced with a classic dilemma—should it preserve the parkland or extract the oil?

To avoid the environmental destruction caused by oil exploration in one of the areas with the greatest biological and cultural diversity in the Amazon, the government proposed permanently forgoing oil production in the Ishpingo-Tambococha-Tiputini (ITT) oil fields, located in Yasuni, if the world community would contribute 50 percent of the forgone income (estimated to be U.S.$3.6 billion over a 13-year period).

Supporters argued that the payments would pay for global climate change benefits resulting from the CO_2 emissions avoided. They calculated 407 million metric tons of CO_2 emissions would be saved due to non-extraction and burning of oil and another 800 million metric tons of CO_2 from avoided deforestation.

Detractors suggested that this was extortion—"pay us or we will destroy the planet."

Regardless of whether it was a good idea, it failed. In August 2013, Ecuador's president announced that, since the initiative had attracted only a fraction of the cash it had aimed to raise, he would end it.

Sources: Ecuador Yasuni ITT Trust Fund. http://mptf.undp.org/yasuni; Ecuador approves Yasuni park oil drilling in Amazon rainforest. www.bbc.co.uk/news/world-latin-america-23722204.

> ### EXAMPLE 5.3
>
> # Trading Water for Beehives and Barbed Wire in Bolivia
>
> Amboro National Park in Bolivia supports a very biologically diverse ecosystem. The park and surrounding areas are under intense pressure from illegal land incursions. Migrants from the surrounding highlands, with encouragement from local political leaders, extract timber from the park and clear areas for agriculture. Lack of well-defined property rights for local communities leaves few alternative options. Due to increased timber harvesting and increased agriculture, the Los Negros River dries up earlier than it did in the past, causing suffering among the local communities that depend on the river for irrigation.
>
> Asquith (2006) describes a unique solution to this property rights problem involving payments for environmental services. Natura Bolivia, an environmental group, helped negotiate an agreement through which downstream water users would pay for the protection of native vegetation in the watershed. Instead of financial compensation, though, payment would be in the form of one beehive and training in honey production per 10 hectares of cloud forest protected. In 2003, 60 beehives were provided to farmers in exchange for 600 hectares of cloud forest conserved. In 2004, the municipal government provided another 11 hives to farmers. By 2006, 2100 hectares had been protected.
>
> The Los Negros scheme is slowly building a market for environmental services and helping to define property rights in the region. In 2006, when contracts were renewed, some farmers requested barbed wire, instead of beehives, in order to help them strengthen their land claims. Combining a market mechanism (payment for environmental services) with developing a local enforcement mechanism and strengthening local property rights has proven to be a successful scheme so far.
>
> *Source*: Asquith, N. (December 2006). Bees and barbed wire for water on the Bolivian frontier. *PERC, 24*(4). www.perc.org/articles/bees-and-barbed-wire-water.

Water is not the only service to be involved in a payments scheme and sometimes the payments can be in kind rather than in cash (see Example 5.3).

Tradable Entitlement Systems

Another program approach recognizes that not only more land but also land better suited for supplying environmental services could be supplied if those services were treated separately in land titles. Some land may be especially good at providing environmental services while having a low opportunity cost, but other land may have a very high opportunity cost. If all land is required to meet the same environmental service provision requirements, the cost of the program will soar. Suppose, however, that the landowner has to supply those services, but not necessarily on the specific piece of land facing the requirement. This is the premise of a number of programs, including wetlands banking and carbon sequestration credits.

Wetlands Banking

Several U.S. administrations, both Republican and Democratic, have pledged that wetlands should experience "no net loss."[6] Despite these bipartisan pledges to protect wetlands, as the pressure on coastal and shorefront properties has increased, the economic benefits from developing wetlands (and political pressures to remove obstacles to development) have significantly increased as well.

One policy instrument for attempting to preserve wetlands in the face of this pressure is known as Wetlands Mitigation Banking and involves providing incentives for creating off-site "equivalent" wetlands services when adverse impacts on the original site are unavoidable and when either on-site compensation is not practical or use of a mitigation bank is environmentally preferable to on-site compensation. According to the U.S. EPA, "The objective of a mitigation bank is to provide for the replacement of the chemical, physical, and biological functions of wetlands and other aquatic resources which are lost as a result of authorized impacts."[7]

Mitigation banks involve wetlands, streams, or other aquatic resource areas that have been restored, established, enhanced, or (in certain circumstances) specifically preserved for the purpose of providing compensation for unavoidable impacts to aquatic resources. Mitigation banks involve a form of "third-party" compensatory mitigation in which the responsibility for compensatory mitigation implementation and success is assumed by someone other than the party who, by causing an adverse impact to a wetland, is required by law to provide mitigation.

A mitigation bank may be created when a government agency, corporation, non-profit organization, or other entity undertakes mitigation activities under a formal agreement with a regulatory agency. The value of those activities is defined in "compensatory mitigation credits." In principle, the number of credits available for sale is based upon the use of ecological assessment techniques to certify that the credited areas provide the specified ecological functions.

How has the program performed? As one recent review (Salzman & Ruhl, 2006) concludes:

> Despite policies mandating that habitat trading ensure equivalent value and function, the experience is that most programs are not administered this way. In practice, most habitat trades to date in wetlands programs have been approved on the basis of acres, in many instances ensuring equivalence in neither value nor function.

This experience is instructive. Merely assuring that the compensation involves a similar number of acres falls short of true equivalence unless the replacement ecological functions supplied by those acres are also the same.

Carbon Sequestration Credits

To the extent that landowners do not receive all the benefits of landownership, they may discount or ignore the benefits that accrue to others. Through photosynthesis, trees absorb (sequester) carbon dioxide, thereby removing it from the atmosphere and lowering its threat to the climate. Carbon sequestration credits are an attempt to rectify one such imbalance. Is this an efficient remedy?

Carbon sequestration credits attempt to internalize the carbon absorption benefit externality by giving forest (or marsh) owners credit for the additional carbon they remove from the atmosphere. They can earn this credit by investing in additional carbon sequestration (by planting new trees, or protecting a salt marsh, for example). This credit (or offset) can be sold to those who can use these reductions in fulfillment of their legal obligations to meet specified carbon-emissions targets. Some evidence suggests that reducing carbon in this way would be cheaper than many other measures. The Reducing Emissions from Deforestation and Forest Degradation (REDD) program, run by the United Nations, is an example of this approach (see Example 5.4).

EXAMPLE 5.4

Reducing Emissions from Deforestation and Forest Degradation (REDD): A Twofer?

According to the United Nations, deforestation and forest degradation, through agricultural expansion, conversion to pastureland, infrastructure development, destructive logging, fires, and so on, account for nearly 20 percent of global greenhouse gas emissions, more than the entire global transportation sector and second only to the energy sector. In response, the United Nations has set up a program to reduce these emissions by reducing the forest degradation in developing countries. REDD is an effort to create a financial value for the carbon stored in forests, offering incentives for developing countries to reduce emissions from forested lands and to invest in low-carbon paths to sustainable development. According to this scheme, nations would receive payments for emissions-reduction credits determined on the basis of actual reductions in forest emissions measured against agreed-upon baselines. These credits can be sold in the international compliance carbon markets (where they could be used in combination with domestic reductions to meet assigned national targets) or voluntary carbon markets (where they could be used to pursue other organizational goals, such as demonstrating carbon neutrality). Data from the Forest Trends Ecosystem Marketplace indicate that as of 2016, forest carbon projects are protecting 28 million hectares of forest.

The promise of this program is that it offers opportunities to make progress on two goals at once: (1) reducing forest degradation and (2) reducing emissions that contribute to climate change. The challenges, which are far from trivial, are to establish baselines that are both fair and effective and to assure that monitoring and verification procedures are rigorous enough to provide reliable, accurate measures of actual emissions reductions. Otherwise the emissions authorized by the credits might exceed the actual emissions reductions that the credits are based upon.

Sources: Government of Norway. (2009). Reducing emissions from deforestation and forest degradation (REDD): An options assessment report. An electronic copy of this report is available at the United Nations REDD website: www.un-redd.org; Forest Trends Ecosystem Marketplace. (2016). View from the understory: State of forest carbon finance 2016. www.forest-trends.org/documents/files/doc_5388.pdf (Accessed February 10, 2017).

Conflict Resolution in Open-Access Resources via
Transferable Entitlements

In a later chapter on fisheries, we will learn about individual transferable quotas (ITQs) and how they are used in fisheries management. When marine resources and services suffer from free-access problems, ITQs are one option for reducing the over-fishing problem.

Arnason (2012) argues that a properly designed ITQ system could also provide another, quite different, benefit, namely facilitating the resolution of marine resource conflicts between recreational and commercial fisheries as well as conflicts between fishing and other marine resource uses. Making the entitlements transferable creates both an economic means and an economic incentive for the entitlements to move to their highest-valued use as circumstances change, but careful design and adequate enforcement would be key to achieving success in conflict resolution.

Have ITQs helped to resolve conflicts? Not yet, but some ITQ holders are beginning to coordinate with other users of marine resources. In New Zealand, for example, the scallop fishery has formed an association that coordinates activities not only with other open-water fisheries, but also with aquaculture (Arnason, 2012).

One difficult international area of conflict involves the management of whale populations. Could tradable entitlements possibly help to resolve this conflict (see Debate 5.2)?

DEBATE 5.2

Tradable Quotas for Whales?

The International Whaling Commission (IWC) banned whaling in 1986. Yet approximately 2000 are still harvested each year—approximately 1000 by Japan for "scientific purposes"; 600 by Iceland and Norway, who do not recognize the ban; and 350 for subsistence (Costello et al., 2012). In 2010, some nations proposed allowing limited whaling with the hope that taking this step would reduce the number of whales actually harvested. This proposal never materialized due to disagreements between whaling and nonwhaling nations.

Costello et al. (2012) argue that this conflict could be reduced using tradable quotas for whale harvesting, thus "creating a market that would be economically, ecologically and socially valuable for whalers and whales alike" (139). Under their scheme both whalers and conservationists could bid for quotas and whalers could earn profits from whaling or from selling their quotas to conservationists. They propose allocating "whale shares" in sustainable numbers to all the member nations of the IWC. (Note that this means that nonwhaling nations would also get a share. These shares could only be acquired by the whaling nations by buying them from the nonwhaling nations.) Shares would be traded in a global market and could be exercised or retired in perpetuity. The size of the harvest would depend on who bought the shares and could fall between zero (conservationists purchase all) and the sustainable total quota. Since trades are voluntary, in princi-ple this market mechanism has the potential to make all parties better off (including the whales)!

Opponents note that multiple challenges exist, including determin-ing the sustainable quota, obtaining agreement on how the shares to this quota would be initially allocated among the parties, and creat-ing a trading system with adequate transparency and enforcement. Additionally, those who oppose putting a price tag on whales as a mat-ter of principle certainly are opposed to this idea. However, as Costello et al. point out, this lack of a real price tag could well be what has hindered anti-whaling operations. Smith et al. (2014) argue that this is flawed analysis. Whales are impure public goods, meaning that there are both private and public benefits to their conservation. A market for whales (or any species) would need to reflect *all* of the values of the species, which would be extremely difficult. Existence values, for example, would need to be summed across individuals, while harvesting benefits only benefit the harvester. They argue that using the market to determine the level of conservation is "akin to using the market to set the level of the 'cap,' rather than solely using the market to allocate permits under a scientifically determined cap" (15). They also argue that creating a market for whales could legitimize the trade in whale meat, exactly the opposite of the policy's intention. Monitoring and enforce-ment would also be inherently challenging for a highly migratory spe-cies. Finally, they question how the quota would be chosen. How high?

What about costs and benefits? Conservation organizations such as Greenpeace spend millions of dollars on anti-whaling campaigns. Costello et al. estimate that Greenpeace USA, Greenpeace International, Sea Shepherd Conservation Society, and the World Wildlife Fund spend approximately $25 million annually on anti-whaling activities. The estimated profit from one minke whale is approximately $13,000, while the profit is $85,000 for a fin whale (2012 market prices and costs). Costello et al. estimate that the 350 whales saved by the Sea Shepherd in 2008 could simply have been purchased for less than $4 million.

Instead of spending money on anti-whaling, these groups would have the option to simply purchase the whales, thereby preventing anyone from harvesting them. Costello et al. think it could be a win–win situation. Do you think they are right?

Source: Costello, C., Gaines, S., & Gerber, L. R. (January 12, 2012). Conservation science: A market approach to saving the whales. *Nature, 481*, 139–140; Smith, M. D., Asche, F., Bennear, L. S., Havice, E., Read, A. J., & Squires, D. (2014). Will a catch share for whales improve social welfare? *Ecological Applications, 24*(1), 15–23; Gerber, L. R., Costello, C., & Gaines, S. D. (2014). Facilitate, don't forbid, trade between conservationists and resource harvesters. *Ecological Applications, 24*(1), 23–24.

Ecotourism

Ecotourism provides another prominent example of an activity that attempts to create a revenue stream based upon environmental services that can serve to fund protection of those services.

According to several organizations such as the International Ecotourism Society and International Union for Conservation of Nature, ecotourism can be defined as follows:

> Environmentally responsible travel to natural areas, in order to enjoy and appreciate nature (and accompanying cultural features, both past and present) that promotes conservation, has a low visitor impact, and provides for beneficially active socioeconomic involvement of local peoples.

Not all ecotourism projects turn out to be consistent with this definition. Increasing the number of visitors to sensitive natural areas in the absence of appropriate oversight and control can threaten the integrity of both ecosystems and local cultures (see Debate 5.3). Additionally, the possible instabilities in this revenue source posed by climate fluctuations, volatile exchange rates, global pandemics, and political and social upheaval could make an excessive reliance upon tourism a risky business.

In the wake of the global COVID-19 pandemic, ecotourism plummeted. Communities relying on ecotourism revenues for conservation efforts were left without those resources to protect ecosystems. On the other hand, many areas experienced fewer crowds and less congestion and damage from human use.

Without revenue from ecotourism, though, incentives for poaching increase. Poaching is a major threat to wildlife. Poaching is the illegal taking of game or domestic livestock. Normally we consider adequate enforcement to be the solution to poaching, but in some settings assuring adequate enforcement is easier said than done. Can trophy hunting help?

DEBATE 5.3

Does Ecotourism Provide a Pathway to Sustainability?

One of the ways ecotourism can promote conservation is by providing the necessary funds to implement an effective conservation program. Take the example of Bolivia's Eduardo Avaroa Reserve. This diverse landscape includes hot springs and geysers surrounded by volcanoes and majestic mountains. Its freshwater and saltwater lakes provide habitat for year-round flocks of pink flamingos and other birds, while nearby 23 types of mammals and almost 200 species of plants flourish in the desert-like environment. With over 40,000 visitors per year, the park is Bolivia's most visited.

When a conservation planning initiative determined that tourism was a major threat to the reserve, The Nature Conservancy worked with the Bolivian National Park System to develop a visitor-fee system.

The program, which reportedly generated over half a million dollars in new funds, allows the reserve to fund efforts to mitigate these tourism-related threats. The visitor-fee approach is now being extended across the Bolivian Park System. It is estimated that the national protected areas system could generate more than $3 million per year in new income for conservation.

Quite a different take on ecotourism is provided by a British academic, Rosaleen Duffy. Speaking about Belize—a popular ecotourist destination in Central America—Duffy relates stories of how scuba diving and snorkeling visitors have spoiled fragile corals and otherwise harassed marine wildlife.

"In their pursuit of reefs, rainforests, and ruins," writes Duffy, "they did not reflect on the environmental impact of the construction of hotels, the use of airlines, the manufacture of diving equipment, the consumption of imported goods or even something as visible as taking a motorboat out to the reef, which polluted the water." As a *Time* article on her book notes, "To Duffy, it seems, the only good tourist is the one who stays home."

Sources: Duffy, D. (2002). *A Trip too Far—Ecotourism, Politics and Exploitation*. Washington, D.C.: Island Press; Bird, M. A. (2002). Ecotourism or egotourism. *TIME* online. http://content.time.com/time/magazine/article/0,9171,338585,00. html (Accessed May 24, 2007); The Nature Conservancy, Ecotourism and Conservation Finance. www.nature.org/aboutus/travel/ecotourism/about/ art14824.html (Accessed May 24, 2007).

Consider, for example, how the economics of poaching might be used to enhance enforcement in the case of African wildlife. From an economic point of view, poaching can be discouraged if it is possible to raise the relative cost of illegal activity. In principle that can be accomplished by increasing the sanctions levied against poachers, but it is effective only if monitoring can not only detect the illegal activity but also apply the sanctions to those who engage in it. In many places that is a tall order, given the large size of the habitat to be monitored and the limited budgets for funding enforcement. Example 5.5 shows, however, how economic incentives can be enlisted to promote more monitoring by local inhabitants as well as to provide more revenue for enforcement activity.

EXAMPLE 5.5

Payments for Ecosystem Services—Wildlife Protection in Zimbabwe

In the late 1980s, an innovative program was initiated in Zimbabwe that stands out as a success among other African wildlife protection schemes. It transformed the role of wildlife from a state-owned treasure to be preserved into an active resource controlled and used by both commercial farmers and smallholders in communal lands. The transformation has been good for the economy and the wildlife.

The initiative is called the Communal Areas Management Program for Indigenous Resources (CAMPFIRE). It was originally sponsored by several different agencies in cooperation with the Zimbabwean government, including the University of Zimbabwe's Center for Applied Study, the Zimbabwe Trust, and the World Wide Fund for Nature (WWF). The U.S. federal government currently provides resources to CAMPFIRE, principally through USAID. Under the CAMPFIRE system, villagers collectively utilize local wildlife resources on a sustainable basis. Trophy hunting by foreigners is perhaps the most important source of revenue, because hunters require few facilities and are willing to pay substantial fees to kill a limited number of large animals. The government sets the prices of hunting permits as well as quotas for the number of animals that can be taken per year in each locality. Individual communities sell the permits and contract with safari operators who conduct photographic and hunting expeditions on community lands.

The associated economic gains accrue to the villages, which then decide how the revenues should be used. The money may either be paid to households in the form of cash dividends, which may amount to 20 percent or more of an average family's income, or they may be used for capital investments in the community, such as schools or clinics. In at least one area, revenues compensate citizens who have suffered property loss due to wild animals. Households may also receive nonmonetary benefits, such as meat from problem animals or culled herds. By consistently meeting their needs from their own resources on a sustainable basis, local communities have become self-reliant. This voluntary program has been steadily expanding since its inception, and now includes 28 wildlife districts, of which 15 are hunting districts.

The program has been working. In 2010, 40 elephants were poached. In 2015, this number had dropped to five. Additionally, it has been estimated that households participating in CAMPFIRE increased their incomes by 15–25 percent. Between 1989 and 2006, CAMPFIRE dividends disbursed to communities were $20.8 million.

In 2014, the United States suspended ivory imports from Tanzania and Zimbabwe in an effort to reduce poaching of elephants. American clients generally constitute 76 percent of hunters in CAMPFIRE areas for all animals hunted each year. The ban resulted in the cancellation of 108 out of 189 (57 percent) elephant hunts booked by U.S. citizens in CAMPFIRE areas. The resulting drop in CAMPFIRE income has been significant. Revenues dropped from $2.3 million in 2013 to $2.1 million in 2014 to $1.6 million in 2015.

The decreased revenues reduce funds for protection of wildlife and also remove the incentives for community members to protect the elephants. While well-intended, the American ban could backfire if poaching resumes.

Sources: Frost, P. G., & Bond, I. (2008). The CAMPFIRE programme in Zimbabwe: Payments for wildlife services. *Ecological Economics*, 65(4), 776–787. http://campfirezimbabwe.org/index.php/news-spotlight; Jonga, C., & Pangeti, G. (2015). https://firstforwildlife.wordpress.com/2015/08/18/the-campfire-program-in-zimbabwe; Barbier, E. (1992). Community based development in Africa. In T. Swanson & E. Barbier (Eds.), *Economics for the Wilds: Wildlife, Diversity, and Development*. Washington, D.C.: Island Press, 107–118; Bojo, J. (February 1996). The economics of wildlife: Case studies from Ghana, Kenya, Namibia and Zimbabwe. *AFTES Working Paper No. 19*. The World Bank; www.Colby.edu/personal/thtieten/end-zim.html.

Other types of incentives have also proved successful. In Kenya, for example, a compensation scheme has helped Maasai tribesmen to transition from hunting lions to protecting them. Maasai from the Mbirikani ranch are now compensated for livestock killed by predators. They receive $80 for each donkey and $200 for each cow killed. The Mbirikani Predator Fund has compensated herders for the loss of 750 head of livestock each year since the program began in 2003. As an additional collective incentive, if any herder kills a lion, no one gets paid.[8]

Rearranging the economic incentives so that local groups have an economic interest in preservation can provide a powerful means of protecting some biological populations. Open access undermines those incentives.

Sometimes, however, the benefits and costs of removing predators that kill livestock are unclear. Perceived costs can surprisingly turn out to be unexpected benefits. As one example, wolves once ranged over most of the Northern hemisphere, but humans nearly wiped out the species in the United States and Europe by 1960 (Boitani, 2003). Why? Policymakers believed that the economic costs of wolves—namely threats to valuable livestock and big game—were too high. Even President Theodore Roosevelt, a famed conservationist, once called the wolf a "beast of waste and desolation" (Roosevelt 1893, 386). Are the economic costs too high? Example 5.6 illustrates a case for the reintroduction of wolves. Reintroducing wolves results in *reduced* predation and reduced human deaths from vehicle collisions with deer!

EXAMPLE 5.6

On the Error of Ignoring Ecosystem Services: The Case of Wolf Recovery in the United States

The ecosystem services wolves provide were unfortunately not obvious to the European settlers of North America until *after* they were lost. Aldo Leopold, widely regarded to be the father of wildlife ecology, notes:

> I have lived to see state after state extirpate its wolves. I have watched the face of many a newly wolfless mountain, and seen the south-facing slopes wrinkle with a maze of new deer trails. I have seen every edible bush and seedling browsed … I have seen every edible tree defoliated to the height of a saddlehorn.
>
> (Leopold, 1949)

Wolves have since returned to at least ten U.S. states and 28 European countries (Chapron et al., 2014; U.S. Fish and Wildlife Service, n.d.), through natural migration and reintroduction programs. Scientists have since documented that wolves can help to reduce deer populations and change deer behavior in ways that benefit vegetation, a phenomenon known as a trophic cascade.

These ecological changes also protect human lives and property by improving roadway safety. Drivers hit 1 to 2 million wild animals on roads every year in the United States, causing 26,000 human injuries, 200 human fatalities, and nearly $11.4 billion in total economic losses (in 2022 U.S. dollars) (Huijser et al., 2008). Most of these collisions are with deer. Economists Jennifer Raynor,

Corbett Grainger, and Dominic Parker (2021) examine whether wolves reduce these losses in the state of Wisconsin, where wolves naturally recolonized starting in the 1970s. They find that wolves reduce the number of vehicle collisions with deer by almost one-quarter, generating an annual economic benefit of about $11 million statewide.

Do these benefits outweigh the costs of predation on domesticated animals? Wisconsin maintains a program that reimburses the costs of verified wolf predation of livestock, hunting dogs, and pets. This program paid $3.1 million in claims from 1985 and 2019, or an average of about $174,000 per year over the last five years (Wisconsin Department of Natural Resources, 2020). The economic benefit of reduced vehicle collisions is 63 times larger than the costs of verified predation losses!

Perhaps even more surprisingly, the number of domesticated animals killed by predators may *fall* as wolves recolonize. Ongoing work by Eyal Frank, Anouch Missirian, Dominic Parker, and Jennifer Raynor (2022) shows that calf predation rates decline sharply when wolves return to an area. How can this be, if wolves are killing calves? It turns out, coyotes are more likely than wolves to kill livestock, and wolves keep coyote populations in check. What was a perceived cost of wolves can be an additional benefit, when considering the broader ecosystem services of wolves.

Wolf management decisions continue to be controversial, and policymakers are grappling with how to balance the economic costs and benefits of the species. As we have seen in other parts of this book, accounting for all of the benefits and costs is important for good decision making.

Sources: Chapron, G., Kaczensky, P., Linnell, J. D. C., von Arx, M., Huber, D., Andrén, H., López-Bao, J. V., et al. (2014). Recovery of large carnivores in Europe's modern human-dominated landscapes. *Science*, 346(6216), 1517–1519. https://doi.org/10.1126/science.1257553; Frank, E. G., Missrian, A., Parker, D. P., & Raynor, J. L. (2022). *Reversing Local Extinctions: The Economic Impacts of Reintroducing Wolves in North America*. Working Paper; Groot Bruinderink, G. W. T. A., & Hazebroek, E. (1996). Ungulate traffic collisions in Europe. *Conservation Biology*, 10(4), 1059–1067. https://doi.org/10.1046/j.1523-1739.1996.10041059.x; Huijser, M. P., McGowen, P., Fuller, J., Hardy, A., Kociolek, A., Clevenger, A. P., Smith, D., & Ament, R. (2008). *Wildlife-Vehicle Collision Reduction Study: Report to Congress*. FHWA-HRT-08-034. McLean, V.A.: Federal Highway Administration. http://www.fhwa.dot.gov/publications/research/.../pavements/.../research/safety/08034/02.cfm; Leopold, A. (1989). *A Sand County Almanac and Sketches Here and There*. Special commemorative ed. New York, NY: Oxford University Press; Raynor, J. L., Grainger, C. A., & Parker, D. P. (2021). Wolves make roadways safer, generating large economic returns to predator conservation. *Proceedings of the National Academy of Sciences*, 118(22), e2023251118. https://doi.org/10.1073/pnas.2023251118; U.S. Fish and Wildlife Service. (n.d.). Gray wolf: Current population in the United States. https://www. fws.gov/midwest/wolf/aboutwolves/WolfPopUS.htm (Accessed July 27, 2020); Wisconsin Department of Natural Resources. (2020). Wisconsin Annual Wolf Damage Payment Summary.

Poverty and Debt

Poverty and debt are major sources of pressure on ecosystem services. In eastern and southern Africa, for example, positive feedback loops have created a downward cycle in which poverty and deforestation reinforce each other. Most natural forests have long since been cut down for timber and fuelwood and for producing crops from the cleared land. As forests disappear, the rural poor are forced to divert more time toward locating new sources of fuel. Once fuelwood is no longer available, dried animal waste is burned, thereby eliminating it as a source of fertilizer to nourish depleted soils. Fewer trees lead to more soil erosion and soil depletion leads to diminished nutrition. Diminished nutrition reinforces the threats to human health posed by an inability to find or afford enough fuel, wood, or animal waste for cooking and boiling unclean water. Degraded health saps energy, increases susceptibility to disease, and reduces productivity. Survival strategies may necessarily sacrifice long-term goals simply to ward off starvation or death; the forest is typically an early casualty.

At the national level, poverty takes the form of staggering levels of debt. Repaying this debt and the interest payments flowing from it reduces the capacity of a nation to accumulate foreign exchange earnings. In periods of high real interest rates, servicing these debts commands most if not all foreign exchange earnings. Using these foreign exchange earnings to service the debt eliminates the possibility of using them to finance imports for sustainable activities to alleviate poverty.

According to the "debt-resource hypothesis," large debts owed by many developing countries encourage these countries to overexploit their resource endowments to raise the necessary foreign exchange. Timber exports represent a case in point. One strategy that has been employed to help and has had some success is debt-for-nature swaps.

Debt-for-Nature Swaps

One strategy involves reducing the pressure on the forests caused by the international debt owed by many developing countries. One of the more innovative policies that explores common ground in international arrangements has become known as the debt-for-nature swap. A *debt-for-nature swap* involves the purchase (at a discounted value in the secondary debt market) of a developing country's debt, frequently by an environmental nongovernmental organization (NGO). The new holder of the debt, the NGO, offers to cancel the debt in return for an environmentally related action on the part of the debtor nation.

The first debt-for-nature swap took place in Bolivia in 1987. Since then debt-for-nature swaps have been arranged or explored in many developing countries, including Ecuador, the Philippines, Zambia, Jamaica, Madagascar, Guatemala, Venezuela, Argentina, Honduras, and Brazil.

A brief examination of the Madagascar case can illustrate how these swaps work. Recognized as a prime source of biodiversity, the overwhelming majority of Madagascar's land mammals, reptiles, and plants are found nowhere else on earth. Madagascar is also one of the poorest countries in the world, burdened with high levels of external debt. Because of its limited domestic financial resources, Madagascar could not counter the serious environmental degradation it was experiencing.

Between 1989 and 1996, Conservation International, the Missouri Botanical Garden, and the World Wildlife Fund negotiated nine commercial debt-for-nature swaps in Madagascar. These arrangements generated $11.7 million in conservation funds. Agreements signed by Madagascar's government and the participating conservation organizations identified the programs to be funded. One such program trained over 320 nature protection agents, who focused on involving local communities in forest management.

Other arrangements involving different governments and different environmental organizations have since followed this lead. The main advantage of these arrangements to the debtor nation is that a significant foreign exchange obligation can be paid off with domestic currency. Debt-for-nature swaps offer the realistic possibility to turn what has been a major force for unsustainable economic activity (the debt crisis) into a force for resource conservation.

Extractive Reserves

One strategy specifically designed to protect the indigenous people of the forest as well as to prevent deforestation involves the establishment of extractive reserves. These areas would be reserved for the indigenous people to engage in their traditional hunting–gathering activities.

Extractive reserves have already been established in the Acre region of Brazil. Acre's main activity comes from the thousands of men who tap the rubber trees scattered throughout the forest, a practice dating back 100 years. Under the leadership of Chico Mendes, a leader of the tappers who was subsequently assassinated, four extractive reserves were established in June 1988 by the Brazilian government to protect the rubber tappers from encroaching development.

The World Heritage Convention

The World Heritage Convention came into being in 1972, with the primary mission of identifying and preserving the cultural and natural heritage of outstanding sites throughout the world and ensuring their protection through international cooperation. Currently, some 178 countries have ratified the convention.

Ratifying nations have the opportunity to have their natural properties of outstanding universal value added to the World Heritage List. The motivation for taking this step is to gain international recognition for this site, using the prestige that comes from this designation to raise awareness for heritage preservation and the likelihood that the site can be preserved.

A ratifying nation may receive both financial assistance and expert advice from the World Heritage Committee as support for promotional activities for the preservation of its properties as well as for developing educational materials.

Responsibility for providing adequate protection and management of these sites falls on the host nations, but a key benefit from ratification, particularly for developing countries, is access to the World Heritage Fund. This fund is financed by mandatory contributions from ratifying nations, calculated at 1 percent of the country's contribution to UNESCO, the administering agency. Annually, about $3 million (U.S.) are made available, mainly to low-income countries, to finance technical assistance and training projects, as well as for assistance preparing their nomination proposals or to develop conservation projects. Emergency assistance may also be made available for urgent action to repair damage caused by human-made or natural disasters.

Royalty Payments

A potential source of revenue for biodiversity preservation involves taking advantage of the extremely high degree of interest by the pharmaceutical industry in searching for new drugs derived from these biologically diverse pools of flora and fauna. Establishing the principle that nations containing these biologically rich resources within their borders would be entitled to a stipulated royalty on any and all products developed from genes obtained from these preserves provides both an incentive to preserve the resources and some revenue to accomplish the preservation.

Nations harboring rich biological preserves have begun to realize their value and to extract some of that value from the pharmaceutical industry. The revenue is in part used for inventorying and learning more about the resource as well as preserving it. For example, in 1996, Medichem Research, an Illinois-based pharmaceutical company, entered into a joint venture with the Sarawak government. The organization created by this joint venture has the right to file exclusive patents on two compounds that offer some promise as cancer treatments.

The agreement specified a 50–50 split from royalties once the drug is marketed. The Sarawak government was given the exclusive right to supply the latex raw material from which the compounds are derived. Furthermore, Sarawak scientists are involved in screening and isolating the compounds and Sarawak physicians are involved in the clinical trials.

This agreement not only provides a strong rationale for protecting the biological source, but also enables the host country to build its capacity for capturing the value of its biodiversity in the future (Laird & Ten Kate, 2002). These arrangements are particularly significant because they facilitate transboundary sharing of the costs of preservation. It is unrealistic to expect countries harboring these preserves to shoulder the entire cost of preservation when the richer countries of the world are the major beneficiaries. It may also be unrealistic to assume that pharmaceutical demand is sufficient to fund efficient preservation (see Example 5.7).

EXAMPLE 5.7

Does Pharmaceutical Demand Offer Sufficient Protection to Biodiversity?

The theory is clear—incentives to protect plants are stronger when the plants are valuable to humans. Is the practice equally clear?

The case of Taxol is instructive. Derived from the slow-growing Pacific yew, Taxol is a substance that has proved effective in treating advanced forms of breast and ovarian cancers. As of 1998, it was the best-selling anticancer drug ever.

Since the major site for this tree was in the old-growth forests of the Pacific Northwest, the hope of environmental groups was that the rise in the importance of Taxol might provide both sustainable employment and some protection for old-growth forests.

In fact, that is not how it worked out. The Taxol for the chemical trials was derived from the bark of the tree. Stripping the tree of its bark killed it. And supplying enough bark for the chemical trials put a tremendous strain on the resource.

Ultimately, the private company that marketed Taxol, Bristol-Squibb, developed a semi-synthetic substitute that could be made from imported renewable tree parts.

The Pacific yew, the original source of one of the most important medical discoveries in the twentieth century, was left completely unprotected. And the industry that had grown up to supply the bark collapsed. In the end, its value proved transitory and its ability to support a sustainable livelihood in the Pacific Northwest was illusory. Not all seemingly good ideas produce the expected outcomes. The details matter.

Source: Goodman, J., & Walsh, V. (2001). *The Story of Taxol: Nature and Politics in the Pursuit of an Anti-Cancer Drug*. New York: Cambridge University Press.

Debt-for-nature swaps, extractive reserves, and royalty payments all involve recognition of the fact that resolving the global externalities component of deforestation requires a rather different approach from resolving the other aspects of the deforestation problem. In general, this approach involves financial transfers from the industrialized nations to the tropical nations, transfers that are constructed so as to incorporate global interests into decisions about the future of tropical forests.

Recognizing the limited availability of international aid for the preservation of biodiversity habitat, nations have begun to tap other revenue sources. Tourist revenues have become an increasingly popular source, particularly where tourism is specifically linked to the resources that are targeted for preservation. Rather than mixing these revenues with other public funds, nations are earmarking them for preservation (see Example 5.8).

EXAMPLE 5.8

Trust Funds for Habitat Preservation

How can local governments finance biodiversity preservation when faced with limited availability of both international and domestic funds? One option being aggressively pursued involves trust funds. Trust funds are moneys that are legally restricted to be used for a specific purpose (as opposed to being placed in the general government treasury). They are administered by trustees to assure compliance with the terms of the trust. Most, but not all, trust funds are protected endowments, meaning that the trustees can spend the interest and dividends from the funds, but not the principal. This assures the continuity of funds for an indefinite period.

Where does the money come from? Many nations that harbor biodiversity preserves cannot afford to spend the resources necessary to protect them. One possibility is to tap into foreign demands for preservation. In Belize, the revenue comes from a "conservation fee" charged to all arriving foreign visitors. The initial fee, $3.75, was passed by Belize's parliament in January 1996, raising $500,000 in revenues each year for the trust fund. These fees, along with grants and donations, provide the Protected Areas Conservation Trust (PACT) with a sustainable source of funding for protected areas.

Currently in Belize, 482 projects in some 103 protected areas form a vast national protected areas system, with categories that encompass forest reserves, nature reserves, national parks, marine reserves, private reserves, wildlife sanctuaries, natural monuments, bird sanctuaries, spawning aggregation reserves, and archaeological reserves. Similar trust funds have been set up in Mexico, Honduras, and Guatemala.

Biodiversity preservation that depends on funds from the general treasury becomes subject to the vagaries of budgetary pressures. When the competition for funds intensifies, the funds may disappear or be severely diminished. The virtue of a trust fund is that it provides long-term, sustained funding targeted specifically on the protection of biodiversity.

Source: www.pactbelize.org (Accessed October 31, 2019)

The Special Problem of Protecting Endangered Species

Suppose a specific species is found to be endangered and listed as such under the U.S. Endangered Species Act (ESA). How can economics help to create incentive-based programs to enhance the likelihood of survival for this species?

Conservation biologists have found that one key to reducing the threat to endangered species is to prevent their habitat from becoming fragmented into smaller parcels. In response, economists have developed programs that attempt to reduce habitat fragmentation.

Conservation Banking

One such program, conservation banking, enlists a tailored transferable credits program into endangered and threatened species conservation. A conservation bank is a parcel of land containing natural-resource values that are conserved and managed, in perpetuity, through a conservation easement held by an entity responsible for enforcing the terms of the easement. Banks of especially suitable land are established for specified listed species (under the Endangered Species Act) and used to offset impacts to the species occurring on nonbank lands by providing a larger, less fragmented habitat for them.

Access to the habitat services provided by these banks is provided by the creation of salable quantified "credits," where each credit provides a specified amount of habitat provision designed to satisfy the requirements of the ESA. Project proponents are, therefore, able to complete their ESA obligations through a one-time purchase of credits from the conservation bank (see Example 5.9).

EXAMPLE 5.9

Conservation Banking: The Gopher Tortoise Conservation Bank

In rapidly growing Mobile County, Alabama, the gopher tortoise faced survival problems due to the disappearance of its habitat. Since the tortoise is federally listed as a threatened species under the Endangered Species Act (ESA), small landowners were forced to observe some rather severe restrictions on their use of the land. Because these restrictions were quite burdensome for the landowners and the resulting fragmented, patchy habitat proved ineffective in protecting the tortoise, these restrictions created quite a conflict in the community.

A conservation bank established by the Mobile Area Water and Sewer System (MAWSS) in 2001 reduced the conflict, allowing development to continue in other areas while restoring and permanently protecting a much more suitable large tract of the long-leaf pine habitat that the tortoise prefers.

MAWSS owns a 7000-acre forest that buffers and protects the county's water supply. Under the terms of its conservation bank, MAWSS has agreed to set aside 222 acres, forgo any development on that land, and manage it in perpetuity

---

for the benefit of gopher tortoises. Landowners who want to build on tortoise habitat elsewhere in Mobile County can purchase "credits" from the bank, and thereby be relieved of their ESA responsibilities to set aside a small patch of their land. The tortoises benefit because the large tract of contiguous, suitable habitat is vastly superior to a network of small, unconnected patches of land, while the landowners can now develop their land by helping to fund (through the purchase of credits) this tortoise habitat.

Source: Environmental Defense's Center for Conservation Incentives. (February 24, 2003). Gopher tortoise conservation bank: Mobile area landowners and wildlife get help. www.edf. org/?from=splash_continue&_ga=1.202011924.401743717.1469651799.

The Agglomeration Bonus

Another strategy to reduce fragmentation, known as the *agglomeration bonus*, has been proposed by Smith and Shogren (2002). The agglomeration bonus is a voluntary incentive mechanism that is designed to protect endangered species and biodiversity by reuniting fragmented habitat across private land in a manner that minimizes landowner resistance.

Many states currently have programs that encourage landowners to conserve land, but how can these owners be further encouraged to give priority to land that connects with other land? Under this bonus payment scheme the landowner receives an additional payment (the bonus) for each retired acre that shares a common border with another retired acre. If both landowners retire land at their common border, both can profit from their neighbor's retired acres. With this bonus each landowner has an explicit incentive to give priority to retiring acres that are adjacent to their neighbor's retired acres. Notice that the agglomeration bonus pays for connected land, not any specific piece of land—landowners are free to select any land that shares a common border with other retired land.

This mechanism provides an incentive for landowners to give preference to land that would form a contiguous reserve across their common border. The government agency's role would be to target the critical habitat and to integrate the agglomeration bonus into the compensation package, but the landowners would have the ultimate power to decide whether to participate.

An analysis of the properties of this mechanism using experimental economics (Parkhurst et al., 2002) found that in the lab the absence of a bonus always created fragmented habitat, whereas with the bonus players cooperated to establish the optimal habitat reserve.

Safe Harbor Agreements

Safe harbor agreements are a means of conserving endangered and threatened species on privately owned land. These agreements approach the problem of landowner incentives from a different perspective, mainly seeking to overcome some rather severe unintended consequences that can flow from the ESA.

Under the ESA many landowners are actually inhibited from implementing practices likely to benefit endangered species because of the repercussions that might arise from these apparently benign activities. Under the approach taken by the ESA, the presence of an endangered species on a property may result in new legally imposed restrictions on any activities deemed harmful to that species. Thus, if landowners were simply to restore wildlife habitats on their property, and those habitats attracted endangered animals, they might find themselves faced with many new restrictions on their use of the land. As a result, some landowners are not only unwilling to take such risks, but they may actually actively manage property to prevent endangered species from occupying their land.

Safe harbor agreements overcome these perverse incentive problems. Any landowner who agrees to carry out activities expected to benefit an endangered species is guaranteed that no added ESA restrictions will be imposed as a result. A landowner's ESA responsibilities are effectively frozen at their current levels for a particular species if they agree to restore, enhance, or create habitat for that species. Safe harbor agreements do not, however, confer a right to harm any endangered species already present when the agreement is entered into (established by the landowner's "baseline" responsibilities). Those responsibilities are unaffected by a safe harbor agreement.

Preventing Invasive Species

Invasive species are nonnative plants and animals that have been introduced (intentionally or accidentally). They tend to spread quickly, causing damage to ecosystem and human health. The literature on the economics of invasive species is relatively new, but there is agreement that prevention is much less expensive than mitigation. As such, prevention is a preferable policy option to control once a species has taken over a new location (see, for example, Finnoff et al., 2007; Kaiser & Burnett, 2010). This is frequently called the *precautionary principle* in economics.

On the other hand, many species have already been introduced or there is a concern they have reached a particular location. Example 5.10 looks at the role of community science in the detection and monitoring of invasive species.

EXAMPLE 5.10

The Changing Economics of Monitoring and its Role in Invasive Species Management

An old adage states that you can't manage what you don't measure. Measurement, however, has typically not been cheap, posing a dilemma for managers who want to make solid decisions with limited budgets.

One area where this has been true is in fisheries. In many cases managers don't even know all the species that inhabit the marine and freshwater environments in their areas.

New technology may change that. Scientists have developed simple techniques involving Environmental DNA or eDNA that allow scientists to extract filtered water from a water course for testing. These tests, which can be done for anywhere from $50 to $150 a test, are powerful enough to detect any species that have been present in that water in the last day or two. The presence of a single cell is sufficient. These costs are sufficiently low and the results sufficiently reliable that the U.S. Forest Service has launched a project to collect DNA from all rivers and streams across the western United States to create an Aquatic Environmental DNA Atlas.

Another common use of this approach is to detect the presence of invasive species. Researchers at Cornell University faced the daunting task of monitoring New York state's 7600 lakes and 70,000 miles of rivers and streams for these species. The challenge was finding a way to acquire the samples at reasonable cost.

To meet this challenge, they started a community science project with cooperating science teachers across the state. Detection kits were sent to participating classes. The students in those classes gathered the water samples as part of their class and sent the collected samples to the university. When the results were returned, the students entered them in a database.

With the low labor costs associated with this form of gathering the samples and the new technology that makes the DNA tests not only possible, but simple enough that community scientist results can be reliable, monitoring can now take place on a scale that was formerly inconceivable. And the community scientists can participate in "hands-on" science.

Source: Robbins, J. (March 9, 2017). A splash of river water now reveals the DNA of all its creatures. *Yale Environment 360*. http://e360.yale.edu/features/edna-rivers-fish-bull-trout-forest-service
(Accessed March 9, 2017).

Moving Forward

Ecosystem goods and services may be the ultimate resources that humans rely on. This chapter has highlighted some of the ways that economic analysis can place values on these goods and services to assist policymakers in decision making. We have also looked at multiple examples of economic incentives and mechanisms to encourage the provision of ecosystem goods and services and to reduce their degradation.

As we have seen with these examples, the theory is relatively straightforward but in practice, developing innovative mechanisms like payments for ecosystem services or carbon sequestration credits is challenging, especially in developing countries.

Summary

Ecosystems provide a host of services to humans, but the continued existence of those services is threatened. In this chapter we explore how two different kinds of economic analysis can contribute to protecting, maintaining, and enhancing these ecosystems.

The first step involves providing quantitative estimates of the value of these ecosystem services both to demonstrate their importance in general and to provide metrics that can be included in benefit-cost analyses that are being used for making choices that affect ecosystems. For commercial species such as fish and forests, and commercial resources such as water, the valuation task is made somewhat easier by the ready availability of prices.

For other ecosystem services the task is more difficult, but over time some of those barriers are beginning to fall as techniques such as avoided cost, stated preference surveys, and travel-cost studies are used to value ecosystem services. These methodologies are increasingly being applied to such different problems as valuing pollination services, assessing the economic impact of ecosystem-degrading events such as oil spills, and quantifying the role and economic benefits of natural water purification systems derived from wetlands or stream buffer zones. Newer methods such as computable general equilibrium (CGE) models allow analysts to capture not only the direct values to humans, but the indirect values as well. These studies not only corroborate and quantify the general sense that ecosystems services are valuable and deserve protection but they also identify the many pathways that provide these provisioning, regulating, supporting, and cultural services.

This chapter also examines the other main protection avenue—designing institutions and mechanisms that can eliminate or at least reduce perverse incentives that intensify degradation. Specifically, we have examined innovative schemes that provide payments from service users to service providers for historically nonmarketed services to assure that the providers have an incentive to refrain from converting the land to some other incompatible use. Another category of approaches focuses on creating new transferable entitlements to service flows. Not only do they give rise to new markets (such as wetlands banking, conservation entitlements for fish, or carbon sequestration credits) that can provide more economic sustainability to these flows by returning revenue to those who protect those services, but they also provide a new venue for potentially reducing resource conflicts.

And finally, we note how economic incentives can be used to protect the most vulnerable species—those that have already been classified as endangered. Environmental organizations have turned to economic approaches such as conservation banking to provide incentives for the market to preserve more of the most suitable endangered species habitat and safe harbor programs to counteract some of the more perverse habitat-destroying incentives for landowners that were inadvertently created by the Endangered Species Act.

As we point out in this chapter, this relatively new subfield is experiencing some growing pains, but early successes and new innovations indicate that its future is promising.

Discussion Questions

1. Consider the issues raised by the debate over Ecuador's proposal to preserve the Yasuni National Park from oil extraction. What is your view? Is this simply another payment for ecosystem services or was this extortion? Is this case different from some of the other payment for services cases described previously? If so, how is it different?

2. Consider the issues raised by the debate over using ecotourism to promote sustainability. What is your view? Is ecotourism always a pathway to sustainability? Never a pathway to sustainability? Sometimes a pathway to sustainability? Does your view suggest an appropriate role for government in managing ecotourism or should the entire process be left to the private sector? Why?

3. In 2016, *Outside Magazine* ran an obituary for the Great Barrier Reef in Australia (www.outside-online.com/2112086/obituary-great-barrier-reef-25-million-bc-2016). It was meant to be in part a spoof, yet recent evidence suggests that, while the whole reef is not dead, large portions of it are, and recovery might not be possible. What is the value of the Great Barrier Reef? Which ecosystem services values might be lost?

4. One approach to protecting ecosystem services involves dedicating specific habitat to wildlife (such as parks or reserves), a strategy that prohibits residential development in those areas. Other strategies (wetlands and conservation banking) accommodate residential development at a specific site, while attempting to offset the adverse effects on that site with requirements for preservation activities at other sites as a condition of allowing development at the original site. In your mind, does one of these strategies always dominate the other? If so, why? If not, does the context matter? How would an economist think about these questions?

Self-Test Exercises

1. Several of the policy options discussed in this chapter rely on transferable entitlements of one kind or another. The prominence of these approaches raises the question of what transferability adds to the mix. For each of the following options describe why making the entitlement transferable increases its efficiency.
   a. Carbon reduction credits.
   b. Conservation banking.

2. Suppose that a fishery has two sectors: (1) a commercial fishery that harvests fish to sell them to a processor and (2) a recreational fishery where boat captains take individuals out to catch some fish for the sport of it. Each sector has a catch share. Suppose further that the demand for sport fishing goes up considerably relative to the commercial fishery. This development would create a conflict because the recreational fishery would no doubt argue that its catch share is now unfairly low. Compare how this conflict might be dealt with depending on whether the catch shares are transferable between sectors or not. Think about how the incentives of each sector to resolve this conflict are affected by the possibility of inter-sector transferability of the catch shares.

Notes

1 The Millennium Development Goals (MDGs) include reducing the world's biodiversity losses and loss of environmental resources, as well as reducing the number of people without access to such services as safe drinking water (https://www.un.org/millenniumgoals).

2 For a description of these approaches and the role they play in ecosystem service evaluation, see Bateman et al. (2011).

3 https://asmith.ucdavis.edu/news/bees-per-almond#:~:text=So%2C%20in%20total%20California%20produces,from%20all%20over%20the%20country, https://www.wcngg.com/2020/11/23/2021-almond-pollination-outlook-economic-outlook-and-other-considerations.

4 https://www.fsa.usda.gov/programs-and-services/conservation-programs/conservation-reserve-program/index.

5 https://www.dcceew.gov.au/water/policy/mdb/commonwealth-water-mdb.

6 This section benefited from Salzman and Ruhl (2006).
7 Conservation International. (June 21, 2007). www.conservation.org/NewsRoom/ pressreleases/Pages/062107-Saving-Africa%E2%80%99s-Free-Roaming-Lions.aspx.
8 https://biglife.org/what-we-do/human-wildlife-conflict-mitigation/predator-compensation.

Further Reading

Agricultural and Resource Economics Review (continues the Northeastern Journal of Agricultural and Resource Economics), 42(1), April 2013. This special issue is devoted entirely to the economics of ecosystem services valuation, measurement, and analysis.

Environmental and Resource Economics. (December 2022). Special issue: The economics of biodiversity: Building on the Dasgupta review. *83*(4). This special issue focuses on the economics of biodiversity and in particular examines the "Dasgupta Review."

Johnson, J. A., Ruta, G., Baldos, U., Cervigni, R., Chonabayashi, S., Corong, E., Gavryliuk, O., Gerber, J., Hertel, T., Nootenboom, C., & Polasky, S. (2021). *The Economic Case for Nature: A Global Earth-Economy Model to Assess Development Policy Pathways*. Washington, DC: World Bank. https://openknowledge.worldbank. org/handle/10986/35882. License: CC BY 3.0 IGO. A report that outlines the economics case for protecting nature, with detailed evidence from around the world and evidence of the inequitable distribution of damages from losses of biodiversity.

Millennium Ecosystem Assessment. (2005). *Ecosystems and Human Well-Being: A Synthesis*. Washington, DC: Island Press. A summary of the findings of the U.N. Ecosystem Assessment.

National Research Council of the National Academies of Science (NRC). (2013). *An Ecosystem Services Approach to Assessing the Impacts of the Deepwater Horizon Oil Spill in the Gulf of Mexico*. Washington, DC: National Academies Press. Discusses the benefits and challenges associated with using an ecosystem services approach to damage assessment and offers suggestions for areas of future research.

Pattanayak, S. K., Wunder, S., & Ferraro, P. J. (2010). Show me the money: Do payments supply environmental services in developing countries? *Review of Environmental Economics and Policy*, 4(2), 254–274. Survey of the literature on payments for ecosystem services with a particular emphasis on their use in developing countries.

Ruckelshaus, M., McKenzie, E., Taillis, H., Guerry, A., Daily, G., Kareiva, P., Polasky, S., Ricketts, T., Bhagabati, N., Wood, S., & Bernhardt, J. (2015). Notes from the field: Lessons learned from using ecosystem service approaches to inform real-world decisions. *Ecological Economics*, 115, 11–21. https://doi.org/10.1016/j. ecolecon.2013.07.009. Offers six lessons from recent assessments of biodiversity and ecosystem services.

TEEB. (September 2009). *The Economics of Ecosystems and Biodiversity: Climate Issues Update*. Geneva: The Economics of Ecosystems and Biodiversity. A report that examines the impacts of climate change on ecosystems and biodiversity with a special emphasis on coral reefs and forests.

Additional references and historically significant references are available on this book's Companion Website: www.routledge.com/cw/Tietenberg

Chapter 6

Dynamic Efficiency and Sustainable Development

Introduction

In previous chapters, we have developed two specific criteria for identifying allocation problems. The first, static efficiency, allows us to evaluate those circumstances where time is not a crucial aspect of the allocation problem. Typical examples might include allocating resources such as an annually replenished water supply or solar energy, where next year's flow is independent of this year's choices. The second, more complicated criterion, dynamic efficiency, is suitable for those circumstances where time is a crucial aspect and subsequent choices are dependent on earlier choices. The combustion of depletable energy resources such as oil is a typical example, since supplies used now are unavailable for future generations.

After defining these criteria and showing how they could be operationally invoked, we demonstrated how helpful they can be. They are useful not only in identifying the misuse of environmental resources and ferreting out their behavioral sources, but also in providing a basis for identifying different types of remedies. These criteria even help design optimal policy instruments for restoring some sense of balance between the economy and the environment.

But the fact that these are powerful and useful tools in the quest for a sense of balance does not imply that they are the only criteria in which we should be interested. In a general sense, the efficiency criteria are designed to prevent wasteful use of environmental and natural resources. That is a desirable attribute, but it is not the only possible desirable attribute. We might care, for example, not only about the value of the environment (the size of the pie), but also about how this value is shared (the size of each piece to recipients). In other words, fairness or justice concerns should accompany efficiency considerations.

In this chapter, we investigate one particular fairness concern—the treatment of future generations. We begin by considering a specific, ethically challenging situation—the allocation of a depletable resource over time.

DOI: 10.4324/9781032689111-7

Specifically, we trace out the temporal allocation of a depletable resource that satisfies the dynamic efficiency criterion and show how this allocation is affected by changes in the discount rate. To lay the groundwork for our evaluation of fairness, we define what we mean by a just allocation among generations. Finally, we consider not only how this theoretical definition can be made operationally measurable, but also how it relates to dynamic efficiency. To what degree is dynamic efficiency compatible with intergenerational fairness?

A Two-Period Model

Dynamic efficiency balances present and future uses of a depletable resource by maximizing the present value of the net benefits derived from its use. This implies a particular allocation of the resource across time. We can illustrate the properties of this allocation with the aid of a simple numerical example. We begin with the simplest of models—deriving the dynamic efficient allocation across two time periods. In subsequent chapters, we show how these conclusions generalize to longer time periods and to more complicated situations.

Assume that we have a fixed supply of a depletable resource to allocate between two periods. Assume further that the demand function is the same in each of the two periods, the marginal willingness to pay is given by the formula $P = 8 - 0.4q$, and the marginal cost of supplying that resource is constant at \$2 per unit. (see Figure 6.1)

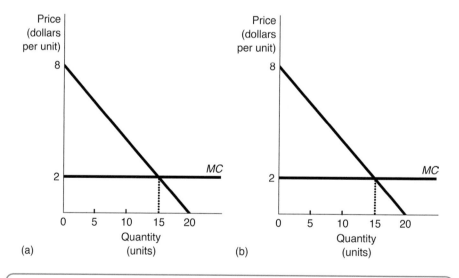

Figure 6.1 The Allocation of an Abundant Depletable Resource: (a) Period 1 and (b) Period 2.

Source: U.S. Bureau of Mines and the U.S. Geological Survey. (1976). Principles of the Mineral Resource Classification System of the U.S. Bureau of Mines and the U.S. Geological Survey. Geological Survey Bulletin, 1450-A.

Note that if the total supply (Q) were 30 or greater, and we were concerned only with these two periods, an efficient allocation would allocate 15 units to each period, *regardless of the discount rate.* Thirty units would be sufficient to cover the demand in both periods; the consumption in Period 1 would not reduce the consumption in Period 2. In this case the static efficiency criterion is sufficient because the allocations are not temporally interdependent—abundance eliminates the scarcity.

Consider, however, what happens when the available supply is less than 30. Suppose it equals 20. How do we determine the efficient allocation? According to the dynamic efficiency criterion, the efficient allocation is the one that maximizes the present value of the net benefit. The present value of the net benefit for both periods is simply the sum of the present values in each of the two periods. To take a concrete example, consider the present value of a particular allocation—15 units in the first period and five in the second. How would we compute the present value of that allocation?

The present value in the first period would be that portion of the geometric area under the demand curve that is over the supply curve; $45.00.[1] The present value in the second period is that portion of the area under the demand curve that is over the supply curve from the origin to the five units received, multiplied by $1/(1 + r)$. If we use $r = 0.10$, then the present value of the net benefit received in the second period is $22.73,[2] and the present value of the net benefits for the 2 years is $67.73.

Having learned how to find the present value of net benefits for any allocation, how does one find the allocation that *maximizes* present value? One way, with the aid of a computer, is to try all possible combinations of q_1 and q_2 that sum to 20. The one yielding the maximum present value of net benefits can then be selected. That is tedious and, for those who have the requisite mathematics, unnecessary.

It turns out that the dynamically efficient allocation of this resource has to satisfy the condition that the present value of the marginal net benefit from the last unit in Period 1 equals the present value of the marginal net benefit from the last unit in Period 2 (see appendix at the end of this chapter for the derivation). Even without the mathematics, this principle is easy to understand, as can be demonstrated with the use of a simple graphical representation of the two-period allocation problem.

Figure 6.2 depicts the present value of the marginal *net* benefit for each of the two periods. The net benefit curve for Period 1 is to be read from left to right. The net benefit (MB − MC) curve intersects the vertical axis at $6; demand would be zero at $8 and the marginal cost is $2, so the difference (marginal net benefit) is $6. The marginal net benefit for the first period goes to zero at 15 units because, at that quantity, the marginal willingness to pay for that unit exactly equals its marginal cost. Can you verify those numbers?

The only challenging aspect of drawing the graph involves constructing the curve for the present value of net benefits in Period 2. Two aspects of Figure 6.2 are worth noting. First, the zero axis for the Period 2 net benefits is on the right, rather than the left, side. Therefore, increases in Period 2 are recorded from right to left. By drawing the two periods this way, all points along the horizontal axis yield a total of 20 units allocated between the two periods. Any point on that axis picks a unique allocation between the two periods.[3]

Second, the present value of the marginal net benefit curve for Period 2 intersects the vertical axis at a different point than does the comparable curve for Period 1. Can you see why? This intersection is lower because the marginal benefits in the second period need to be discounted (multiplied by $1/(1 + r)$) to convert them into present value. This follows from the fact that they are received one year later. Thus, with the 10 percent discount rate we are using, the marginal net benefit on the right-hand axis

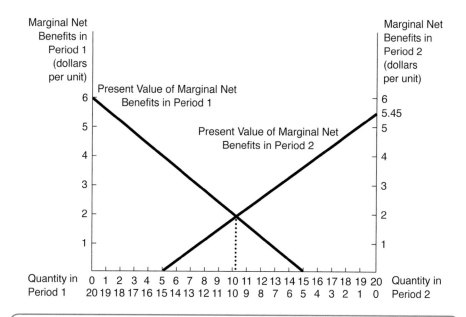

Figure 6.2 **The Dynamically Efficient Allocation.**

is $6 and its present value is $6/1.10 = \$5.45$. Note that larger discount rates $(r > .10)$ would rotate the Period 2 marginal benefit curve around the point of zero net benefit $(q_1 = 5, q_2 = 15)$ toward the right-hand axis. We shall use this fact in a moment.

The efficient allocation is now readily identifiable as the point where the two curves representing present value of marginal net benefits cross (since that is the allocation where the two marginal present values of net benefits for the two periods are equal). The total present value of net benefits is then the area under the marginal net benefit curve for Period 1 up to the efficient allocation, plus the area under the present value of the marginal net benefit curve for Period 2 from the right-hand axis up to its efficient allocation. Because we have an efficient allocation, the sum of these two areas is maximized.[4]

Since we have developed our efficiency criteria independent of an institutional context, these criteria are equally appropriate for evaluating resource allocations generated by markets, government rationing, or even the whims of a dictator. While *any* efficient allocation method must take scarcity into account, the details of precisely how that is done depend on the context.

Intertemporal scarcity imposes an opportunity cost that we henceforth refer to as the *marginal user cost*. When resources are scarce, greater current use diminishes future opportunities. The marginal user cost is the present value of these forgone future opportunities at the margin. To be more specific, uses of those resources, which would have been appropriate in the absence of scarcity, may no longer be appropriate once scarcity is present.

Consider a practical example. Using large quantities of water to keep lawns lush and green may be wholly appropriate for an area with sufficiently large replenishable water supplies, but quite inappropriate when it denies drinking water to future generations. Failure to take the higher future scarcity value of water into account in the present would lead to inefficiency due to the additional cost resulting from the increased scarcity imposed on the future. This additional marginal value created by scarcity is the marginal user cost.

We can illustrate this concept by returning to our numerical example. With 30 or more units, each period would be allocated 15 units, the resource would *not* be scarce, and the marginal user cost would therefore be zero.

With 20 units, however, scarcity emerges. No longer can 15 units be allocated to each period; each period will have to be allocated less than would be the case with abundance. Due to this scarcity, the marginal user cost for this case is not zero. As can be seen from Figure 6.2, the present value of the marginal user cost—the additional value created by scarcity—is graphically represented by the vertical distance between the quantity (horizontal) axis and the intersection of the two present-value curves. Notice that the present value of the marginal net benefit for Period 1 is equal to the present value of the marginal net benefit for Period 2. This common value can either be read off the graph or determined more precisely, as demonstrated in the chapter appendix, to be $1.905.

We can make this concept of marginal user cost even more concrete by considering its use in a market context. An efficient market would have to consider not only the marginal cost of extraction for this resource but also the marginal user cost. Whereas in the absence of scarcity, the price would equal only the marginal cost of extraction, with scarcity, the price would equal the sum of marginal extraction cost and marginal user cost.

To see this, solve for the prices that would prevail in an efficient market facing scarcity over time. The mathematics simply calculates the intersection of MNB_0 and $PVMNB_1$. This is the place where total net benefits (area under the curves) are maximized. Setting the two equations equal to each other, remembering to discount the second time period, will leave you with one equation and two unknowns. But recall, you also know that Q_0 and $Q_1 = 20$ in this example. You can now sub in for Q_0 or Q_1 to calculate your efficient quantities.

Inserting the efficient quantities for the two periods (10.238 and 9.762, respectively) into the willingness-to-pay function ($P = 8 - 0.4q$) yields $P_1 = 3.905$ and $P_2 = 4.095$. The corresponding supply-and-demand diagrams are given in Figure 6.3. Compare Figure 6.3 with Figure 6.1 to see the impact of scarcity on price.

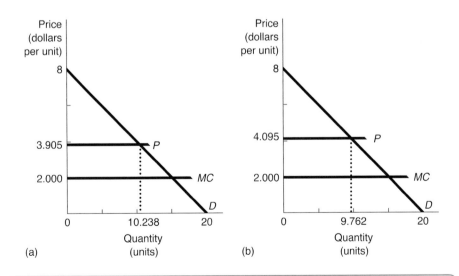

Figure 6.3 **The Efficient Market Allocation of a Depletable Resource: The Constant-Marginal-Cost Case: (a) Period 1 and (b) Period 2.**

Note that marginal user cost is zero in Figure 6.1, as expected from the absence of scarcity. In an efficient allocation involving scarcity, the marginal user cost for each period is the difference between the price and the marginal cost of extraction. Notice that it takes the value $1.905 in the first period and $2.095 in the second. In both periods, the *present value* of the marginal user cost is $1.905. In the second period, the actual marginal user cost is $1.905(1 + r)$. Since $r = 0.10$ in this example, the actual (as opposed to present value) marginal user cost for the second period is $2.095.[5] Thus, while the *present value* of marginal user cost is equal in both periods, the actual marginal user cost rises over time.

Both the size of the marginal user cost and the allocation of the resource between the two periods are affected not only by the degree of scarcity, but also by the discount rate. In Figure 6.2, because of discounting, the efficient allocation allocates somewhat more to Period 1 than to Period 2. A discount rate larger than 0.10 would be incorporated in this diagram by rotating (not shifting) the Period 2 curve an appropriate amount toward the right-hand axis, holding fixed the point at which it intersects the horizontal axis. (Can you see why?) The larger the discount rate, the greater the amount of rotation required.

The implication is clear—the amount allocated to the second period would be necessarily smaller with larger discount rates. The general conclusion, which holds for all models we consider, is that higher discount rates tend to skew resource extraction toward the present because they give the future less weight in balancing the relative value of present and future resource use. The choice of what discount rate to use, then, becomes a very important consideration for decision makers.

Defining Intertemporal Fairness

While no generally accepted standards of fairness or justice exist, some have more prominent support than others. One such standard concerns the treatment of future generations. What legacy should earlier generations leave to later ones? This is a particularly difficult issue because, in contrast to other groups for which we may want to ensure fair treatment, future generations cannot articulate their wishes, much less negotiate with current generations. ("We'll accept your radioactive wastes if you leave us plentiful supplies of titanium.")

One starting point for intergenerational equity is provided by philosopher John Rawls in his monumental work, *A Theory of Justice*. Rawls suggests that one way to derive general principles of justice is to place, hypothetically, all people into an original position behind a "veil of ignorance." This veil of ignorance would prevent them from knowing their eventual position in society. Once behind this veil, people would be asked to decide on rules to govern the society that they would, after the decision, be forced to inhabit.

In our context, this approach would suggest a hypothetical meeting of all members of present and future generations to decide on rules for allocating resources among generations. Because these members are prevented by the veil of ignorance from knowing the generation to which they will belong after the rules are defined, they will not be excessively conservationist (lest they turn out to be a member of an earlier generation) or excessively exploitative (lest they become a member of a later generation).

What kind of rule would emerge from such a meeting? One possibility is the sustainability criterion. The *sustainability criterion* suggests that, at a minimum, future generations should be left no worse off than current generations. Allocations that impoverish future generations in order to enrich current generations are, according to this criterion, patently unfair.

In essence, the sustainability criterion suggests that earlier generations are at liberty to use resources that would thereby be denied to future generations as long as the well-being of future generations remains just as high as that of all previous generations. On the other hand, diverting resources from future use would violate the sustainability criterion if it reduced the well-being of future generations below the level enjoyed by preceding generations.

One of the implications of this definition of sustainability is that it is possible for the current generation to use resources (even depletable resources) as long as the interests of future generations could be protected. Do our institutions provide adequate protection for future generations? We begin with examining the conditions under which efficient allocations satisfy the sustainability criterion. Are all efficient allocations sustainable?

Are Efficient Allocations Fair?

In the numerical example we have constructed, it certainly does not appear that the efficient allocation satisfies the sustainability criterion. In the two-period example, more resources are allocated to the first period than to the second. Therefore, net benefits in the second period are lower than in the first. Sustainability does not allow earlier generations to profit at the expense of later generations, and this example certainly appears to be a case where that is happening.

Yet appearances can be deceiving. Choosing this particular extraction path does not prevent those in the first period from saving some of the net benefits for those in the second period. If the allocation is dynamically efficient, it will always be possible to set aside sufficient net benefits accrued in the first period for those in the second period, so that those in both periods will be at least as well off as they would have been with any other extraction profile and one of the periods will be better off.

We can illustrate this point with a numerical example that compares a dynamic efficient allocation with sharing to an allocation where resources are committed equally to each generation. Suppose, for example, you believe that setting aside half (10 units) of the available resources for each period would be a better allocation than the dynamic efficient allocation. The net benefits to each period from this alternative scheme would be $40. Can you see why?

Now let's compare this to an allocation of net benefits that could be achieved with the dynamic efficient allocation. For the dynamic efficient allocation to satisfy the sustainability criterion, we must be able to show that it can produce an outcome such that each generation would be at least as well off as it would be with the equal allocation and one will be better off. Can that be demonstrated?

In the dynamic efficient allocation with no sharing, the net benefits to the first period were $40.466, while those for the second period were $39.512.[6] Clearly, in the absence of sharing between the periods, this example would violate the sustainability criterion; the second generation is worse off than it would be with equal sharing. (While it would receive $40.00 from equal resource allocation across the two periods, it receives only $39.512 from the dynamic efficient allocation in the absence of any benefit sharing.)

But suppose the first generation was willing to share some of the net benefits from the extracted resources with the second generation. If the first generation keeps net benefits of $40 (thereby making it just as well off as if equal amounts were extracted in each period) and saves the extra $0.466 (the $40.466 net benefits earned during the first period in the dynamic efficient allocation minus the $40 reserved for itself) at 10 percent interest for those in the next period, this saving would grow to $0.513 by the second period [0.466(1.10)]. Add this to the net benefits received directly from the dynamic efficient allocation ($39.512), and the second generation would receive $40.025. Those in the second period would be better off by accepting the dynamic efficient allocation with sharing than they would if they demanded that resources be allocated equally between the two periods.

This example demonstrates that, although dynamic efficient allocations do not automatically satisfy sustainability criteria, they could be compatible with sustainability, even in an economy relying heavily on depletable resources. The possibility that the second period can be better off is not a guarantee; the required degree of sharing must take place. Example 6.1 points out that under some conditions this sharing does take place, although, as we shall see, such sharing is more likely to be the exception rather than the norm. In subsequent chapters, we shall examine both the conditions under which we could expect the appropriate degree of sharing to take place and the conditions under which it would not.

EXAMPLE 6.1

The Alaska Permanent Fund

One interesting example of an intergenerational sharing mechanism currently exists in the state of Alaska. Extraction from Alaska's oil fields generates significant income, but it also depreciates one of the state's main environmental assets. To protect the interests of future generations as the Alaskan pipeline construction neared completion in 1976, Alaska voters approved a constitutional amendment that authorized the establishment of a dedicated fund: the Alaska Permanent Fund. This fund was designed to capture a portion of the rents received from the sale of the state's oil to share with future generations. The amendment requires:

> At least 25 percent of all mineral lease rentals, royalties, royalty sales proceeds, federal mineral revenue-sharing payments and bonuses received by the state be placed in a permanent fund, the principal of which may only be used for income-producing investments.

The principal of this fund cannot be used to cover current expenses without a majority vote of Alaskans.

The fund is fully invested in capital markets and diversified among various asset classes. It generates income from interest on bonds, stock dividends, real estate rents, and capital gains from the sale of assets. To date, the legislature has used some of these annual earnings to provide dividends to every eligible Alaska resident, while retaining the rest in the fund in order to increase the size of the endowment, thereby assuring that it is not eroded by inflation. As of December 2022, the market value of the fund was $74.46 billion and the dividend to every resident in that year was $3,284.00.

Although this fund does preserve some of the revenue for future generations, two characteristics are worth noting. First, the principal could be used for current expenditures if a majority of current voters agreed. To date, that has not happened, but it has been discussed. Second, only 25 percent of the oil net revenue is placed in the fund; assuming that net revenue reflects scarcity rent, full sustainability would require dedicating 100 percent of it to the fund. Because the current generation not only gets its share of the income from the permanent fund, but also receives 75 percent of the proceeds from current oil sales, this sharing arrangement falls short of full sustainability.

Source: The fund is managed by the Alaska Permanent Fund Corporation, https://apfc.org
(Accessed January 19, 2023); the Alaska Permanent Fund Website: https://pfd.alaska.gov
(Accessed January 19, 2023).

Applying the Sustainability Criterion

One of the difficulties in assessing the fairness of intertemporal allocations using this version of the sustainability criterion is that it is so difficult to apply. Discovering whether the well-being of future generations would be lower than that of current generations requires us not only to know something about the allocation of resources over time, but also to know something about the preferences of future generations (in order to establish how valuable various resource streams are to them). That is a tall (impossible?) order!

Is it possible to develop a version of the sustainability criterion that is more operational? Fortunately it is, thanks to what has become known as the "Hartwick Rule." In an early article, John Hartwick (1977) demonstrated that a constant level of consumption could be maintained perpetually from an environmental endowment if all the scarcity rent derived from resources extracted from that endowment were invested in capital. That level of investment would be sufficient to assure that the value of the total capital stock would not decline.

Two important insights flow from this reinterpretation of the sustainability criterion. First, with this version, it is possible to judge the sustainability of an allocation by examining whether or not the value of the total capital stock is declining—a declining capital stock violates the rule. That test can be performed each year without knowing anything about future allocations or preferences. Second, this analysis suggests the specific degree of sharing that would be necessary to produce a sustainable outcome, namely, all scarcity rent must be invested.

Let's pause to be sure we understand what is being said and why it is being said. Although we shall return to this subject later in the book, it is important now to have at least an intuitive understanding of the implications of this analysis. Consider an analogy. Suppose a grandparent left you an inheritance of $10,000 and you put it in a bank where it earns 10 percent interest.

What are the choices for allocating that money over time and what are the implications of those choices? If you withdrew exactly $1,000 per year, the amount in the bank would remain $10,000 and the income would last forever; you would be spending only the interest, leaving the principal intact. If you spend more than $1,000 per year, the principal would necessarily decline over time and eventually the balance in the account would go to zero. In the context of this discussion, spending $1,000 per year or less would satisfy the sustainability criterion, while spending more would violate it.

What does the Hartwick Rule mean in this context? It suggests that one way to tell whether an allocation (spending pattern) is sustainable or not is to examine what is happening to the value of the principal over time. If the principal is declining, the allocation (spending pattern) is not sustainable. If the principal is increasing or remaining constant, the allocation (spending pattern) is sustainable.

How do we apply this logic to the environment? In general, the Hartwick Rule suggests that the current generation has been given an endowment. Part of the endowment consists of environmental and natural resources (known as natural capital) and another part consists of physical capital (such as buildings, equipment, schools, and roads). Sustainable use of this endowment implies that we should keep the principal (the value of the natural and physical endowment) intact and live off only the flow of services provided. We should not, in other words, chop down all the trees and use up all the oil, leaving future generations to fend for themselves. Rather, we need to assure that the value of the total capital stock is maintained, not depleted.

The desirability of this version of the sustainability criterion depends crucially on how substitutable the two forms of capital are. If physical capital can readily substitute for natural capital, then maintaining the value of the sum of the two is sufficient. If, however, physical capital cannot completely substitute for natural capital, investments in physical capital alone may not be enough to assure sustainability.

How tenable is the assumption of complete substitutability between physical and natural capital? Clearly, it is untenable for certain essential categories of environmental resources. Although we can contemplate the replacement of natural breathable air with universal air-conditioning in domed cities, both the expense and the artificiality of this approach make it an absurd compensation device. Obviously, intergenerational compensation must be approached carefully (see Example 6.2).

EXAMPLE 6.2

Nauru: Weak Sustainability in the Extreme

The weak sustainability criterion is used to judge whether the depletion of natural capital is offset by sufficiently large increases in physical or financial capital so as to prevent total capital from declining. It seems quite natural to suppose that a violation of that criterion does demonstrate *unsustainable* behavior. But does fulfilment of the weak sustainability criterion provide an adequate test of *sustainable* behavior? Consider the case of Nauru.

Nauru is a small Pacific island that lies some 3000 kilometers northeast of Australia. It contains one of the highest grades of phosphate ever discovered. Phosphate is a prime ingredient in fertilizers.

Over the course of a century, first colonizers and then, after independence, the citizens of Nauru decided to extract massive amounts of this deposit. This decision has simultaneously enriched the remaining inhabitants (including the creation of a trust fund believed to contain over $1 billion) and destroyed most of the local ecosystems. Local needs are now mainly met by imports financed by the sales of the phosphate.

However wise or unwise the choices made by the people of Nauru were, they could not be replicated globally. An entire population cannot subsist solely on imports financed with trust funds; every import must be exported by someone! The story of Nauru demonstrates the value of complementing the weak sustainability criterion with other, more demanding criteria. Satisfying the weak sustainability criterion may be a necessary condition for sustainability, but it is not always sufficient.

Source: Gowdy, J. W., & McDaniel, C. N. (1999). The physical destruction of Nauru: An example of weak sustainability. *Land Economics, 75*(2), 333–338.

Recognizing the weakness of the constant total capital definition in the face of limited substitution possibilities has led some economists to propose a new, additional definition. According to this new definition, an allocation is sustainable if it maintains the value of the stock of *natural* capital. This definition assumes that it is natural capital that drives future well-being and further assumes that little or no substitution between physical and natural capital is possible. To differentiate these two definitions, the maintenance of the value of total capital is known as the "weak sustainability" (less restrictive) definition, while maintaining the value of natural capital is known as the "strong sustainability" (more restrictive) definition.

A final, additional definition, known as "environmental sustainability," requires that certain *physical flows* of certain key *individual* resources be maintained. This definition suggests that it is not sufficient to maintain the *value* of an *aggregate*. For a fishery, for example, this definition would require catch levels that did not exceed the growth of the biomass for the fishery. For a wetland, it would require the preservation of specific ecological functions.

Implications for Environmental Policy

In order to be useful, guides to policy, our sustainability, and efficiency criteria must be neither synonymous nor incompatible. Do these criteria meet that test?

They do. As we shall see later in the book, not all efficient allocations are sustainable and not all sustainable allocations are efficient. Yet some sustainable allocations are efficient and some efficient allocations are sustainable. Furthermore, market allocations may be either efficient or inefficient and either sustainable or unsustainable.

Do these differences have any policy implications? Indeed they do. In particular they suggest a specific strategy for policy. Among the possible uses for resources that fulfill the sustainability criterion, we choose the one that maximizes either dynamic or static efficiency as appropriate. In this formulation the sustainability criterion acts as an overriding constraint on social decisions. Yet, by itself, the sustainability criterion is insufficient because it fails to provide any guidance on which of the infinite number of sustainable allocations should be chosen. That is where efficiency comes in. It provides a means for maximizing the wealth derived from all the possible sustainable allocations.

This combination of efficiency with sustainability turns out to be very helpful in guiding policy. Many unsustainable allocations are the result of inefficient behavior.

Correcting the inefficiency can either restore sustainability or move the economy a long way in that direction. Furthermore, and this is important, correcting inefficiencies can frequently produce win–win situations. In win–win changes, the various parties affected by the change can all be made better off after the change than before. This contrasts sharply with changes in which the gains to the gainers are smaller than the losses to the losers.

Win–win situations are possible because moving from an inefficient to an efficient allocation increases net benefits. The increase in net benefits provides a means for compensating those who might otherwise lose from the change. Compensating losers reduces the opposition to change, thereby making change more likely. Do our economic and political institutions normally produce outcomes that are both efficient and sustainable? In upcoming chapters we will provide explicit answers to this important question.

Summary

Both efficiency and ethical considerations can guide the desirability of private and social choices involving the environment. Whereas the former is concerned mainly with eliminating waste in the use of resources, the latter is concerned with assuring the fair treatment of all parties.

The present chapter examines one globally important characterization of the obligation previous generations owe to generations that follow and the policy implications that flow from acceptance of that obligation. Examples later in the book will focus on the environmental justice implications of environmental degradation and remediation for members of the current generation.

The specific obligation examined in this chapter—sustainable development—is based upon the notion that earlier generations should be free to pursue their own well-being as long as in so doing they do not diminish the welfare of future generations. This notion gives rise to three alternative definitions of sustainable allocations:

Weak Sustainability. Resource use by previous generations should not exceed a level that would prevent subsequent generations from achieving a level of well-being at least as great. One operational implication of this definition is that the value of the capital stock (natural plus physical capital) should not decline. Individual components of the aggregate could decline in value as long as other components were increased in value (normally through investment) sufficiently to leave the aggregate value unchanged.

Strong Sustainability. According to this interpretation, the value of the remaining stock of natural capital should not decrease. This definition places special emphasis on preserving natural (as opposed to total) capital under the assumption that natural and physical capital offer limited substitution possibilities. This definition retains two characteristics of the previous definition: it preserves value (rather than a specific level of physical flow), and it preserves an aggregate of natural capital (rather than any specific component).

Environmental Sustainability. Under this definition, the *physical* flows of *individual* resources should be maintained, not merely the *value* of the *aggregate*. For a fishery, for example, this definition would emphasize maintaining a constant fish catch (referred to as a sustainable yield), rather than a constant value of the fishery. For a wetland, it would involve preserving specific ecological functions, not merely their aggregate value.

It is possible to examine and compare the theoretical conditions that characterize various allocations (including market allocations and efficient allocations) to the necessary conditions for an allocation to be sustainable under these definitions. According to the theorem that is now known as the "Hartwick Rule," if all the scarcity rent from the use of scarce resources is invested in capital, the resulting allocation will satisfy the first definition of sustainability.

In general, not all efficient allocations are sustainable and not all sustainable allocations are efficient. Furthermore, market allocations can be (1) efficient, but not sustainable; (2) sustainable, but not efficient; (3) inefficient and unsustainable; or (4) efficient and sustainable. One class of situations, known as "win–win" situations, provides an opportunity to increase simultaneously the welfare of both current and future generations.

We shall explore these themes much more intensively as we proceed through the book. In particular, we shall inquire into when market allocations can be expected to produce allocations that satisfy the sustainability definitions and when they cannot. We shall also see several specific examples of how the skillful use of economic incentives can allow policymakers to exploit "win–win" situations to promote a transition onto a sustainable path for the future.

Discussion Question

1. The environmental sustainability criterion differs in important ways from both strong and weak sustainability. Environmental sustainability frequently means maintaining a constant physical flow of individual resources (e.g., fish from the sea or wood from the forest), while the other two definitions call for maintaining the *aggregate value* of those service flows. When might the two criteria lead to different choices? Why?

Self-Test Exercises

1. In the numerical example given in the text, the inverse demand function for the depletable resource is $P = 8 - 0.4q_t$ and the marginal cost of supplying it is $2. (a) If 20 units are to be allocated between two periods, in a dynamic efficient allocation how much would be allocated to the first period and how much to the second period when the discount rate is zero? (b) Given this discount rate, what would be the efficient price in the two periods? (c) What would be the marginal user cost in each period?

2. Assume the same demand conditions as stated in Problem 1, but let the discount rate be 0.10 and the marginal cost of extraction be $4. How much would be produced in each period in an efficient allocation? What would be the marginal user cost in each period? Would the static and dynamic efficiency criteria yield the same answers for this problem? Why?

3. Compare two versions of the two-period depletable resource model that differ only in the treatment of marginal extraction cost. Assume that in the second version the constant marginal extraction cost is lower in the second period than the first (perhaps due to the anticipated arrival of a new, superior extraction technology). The constant marginal extraction cost is the same in both periods in the first

version and is equal to the marginal extraction cost in the first period of the second version. In a dynamic efficient allocation, how would the extraction profile in the second version differ from the first? Would relatively more or less be allocated to the second period in the second version than in the first version? Would the marginal user cost be higher or lower in the second version? Why?

a.   Consider the general effect of the discount rate on the dynamic efficient allocation of a depletable resource across time. Suppose we have two versions of the two-period model discussed in this chapter. The two versions are identical except for the fact that the second version involves a higher discount rate than the first version. What effect would the higher discount rate have on the allocation between the two periods and the magnitude of the present value of the marginal user cost?

b.   Explain the intuition behind your results.

c.   Consider the effect of population growth on the dynamic efficient allocation of a depletable resource across time. Suppose we have two versions of the two-period model, discussed in this chapter, that are identical except for the fact that the second version involves a higher demand for the resource in the second period (e.g., the demand curve shifts to the right due to population growth) than the first version. What effect would the higher demand in the second period have on the allocation between the two periods and the magnitude of the present value of the marginal user cost?

d.   Explain the intuition behind your results.

Appendix: The Simple Mathematics of Dynamic Efficiency

Assume that the demand curve for a depletable resource is linear and stable over time. Thus, the inverse demand curve in year t can be written as

$$P_t = a - bq_t \tag{A.1}$$

The total benefits from extracting an amount q_t in year t are then the integral of this function (the area under the inverse demand curve):

$$(\text{Total benefits})\, t = \int_0^{qt} (a - bq)\, dq$$

$$= aq_t - \frac{b}{2} q_t^2 \tag{A.2}$$

Further assume that the marginal cost of extracting that resource is a constant c and therefore the total cost of extracting any amount q_t in year t can be given by

$$(\text{Total cost})_t = cq_t \tag{A.3}$$

If the total available amount of this resource is $\bar{Q}$, then the dynamic efficient allocation of a resource over n years is the one that satisfies the maximization problem:

$$\text{Max}_q \sum_{i=1}^{n} \frac{aq_i - \frac{bq_i^2}{2} - cq_i}{(1+r)^{i-1}} + \lambda \left(\bar{Q} - \sum_{i=1}^{n} q_i \right) \quad \text{(A.4)}$$

Assuming that $\bar{Q}$ is less than would normally be demanded, the dynamic efficient allocation must satisfy

$$\frac{a - bq_i - c}{(1+r)^{i-1}} - \lambda = 0, i = 1, \ldots, n$$

$$\bar{Q} - \sum_{i=1}^{n} q_i = 0 \quad \text{(A.5)}$$

An implication of the first of these two equations is that $(P - MC)$ increases over time at rate r. This difference, which is known as the marginal user cost, will play a key role in our thinking about allocating depletable resources over time.

An exact solution to the two-period model can be illustrated using these solution equations and some assumed values for the parameters.

The following parameter values are assumed by the two-period example:

$$a = 8, c = 2, b = 0.4, Q = 20, \text{ and } r = 0.10.$$

Inserting these parameters into the two equations (one for each period), we obtain

$$8 - 0.4q_1 - 2 - \lambda = 0,$$

$$\frac{8 - 0.4q_2 - 2}{1.10} - \lambda = 0$$

$$q_1 + q_2 = 20.$$

It is now readily verified that the solution (accurate to the third decimal place) is

$$q_1 = 10.238, q_2 = 9.762, \lambda = 1.905.$$

We can now demonstrate the propositions discussed in this text.

1. Verbally, in a dynamic efficient allocation, the present value of the marginal net benefit in Period 1 $(8 - 0.4q_1 - 2)$ has to equal λ. In addition, the present value of the marginal net benefit in Period 2 should also equal λ. Therefore, they must equal each other. This demonstrates the proposition shown graphically in Figure 6.2.
2. The present value of marginal user cost is represented by λ. Thus, the price in the first period $(8 - 0.4q_1)$ should be equal to the sum of marginal extraction cost ($2) and marginal user cost ($1.905). Multiplying λ by $1 + r$, it becomes clear that price in the second period $(8 - 0.4q_2)$ is equal to the marginal extraction cost ($2) plus the higher marginal user cost $[\lambda (1 + r) = (1.905) (1.10) = \$2.095]$ in Period 2. These results show why the graphs in Figure 6.3 have the properties they do. They also illustrate the point that, in this case, marginal user cost rises over time.

Notes

1 The height of the triangle is $6 [$8 – $2] and the base is 15 units. The area is therefore $(1/2)(\$6)(15) = \$45$.
2 The undiscounted net benefit is $25. The calculation is $((6 - 2) \times 5) + (1/2 \times (8 - 6) \times 5) = \$25$. The discounted net benefit is therefore $25/1.10 = 22.73$.
3 Note that the sum of the two allocations in Figure 6.2 is always 20. The left-hand axis represents an allocation of all 20 units to Period 2 and the right-hand axis represents an allocation entirely to Period 1.
4 Demonstrate that this point is the maximum by first allocating slightly more to Period 2 (and therefore less to Period 1) and showing that the total area decreases. Conclude by allocating slightly less to Period 2 and showing that, in this case as well, total area declines.
5 You can verify this by taking the present value of $2.095 and showing that it equals $1.905.
6 The supporting calculations are $(1.905)(10.238) + 0.5(4.095)(10.238)$ for the first period and $(2.095)(9.762) + 0.5(3.905)(9.762)$ for the second period.

Further Reading

Heal, G. (2012). Reflections—Defining and measuring sustainability. *Review of Environmental Economics and Policy*, 6(1), 147–163. An examination of the concept of sustainability and the possibility of quantifying it.

Kiron, D., Kruschwitz, N., Haanæs, K., & Velken, I. V. S. (2012). Sustainability nears a tipping point. *MIT Sloan Management Review*, 53(2), 69–74. What is the role for the private sector in sustainable development? Is concern over the "bottom line" consistent with the desire to promote sustainable development?

Lopez, R., & Toman, M. A. (Eds.). (2006). *Economic Development and Environmental Sustainability*. New York: Oxford University Press. Thirteen essays that explore how the principles of sustainability can be implemented in the context of reducing poverty through development.

Pezzey, J. V. C., & Toman, M. A. (2002). Progress and problems in the economics of sustainability. In T. Tietenberg & H. Folmer (Eds.), *The International Yearbook of Environmental and Resource Economics: A Survey of Current Issues*. Cheltenham: Edward Elgar, 165–232. An excellent technical survey of the economics literature on sustainable development.

USEPA Sustainability website: www.epa.gov/sustainability/learn-about-sustainability #what. A description of how the concept of sustainability affects the work of the United States Environmental Protection Agency.

World Bank. (2011). *The Changing Wealth of Nations: Measuring Sustainable Development in the New Millennium*. Washington, DC: World Bank. This study presents, for the first time, a set of "wealth accounts" for over 150 countries for 1995, 2000, and 2005. This set of accounts allows a longer-term assessment of global, regional, and country performance within the weak sustainability context.

Chapter 7

Depletable Resource Allocation

The Role of Longer Time Horizons, Substitutes, and Extraction Cost

The whole machinery of our intelligence, our general ideas and laws, fixed and external objects, principles, persons, and gods, are so many symbolic, algebraic expressions. They stand for experience; experience which we are incapable of retaining and surveying in its multitudinous immediacy. We should flounder hopelessly, like the animals, did we not keep ourselves afloat and direct our course by these intellectual devices. Theory helps us to bear our ignorance of fact.

George Santayana, *The Sense of Beauty* (1896)

Introduction

How do societies react when finite stocks of depletable resources become scarce? Is it reasonable to expect that self-limiting feedbacks would facilitate the transition to a sustainable, steady state? Or is it more reasonable to expect that self-reinforcing feedback mechanisms would cause the system to overshoot the resource base, possibly even precipitating a societal collapse?

We begin to seek answers to these questions by studying the implications of both efficient and profit-maximizing decision making. What kinds of feedback mechanisms are implied by decisions motivated by efficiency and by profit maximization? Are they compatible with a smooth transition or are they more likely to produce overshoot and collapse?

We approach these questions in several steps, beginning by defining and discussing a simple but useful *resource taxonomy* (classification system), as well as explaining the dangers of ignoring the distinctions made by this taxonomy. We initiate the analysis by defining an efficient allocation of an exhaustible resource over time in the absence

DOI: 10.4324/9781032689111-8

of any renewable substitute and explore the conditions any efficient allocation must satisfy. Numerical examples illustrate the implications of these conditions.

Renewable resources are integrated into the analysis by relying on the simplest possible case—the resource is assumed to be supplied at a fixed, abundant rate and can be accessed at a constant marginal cost. Solar energy and replenishable surface water are two examples that seem roughly to fit this characterization. Integrating a renewable resource backstop into our basic depletable resource model allows us to characterize efficient extraction paths for both types of resources, assuming that they are perfect substitutes. We also explore how these efficient paths are affected by changes in the nature of the cost functions as well as by the presence or absence of externalities. Succeeding chapters will use these principles to examine the allocation of such diverse resources as energy, minerals, land, and water and to provide a basis for developing more elaborate models of renewable biological populations, such as fisheries and forests.

A Resource Taxonomy

Three separate concepts are used to classify the stock of depletable resources: (1) *current reserves*, (2) *potential reserves*, and (3) *resource endowment*. The U.S. Geological Survey (USGS) has the official responsibility for keeping records of the U.S. resource base and has developed the classification system described in Figure 7.1.

Note the two dimensions—one economic and one geological. A movement from top to bottom represents movement from cheaply extractable resources to those extracted at substantially higher costs. By contrast, a movement from left to right represents increasing geological uncertainty about the size of the resource base.

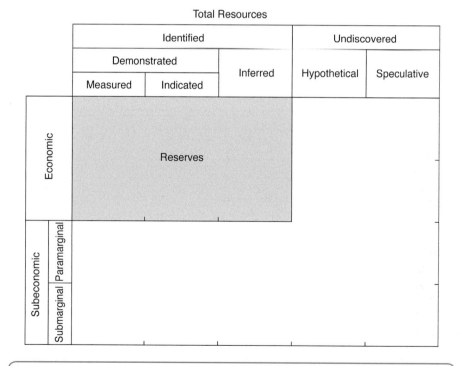

Figure 7.1 A Categorization of Resources.

Current reserves (shaded area in Figure 7.1) are defined as known resources that can profitably be extracted at current prices. The magnitude of these current reserves can be expressed as a number.

Potential reserves, on the other hand, are most accurately defined as a function rather than a number. The amount of reserves potentially available depends upon the price people are willing to pay for those resources—the higher the price, the larger the potential reserves. Higher prices enable not only more expensive measures to recover more of the resource from conventional sources, but also measures to extract resources from previously untapped unconventional sources.

The *resource endowment* represents the natural occurrence of resources in the earth's crust. Since prices have nothing to do with the size of the resource endowment, it is a geological, rather than an economic, concept. This concept is important because it represents a physical upper limit on the availability of terrestrial resources.

The distinctions among these three concepts are significant. One common mistake in failing to respect these distinctions is using data on current reserves as if they represented the maximum potential reserves. This fundamental error can cause a huge understatement of the time until exhaustion.

A second common mistake is to assume that the entire resource endowment can be made available as potential reserves at a price people would be willing to pay. Clearly, if an infinite price were possible, the entire resource endowment could be exploited, but don't hold your breath until the arrival of infinite prices.

Other distinctions among resource categories are also useful. The first category includes all depletable, recyclable resources, such as copper. A *depletable resource* is one for which the natural replenishment feedback loop can safely be ignored. The rate of replenishment for these resources is so low that it does not offer a potential for augmenting the stock in any reasonable time frame.

A *recyclable resource* is one that, although currently being used for some particular purpose, exists in a form allowing its mass to be recovered once that original purpose is no longer necessary or desirable. For example, copper wiring from an automobile can be recovered after the car has been shipped to the junkyard. The degree to which a recyclable resource is actually recycled is determined by economic conditions.

TERMS

Identified resources: specific bodies of mineral-bearing material whose location, quality, and quantity are known from geological evidence, supported by engineering measurements.

Measured resources: material for which quantity and quality estimates are within a margin of error of less than 20 percent, from geologically well-known sample sites.

Indicated resources: material for which quantity and quality have been estimated partly from sample analyses and partly from reasonable geological projections.

Inferred resources: material in unexplored extensions of demonstrated resources based on geological projections.

Undiscovered resources: unspecified bodies of mineral-bearing material surmised to exist on the basis of broad geological knowledge and theory.

> **Hypothetical resources**: undiscovered materials reasonably expected to exist in a known mining district under known geological conditions.
>
> **Speculative resources**: undiscovered materials that may occur in either known types of deposits in favorable geological settings where no discoveries have been made, or in yet unknown types of deposits that remain to be recognized.
>
> *Source*: U.S. Bureau of Mines and the U.S. Geological Survey. (1976). Principles of the Mineral Resource Classification System of the U.S. Bureau of Mines and the U.S. Geological Survey. *Geological Survey Bulletin*, 1450-A.

The current reserves of a depletable, recyclable resource can be augmented by economic replenishment, as well as by recycling. Economic replenishment takes many forms, all sharing the characteristic that they turn previously unrecoverable resources into recoverable ones. One obvious stimulant for this replenishment is price. As price rises, producers find it profitable to explore more widely, dig more deeply, and use lower-concentration ores.

Higher prices also stimulate technological progress. Technological progress simply refers to an advancement in the state of knowledge that allows us to expand the set of feasible possibilities. Harnessing nuclear power and the advent of both horizontal drilling and hydraulic fracturing are two obvious examples. (Both are discussed in Chapter 11.)

The potential reserves of depletable, recyclable resources, however, can be exhausted. The depletion rate is affected by the demand for and the durability of the products built with the resource, and the ability to reuse the products. Except where demand is totally price-inelastic (i.e., insensitive to price), higher prices tend to reduce the quantity demanded. Durable products last longer, reducing the need for newer ones. Reusable products (e.g., rechargeable batteries or products sold at flea markets) provide a substitute for new products.

For some resources, the size of the potential reserves depends explicitly on our ability to store the resource. For example, helium is generally found commingled with natural gas in common fields. As the natural gas is extracted and stored, unless the helium is simultaneously captured and stored, it diffuses into the atmosphere. This diffusion results in such low atmospheric concentrations that extraction of helium from the air is not economical at current or even likely future prices. Thus, the useful stock of helium depends crucially on how much we decide to store.

Not all depletable resources can be recycled or reused. Depletable energy resources such as coal, oil, and gas are irreversibly transformed when they are combusted. Once turned into heat energy, the heat dissipates into the atmosphere and becomes nonrecoverable.

The endowment of depletable resources is of finite size. Current use of depletable, nonrecyclable resources precludes future use; hence, the issue of how they should be shared among generations is raised in the starkest, least forgiving form.

Depletable, recyclable resources raise this same issue, though somewhat less starkly, since recycling and reuse make the useful stock last longer, all other things being equal. It is tempting to suggest that depletable, recyclable resources could last forever with 100 percent recycling, but unfortunately the physical theoretical upper limit on recycling is less than 100 percent. Some of the mass is always lost during recycling or use.

Because less than 100 percent of the mass is recycled, the useful stock must eventually decline to zero. Therefore, even for recyclable, depletable resources, the cumulative useful stock is finite, and current consumption patterns still have some effect on future generations.

Renewable resources are differentiated from depletable resources primarily by the fact that natural replenishment augments the flow of renewable resources at a non-negligible rate. Solar energy, water, and biological populations are all examples of renewable resources. For this class of resources it is possible, though not inevitable, that a flow of these resources could be maintained perpetually.[1]

For some renewable resources, the continuation and volume of their flow depend crucially on humans. Soil erosion and nutrient depletion reduce the flow of food. Excessive fishing reduces the stock of fish, which in turn reduces the rate of natural increase of the fish population. What other examples can you come up with?

For other renewable resources, such as solar energy, the flow is independent of humans. The amount consumed by one generation does not reduce the amount that can be consumed by subsequent generations.

Some renewable resources can be stored; others cannot. For those that can, storage provides an additional way to manage the allocation of the resource over time; we are not left simply at the mercy of natural ebbs and flows. Food, without proper care, perishes rapidly, but under the right conditions stored food can be used to feed the hungry in times of famine. Unstored solar energy radiates off the earth's surface and dissipates into the atmosphere. While solar energy can be stored in many forms, the most common natural form of storage occurs when it is converted to biomass by photosynthesis.

Storage of renewable resources usually provides a different service than storage of depletable resources. Storing depletable resources prolongs their economic life; storing renewable resources, on the other hand, can serve as a means of smoothing out the cyclical imbalances of supply and demand. Surpluses can be stored for use during periods when deficits occur. Familiar examples include food stockpiles and the use of dams to store water to use for hydropower.

Managing renewable resources presents a different challenge from managing depletable resources, although an equally significant one. The challenge for depletable resources involves allocating dwindling stocks among generations while meeting the ultimate transition to renewable resources. In contrast, the challenge for managing renewable resources involves the maintenance of an efficient, sustainable flow. Chapters 8 through 10 deal with how the economic and political sectors have responded to these challenges for particularly significant types of resources.

Efficient Intertemporal Allocations

If we are to judge the efficiency of market allocations, we must define what is meant by efficiency in relation to the management of depletable and renewable resources. Because allocation over time is the crucial issue, dynamic efficiency becomes the core concept. The dynamic efficiency criterion assumes that society's objective is to maximize the present value of net benefits coming from the resource. For a depletable, nonrecyclable resource, this requires a balancing of the current and subsequent uses of the resource. In order to refresh our memories about how the dynamic efficiency criterion defines this balance, we shall begin with recalling and elaborating on the very simple two-period model developed in Chapter 6. We can then proceed to demonstrate how conclusions drawn from that model generalize to longer planning horizons and more complicated situations.

The Two-Period Model Revisited

In Chapter 6, we defined a situation involving the allocation, over two periods, of a finite resource that could be extracted at constant marginal cost. With a stable demand curve for the resource, an efficient allocation involved allocating more than half of the resource to the first period and less than half to the second period. How the resources were divided between the two periods was affected by the marginal cost of extraction, the marginal user cost, and the discount rate.

Due to the fixed and finite nature of depletable resources, use of a unit today precludes use of that unit tomorrow. Therefore, production decisions today must take forgone future net benefits into account. Marginal user cost is the opportunity cost measure that allows intertemporal balancing to take place.

In our two-period model, the marginal cost of extraction is assumed to be constant, but the value of the marginal user cost was shown to rise over time. In fact, as was demonstrated mathematically in the appendix to Chapter 6, when the demand curve is stable over time and the marginal cost of extraction is constant, the rate of increase in the current value of the marginal user cost is equal to r, the discount rate. Thus, in Period 2, the marginal user cost would be $1 + r$ times as large as it was in Period 1.[2] Marginal user cost rises at rate r in an efficient allocation in order to preserve the balance between present versus future production.

In summary, our two-period example suggests that an efficient allocation over time of a finite resource with a constant marginal cost of extraction involves rising marginal user cost and falling quantities consumed. How can we generalize to longer time periods and different extraction circumstances?

The N-Period Constant-Cost Case

We begin this generalization by retaining the constant-marginal-extraction-cost assumption while extending the time horizon within which the resource is allocated. In the numerical example shown in Figures 7.2a and 7.2b, the demand curves and the marginal cost curve from the two-period case are retained. The only changes in this numerical example from the two-period case involve spreading the allocation over a larger number of years and increasing the total recoverable supply from 20 to 40. (The specific mathematics behind this and subsequent examples is presented in the appendix at the end of this chapter, but we shall guide you through the intuition that follows from that analysis in this section.)

Figure 7.2a demonstrates how the efficient quantity extracted varies over time, while Figure 7.2b shows the behavior of the marginal user cost and the marginal cost of extraction. We shall use the term "total marginal cost" to refer to the sum of the two. The marginal cost of extraction is represented by the lower line, and the marginal user cost is depicted as the vertical distance between the marginal cost of extraction and the total marginal cost. To avoid confusion, note that the horizontal axis is defined in terms of time, not the more conventional designation—quantity.

Several trends are worth noting. First of all, in this case, as in the two-period case, the efficient marginal user cost rises steadily in spite of the fact that the marginal cost

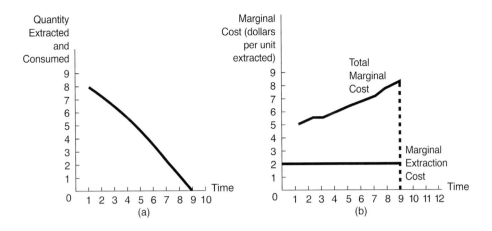

Figure 7.2 (a) Constant Marginal Extraction Cost with No Substitute Resource: Quantity Profile (b) Constant Marginal Extraction Cost with No Substitute Resource: Marginal Cost Profile.

of extraction remains constant. This rise in the efficient marginal user cost reflects increasing scarcity and the resulting rise in the opportunity cost of current consumption (reflecting forgone future opportunities) as the remaining stock dwindles.

In response to these rising costs over time, the extracted quantity falls over time until it finally becomes zero, which occurs precisely at the moment when the total marginal cost becomes $8. At this point, total marginal cost is equal to the highest price anyone is willing to pay, so demand and supply simultaneously equal zero. Thus, even in this challenging case involving no increase in the cost of extraction, an efficient allocation envisions a smooth transition to the exhaustion of a resource. The resource does not "suddenly" run out (because prices have signaled the increasing scarcity), although in this case it does run out.

Transition to a Renewable Substitute

So far we have discussed the allocation of a depletable resource when no substitute is available to take its place. Suppose, however, we consider the nature of an efficient allocation when a substitute renewable resource is available at constant marginal cost. This case, for example, could describe the efficient allocation of oil or natural gas with a solar or wind substitute or the efficient allocation of exhaustible groundwater with a surface-water substitute. How could we define an efficient allocation in this circumstance?

Since this problem is very similar to the one already discussed, we can use what we have already learned as a foundation for mastering this new situation. Just as in the previous case, in this case the depletable resource would also be exhausted, but now the exhaustion will pose less of a problem, since we'll merely switch to the renewable substitute at the appropriate time.

For the purpose of our numerical example, assume the existence of a perfect substitute for the depletable resource that is infinitely available at a cost of $6 per unit. The transition from the depletable resource to this renewable resource would ultimately transpire because the renewable resource marginal cost ($6) is less than the maximum willingness to pay ($8). (Can you figure out what the efficient allocation would be if the marginal cost of this substitute renewable resource was $9, instead of $6?)

The total marginal cost for the depletable resource in the presence of a $6 perfect substitute would never exceed $6, because society could always substitute the renewable resource whenever it was cheaper. Thus, while the maximum willingness to pay ($8, the *choke price*) sets the upper limit on total marginal cost when no substitute is available, the marginal cost of extraction of the substitute ($6 in our example) sets the upper limit in this new case as long as the perfect substitute is available at a marginal cost lower than the choke price. The efficient path for this situation is given in Figures 7.3a and 7.3b.

In this efficient allocation, the transition is once again smooth. Quantity extracted per unit of time is gradually reduced as the marginal user cost rises until the switch is made to the substitute. No abrupt change is evident once again in either marginal cost or quantity profiles.

What about the timing of the extraction of the depletable resource? When a renewable resource is available, more of the depletable resource would be extracted in the earlier periods than was the case without a renewable resource. Do you see why?

In this example, the switch is made during the sixth period, whereas in the previous example (involving no renewable substitute) the last units were exhausted at the end of the eighth period. That seems consistent with common sense. When a substitute is available, the need to save some of the depletable resource for the future is certainly less pressing. The opportunity cost is lower.

At the switch point, consumption of the renewable resource begins. Prior to the switch point, only the depletable resource is consumed, while after the switch point only the renewable resource is consumed. This sequencing of consumption patterns results from the costs of the choices. Prior to the switch point, the depletable resource is cheaper. At the switch point, the total marginal cost of the depletable

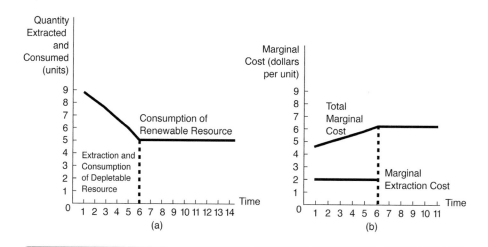

Figure 7.3 (a) Constant Marginal Extraction Cost with Substitute Resource: Quantity Profile (b) Constant Marginal Extraction Cost with Substitute Resource: Marginal Cost Profile.

resource (including marginal user cost) rises to meet the marginal cost of the substitute, and the transition occurs. Due to the availability of the substitute resource, after the switch point consumption never drops below five units in any time period.

Why five? Five is the amount that maximizes the net benefit when the marginal cost equals $6 (the price of the substitute). (Convince yourself of the validity of this statement by substituting $6 into the willingness-to-pay function and solving for the quantity demanded.)

We shall not show the numerical example here, but it is not difficult to see how an efficient allocation would be defined when the transition is from one constant marginal-cost depletable resource to another depletable resource with a constant, but higher, marginal cost (see Figure 7.4). The total marginal cost of the first resource would rise over time until it equaled that of the second resource at the time of transition (T^*). In the period of time prior to transition, only the cheapest resource would be consumed; all of it would have been consumed by T^*.

A close examination of the total-marginal-cost path reveals two interesting characteristics worthy of our attention. First, even in this case, the transition is a smooth one; total marginal cost never jumps to the higher level. Second, the slope of the total marginal cost curve over time is flatter after transition.

The first characteristic is easy to explain. The total marginal costs of the two resources have to be equal at the time of transition. If they weren't equal, the net benefit could be increased by switching to the lower-cost resource from the more expensive resource. Total marginal costs are not equal in the other periods. In the period before transition, the first resource is cheaper and therefore used exclusively, whereas after transition the first resource is exhausted, leaving only the second resource.

The slope of the marginal cost curve over time is flatter after transition simply because the component of total marginal cost that is growing (the marginal user cost) represents a smaller portion of the total marginal cost of the second resource than of the first. The total marginal cost of each resource is determined by the marginal

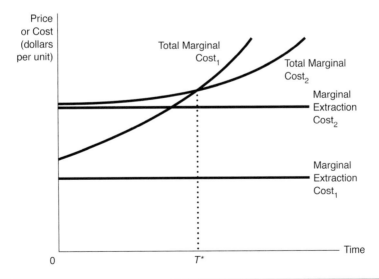

Figure 7.4 The Transition from One Constant-Cost Depletable Resource to Another.

extraction cost plus the marginal user cost. In both cases the marginal user cost is increasing at rate r, and the marginal cost of extraction is constant. As you can see in Figure 7.4, the marginal cost of extraction, which is constant, constitutes a much larger proportion of total marginal cost for the second resource than for the first. Hence, total marginal cost rises more slowly for the second resource, at least initially.

Increasing Marginal Extraction Cost

We have now expanded our examination of the efficient allocation of depletable resources to include longer time horizons and the availability of other depletable or renewable resources that could serve as perfect substitutes. As part of our trek toward increasing realism, we will now consider a situation in which the marginal cost of extracting the depletable resource rises with the cumulative amount extracted. This is commonly the case, for example, with minerals, where the higher-grade ores are extracted first, followed by an increasing reliance on lower-grade, higher marginal cost ones.

Analytically, this case is handled in the same manner as the previous case, except that the function describing the marginal cost of extraction is slightly more complicated[3]—it increases with the cumulative amount extracted. The dynamic efficient allocation of this resource is once again found by maximizing the present value of the net benefits, but in this case using this modified cost of extraction function. The results of that maximization are portrayed in Figures 7.5a and 7.5b.

The most significant difference between this case and those that preceded it lies in the behavior of marginal user cost. In the constant marginal cost cases we noted that marginal user cost rose over time at rate r. When the marginal cost of extraction increases with the cumulative amount extracted, as in this case, marginal user cost *declines* over time until, at the time of transition to the renewable resource, it goes to zero. Can you figure out why?

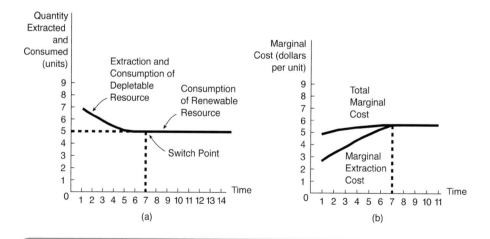

Figure 7.5 (a) Increasing Marginal Extraction Cost with Substitute Resource: Quantity Profile (b) Increasing Marginal Extraction Cost with Substitute Resource: Marginal Cost Profile.

Remember that marginal user cost is an opportunity cost reflecting forgone future marginal net benefits. In contrast to the constant marginal-cost case, in the increasing marginal-cost case every unit extracted now raises the cost of future extraction. Therefore, as the current marginal cost rises over time, the sacrifice made by future generations diminishes as an additional unit is consumed earlier; the net benefit that would be received by a future generation, if a unit of the resource were saved for them, gets smaller and smaller as the marginal extraction cost of that resource gets larger and larger. By the last period, the marginal extraction cost is so high that earlier consumption of one more unit imposes no sacrifice at all. At the switch point, the opportunity cost of current extraction (as reflected in the marginal user cost) drops to zero, and total marginal cost equals the marginal extraction cost.[4]

The increasing-cost case differs from the constant-cost case in another important way as well. In the constant-cost case, the depletable resource reserve is ultimately completely exhausted. In the increasing-cost case, however, the reserve is not exhausted; some is left in the ground because it is more expensive than the substitute.

Up to this point in our analysis, we have examined what an efficient allocation would look like in a number of circumstances. First, we examined a situation in which a finite amount of a resource is extracted at constant marginal cost. Despite the absence of increasing extraction cost, an efficient allocation involves a smooth transition to a substitute, when one is available, or to abstinence, when one is not. The complication of increasing marginal cost changes the time profile of the marginal user cost, but it does not alter the basic finding of declining consumption of depletable resources coupled with rising total marginal cost.

Can this analysis be used as a basis for judging whether current extraction profiles are efficient? As a look at the historical record reveals, the consumption patterns of most depletable resources have involved increases, not decreases, in consumption over time. Is this prima facie evidence that the resources are not being allocated efficiently?

Exploration and Technological Progress

Using the historical patterns of increasing consumption to conclude that depletable resources are not being allocated efficiently would not represent a valid conclusion. As we have noted earlier, the conclusions of any model depend on the structure of that model. The models considered to this point have not yet included a consideration of the role of population and income growth, which could cause demand to shift upward over time, or of the exploration for new resources or technological progress. These are historically significant factors in the determination of actual consumption paths.[5]

Consider how these factors might influence the efficient extraction profile. The search for new resources is expensive. As easily discovered resources are exhausted, searches are initiated in less rewarding, more costly, environments, such as the bottom of the ocean or locations deep within the earth. This suggests the *marginal cost of exploration*, which is the marginal cost of finding additional units of the resource, should be expected to rise over time, just as the marginal cost of extraction does.

As the total marginal cost for a resource rises over time, society should actively explore possible new sources of that resource. Larger increases in the marginal cost of extraction for known sources trigger larger potential increases in net benefits from finding new sources that previously would have been unprofitable to extract.

Some of this exploration would be successful: new sources of the resource would be discovered. If the marginal extraction cost of the newly discovered resources is low enough, these discoveries could lower, or at least delay, the increase in the total marginal cost of production. As a result, the new finds would tend to encourage more consumption and more extraction. Compared to a situation with no exploration possible, the model with exploration would show a smaller and slower decline in consumption, while the rise in total marginal cost would be dampened.

It is also not difficult to expand our concept of efficient resource allocations to include *technological progress*, the general term economists give to advances in the state of knowledge. In the present context, technological progress would be manifested as reductions over time in the cost of extraction. For a resource that can be extracted at constant marginal cost, a one-time breakthrough lowering the marginal cost of extraction would hasten the time of transition. Furthermore, for an increasing-cost resource, more of the total available resource would be recovered in the presence of technological progress than would be recovered without it. (Why?)

The most pervasive effects of technological progress involve continuous downward shifts in the cost of extraction over some time period. The total marginal cost of the resource could actually fall over time if the cost-reducing nature of technological progress became so potent that, in spite of increasing reliance on inferior ore, the marginal cost of extraction decreased (see Example 7.1). With a finite amount of this resource, the fall in total marginal cost would be transitory, since ultimately it would have to rise. As we shall see in the next few chapters, however, this period of transition can last quite a long time.

EXAMPLE 7.1

Historical Example of Technological Progress in the Iron Ore Industry

The term *technological progress* plays an important role in the economic analysis of mineral resources. Yet, at times, it can appear abstract, even mystical. It shouldn't! Far from being a blind faith detached from reality, technological progress refers to a host of ingenious ways in which people have reacted to impending shortages with sufficient imagination that the available supply of resources has been expanded by an order of magnitude and at reasonable cost. An interesting case from economic history illustrates how concrete a notion technological progress is.

In 1947, the president of Republic Steel, C. M. White, calculated the expected life of the Mesabi Range of northern Minnesota (the source of some 60 percent of iron ore consumed during World War II) as being in the range from 5 to 7 years. By 1955, only 8 years later, *U.S. News and World Report* concluded that worry over the scarcity of iron ore could be forgotten. The source of this remarkable transformation of a problem of scarcity into one of abundance was the discovery of a new technique of preparing iron ore, called *pelletization*.

Prior to pelletization, the standard ores from which iron was derived contained from 50 to more than 65 percent iron in crude form. A significant percentage of taconite ore containing less than 30 percent iron in crude form was available, but no one knew how to produce it at reasonable cost.

Pelletization, a process by which these ores are processed and concentrated at the mine site prior to shipment to the blast furnaces, allowed the profitable use of the taconite ores. While expanding the supply of iron ore, pelletization reduced its cost in spite of its inferior grade.

There were several sources of the cost reduction. First, substantially less energy was used; the shift in ore technology toward pelletization produced net energy savings of 17 percent in spite of the fact that the pelletization process itself required more energy. The reduction came from the discovery that the blast furnaces could be operated much more efficiently using pelletized inputs. The process also reduced labor requirements per ton by some 8.2 percent while increasing the output of the blast furnaces. A blast furnace owned by Armco Steel in Middletown, Ohio, which had a rated capacity of approximately 1500 tons of molten iron per day, was able, by 1960, to achieve production levels of 2700–2800 tons per day when fired with 90 percent pellets. Pellets nearly doubled the blast furnace productivity!

Sources: Kakela, P. J. (December 15, 1978). Iron ore: Energy, labor, and capital changes with technology. *Science*, 202, 1151–1157; Kakela, P. J. (April 10, 1981). Iron ore: From depletion to abundance. *Science*, 212, 132–136.

Market Allocations of Depletable Resources

In the preceding sections, we have examined in detail how the efficient allocation of substitutable, depletable, and renewable resources over time would be defined in a variety of circumstances. We must now address the question of whether actual markets can be expected to produce an efficient allocation. Can the private market, involving millions of consumers and producers, each reacting to their own unique preferences, ever result in a dynamically efficient allocation? Is profit maximization compatible with dynamic efficiency?

Appropriate Property Rights Structures

The most common misconception of those who believe that even a perfect market could never achieve an efficient allocation of depletable resources is based on the idea that producers want to extract and sell the resources as fast as possible, since that is how they derive the value from the resource. This misconception makes people see markets as myopic and unconcerned about the future.

As long as the property rights governing natural resources have the characteristics of exclusivity, transferability, and enforceability (Chapter 2), the markets in which those resources are bought and sold will not necessarily lead to myopic choices for the simple reason that myopia would reduce profits. By taking marginal user cost into account, the producer maximizes profits by acting efficiently.

A resource in the ground has two potential sources of value to its owner: (1) a use value when it is sold (the only source considered by those diagnosing inevitable myopia) and (2) an asset value when it remains in the ground. As long as the price of a resource continues to rise, the resource in the ground is becoming more valuable. The owner of this resource accrues this capital gain, however, only if the resource is conserved for later sale. A producer who sells all resources in the earlier periods loses the chance to take advantage of higher prices in the future.

A profit-maximizing producer attempts to balance present and future production in order to maximize the value of the resource and, hence, profits. Since higher prices in the future provide an incentive to conserve, a producer who ignores this incentive would not be maximizing the value of the resource. Resources sold by a myopic producer would be bought by someone willing to delay extraction in order to maximize their value. As long as social and private discount rates coincide, property rights structures are well defined (no externalities), and reliable information about future prices is available, a producer who pursues maximum profits simultaneously provides the maximum present value of net benefits for society.

The implication of this analysis is that, in competitive resource markets, the price of the resource equals the total marginal cost of extracting and using the resource. Thus, Figures 7.2a through 7.5b can illustrate not only an efficient allocation but also the allocation produced by an efficient market. When used to describe an efficient market, the total marginal cost curve describes the time path that prices could be expected to follow.

Environmental Costs

Not all actual situations, however, satisfy the conditions necessary for this harmonious outcome. One of the most important situations in which property rights structures may not be well defined occurs when the extraction of a natural resource imposes an environmental cost on society that is not internalized by the producers. The aesthetic costs of strip mining, the health risks associated with uranium tailings, and the acids leached into streams from mine operations are all examples of associated environmental costs. The presence of environmental costs is both empirically and conceptually important, since it forms one of the bridges between the traditionally separate fields of environmental economics and natural resource economics.

Suppose, for example, that the extraction of a depletable resource caused some damage to the environment that was not adequately reflected in the costs faced by the extracting firms. This would be, in the context of the discussion in Chapter 2, an external cost. The cost of getting the resource out of the ground, as well as processing and shipping it, is borne by the resource owner and considered in the calculation of how much of the resource to extract. The environmental damage, however, may not be borne by the owner and, in the absence of any outside attempt to internalize that external cost, will not normally be part of the extraction decision. How would the market allocation, based on only the costs borne by the owner, differ from the efficient allocation, which is based on all costs, regardless of who ultimately bears them?

We can examine this issue by modifying the numerical example used earlier in this chapter. Assume the environmental damage can be represented by increasing the marginal cost by $1.[6] The additional dollar reflects the cost of the environmental damage caused by producing another unit of the resource. What effect do you think this external cost would have on the efficient time profile for quantities extracted?

The answers are given in Figures 7.6a and 7.6b. The result of including environmental cost in the timing of the switch point is especially interesting because it involves two different effects that work in opposite directions. On the demand side, the internalization of environmental costs results in higher prices, which tend to dampen demand. This lowers the rate of consumption of the resource, which, all other things being equal, would make it last longer.

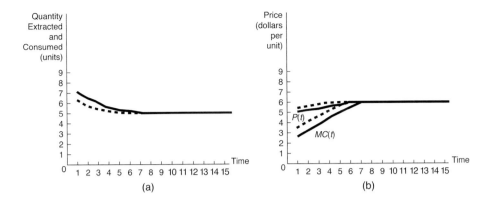

Figure 7.6 (a) Increasing Marginal Extraction Cost with Substitute Resource in the Presence of Environmental Costs: Quantity Profile (b) Increasing Marginal Extraction Cost with Substitute Resource in the Presence of Environmental Costs: Price Profile (Solid Line—without Environmental Costs; Dashed Line—with Environmental Costs).

All other things are not equal, however. The higher marginal cost also means that a smaller cumulative amount of the depletable resource would be extracted in an efficient allocation. (Can you see why?) As shown in Figures 7.6a and 7.6b, the efficient cumulative amount extracted would be 30 units instead of the 40 units extracted in the case where environmental costs were not included. This supply-side effect tends to hasten the time when a switch to the renewable resource is made, all other things being equal.

Which effect dominates—the rate-of-consumption effect or the supply effect? In our numerical example, the supply-side effect dominates and, as a result, the time of transition for an efficient allocation is sooner than for the market allocation. In general, the answer depends on the shape of the marginal-extraction-cost function. With constant marginal cost, for example, there would be no supply-side effect and the market would unambiguously transition later. If the environmental costs were associated with the use of the renewable resource, rather than the depletable resource, the time of transition for the efficient allocation would have been later than the market allocation. Can you see why?

What can we learn from this analysis of the increasing-cost case about the allocation of depletable resources over time when environmental side effects are *not* borne by the agent determining the extraction rate? Ignoring external costs leaves the market price of the depletable resource too low, too much of the resource would be extracted, and the rate at which it would be extracted would be too high relative to an efficient extraction profile.

Since policies that internalize these external costs can affect both the quantity extracted and price profiles, they can sometimes produce unexpected outcomes (see Example 7.2).

This once again demonstrates the interdependencies among the various decisions we have to make about the future. Environmental and natural resource decisions are intimately and inextricably linked.

EXAMPLE 7.2

The Green Paradox

Common sense indicates that when pollution taxes to promote nonpolluting technology are imposed, they would lower emissions and improve welfare as long as the taxes weren't excessive. In an intriguing article, Sinn (2008) argues that in the case of global warming these demand-reducing policies could trigger (under certain conditions) price effects that could actually reduce welfare. Because this analysis suggests that policies designed to internalize an externality could actually result in lower economic welfare, this outcome was labeled "the green paradox."

The basic logic behind this finding is easily explained in terms of the depletable resource models developed in this chapter. The specific policy case examined by Sinn was a carbon tax rate that rises over time faster than the rate of interest. This carbon tax design changes the relative prices between current and future sales, increasing the relative profitability of earlier extraction. (Remember, one reason for delaying extraction was the higher prices extractors would gain in the future. With this specific tax profile the after-tax return is falling, not rising.) This policy would not only change the profit-maximizing extraction profile so that more is extracted earlier, but the present value of net benefits could fall.

Notice that this result depends on earlier, not larger, cumulative damages. In the constant marginal extraction cost (MEC) model, cumulative extraction (and hence, cumulative damages) is fixed so these policies would affect the timing, but not the magnitude, of the cumulative emissions. In the increasing-cost MEC case, however, the cumulative emissions would actually be less; the imposition of the carbon tax would ultimately result in more of the depletable resource being left in the ground.

Is the green paradox a serious obstacle to climate policy? So far the verdict seems to be no (van der Ploeg, 2013; Jensen et al., 2015), but the dearth of empirical evidence pointing either one way or the other leaves the door ajar.

Sources: Sinn, H.-W. (2008). Public policies against global warming: A supply side approach. *International Tax and Public Finance, 15*, 360–394; van der Ploeg, F. (2013). Cumulative carbon emissions and the green paradox. *Annual Review of Resource Economics, 5*, 281–300; Jensen, S., Mohliny, K., Pittelz, K., & Sterner, T. (2015). An introduction to the green paradox: The unintended consequences of climate policies. *Review of Environmental Economics and Policy, 9*, 246–265. doi: 10.1093/reep/rev010.

Summary

The efficient extraction profiles for depletable and renewable resources depend on the circumstances. In the standard treatments when the resource can be extracted at a constant marginal cost, the efficient quantity of the depletable resource extracted declines over time. If no substitute is available, the quantity declines smoothly to zero. If a renewable constant-cost substitute is available, the quantity of the depletable resource extracted will decline smoothly to the quantity available from the renewable resource. In each case, all of the available depletable resource would be eventually used up and marginal user cost would rise over time, reaching a maximum when the last unit of depletable resource was extracted.

The efficient allocation of an increasing marginal-cost resource is similar in that the quantity extracted declines over time but differs with respect to the behavior of marginal user cost and the cumulative amount extracted. Whereas marginal user cost typically rises over time when the marginal cost of extraction is constant, it declines over time when the marginal cost of extraction rises with the cumulative amount extracted. Furthermore, in the constant-cost case the cumulative amount extracted is equal to the available supply; in the increasing-cost case it depends on the relationship between the marginal extraction cost function and the cost of the substitute, and some of the resource may be left in the ground unused.

Introducing technological progress and exploration activity into the model tends to delay the transition to renewable resources. Exploration expands the size of current reserves, while technological progress keeps marginal extraction cost from rising as fast as it otherwise would. If these effects are sufficiently potent, marginal cost could actually decline for some period of time, causing the quantity extracted to rise.

In the absence of environmental costs when property rights structures are properly defined, market allocations of depletable resources can be efficient. In this case profit maximization and efficiency can be compatible.

When the extraction of resources imposes an external environmental cost, however, generally market allocations will not be efficient. The market price of the depletable resource would be too low, the rate of extraction would be excessive, and too much of the resource would ultimately be extracted. (Think of this model when you read about the effects of fracking in Chapter 11.)

In an efficient market allocation, the transition from depletable to renewable resources is smooth and exhibits no overshoot-and-collapse characteristics. Whether the actual market allocations of these various types of resources are efficient remains to be seen. To the extent markets negotiate an efficient transition, a laissez-faire policy would represent an appropriate response by the government. On the other hand, when the market is not capable of yielding an efficient allocation, some form of government intervention may be necessary. In the next few chapters, we shall examine these questions for a number of different types of depletable and renewable resources.

Discussion Question

1. One current practice is to calculate the years remaining for a depletable resource by taking the prevailing estimate of current reserves and dividing it by current annual consumption. How useful is that calculation? Why?

Self-Test Exercises

1. To anticipate subsequent chapters where more complicated renewable resource models are introduced, consider a slight modification of the two-period depletable resource model. Suppose a biological resource is renewable in the sense that any of it left unextracted after Period 1 will grow at rate k. Compared to the case where the total amount of a constant-MEC resource is fixed, how would the efficient allocation of this resource over the two periods differ? (*Hint*: It can be shown that $MNB_1/MNB_2 = (1 + k)/(1 + r)$, where MNB stands for marginal net benefit.)

2. Consider an increasing marginal-cost depletable resource with no effective substitute. (a) Describe, in general terms, how the marginal user cost for this resource in the earlier time periods would depend on whether the demand curve for that resource was stable or shifting outward over time. (b) How would the allocation of that resource over time be affected?

3. Many states are now imposing severance taxes on resources being extracted within their borders. In order to understand the effect of these taxes on the allocation of a mineral over time, assume a stable demand curve. (a) How would the competitive allocation of an increasing marginal-cost depletable resource be affected by the imposition of a per-unit tax (e.g., $4 per ton) if there exists a constant-marginal-cost substitute? (b) Comparing the allocation without a tax to one with a tax, in general terms, what are the differences in cumulative amounts extracted and the price paths?

4. For the increasing marginal-extraction-cost model of the allocation of a depletable resource, how would the ultimate cumulative amount taken out of the ground be affected by (a) an increase in the discount rate, (b) the extraction by a monopolistic, rather than a competitive, industry, and (c) a per-unit subsidy paid by the government for each unit of the abundant substitute used?

5. Suppose you wanted to hasten the transition from a depletable fossil fuel to solar energy. Compare the effects of a per-unit tax on the depletable resource to an equivalent per-unit subsidy on solar energy. Would they produce the same switch point? Why or why not?

6. Suppose a tax on the extraction of a depletable resource is enacted and it will first take effect 10 years in the future. This resource is assumed to have a renewable, constant MEC substitute that will remain untaxed.

   a. For a depletable resource characterized by a constant MEC, how would, if at all, this pending law affect the extraction profile over time in terms of both the timing of the extraction and the cumulative amount extracted? Why?

   b. If the depletable resource is characterized by an increasing MEC, how would your answer in (a) change, if at all? Why?

Appendix: Extensions of the Constant-Extraction-Cost Depletable Resource Model: Longer Time Horizons and the Role of an Abundant Substitute

In the appendix to Chapter 6, we derived a simple model to describe the efficient allocation of a constant-marginal-cost depletable resource over time and presented the numerical solution for a two-period version of that model. In this appendix, the mathematical derivations for the extension to that basic model will be documented, and the resulting numerical solutions for these more complicated cases will be explained.

The *N*-Period, Constant-Cost, No-Substitute Case

The first extension involves calculating the efficient allocation of the depletable resource over time when the number of time periods for extraction is unlimited. This is a more difficult calculation because how long the resource will last is no longer predetermined; the time of exhaustion must be derived as well as the extraction path prior to exhaustion of the resource.

The equations describing the allocation that maximizes the present value of net benefits are

$$\frac{a - bq_t - c}{(1+r)^{t-1}} - \lambda = 0, t = 1, \ldots, T \tag{A.1}$$

$$\sum_{t=1}^{n} q_t = \bar{Q} \tag{A.2}$$

The parameter values assumed for the numerical example presented in the text are

$$a = \$8, b = 0.4, c = \$2, \bar{Q} = 40, \text{and } r = 0.10$$

The allocation that satisfies these conditions is

q_1 = 8.004	q_4 = 5.689	q_7 = 2.607	T = 9
q_2 = 7.305	q_5 = 4.758	q_8 = 1.368	λ = 2.7983
q_3 = 6.535	q_6 = 3.733	q_9 = 0.000	

The optimality of this allocation can be verified by substituting these values into the preceding equations. (Due to rounding, these add to 39.999, rather than 40.000.)

Practically speaking, solving these equations to find the optimal solution is not a trivial matter, but neither is it very difficult. One method of finding the solution for those without the requisite mathematics involves developing a computer algorithm (computation procedure) that converges on the correct answer. One such algorithm for this example can be constructed as follows: (1) assume a value for λ; (2) using Equation set (A.1) solve for all q's based upon this λ; (3) if the sum of the calculated q's exceeds $\bar{Q}$, adjust λ upward or if the sum of the calculated q's is less than $\bar{Q}$, adjust λ downward (the adjustment should use information gained in previous steps to ensure that the new trial will be closer to the solution value); (4) repeat steps (2) and (3) using the new λ; (5) when the sum of the q's is sufficiently close to $\bar{Q}$ stop the calculations. As an exercise, those interested in computer programming might construct a program to reproduce these results.

Constant Marginal Cost with an Abundant Renewable Substitute

The next extension assumes the existence of an abundant, renewable, perfect substitute, available in unlimited quantities at a cost of $6 per unit. To derive the dynamically efficient allocation of both the depletable resource and its substitute, let q_t be the amount of a constant-marginal-cost depletable resource extracted in year t and q_{st} the amount used of another constant-marginal-cost resource that is perfectly substitutable for the depletable resource. The marginal cost of the substitute is assumed to be $d.

With this change, the total benefit and cost formulas become

$$\text{Total benefit} = \sum_{t=1}^{T} a(q_t + q_{st}) - \frac{b}{2}(q_t + q_{st})^2 \tag{A.3}$$

$$\text{Total cost} = \sum_{t=1}^{T}(cq_t + dq_t) \tag{A.4}$$

The objective function is thus

$$\text{PVNB} = \sum_{t=1}^{T}\frac{a(q_t + q_{st}) - \dfrac{b}{2}(q_t^2 + q_{st}^2 + 2q_t q_{st}) - cq_t - dq_{st}}{(1+r)^{t-1}} \tag{A.5}$$

subject to the constraint on the total availability of the depletable resource

$$\bar{Q} - \sum_{t=1}^{T}q_t \geq 0 \tag{A.6}$$

Necessary and sufficient conditions for an allocation maximizing this function are expressed in Equations (A.7), (A.8), and (A.9):

$$\frac{a - b(q_t + q_{st}) - c}{(1+r)^{t-1}} - \lambda \leq 0, \; t = 1, \ldots, T \tag{A.7}$$

Any member of Equation set (A.7) will hold as an equality when $q_t > 0$ and will be negative when

$$a - b(q_t + q_{st}) - d \leq 0, \; t = 1, \ldots, T \tag{A.8}$$

Any member of Equation set (A.8) will hold as an equality when $q_{st} > 0$ and will be negative when $q_{st} = 0$

$$\bar{Q} - \sum_{t=1}^{T}q_t \geq 0 \tag{A.9}$$

For the numerical example used in the text, the following parameter values were assumed: $a = \$8$, $b = 0.4$, $c = \$2$, $d = \$6$, $Q = 40$, and $r = 0.10$. It can be readily verified that the optimal conditions are satisfied by

$$q_1 = 8.798 \qquad q_3 = 7.495 \quad q_5 = 5.919$$
$$q_2 = 8.177 \qquad q_4 = 6.744$$
$$q_{s6} = 2.137 \qquad q_{st} = \begin{pmatrix} 5.000 \text{ for } t > 6 \\ 0 \text{ for } t < 6 \end{pmatrix}$$
$$q_6 = 2.863 \qquad \lambda = 2.481$$

The depletable resource is used up before the end of the sixth period and the switch is made to the substitute resource at that time. From Equation set (A.8), in competitive markets the switch occurs precisely at the moment when the resource price rises to meet the marginal cost of the substitute.

The switch point in this example is earlier than in the previous example (the sixth period rather than the ninth period). Since all characteristics of the problem except for the availability of the substitute are the same in the two numerical examples, the difference can be attributed to the availability of the renewable substitute.

Notes

1 Even renewable resources are ultimately finite because their renewability depends on energy from the sun and the sun is expected to serve as an energy source for only the next 5 or 6 billion years. Because the finiteness of renewable resources is sufficiently far into the future, the distinction between depletable and renewable resources remains useful as a practical matter.

2 The condition that marginal user cost rises at rate r turns out to be true only when the marginal cost of extraction is constant. Later in this chapter we show how the marginal user cost is affected when marginal extraction cost is not constant. Remember in Chapter 1 how we noted that the outcome of any model depends upon the assumptions that undergird it? This is one example of that point.

3 The new marginal cost of extraction is $MCt = \$2 + 0.1Q_t$, where Q_t is cumulative extraction to date.

4 Total marginal cost cannot be greater than the marginal cost of the substitute. Yet, in the increasing marginal extraction cost case, at the time of transition the marginal extraction cost must also <u>equal</u> the marginal cost of the substitute. If that weren't true, it would imply that some of the resource that was available at a marginal cost lower than the substitute would remain unused. This would clearly be inefficient, since net benefits could be increased by simply using it instead of the more expensive substitute. Hence, at the switch point, in the rising marginal-cost case, the marginal extraction cost has to equal total marginal cost, implying a zero marginal user cost.

5 To derive how a rising demand curve over time due to either rising income or population growth would affect the extraction profile, complete self-test exercise (2) at the end of this chapter.

6 Including environmental damage, the marginal cost function would be raised to $\$3 + 0.1Q$ instead of $\$2 + 0.1Q$.

Further Reading

Andre, F., & Cerda, E. (2006). On the dynamics of recycling and natural resources. *Environmental & Resource Economics*, 33(2), 199–221. This article provides a formal examination of how the recyclability of depletable resources affects extraction profiles and sustainability.

Banzhaf, H. S. (July 2016). The environmental turn in natural resource economics: John Krutilla and "conservation reconsidered." Resources for the Future Discussion paper DP 16–27. www.rff.org/files/document/file/RFF-DP-16-27.pdf. A discussion of how a classic paper in the early twentieth century used economics to unify the traditionally separate views of conservationists and preservationists.

Conrad, J. M., & Clark, C. W. (1987). *Natural Resource Economics: Notes and Problems*. Cambridge: Cambridge University Press. Reviews techniques of dynamic optimization and shows how they can be applied to the management of various resource systems.

Fischer, C., & Laxminarayan, R. (2005). Sequential development and exploitation of an exhaustible resource: Do monopoly rights promote conservation? *Journal of Environmental Economics and Management*, 49(3), 500–515. Examines the conditions under which a monopolist would extract a depletable resource more quickly or more slowly than a competitive industry.

Strand, J. (2010). Optimal fossil-fuel taxation with backstop technologies and tenure risk. *Energy Economics*, 32(2), 418–422. This article examines the time paths for optimal taxes and extraction profiles for a depletable resource that creates a negative stock externality (think climate change), involves increasing marginal extraction cost, and is subject to competition from an unlimited backstop resource causing no externality.

Chapter 8

Common-Pool Resources
Commercially Valuable Fisheries

Introduction

In 2009, the World Bank and the Food and Agriculture Organization of the United Nations (FAO) released a report called *The Sunken Billions: The Economic Justification for Fisheries Reform*. According to this report, economic losses in marine fisheries due to overfishing, poor management, and economic inefficiency are approximately US$50 billion per year. Over the last 30 years, those losses sum to over $2 trillion! The report goes on to argue that well-managed marine fisheries could provide sustainable economic benefits for millions of fisheries, coastal villages, and cities. In this chapter we explore the role of economics in designing well-managed fisheries.

Humans share the planet with many other living species. How those biological populations are treated depends in part on whether they are commercially valuable and whether the institutional framework set up to manage the harvesting of a given resource provides sufficient conservation incentives to those who are best positioned to protect the resource.

In an earlier chapter we considered the broader concept of ecosystem services that may or may not be commercially valuable but are crucially important for ecosystem health and human welfare. In the next few chapters, we examine environmental goods and services that are commercially valuable. Let's start with fisheries. In this chapter we consider how the process of fisheries management could be reformed to improve both efficiency and sustainability. A commercially valuable species is like a double-edged sword. On one hand, the value of the species to humans provides a strong and immediate reason for human concern about its future. On the other hand, its value may promote excessive harvest. Commercially exploited biological resources can become depleted to the point of commercial extinction if the population is drawn down beyond a critical threshold.

Extinction, although important, is not the only critical renewable resource-management issue. How do we choose among sustainable levels of harvest? What sustainable level of harvest is appropriate?

DOI: 10.4324/9781032689111-9

Biological populations belong to a class of renewable resources we will call *interactive resources*, wherein the size of the resource stock (population) is determined jointly by biological considerations and by actions taken by society. The postharvest size of the population, in turn, determines the availability of resources for the future. Thus, humanity's actions affect the flow of these resources over time. Because this flow is not purely a natural phenomenon, the rate of harvest has intertemporal effects. Tomorrow's harvesting choices are affected by today's harvesting behavior.

Using the fishery as a case study, we begin by examining what is meant by an efficient and sustainable level of harvest. We then investigate whether efficiency is a sufficiently strong criterion to avoid extinction. Will efficient harvests always result in sustainable outcomes? Having shown how our two social choice criteria apply to fisheries, we turn to an examination of how well our institutions fulfill those criteria. Are normal incentives compatible with efficient sustainable harvest levels?

Unfortunately, we shall discover that in many cases normal incentives are compatible with neither efficiency nor sustainability. Many commercial fisheries can be classified as open-access, common-pool resources, and, as such, suffer from overharvesting. According to the FAO, total fisheries and aquaculture production reached 214 million metric tons in 2020, an all-time record. This number includes 178 million metric tons of aquatic animals and 36 million metric tons of algae (Figure 8.1). The world's seven largest fishing fleets account for 49 percent of the global capture (China, Indonesia, Peru, India, Russian Federation, United States, and Vietnam). The FAO estimates that over 92 percent of the world's fish stocks are either fully exploited or overexploited (FAO, 2021). About one-third are overexploited or depleted. The FAO also reports that

In 2019, the fraction of fish stocks sustainably fished decreased to 64.6 percent, that is 1.2 percent lower than in 2017. This worsening trend in the percentage of overfished stocks (by number) should not detract from the fact that sustainably fished stocks provided 82.5 percent of the total 2019 fish landings. That's a 3.8 percent increase since 2017 and demonstrates larger stocks are being managed more effectively.[1]

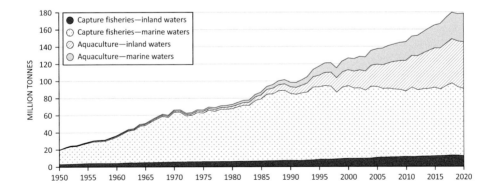

Figure 8.1 World Capture Fisheries and Aquaculture Production.

Source: Food and Agriculture Organization of the United Nations. Reproduced with permission.

That is good news. The bad news is that the most recent data from the FAO maintain that 35.4 percent of global stocks are overfished. In 1974, that number was 10 percent. Almost 40 million people rely on capture fisheries for their livelihood. Maintaining healthy fisheries will continue to provide challenges. When the asset value of the resource cannot be protected by existing institutions, a *tragedy of the commons*[2] can result. As we shall see, with so many fisheries experiencing overfishing, finding solutions that meet both efficiency and sustainability criteria is challenging.

Efficient Allocations—Bioeconomics Theory

The Biological Dimension

Like many other studies, our characterization of the fishery rests on a biological model originally proposed by Schaefer (1957). The Schaefer model posits a particular average relationship between the growth of the fish population and the size of the fish population. This is an average relationship in the sense that it abstracts from such influences as water temperature and the age structure of the population. The model therefore does not attempt to characterize the fishery on a day-to-day basis, but rather in terms of some long-term average in which these various random influences tend to counterbalance each other (see Figure 8.2).

The size of the population is represented on the horizontal axis and the growth of the population on the vertical axis. The graph suggests that there is a range of population sizes $(\underline{S} - S^*)$ where population growth increases as the population increases and a range $(S*-\bar{S})$ where initial increases in population lead to eventual declines in growth. We can shed further light on this relationship by examining more closely the two points $(\underline{S}\,\bar{S})$ where the function intersects the horizontal axis and therefore growth in the stock is zero. $\bar{S}$ is known as the natural equilibrium, since this is the population size that would persist in the absence of outside influences. Reductions in the stock due to mortality or out-migration would be exactly offset by increases in the stock due to births, growth of the fish in the remaining stock, and in-migration.

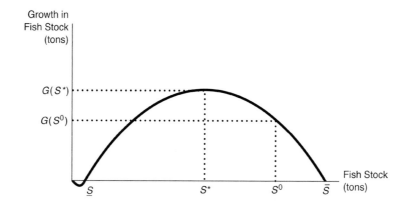

Figure 8.2 **Relationship between the Fish Population (Stock) and Growth.**

This natural equilibrium would persist because it is stable. A *stable equilibrium* is one in which movements away from this population level set forces in motion to restore it. If, for example, the stock temporarily exceeded $\bar{S}$, it would be exceeding the capacity of its habitat (called *carrying capacity*). As a result, mortality rates or out-migration would increase until the stock was once again within the confines of the carrying capacity of its habitat at $\bar{S}$

This tendency for the population size to return to $\bar{S}$ works in the other direction as well. Suppose the population is temporarily reduced below $\bar{S}$. Because the stock is now smaller, growth would be positive and the size of the stock would increase. Over time, the fishery would move along the curve to the right until $\bar{S}$ is reached again.

What about the other points on the curve? $\underline{S}$, known as the *minimum viable population*, represents the level of population below which growth in population is negative (deaths and out-migration exceed births and in-migration). In contrast to $\bar{S}$, this equilibrium is unstable. Population sizes to the right of $\underline{S}$ lead to positive growth and a movement along the curve toward $\bar{S}$ and away from $\underline{S}$. When the population moves to the left of $\underline{S}$, the population declines until it eventually becomes extinct. In this region, no forces act to return the population to a viable level.

A catch level is said to represent a *sustainable yield* whenever it equals the growth rate of the population, since it can be maintained over time. As long as the population size remains constant, the growth rate (and hence the catch) will remain constant as well.

S^* is known in biology as the *maximum sustainable yield population*, defined as the population size that yields the maximum growth; hence, the maximum sustainable yield (catch) is equal to this maximum growth and it represents the largest catch that can be perpetually sustained. Since the catch is equal to the growth, the sustainable yield for any population size (between $\underline{S}$ and $\bar{S}$) can be determined by drawing a vertical line from the stock size of interest on the horizontal axis to the point at which it intersects the function and drawing a horizontal line over to the vertical axis. The sustainable yield is the growth in the biomass defined by the intersection of this line with the vertical axis. Thus, in terms of Figure 8.2, $G\,(S^0)$ is the sustainable yield for population size S^0. Since the catch is equal to the growth, population size (and next year's growth) remains the same.

It should now be clear why $G(S^*)$ is the maximum sustainable yield. Larger catches would be possible in the short run, but these could not be sustained; they would lead to reduced population sizes and eventually, if the population were drawn down to a level smaller than $\underline{S}$, to the extinction of the species.

Static Efficient Sustainable Yield

Is the maximum sustainable yield synonymous with efficiency? The answer is no. Recall that efficiency is associated with maximizing the *net* benefit from the use of the resource. If we are to define the efficient allocation, we must include the costs of harvesting as well as the benefits.

Let's begin by defining the efficient sustainable yield without worrying about discounting. The static efficient sustainable yield is the catch level that, if maintained perpetually, would produce the largest annual net benefit. We shall refer to this as the *static efficient sustainable yield* to distinguish it from the *dynamic efficient sustainable yield*, which incorporates discounting. The initial use of this static concept enables us to fix the necessary relationships firmly in mind before dealing with the more complex role discounting plays. Subsequently, we raise the question of whether efficiency always dictates the choice of a sustainable yield, as opposed to a catch that changes over time.

We condition our analysis on three assumptions that simplify the analysis without sacrificing too much realism: (1) the price of fish is constant and does not depend on the amount sold, (2) the marginal cost of a unit of fishing effort is constant, and (3) the amount of fish caught per unit of effort expended is proportional to the size of the fish population (the smaller the population, the fewer fish caught per unit of effort).

Given these assumptions, we can construct the economic model. Under assumption (3), we can overlay harvest-effort functions onto the population function in Figure 8.2. Since the amount of fish caught per unit of effort is held constant, the relationship between catch and stock for given levels of effort can be portrayed by the linear functions in Figure 8.3. (For the mathematically inclined, the formula is Equation 8.3 in the appendix to this chapter.) Notice that increasing effort rotates the harvest function up and to the left (E2 > E1). The sustained yield associated with each level of effort is the point of intersection of these two curves. If we plot the series of points associated with the possible levels of effort and the sustained yield associated with each effort level, we will have our sustainable yield function defined in terms of effort rather than population, as portrayed in Figure 8.4. (Effort could be measured in vessel years, hours of fishing, or some other conventional metric.)

To avoid confusion, notice that increasing fishing effort in Figure 8.3 would result in smaller population sizes and would be recorded as a movement from right to left. Because the variable on the horizontal axis in Figure 8.4 is effort, and not population, an increase in fishing effort is recorded as a movement from left to right.

So far so good. To turn this into a complete economic model, we need to determine benefits and costs or, equivalently in this case, total revenue and total costs. From assumption (1) we know that the shape of the biological function dictates the shape of the revenue function. Simply multiplying each sustained yield (harvest) in Figure 8.4 by the constant price, we can turn the physical units (harvest) into monetary units

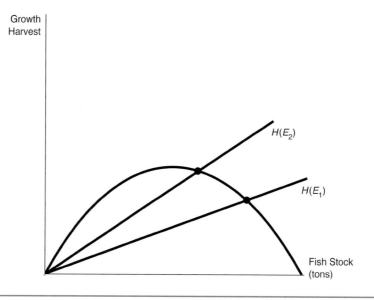

Figure 8.3 Relating Equilibrium Effort, Harvest, and Stock Size.

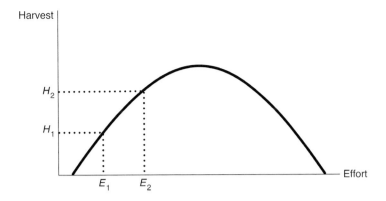

Figure 8.4 Sustainable Harvest (Yield).

(total revenue). Under assumption (2) we can characterize the final component of our model; the linear function that depicts the total cost is simply calculated as the level of effort times the constant marginal cost of each unit of effort. The resulting figure (8.5) portrays the benefits (revenues) and costs as a function of fishing effort.

In any sustainable yield, annual catches, population, effort levels, and net benefits, by definition, remain constant over time. The static efficient sustainable yield allocation maximizes the constant annual net benefit.

As sustained levels of effort are increased, eventually a point is reached (E^m) at which further effort reduces the sustainable catch (and revenue) for all years. That point, of course, corresponds to the maximum sustainable yield on Figure 8.2(S^*), meaning that both points reflect the same population and growth levels. Every effort level portrayed in Figures 8.4 and 8.5 corresponds to a specific population level in Figure 8.2.

The net benefit is presented in the diagram as the difference (vertical distance) between benefits (price times the quantity caught) and costs (the constant marginal cost of effort times the units of effort expended). The efficient level of effort is E^e, or the point in Figure 8.5 at which the vertical distance between benefits and costs is maximized.

E^e is the efficient level of effort because it is where marginal benefit (which graphically is the slope of the total benefit curve) is equal to marginal cost (the *constant* slope of the total cost curve). Levels of effort higher than E^e are inefficient because the additional cost associated with them exceeds the additional value of the fish obtained. Can you see why lower levels of effort are also inefficient?

Now we are armed with sufficient information to determine whether the maximum sustainable yield is efficient. The answer is clearly no. The maximum sustainable yield would be efficient only if the marginal cost of additional effort were zero. Can you see why? (*Hint*: what is the marginal benefit at the maximum sustainable yield?) Since at E^m the marginal benefit is lower than marginal cost, the efficient level of effort is *less* than that necessary to harvest the maximum sustainable yield. Thus, the static efficient level of effort leads to a *larger* fish population, but a lower annual catch than the maximum sustainable yield level of effort.

To fix these concepts firmly in mind, consider what would happen to the static efficient sustainable yield if a technological change were to occur (e.g., better sonar

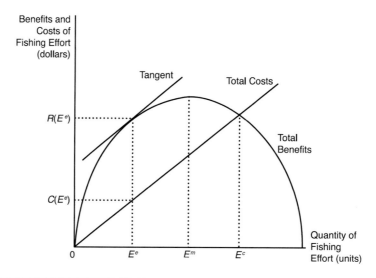

Figure 8.5 Efficient Sustainable Yield for a Fishery.

detection) that lowered the marginal cost of fishing. The lower marginal cost would result in a rotation of the total cost curve to the right. With this new cost structure, the old level of effort would no longer be efficient. The marginal cost of fishing (slope of the total cost curve) would now be lower than the marginal benefit (slope of the total benefit curve). Since the marginal cost is constant, the equality of marginal cost and marginal benefit can result only from a decline in marginal benefits. This implies an increase in effort. The new static efficient sustainable yield equilibrium implies more annual effort, a lower population level, a larger annual catch, and a higher net benefit for the fishery.

Dynamic Efficient Sustainable Yield

The static efficient sustainable yield turns out to be the special case of the dynamic efficient sustainable yield where the discount rate is zero. It is not difficult to understand why: the static efficient sustained yield is the allocation that maximizes the (identical) net benefit in every period. Any effort levels higher than this would yield temporarily larger catches (and net benefit), but this would be more than offset by a reduced net benefit in the future as the stock reached its new lower level. Thus, the undiscounted net benefits would be reduced.

The effect of a positive discount rate for the management of a fishery is similar to its influence on the allocation of depletable resources—the higher the discount rate, the higher the cost (in terms of forgone current income) to the resource owner of maintaining any given resource stock. When positive discount rates are introduced, the efficient level of effort increases beyond that suggested by the static efficient sustained yield with a corresponding decrease in the equilibrium population level.

The increase in the yearly effort beyond the efficient sustained yield level would *initially* result in an increased net benefit from the increased catch. (Remember that the amount of fish caught per unit of effort expended is proportional to the size of the population.) However, since this catch exceeds the sustained yield for that population size, the population of fish would be reduced and future population and catch levels would be lower. Eventually, as that level of effort is maintained, a new, lower equilibrium level would be attained when the size of the catch once again equals the growth of the population. Colin Clark (1976) has shown mathematically that, in terms of Figure 8.5, as the discount rate is increased, the dynamic efficient level of effort is increased until, with an infinite discount rate, it would become equal to E^c, the point at which net benefits go to zero.

It is easy to see why the use of an infinite discount rate to define the dynamic efficient sustainable yield results in allocation E^c. We have seen that temporally interdependent allocations over time give rise to a marginal user cost measuring the opportunity cost of increasing current effort. This opportunity cost reflects the forgone future net benefits when more resources are extracted in the present. For efficient interdependent allocations, the marginal willingness to pay is equal to the marginal user cost plus the marginal cost of extraction.

With an infinite discount rate, this marginal user cost is zero, because no value is received from future allocations. (Do you see why?) This implies that (1) the marginal cost of extraction equals the marginal willingness to pay, which equals the constant price; and (2) total benefits equal total costs.[3] Earlier we demonstrated that the static efficient sustained yield implies a larger fish population than the maximum sustainable yield. Once discounting is introduced, it is inevitable that the dynamic efficient sustainable yield would imply a smaller fish population than the static efficient sustainable yield and it is possible, though not inevitable, that the sustained catch would be smaller. Can you see why? In Figure 8.5 the sustained catch clearly is lower for an infinite discount rate.

The likelihood of the population being reduced below the level supplying the maximum sustainable yield depends on the discount rate. In general, the lower the extraction costs and the higher the discount rate, the more likely it is that the dynamic efficient level of effort will exceed the level of effort associated with the maximum sustainable yield. This is not difficult to see if we remember the limiting case discussed earlier. When the marginal extraction cost is zero, the static efficient sustainable yield and the maximum sustainable yield are equal.

Thus, with zero marginal extraction costs and a positive discount rate, the dynamic efficient level of effort necessarily exceeds not only the static efficient level of effort, but also the level of effort associated with the maximum sustainable yield. Higher extraction costs reduce the static efficient sustainable yield but not the maximum sustainable yield. (Remember that it is a biological, not an economic, concept.) By reducing efficient effort levels, higher extraction costs reduce the likelihood that discounting would cause the population to be drawn below the maximum sustainable yield level.

Could a dynamically efficient management scheme lead to extinction of the fishery? As Figure 8.5 shows, it would not be possible under the circumstances described here because E^c is the highest dynamically efficient level possible in this model, and that level falls short of the level needed to drive the population to extinction. However, in more complex models, extinction certainly can be an outcome.

For extinction to occur under a dynamic efficient management scheme, the benefit from extracting the very last unit would have to exceed the cost of extracting that unit (including the costs on future generations). As long as the fish population growth rate exceeds the discount rate, this will not be the case. If, however, the growth rate is lower than the discount rate, extinction can occur even in an efficient management scheme if the costs of extracting the last unit are sufficiently low.

Why does the biomass rate of growth have anything to do with whether an efficient catch profile leads to overfishing or extinction? Rates of growth determine the productivity of conservation efforts. With high rates of growth, future generations can be easily satisfied. On the other hand, when the rate of growth is very low, it takes a large sacrifice by current generations to produce more fish for future generations. In the limiting case, where the rate of growth is zero, we have a resource with fixed supply and therefore this fishery would become an exhaustible resource. Total depletion would occur whenever the price commanded by the resource is high enough to cover the marginal cost of extracting the last unit.

We have shown that the dynamic efficiency criterion is not automatically consistent with sustaining constant yields perpetually for an interactive renewable resource, since it is mathematically possible for an efficient allocation of a fishery to lead to extinction of the resource. How likely are these criteria to conflict in practice?

It is not as likely as this basic model might imply. Actual fisheries differ from the standard model in two key ways. First, harvesting marginal costs are typically not constant (as they are in the model discussed previously), but rather increase as the remaining stock size diminishes. Second, while the model we discussed holds prices constant, the size of the harvest can affect prices; larger harvests can depress them. Both of these modifications of the basic model suggest additional incentives for conserving the stock.

How empirically important are these incentives? Grafton et al. (2007) examine their importance for four specific fisheries and find not only that extinction is not the efficient outcome in any of the four fisheries but also in general, in this reformulated model, the stock level that maximizes the present value of net benefits is actually *larger* than the stock level that supports the maximum sustainable yield. Their results seem to hold both for relatively high discount rates and for relatively long-lived fish. (The orange roughy fishery, discussed in more detail later in the chapter, was one of the four they studied.)

Appropriability and Market Solutions

We have defined an efficient allocation of the fishery over time. The next step is to characterize the normal market allocation and to contrast these two allocations. Where they differ we can entertain the possibility of various public policy corrective means.

Let's first consider the allocation resulting from a fishery managed by a competitive sole owner. A sole owner would have a well-defined property right to the fish. We can establish the behavior of a sole owner by elaborating on Figure 8.5 as is done in Figure 8.6. Note that the two panels share a common horizontal axis, a characteristic that allows us to examine the effect of various fishing effort levels on both graphs.

A sole owner would want to maximize their profits.[4] Ignoring discounting for the moment, the owner can increase profits by increasing fishing effort until marginal revenue equals marginal cost. This occurs at effort level E^e, the static efficient sustainable yield, and yields positive profits equal to the difference between $R(E^e)$ and $C(E^e)$.

In ocean fisheries, however, sole owners are unlikely. Ocean fisheries are typically open-access resources—no one exercises complete control over them. Since the property rights to the fishery are not conveyed to any single owner, no fisher can exclude others from exploiting the fishery.

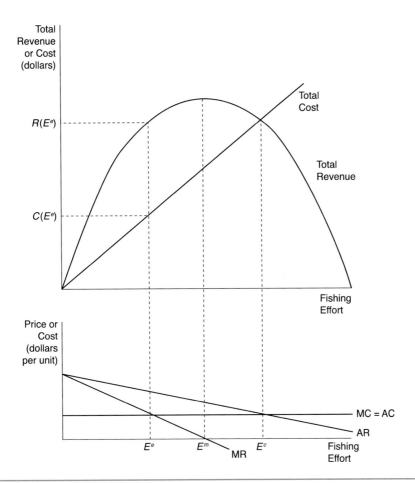

Figure 8.6 Market Allocation in a Fishery.

What problems arise when access to the fishery is completely unrestricted? Open-access resources create two kinds of external costs: a contemporaneous external cost and an intergenerational external cost. The contemporaneous external cost, which is borne by the current generation, involves the over-commitment of resources to fishing—too many boats, too many fishers, too much effort. As a result, current fishers earn a substantially lower rate of return on their efforts. The intergenerational external cost, borne by future generations, occurs because overfishing reduces the stock, which, in turn, lowers future profits from fishing.[5]

We can use Figure 8.6 to see how these external costs arise.[6] Once too many fishers have unlimited access to the same common-pool fishery, the property rights to the fish are no longer efficiently defined. At the efficient level, each boat would receive a profit equal to its share of the scarcity rent. This rent, however, serves as a stimulus for new fishers to enter, pushing up costs and eliminating the rent. Open access results in overexploitation.

The sole owner chooses not to expend more effort than E^e because to do so would reduce the profits of the fishery, resulting in a personal loss. When access to the fishery is unrestricted, a decision to expend effort beyond E^e reduces profits to the fishery as a whole but not to that individual fisher. Most of the decline in profits falls on the other fishers.

In an open-access resource, the individual fisher has an incentive to expend further effort until profits are zero. In Figure 8.6, that point is at effort level E^c, at which average revenue and average cost are equal. It is now easy to see the contemporaneous external cost—too much effort is being expended to catch too few fish, and the cost is substantially higher than it would be in an efficient allocation.

If this point seems abstract, it shouldn't. Many fisheries are plagued by precisely these problems. In a productive fishery in the Bering Sea and Aleutian Islands, for example, one early study (Huppert, 1990) found significant overcapitalization. While the efficient number of motherships (used to take on and process the catch at sea, so the catch boats do not have to return to port as often) was estimated to be nine, the actual level was 140. As a result, a significant amount of net benefits was lost ($124 million a year). Had the fishery been harvested more slowly, the same catch could have been achieved with fewer boats used closer to their capacity.

When a resource owner can exclude others (private property), the owner can balance the use value of the resource against the asset value. When access to the resource is unrestricted, exclusivity is lost. As a result, it is rational for a fisher to ignore the asset value, since they can never appropriate it, and simply maximize the use value. In the process, all the scarcity rent is dissipated. The allocation that results from allowing unrestricted access to the fishery is identical to that resulting from a dynamic efficient sustainable yield when an infinite discount rate is used. Can you see why?

Open-access resources do not automatically lead to a stock lower than (S^*), the one that maximizes the sustained yield. It is possible to draw a cost function with a slope sufficiently steep that it intersects the benefit curve at a point to the left of E^m. Nonetheless, mature, open-access fisheries can be exploited well beyond the point of maximum sustainable yield.

Open-access fishing may or may not pose the threat of species extinction. It depends on the nature of the species and the benefits and costs of an effort level above E^m that would have the effect of driving the stock level below the minimum viable population. One species that may face that risk is the northern bluefin tuna. Northern bluefin tuna include Atlantic bluefin and Pacific bluefin. Once considered critically endangered, the species has recently recovered, but it is still at risk of being harvested at unsustainable levels due to the high market price fishers receive because of its popularity in sushi restaurants. Later in the chapter, we will examine the case of bluefin tuna and its remarkable recovery. The threat of extinction cannot be determined purely from theory; it must be determined by empirical studies on a case-by-case basis.

Are open-access resources and common-pool resources synonymous concepts? They are not. Not all common-pool resources allow unlimited access. Informal arrangements among those harvesting the common-pool resource, which may be fostered by harvester cooperation, can serve to limit access (Example 8.1 presents one such arrangement).

Open-access resources generally violate the efficiency criterion and may violate the sustainability criteria. If these criteria are to be fulfilled, some restructuring of the decision-making environment may be necessary. The next section examines the possible role for government in accomplishing that outcome.

Public Policy toward Fisheries

What can be done? A variety of public policy responses is possible. Perhaps it is appropriate to start with circumstances where allowing the market to work can improve the situation.

EXAMPLE 8.1

Harbor Gangs of Maine and Other Informal Arrangements

Unlimited access to common-pool resources reduces net benefits so drastically that this loss encourages those harvesting the resource to band together to restrict access, if possible. The Maine lobster fishery is one setting where those informal arrangements have served to limit access with some considerable success.

Key among these arrangements is a system of territories that establishes boundaries between fishing areas. Particularly near the offshore islands, these territories tend to be exclusively harvested by close-knit, disciplined groups of harvesters. These "gangs" restrict access to their territory by various means. (Some methods, although effective, are covert and illegal, such as the practice of cutting the lines to lobster traps owned by new entrants, thereby rendering the traps irretrievable.)

Acheson (2003) found that in every season of the year the pounds of lobster caught per trap and the size of those lobsters were greater in defended areas. Not only did the larger number of pounds result in more revenue, but also the bigger lobsters brought in a higher price per pound. Informal arrangements were successful in this case, in part, because the Maine lobster stock is also protected by regulations limiting the size of lobsters that can be taken (imposing both minimum and maximum sizes) and prohibiting the harvest of egg-bearing females.

It turns out that many other examples of community *co-management* also offer encouraging evidence for the potential of sustainability. One example: the Chilean abalone (a type of snail called *loco*) is Chile's most valuable fishery. Local fishers began cooperating in 1988 to manage a small stretch (2 miles) of coastline. Today, the co-management scheme involves 700 co-managed areas, 20,000 artisanal fishers, and 2500 miles of coastline.

While it would be a mistake to assume that all common-pool resources are characterized by open access, it would also be a mistake to assume that all informal co-management arrangements automatically provide sufficient social means for producing efficient harvests such that stronger public policy would be unnecessary. One study (Gutiérrez et al., 2011) examined 130 fisheries in 44 developed and developing countries. It found that co-management can work, but only in the presence of strong leadership, social cohesion, and complementary incentives such as individual or community quotas. They find that effective community-based co-management can both sustain the resource and protect the livelihoods of nearby fishers and fishing communities. The existence of nearby protected areas was also found to be an important determinant of success.

Sources: Acheson, J. M. (2003). *Capturing the Commons: Devising Institutions to Manage the Maine Lobster Fishery*. Hanover, N.H.: University Press of New England; Gutiérrez, N. L., Hilborn, R., & Omar Defeo, O. (February 17, 2011). Leadership, social capital and incentives promote successful fisheries. *Nature, 470*, 386–389. www.nature.com/nature/journal/v470/n7334/full/nature09689.html.

Raising the Real Cost of Fishing

Perhaps one of the best ways to illustrate the virtues of using economic analysis to help design policies is to show the harsh effects of policy approaches that ignore it. Because the earliest approaches to fishery management had a single-minded focus on attaining the maximum sustainable yield, with little or no thought given to maximizing the net benefit, they provide a useful contrast.

One striking concrete example is the set of policies originally designed to deal with overexploitation of the Pacific salmon fishery in the United States. The five species of Pacific salmon are particularly vulnerable to overexploitation and even extinction because of their migration patterns. Pacific salmon are anadromous (sea run) spawned in the gravel beds of rivers. As juvenile fish, they migrate to the ocean, only to return as adults to spawn in the rivers of their birth. After spawning, they die. When the adults swim upstream, with an instinctual need to return to their native streams, they can easily be captured by traps, nets, or other catching devices.

Recognizing the urgency of the problem, the government took action. To reduce the catch, they raised the cost of fishing. Initially this was accomplished by preventing the use of any barricades on the rivers and by prohibiting the use of traps (the most efficient catching devices) in the most productive areas. These measures proved insufficient, since mobile techniques (trolling, nets, and so on) proved quite capable by themselves of overexploiting the resource. Officials then began to close designated fishing areas and suspend fishing in other areas for stipulated periods of time. In Figure 8.5, these measures would be reflected as a rotation of the total cost curve to the left until it intersected the total benefits (revenue) curve at a level of effort equal to E^e. The aggregate of all these regulations had the desired effect of curtailing the yield of salmon.

Were these policies efficient? They were not, even though they resulted in the efficient catch! This statement may seem inconsistent, but it is not. Efficiency implies not only that the catch must be at the efficient level, but also it must be extracted at the lowest possible cost. It was this latter condition that was violated by these policies (see Figure 8.7).

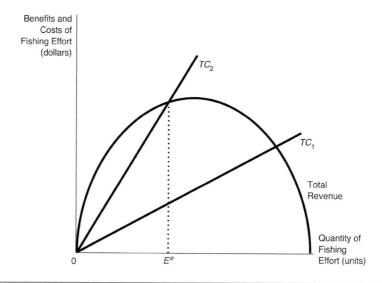

Figure 8.7 Effect of Regulation.

Figure 8.7 reflects the total cost in an unregulated fishery (TC_1) and the total cost after these policies were imposed (TC_2). The net benefit received from an efficient policy is shown graphically as the vertical distance between total cost and total benefit. After the policy, however, the net benefit was reduced to zero; the net benefit (represented by vertical distance) was lost to society. Why?

The net benefit was squandered on the use of excessively expensive means to catch the desired yield of fish. Rather than use traps to reduce the cost of catching the desired number of fish, traps were prohibited. Larger expenditures on capital and labor were required to catch the same number of fish. This additional capital and labor represent one source of the waste.

The limitations on fishing times had a similar effect on cost. Rather than allowing fishers to spread their effort out over time so the boats and equipment could be more productively utilized, fishers were forced to buy larger boats to allow them to take as much as possible during the shorter seasons. There are many examples of seasons lasting only a few hours or days with the catch still exceeding the quota.[7] Significant overcapitalization produces gross inefficiency.

Regulation imposed other costs as well. It was soon discovered that while regulations were adequate to protect the depletion of the fish population, they failed to curb the incentive for individual fishers to increase their share of the take. Even though the profits would be small because of high costs, new technological change would allow adopters to increase their shares of the market and put others out of business.

To protect themselves, the fishers were eventually driven to introducing bans on new technology. These restrictions took various forms, but two are particularly noteworthy. The first was the banning of the use of thin-stranded, monofilament net. The coarse-stranded net it would have replaced was visible to the salmon in the daytime and therefore could be avoided by them. As a result, it was useful only at night. By contrast, the thinner monofilament nets could be successfully used during the daylight hours as well as at night. Monofilament nets were banned in Canada and the United States soon after they appeared.

The most flagrantly inefficient regulation was one in Alaska that barred gill netters in Bristol Bay from using engines to propel their boats. This regulation lasted until the 1950s and heightened the public's awareness of the anachronistic nature of this regulatory approach. The world's most technologically advanced nation was reaping its harvest from the Bering Sea in sailboats, while the rest of the world—particularly Japan and the Soviet Union—was modernizing their fishing fleets at a torrid pace!

Guided by a narrow focus on biologically determined sustainable yield that ignored costs, these policies led to a substantial loss in the net benefit received from the fishery. Costs are an important dimension of the problem, and when they are ignored, the incomes of fishers suffer. When incomes suffer, further conservation measures become more difficult to implement, and incentives to violate the regulations are intensified.

Technical change presents further challenges to attempts to use cost-increasing regulations to reduce fishing effort. Technical innovations can lower the cost of fishing, thereby offsetting the increases imposed by the regulations. In the New England fishery, for example, Jin et al. (2002) report that the introduction of new technologies such as fish finders and electronic navigation aids in the 1970s and 1980s led to higher catches and declines in the abundance of the stocks despite the extensive controls in place at the time.

Taxes

Is it possible to provide incentives for cost reduction while assuring that the yield is reduced to the efficient level? Can a more efficient policy be devised? Economists who have studied the question believe that more efficient policies are possible.

Consider a tax on effort. In Figure 8.7, taxes on effort would also be represented as a rotation of the total cost line and the after-tax cost to the fishers would be represented by line TC_2. Since the after-tax curve coincides with TC_2, the cost curve for all those inefficient regulations, doesn't this imply that the tax system is just as inefficient? No! The key to understanding the difference is the distinction between *transfer costs* and *real resource costs*.

Under a regulation system of the type described earlier in this chapter, all of the costs included in TC_2 are real resource costs, which involve utilization of resources. Transfer costs, by contrast, involve transfers of resources from one part of society to another, rather than their dissipation. Transfers do represent costs to that part of society bearing them but are exactly offset by the gain received by the recipients. Unlike real resource costs, resources are not used up with transfers. Thus, the calculation of the size of the net benefit should subtract real resource costs, but not transfer costs, from benefits. For society as a whole, transfer costs are retained as part of the net benefit; who receives it is affected, but not the size of the net benefit.

A tax on catch would yield a similar result, but in this case the total revenue curve would shrink (price minus tax) rather than total cost increasing. Both types of taxes would help move the equilibrium toward E^*. Can you draw this using Figure 8.7?

In Figure 8.7, the net benefit under a tax system is identical to that under an efficient allocation. The net benefit represents a transfer cost to the fisher that is exactly offset by the revenues received by the tax collector. This discussion should not obscure the fact that, as far as the individual fisher is concerned, tax payments are very real costs. Rent normally received by a sole owner is now received by the government. Since the tax revenues involved can be substantial, fishers wishing to have the fishery efficiently managed may object to this particular way of doing it. They would prefer a policy that restricts catches while allowing them to keep the rents. Is that possible?

Perverse Incentives? Subsidies

Perhaps ironically, it has been much more common to subsidize the fishery sector rather than tax it. The OECD estimates that worldwide, governments spend about $35 billion per year to support the fisheries sector. That is equivalent to about 20 percent of the value of global marine capture.[8]

Many of these subsidies simply reduce operating costs for fishers. This is the opposite of what the economics tells us is the best policy (raising the real cost of fishing). These kinds of perverse incentives include things like fuel subsidies and support for vessels and gear. Martini and Innes (2018) find that all of these types of subsidies can lead to overfishing, lead to stocks being overfished, and encourage illegal, unreported, or unregulated (IUU) fishing. They find that the worst offender in this category is supports that reduce the costs of inputs such as fuel subsidies. Fuel subsidies are also the least effective means of transferring income to fishers. They find that subsidies or payments that focus on improving fishers' business operations (business and human capital) have the lowest tendency to increase fishing effort *and* provide the greatest benefit to fishers. In particular, they find:

> If only US$5 billion in fuel support was converted into support of this type, fishers would see increased income of more than US$2 billion, while at the same time reducing effort and improving fish stocks. (2)

In June of 2022, the World Trade Organization (WTO) announced the adoption of an Agreement on Fisheries Subsidies. This agreement includes the following stipulations:

- No Member shall grant or maintain any subsidy to a vessel or operator engaged in illegal, unreported, and unregulated (IUU) fishing or fishing related activities in support of IUU fishing.
- No Member shall grant or maintain subsidies for fishing or fishing related activities regarding an overfished stock.
- A Member shall take special care and exercise due restraint when granting subsidies to fishing or fishing related activities regarding stocks the status of which is unknown.
- Targeted technical assistance and capacity building assistance to developing country Members, including LDC Members, shall be provided for the purpose of implementation of the disciplines under this Agreement.

Further, the agreement creates a committee to oversee the rules of the agreement. It also creates a funding mechanism to support the program. By prohibiting harmful fishing subsidies, this agreement suggests we can look to the future with more optimism.

Catch Share Programs

Catch share programs allocate a portion of the total allowable catch to individuals, communities, or cooperatives. Programs in this category include individual fishing quotas (IFQs), individual transferable quotas (ITQs), individual vessel quotas (IVQs), territorial use rights fisheries (TURFs), fishing cooperatives, and community fishing quotas.[9] An ITQ program is a specific IFQ program where harvesting privileges can be transferred subsequent to initial allocations, IVQs are sometimes transferable, while TURFs grant rights to a geographic area. All of these create a type of harvest entitlement either in the fishery as a whole or in a specific geographic area.[10] As of 2013, there were nearly 200 rights-based management programs worldwide in 40 countries covering more than 500 species. As more fisheries convert to rights-based management, the number of programs has increased.

Catch share programs exist in 22 countries and on all continents (Table 8.1).

Table 8.1 Countries with Individual Transferable Quota Systems

Country	Number of Species Covered
Argentina	1
Australia	26
Canada	52
Chile	9
Denmark	1
Estonia	2
Falkland Islands	4
Greenland	1
Iceland	25
Italy	1
Mauritius	1*
Morocco	1*
Mozambique	4
Namibia	10
The Netherlands	7
New Zealand	97
Portugal	1*
South Africa	1*
United States	6

Complete species list unavailable. Norway, Peru, and Russia also use ITQ systems as part of their fisheries management.

Sources: Adapted from Chu, C. (2009). Thirty years later: The global growth of ITQs and their influence on stock status in marine fisheries. *Fish and Fisheries, 10,* 217–230; Arnason, R. (Summer 2012). Property rights in fisheries: How much can individual transferable quotas accomplish? *Review of Environmental Economics and Policy, 6*(2), 217–236; Jardine, S. L., & Sanchirico, J. N. (2012). Catch share programs in developing countries: A survey of the literature. *Marine Policy, 36,* 1242–1254.

Let's first consider individual transferable quotas (ITQs). Several of their identifiable characteristics serve to enhance efficiency:

1. The quotas entitle the holder to catch a specified share of the total authorized catch of a specified type of fish.
2. The catch authorized by the quotas held by all fishers should be equal to the efficient catch for the fishery.

3. The quotas should be freely transferable among fishers and markets should send appropriate price signals about the value of the fishery.

Each of these three characteristics plays an important role in obtaining an efficient allocation. Suppose, for example, the quota was defined in terms of boats rather than in terms of catch—not an uncommon type of quota. With a limit on the number of boats an inefficient incentive still remains for each boat owner to build larger boats, to place extra equipment on them, and to spend more time fishing. These actions would expand the capacity of each boat and cause the actual catch to exceed the target (efficient) catch. In a nutshell, the boat quota limits the number of boats fishing but does not limit the amount of fish caught by each boat. If we are to reach and sustain an efficient allocation, the catch must ultimately be limited.

While the purpose of the second characteristic (setting the right catch quota) is obvious, the role of transferability deserves more consideration. With transferability, the entitlement to fish flows naturally to those gaining the most benefit from it because their costs are lower. Because it is valuable, the transferable quota commands a positive price. Those who have quotas but also have high costs find they make more money selling the quotas than using them. Meanwhile, those who have lower costs find they can purchase more quotas and still make money.

Transferable quotas also encourage technological progress. Adopters of new cost-reducing technologies can make more money on their existing quotas and make it profitable to purchase new quotas from others who have not adopted the technology. Therefore, in marked contrast to the earlier regulatory methods used to raise costs, both the tax system and the transferable quota system encourage the development of new technologies without threatening the sustainability of the fishery.

How about the distribution of the rent? In a quota system, the distribution of the rent depends crucially on how the quotas are initially allocated. There are many possibilities with different outcomes. The first possibility is for the government to auction off these quotas. With an auction, the government would appropriate all the rent and the outcome would be very similar to the outcome of the tax system. If the fishers do not like the tax system, they would not like the auction system either.

In an alternative approach, the government could give the quotas to the fishers, for example, in proportion to their historical catch. The fishers could then trade among themselves until a market equilibrium is reached. All the rent would be retained by the current generation of fishers. Fishers who might want to enter the market would have to purchase the quotas from existing fishers. Competition among the potential purchasers would drive up the price of the transferable quotas until it reflected the market value of future rents, appropriately discounted.[11] Rising prices raise concerns about equity if smaller fishers cannot afford to buy quotas or enter the market or quotas cause consolidation with most quotas going to large fleets.

Thus, this type of quota system allows the rent to remain with the fishers, but only the current generation of fishers. Future generations see little difference between this quota system and a tax system; in either case, they have to pay to enter the industry, whether it is through the tax system or by purchasing the quotas.

Worldwide, ITQs are used by 22 countries to manage hundreds of different species (Table 8.1). The annual global catch taken under ITQs may be as large as a quarter of the global harvest (Arnason, 2012). The fact that ITQ systems are spreading to new fisheries rapidly suggests that their potential is being increasingly recognized. This expansion does not mean the absence of any concerns. In 1997, the United States issued a moratorium on the implementation of new ITQ programs,

Table 8.2 Catch Shares in the United States by Fisheries Managements Region

New England	Mid-Atlantic
Atlantic Sea Scallops IFQ (2010)	• Surf Clam & Ocean Quahog ITQ (1990)
• New England Multispecies Sectors (2010)	• Golden Tilefish IFQ (2009)
• Atlantic Deep-Sea Red Crab (2021)	• Monkfish IFQ (2021)
• Atlantic Shark IFQ (2021)	• Atlantic Shark IFQ (2021)
South Atlantic	**Pacific**
Wreckfish ITQ (1991)	• Pacific Sablefish Permit Stacking IFQ (2001)
	• Pacific Coast Groundfish Trawl Rationalization IFQ (2011)
North Pacific	**Gulf of Mexico**
Halibut & Sablefish IFQ (1995)	• Red Snapper IFQ (2007)
• Western Alaska CDQ (1992)	• Grouper & Tilefish IFQ (2010)
• Bering Sea AFA Pollock Cooperative (1999)	• Atlantic Shark IFQ (2021)
• Bering Sea King & Tanner Crab IFQ (2005)	***Atlantic Highly Migratory Species***
• Aleutian Islands Pollock IFQ (2005)	• Individual Bluefin Tuna Quota (2015)
• Groundfish (non-Pollock) Cooperatives (2008)	
• Central Gulf of Alaska Rockfish Cooperative (2011)	
Caribbean	**Western Pacific**
Atlantic Shark IFQ (2021)	• No Catch Share Programs

Sources: https://www.federalregister.gov/documents/2021/11/12/2021-24721/atlantic-highly-migratory-species-2022-atlantic-shark-commercial-fishing-year; https://www.federalregister.gov/documents/2021/03/12/2021-05123/fisheries-of-the-northeastern-united-states-monkfish-fishery-2021-monkfish-specifications; https://www.federalregister.gov/documents/2021/03/26/2021-06287/fisheries-of-the-northeastern-united-states-atlantic-deep-sea-red-crab-fishery-final-2021-atlantic.

which expired in 2002. Issues about the duration of catch shares, whether shareholders need to be active in the fishery, and the distributional implications all remain contentious. As of 2021, there were 23 catch share programs in the United States (Table 8.2).

One of the most established ITQ programs is in New Zealand. In 1986, a limited ITQ system was established in New Zealand to protect its deep-water trawl fishery (Newell et al., 2005). Although this was far from being the only, or even the earliest, application of ITQs, it is the world's largest and provides an unusually rich opportunity to study how this approach works in practice. Some 130 species are fished commercially in New Zealand.[12] The Fisheries Amendment Act of 1986 that set up the program covered 17 inshore species and nine offshore species.

Because this program was newly developed, allocating the quotas proved relatively easy. The New Zealand Exclusive Economic Zone (EEZ) was divided geographically into quota-management regions. The total allowable catches (TACs) for the seven basic species were divided into individual transferable quotas by the quota-management regions. By 2000, 275 quota markets were in existence.

Quotas were initially allocated to existing firms based on their average historical catch. However, because fishing is characterized by economies of scale, simply reducing everyone's catch proportionately wouldn't make much sense. That would simply place higher costs on everyone and waste a great deal of fishing capacity as all boats sat around idle for a significant proportion of time. A better solution would clearly be to have fewer boats harvesting the stock. That way each boat could be used closer to its full capacity without depleting the population. Which fishers should be asked to give up their livelihood and leave the industry?

The economic incentive approach addressed this problem by having the government buy back catch quotas from those willing to sell them. Initially, this was financed out of general revenues; subsequently, it was financed by a fee on catch quotas. Essentially, each fisher stated the lowest price that they would accept for leaving the industry; the regulators selected those who could be induced to leave at the lowest price, paid the stipulated amount from the fee revenues, and retired their licenses to fish for this species. It wasn't long before a sufficient number of licenses had been retired and the population was protected. Because the program was voluntary, those who left the industry did so only when they felt they had been adequately compensated. Meanwhile, those who paid the fee realized that this small investment would benefit them greatly in the future as the population recovered. A difficult and potentially dangerous pressure on a valuable natural resource had been alleviated by the creative use of an approach that changed the economic incentives.

Toward the end of 1987, however, a new problem emerged. The stock of one species (orange roughy) turned out to have been seriously overestimated by biologists. Since the total allocation of quotas was derived from this estimate, the practical implication was that an unsustainably high level of quotas had been issued; the stock was in jeopardy. The New Zealand government began buying some quotas back from fishers, but this turned out to be quite expensive with NZ$45 million spent on 15,000 tons of quotas from inshore fisheries.

Faced with the unacceptably large budget implications of buying back a significant amount of quotas, the government ultimately shifted to a percentage-share allocation of quotas. Under this system, instead of owning quotas defined in terms of a specific quantity of fish, fishers own percentage shares of a total allowable catch. The total allowable catch was determined annually by the government. In this way the government could annually adjust the total allowable catch, based on the latest stock assessment estimates, without having to buy back (or sell) large amounts of quota. This approach affords greater protection to the stock but increases the financial risk to the fishers. By 2004, New Zealand's ITQ program had expanded to cover 70 species. Newell et al. (2005) found that the export value of these species ranged from NZ$700/metric ton for jack mackerel to NZ$40,000/metric ton for rock lobster. They also found that by 2000, some 70 percent of quota holders engaged in transactions in the ITQ market.

Despite this activity, some implementation problems have emerged. Fishing effort is frequently not very well targeted. Species other than those sought (known as "bycatch") may well end up as part of the catch. If those species are also regulated by quotas and the fishers do not have sufficient ITQs to cover the bycatch, they are faced with the possibility of being fined when they land the unauthorized fish. Dumping the bycatch overboard avoids the fines, but the jettisoned fish frequently do not survive. Dumping the bycatch represents a double waste—not only is the stock reduced, but also the harvested fish are wasted.

Managers have also had to deal with "high-grading," which can occur when quotas specify the catch in terms of weight of a certain species, but the value of the catch is affected greatly by the size of the individual fish. To maximize the value of the quota, fishers have an incentive to throw back the less valuable (typically smaller) fish, keeping only the most valuable individuals. As with bycatch, when release mortality is high, high-grading results in both smaller stocks and wasted harvests.

Although ITQ systems are far from perfect, frequently they offer the opportunity to improve on traditional fisheries management (see Example 8.2). In its 2012 annual report to Congress, the NOAA reported that 32 stocks have been rebuilt. Some 41 stocks (19 percent) are still overfished, but that is down from 45 just a year earlier.

Costello, Gaines, and Lynham (2008) examined the global effectiveness of these policies in over 11,000 fisheries from 1950 to 2003. Fisheries with catch share rules, including ITQs, experienced much less frequent collapse than fisheries without them. In fact, they found that by 2003 the fraction of fisheries with ITQs that had collapsed was only half that of non-ITQ fisheries. They suggest that this might be an underestimate since many fisheries with ITQs have not had them for very long. This large study suggests that well-designed property rights regimes (catch shares or ITQs more specifically) may help prevent fisheries collapse and/or help stocks of some species recover. Chu (2009) examined 20 stocks after ITQ programs were implemented and found that 12 of those had improvements in stock size. Eight, however, continued to decline. Apparently, ITQs can sometimes help, but they are no panacea. Recall in Chapter 5 we considered whether ITQs can help to conserve different marine species such as whales.

Catch Share Programs in the United States. In the United States, the Magnuson–Stevens Act authorizes several types of catch share approaches under its "limited access

EXAMPLE 8.2

The Relative Effectiveness of Transferable Quotas and Traditional Size and Effort Restrictions in the Atlantic Sea Scallop Fishery

Theory suggests that individual transferable quotas will produce more cost-effective outcomes in fisheries than traditional restrictions, such as minimum legal size and maximum effort controls. Is this theoretical expectation compatible with the actual experience in implemented systems?

In a fascinating study, economist Robert Repetto (2001) examined this question by comparing Canadian and American approaches to controlling the sea scallop fishery off the Atlantic coast. While Canada adopted a transferable quota system, the United States adopted a mix of size, effort, and area controls. The comparison provides a rare opportunity to exploit a natural experiment since scallops are not migratory and the two countries use similar fishing technologies. Hence, it is reasonable to presume that the differences in experience are largely due to the difference in management approaches.

What were the biological consequences of these management strategies for the two fisheries?

- The Canadian fishery was not only able to maintain the stock at a higher level of abundance, but it was also able to deter the harvesting of undersized scallops.
- In the United States, stock abundance levels declined and undersized scallops were harvested at high levels.

What were the economic consequences of these differences?

- Revenue per sea-day increased significantly in the Canadian fishery, due largely to the sevenfold increase in catch per sea-day made possible by the larger stock abundance.
- In the United States, fishery revenue per sea-day fell, due not only to the fall in the catch per day that resulted from the decline in stock abundance, but also to the harvesting of undersized scallops.
- Although the number of Canadian quota holders was reduced from nine to seven over a 14-year period, 65 percent of the quota remained in its original hands. The evidence suggests that smaller players were apparently not at a competitive disadvantage.

What were the equity implications?

- Both U.S. and Canadian fisheries have traditionally operated on the "lay" system, which divides the revenue among crew, captain, and owner according to preset percentages, after subtracting certain operating expenditures. This means that all parties remaining in the fishery after regulation shared in the increasing rents.

In these fisheries at least, it seems that the expectations flowing from the theory were borne out by the experience.

Source: Repetto, R. (2001). A natural experiment in fisheries management. *Marine Policy, 25*, 252–264.

privilege" program. In the United States there are 23 active or planned catch share programs (Table 8.2). Most of these are individual fishing quotas (IFQs), but more recently cooperatives and community development quotas (CDCs) have emerged.

European Common Fisheries Policy. The Common Fisheries Policy is the fisheries policy of the European Union. It sets total allowable catch (TAC) for member states. Each country receives a national quota based on a percentage of the TAC. For each stock, different allocation percentages per country are applied. E.U. member countries can trade these quotas with other E.U. countries. Each member state is then responsible for enforcing its quota.[13] The 2015 TACs covered 36 species.[14]

Territorial Use Rights Fisheries (TURFs). An alternative to ITQs is to allocate rights to a specific area for a specific species or group of species, rather than to a portion of the total allowable catch. Such geographic-based rights systems are called territorial use rights fisheries or TURFs. Like ITQs, TURFs typically grant access rights, not ownership rights, to harvesters.

TURFs could allow access to a layer of the water column (such as the bottom of the ocean or the surface) in a specific zone. They could also allow access to a specific oyster bed or a raft for mollusks. They could be granted to individuals, communities, corporations, or even to nations. An economic exclusion zone (EEZ) is a TURF granted to an individual nation.

Early examples of operating TURFs can be found in Japan. These now well-established TURFs allocate zones to local fisher organizations called Fishery Cooperative Associations (FCAs). Approximately 1300 FCAs now operate in Japan (Wilen et al., 2012). They can also be found in Chile. With its 3000-mile shoreline, Chile has created management and exploitation areas (MEAs) along its nearshore. These TURFs help manage the economically important Chilean abalone and sea urchin (Wilen et al., 2012). Other examples of TURFs can be found in Bangladesh, Fiji, Grenada, India, Papua New Guinea, Philippines, Solomon Islands, Turkey, and Vietnam (Jardine & Sanchirico, 2012).

TURFs can allow for more economically efficient use of the fishery resource by creating a form of property right, albeit a different property right from that conveyed by an ITQ. Despite their differences, both types of property rights create incentives to protect the future value of the resource, which in turn can incentivize self-enforcement mechanisms. They also can improve the welfare of small fishing communities.

While TURFs do help reduce the open-access problem, the value of a TURF is complicated by the fact that fish are mobile and therefore do not stay in one location. Since a TURF is site-specific, its value is impacted by capture outside of the TURF. Obviously, for stocks that do not migrate far, the value of a TURF is enhanced.

Some researchers have suggested that some combination of TURF and ITQ policies may be most efficient. Debate 8.1 considers this question.

DEBATE 8.1

ITQs or TURFs? Species, Space, or Both?

ITQs and TURFs can improve economic efficiency and help protect fisheries from overexploitation. Is one management method better than another? Can they be usefully combined?

Species-based ITQs have proven very popular and they can, in theory, create efficient harvesting and conservation incentives. However, in practice enforcement can be challenging and they suffer from several externalities. Some of the most prominent externalities, including gear impacts on ecosystems, spatial externalities, and cross-species interactions, might actually be increased by ITQs. Let's see how.

Typically, the total allowable catch (TAC) is divided amongst several, perhaps numerous, owners. Although they do not compete over the size of their catch (since that is fixed by their catch share), they do still compete over the timing of that catch. Timing might matter a great deal when the most productive harvesting periods (in terms of reducing the private effort required per unit of catch) turn out to be precisely the periods that impose the largest external costs (say by increasing the likelihood of bycatch or negatively impacting the juvenile stock). As such, they help solve one problem (assuring a sustainable total catch), while creating another (encouraging a harvest timing that increases external costs).

The Coase theorem suggests that these ownership rights should, in principle, create incentives to solve the remaining externalities as well, but in practice, the transaction costs of such negotiations are apparently prohibitively high.

What about TURFs? TURFs help solve the problem of managing harvests over time and space and can help protect sensitive areas, given that an individual or group has sole rights to that area. Local cooperatives have the advantage of being able in principle to manage interspecies interactions and habitat destruction, but in practice TURFs tend to suffer from conflict and coordination problems. Another common criticism of TURFs is that the scale must match the range of the species and many TURFs do not (or cannot) achieve this size.

Rather than framing the issue as whether ITQs or TURFs are the best choice, it may be that each has its own niche. Certainly, in developing countries with weak institutional structures, TURFs offer many advantages over species-based ITQs. TURFs also may be most appropriate for small, local populations. On the other hand, ITQs have been used successfully for many marine fisheries.

Clearly, one size does not fit all for fisheries policy.

Source: Wilen, J. E., Cancino, J., & Uchida, H. (Summer 2012). The economics of territorial use rights fisheries, or TURFs. *Review of Environmental Economics and Policy, 6*(2), 237–257.

Aquaculture

Having demonstrated that inefficient management of the fishery results from treating it as an open-access resource, one obvious solution is to allow some fisheries to be privately held. This approach can work when the fish are not very mobile, when they can be confined by artificial barriers, or when they instinctively return to their place of birth to spawn.

The advantages of such a move go well beyond the ability to preclude overfishing. The owner is encouraged to invest in the resource and undertake measures that will increase the productivity (yield) of the fishery. (For example, adding certain nutrients to the water or controlling the temperature can markedly increase the yields of some species.) The controlled raising and harvesting of fish is called *aquaculture*. Probably the highest yields ever attained through aquaculture have resulted from using rafts to raise mussels. Some 300,000 kilograms per hectare of mussels, for example, have been raised in this manner in the Galician bays of Spain. This productivity level approximates those achieved in poultry farming, widely regarded as one of the most successful attempts to increase the productivity of farm-produced animal protein.

Japan became an early leader in aquaculture, undertaking some of the most advanced aquaculture ventures in the world. The government has been supportive of these efforts, mainly by creating private property rights for waters formerly held in common. The governments of the prefectures (which are comparable to states in the United States) initiate the process by designating the areas to be used for aquaculture. The local fishers' cooperative associations then partition these areas and allocate the subareas to individual fishers for exclusive use. This exclusive control allows the individual owner to invest in the resource and to manage it effectively and efficiently.

Another market approach to aquaculture involves *fish ranching* rather than *fish farming*. Whereas fish farming involves cultivating fish over their lifetime in a controlled environment, fish ranching involves holding them in captivity only for the first few years of their lives.

Fish ranching relies on the strong homing instincts in certain fish, such as Pacific salmon or ocean trout, which permit their ultimate return and capture. The young salmon or ocean trout are hatched and confined in a convenient catch area for approximately 2 years. When released, they migrate to the ocean. Upon reaching maturity, they instinctually return to the place of their births, where they are harvested.

Fish farming has certainly affected the total supply of harvested fish. Aquaculture is currently the fastest-growing animal food production sector. In China, aquaculture now represents more than two-thirds of fisheries production. China is the largest producer (and exporter) of seafood, producing 62 percent of the global supply of farmed fish, representing almost 20 percent of global marine capture. Shrimp, eel, tilapia, sea bass, and carp are all intensively farmed. Aquaculture is certainly not the answer for all fish. Today, it works well for certain species, but other species will probably never be harvested domestically. Furthermore, fish farming can create intensive environmental problems. Salmon farming and shrimp farming, especially, create negative externalities, as do fish farmed in contaminated water (see Debate 8.2). Nonetheless, it is comforting to know that aquaculture can provide a safety valve in some regions and for some fish and in the process take some of the pressure off the overstressed natural fisheries. The challenge will be to keep aquaculture sustainable.

Subsidies and Buybacks

Excess fleet capacity or overcapitalization is prevalent in many commercial fisheries. Overcapacity encourages overfishing. Many subsidies exacerbate this effect by encouraging overcapacity and overcapitalization. Fuel subsidies, tax exemptions, fish price supports, and grants for new vessels are common forms of subsidies in fisheries. By enhancing profits, these subsidies create perverse incentives to continue fishing even while stocks are declining.

A rather different type of subsidy is intended to discourage overfishing. If vessel owners do not have alternative uses for their vessels, they may resist catch restrictions or other measures meant to help depleted stocks. Management options have included buybacks or, equivalently, decommissioning subsidies to reduce fishing capacity.

DEBATE 8.2

Aquaculture: Does Privatization Cause More Problems Than It Solves?

Privatization of commercial fisheries, namely through fish farming, has been touted as a solution to the overfishing problem. For certain species, it has been a great success. Some types of shellfish, for example, are easily managed and farmed through commercial aquaculture. For other species, however, the likelihood of success is not so clear-cut.

Atlantic salmon is a struggling species in the northeastern United States and, for several rivers, is listed as "endangered." Salmon farming takes the pressure off of the wild stocks. Atlantic salmon are intensively farmed off the coast of Maine, in northeastern Canada, in Norway, and in Chile. Farmed Atlantic salmon make up almost all of the farmed salmon market and more than half of the total global salmon market. While farmed salmon offer a good alternative to wild salmon and aquaculture has helped meet the demand for salmon from consumers, it is not problem free.

Farmed fish escapees from the pens threaten native species, pollution that leaks from the pens creates a large externality, and pens that are visible from the coastline degrade the view of coastal residents. The crowded pens also facilitate the prevalence and diffusion of several diseases and illnesses, such as sea lice and salmon anemia. Antibiotics used to keep the fish healthy are considered dangerous for humans. Diseases in the pens can also be transferred to wild stocks. In 2007, the Atlantic Salmon Federation and 33 other conservation groups called on salmon farms to move their pens farther away from sensitive wild stocks.

And the concerns do not end there. Currently, many small species of fish, like anchovies or herring, are being harvested to feed carnivorous farmed fish. Scientists argue that this is not an efficient way to produce protein, since it takes 3–5 pounds of smaller fish to produce 1 pound of farmed salmon.

Pollution externalities associated with the increased production include contaminated water supplies for the fishponds and heavily polluted wastewater. Some farmers raising their fish in contaminated water have managed by adding illegal veterinary drugs and pesticides to the fish feed, creating food safety concerns. Some tested fish flesh has been found to contain heavy metals, including mercury, and flame retardants.

While solving some problems, intensive aquaculture has created others. Potential solutions include open-ocean aquaculture (moving pens out to sea), closing pens, monitoring water quality, and improving enforcement. Clearly, sole ownership of the fishery isn't a silver bullet when externalities are prevalent.

Is shrimp farming any better? Over half of the shrimp consumed worldwide are farmed, mostly in Asia and Central America, while the markets are mostly in the United States and China. Developing countries that farm shrimp have cut down valuable mangroves in order to create fish farms. These mangroves provide storm protection and important coastal habitat. Things are changing, however. Some shrimp farms are experimenting with inland ponds that treat their own waste. They are also exploring using vegetable protein as a food source. The challenge will be scale. Can new technology be expanded to meet the demand?

Sources: Atlantic Salmon Federation. www.asf.ca/main.html; Barboza, D. (December 15, 2007). China's seafood industry: Dirty water, dangerous fish. *New York Times*; Urry, A. (2014). Grist. http://grist.org/food/is-there-a-sustainable-future-for-americas-most-popular-seafood.

In 2004, the U.S. government spent $100 million to buy out 28 of the 260 Alaskan snow crab fishery vessels. Payments used to buy out excess fishing capacity are useful subsidies in that they reduce overcapacity, but if additional capacity seeps in over time, they are not as effective as other management measures. If fishers come to anticipate a buyback, they may acquire more vessels than they otherwise would have, which would lead to even greater levels of overcapacity.

Exclusive Economic Zones—The 200-Mile Limit

The final policy dimension concerns the international aspects of the fishery problem. Obviously, the various policy approaches to effective management of fisheries require some governing body to have jurisdiction over a fishery so that it can enforce its regulations.

Currently, this is not the case for many of the ocean fisheries. Much of the open water of the oceans is a common-pool resource to governments as well as to individual fishers. No single body can exercise control over it. As long as that continues to be the case, the corrective action will be difficult to implement. In recognition of this fact, there is now an evolving law of the sea defined by international treaties. One of the concrete results of this law, for example, has been some limited restrictions on whaling. Whether this process ultimately yields a consistent and comprehensive system of management remains to be seen, but it is certainly an uphill battle.

The United Nations Convention on the Law of the Sea grants countries bordering the sea ownership rights that extend some 200 miles out to sea. Within these exclusive economic zones (EEZs), the countries have exclusive jurisdiction and can implement effective management policies. These zones are essentially very large TURFs. These "exclusive zone" declarations have been upheld and are now firmly entrenched in international law. Thus, very rich fisheries in coastal waters can be protected, while those in the open waters await the outcome of an international negotiations process. The European Union has the largest EEZ in the world.

Unfortunately, EEZs do not sufficiently protect highly migratory fish stocks such as tunas and sharks, and as such, 58 percent of the ocean (the high seas) is overexploited and overfished for many species (White & Costello, 2014).

Marine Protected Areas and Marine Reserves

Regulating only the amount of catch leaves the type of gear that is used and locations where the harvests take place uncontrolled. Failure to control those elements can lead to environmental degradation of the habitat on which the fishery depends, even if catch is successfully regulated. Some gear may be particularly damaging, not only to the targeted species (e.g., by capturing juveniles that cannot be sold but that don't survive capture), but also to nontargeted species (bycatch). Similarly, harvesting in some geographic areas (such as those used for spawning) might have a disproportionately large detrimental effect on the sustainability of the fishery.

Conservation biologists have suggested complementing current policies with the establishment of a system of marine protected areas (MPAs). The U.S. federal government defines MPAs as "any area of the marine environment that has been reserved by federal, state, tribal, territorial, or local laws or regulations to provide lasting protection for part or all of the natural and cultural resources therein."[15] Restrictions range from minimal to full protection. A marine reserve, a marine protected area with full protection, is an area that prohibits harvesting and enjoys a very high level of protection from other threats, such as pollution.

Biologists believe that marine protected areas can perform several maintenance and restorative functions. First, they protect *individual species* by preventing harvest within the reserve boundaries. Second, they reduce *habitat damage* caused by fishing gear or practices that alter biological structures. Third, in contrast to quotas on single species, reserves can promote *ecosystem balance* by protecting against the removal of ecologically pivotal species (whether targeted species or bycatch) that could throw an ecosystem out of balance by altering its diversity and productivity (Palumbi, 2002).

Reducing harvesting in these areas protects the stock, the habitat, and the ecosystem on which it depends. This protection results in a larger population and, ultimately, if the species swim beyond the boundaries of the reserve, larger catches in the remaining harvest areas. Medoff et al. (2022) find evidence of such "spillover benefits" in the largest MPA in the world, the Papahānaumokuākea Marine National Monument. Using a natural experiment in which they can analyze catch rates from individual vessels before and after the 2016 expansion of this MPA, they find evidence of spillover benefits to both yellowfin and bigeye tuna.

Simply put, reserves promote sustainability by allowing populations to recover. Their relationship to the welfare of current users, however, is less clear. Proponents of MPAs suggest that they can promote sustainability in a win–win fashion (meaning current users benefit as well). This is an important point because users who did not benefit might mount political opposition to marine reserve proposals, thereby making their establishment very difficult.

Would the establishment of a marine protected area maximize the present value of net benefits for fishers? If MPAs work as planned, they reduce harvest in the short run (by declaring areas previously available for harvest off-limits), but they increase it in the long run (as the population recovers and spills over the boundaries of the protected areas). However, the delay would impose costs. (Remember how discounting affects present value?) To take one concrete example of the costs of delay to harvesters, they may have to pay off a mortgage on their boat. Even if the bank grants them a delay in making payments, total payments will rise due to interest. So, by itself, a future rise in harvests does not guarantee that establishing the reserve maximizes present value unless the rise in catch is large enough and soon enough to compensate for the costs imposed by the delay.[16]

Does this mean that MPAs or marine reserves are a bad idea? Certainly not! In some areas, they may be a necessary step for achieving sustainability; in others, they may represent the most efficient means of achieving sustainability. It does mean, however, that we should be wary of the notion that they always create win–win situations; sacrifices by local harvesters might be required. MPA policies must recognize the possibility of this burden and deal with it directly, not just assume it doesn't exist.

Some international action on marine reserves is taking place as well. The 1992 international treaty called the Convention on Biological Diversity lists as one of its goals the conservation of at least 10 percent of the world's ecological regions, including, but not limited to, marine ecoregions. Progress has been significant for terrestrial ecoregions, but less so for coastal and marine ecoregions.

One creative proposal to incentivize the creation of new MPAs as well as incentivize sustainable fishing practices is to link eco-labeling to adjacent MPAs. Lester et al. (2013) propose building on recent surges in demand for green products and sustainable fisheries eco-labeling such as the Marine Stewardship Council's (MSC) label and the Monterey Aquarium Seafood Watch Program. They explore providing credit for adjacent MPAs in seafood certification and labeling. The impact of MPAs on fish stocks is clear and could be used to provide "sustainability credits." They argue that making this link more explicit in labeling could help protect fish stocks.

Enforcement—Illegal, Unreported, and Unregulated Fish Stocks

Illegal, unreported, and unregulated (IUU) fishing is a growing global problem. Approximately 90 percent of the seafood consumed in the United States is imported, either caught by foreign fishing vessels or sent abroad for processing and then reimported. Half of this is wild-caught seafood. It has been estimated that 20–32 percent of wild-caught seafood imports into the United States are from IUU sources (Pramod et al., 2014; World Economic Forum, 2022). The global market is complex and large and when seafood changes hands multiple times, it seems likely that even perceived legal imports contain IUU catch. Some regulations are difficult to enforce, such as the High Seas Driftnet Moratorium Protection Act, which specifies that commerce in products caught with driftnets is illegal. Monitoring, control, and surveillance are prohibitively expensive in many cases.

Another illegal activity is "high-grading," which can occur when fishers have already met their quota, but then catch larger, more valuable fish and discard the low-valued fish overboard. Often, quotas specify the catch in terms of weight of a certain species, but the value of the catch is affected greatly by the size of the individual fish. One possible strategy is simply banning discarding, but due to the difficulties of monitoring and enforcement, that is not as straightforward a solution as it may seem. Kristofersson and Rickertsen (2009) examine whether a ban on discarding has been effective in the Icelandic cod fishery. They use a model of a fishery with an ITQ program and apply it to the Icelandic cod fishery. They estimate that longline vessels would discard up to 25 percent of the catch of small cod and gillnet vessels up to 67 percent. Their analysis found that quota price did not seem to be an influencing factor, but the existence of a system of quotas and the size of the hold in which the harvested fish are kept do matter. They suggest that to get the "most bang for the buck," enforcement efforts should be directed at gillnet vessels and on fisheries with small hold capacities.

Some fisheries managers have successfully solved both problems by allowing fishers to cover temporary overages with allowances subsequently purchased or leased from others. As long as the market value of the "extra" fish exceeds the cost of leasing quotas, the fishers will have an incentive to land and market the fish and the stock will not be placed in jeopardy. The 2022 WTO agreement banning harmful subsidies for IUU fishing should also help reduce the size of the problem.

Clearly, high-grading and other discards are still a significant problem. Zeller et al. (2017) estimate discards at 10–20 percent of global catch. Some of this is high-grading, while other discards are from catch that is diseased or isn't the target species.

Poaching (illegal harvesting) can introduce the possibility of unsustainability even when a legal structure to protect the population has been enacted. For example, in 1986 the International Whaling Commission set a ban on commercial whaling, but under a loophole in this law, Japan continued to kill hundreds of whales each year. In November 2007, a fleet embarked on a 5-month hunt in the Antarctic despite numerous international protests. While originally intending to target humpback whales, in response to the protests Japan eventually stopped harvesting that species. Since humpback whales are considered "vulnerable," commercial hunts have been banned since 1966, but Japan had claimed that harvests for research were not covered by this ban.

Bluefin tuna is another very valuable commercial species that has been brought under international control. Its recovery has been remarkable. The population of bluefin tuna started to decline in the mid-1970s. By the 1990s, the market for bluefin tuna had grown so fast that catches of 50,000 metric tons or more were being recorded. A 2006 stock assessment showed a substantial decline in biomass. The species was at risk of complete collapse. Quotas were reduced, but much of the decline was due to overfishing and illegal harvesting (harvesting more than the quota allotment). Japan is the largest consumer of bluefin tuna, which is prized for sushi. Fleets from Spain, Italy, and France are the primary suppliers.

In the United States, the National Marine Fisheries Service manages the Atlantic Highly Migratory Species regulations, which include a catch share program for the U.S. portion of the International Commission for the Conservation of Atlantic Tunas (ICCAT) quota of endangered bluefin tuna. The rules also include individual bluefin quotas (IBQs) and a closure of the pelagic longline fishery when the annual quota is reached.[17] They also require vessels to account for incidental bluefin tuna landings and dead discards using individual bluefin quota allocation.

A rather different approach to protect the species was tried in the international forum. In 2009, a petition to ban trade in the Atlantic bluefin tuna went before the U.N. Convention on International Trade in Endangered Species (CITES). This was the first time that a major commercial fishery has been addressed by CITES. While conservationists and biologists supported the CITES listing, many industry groups were opposed. The National Fisheries Institute president, John Connelly, wrote in opposition:

> Commercially-exploited aquatic species are fundamentally different from the other species that CITES regulates. … Unlike these other species, fish and

seafood stocks are not generally threatened with biological extinction. While they can and do become overfished, the resulting loss of return on investment for fishers prevents them from driving commercial fish stocks toward biological extinction.

(Gronewold, 2009)

In early 2010, CITES voted against the ban. In January 2011, a record price was set for a northern bluefin. A giant, 754-pound bluefin brought 32.5 million yen, or nearly $400,000. Do you think this price is a sufficient incentive to protect the bluefin tuna from extinction? Why or why not? See Debate 8.3.

DEBATE 8.3

Bluefin Tuna: Difficulties in Enforcing Quotas for High-Value Species

The International Commission for the Conservation of Atlantic Tunas (ICCAT) is responsible for the conservation of highly migratory species, including several species of tuna. ICCAT reports fish biomass as well as catch statistics and is responsible for setting total allowable catch by species each year.

Since ICCAT has never successfully enforced its quotas, it is not clear that it has a credible enforcement capability. Monitoring statistics consistently show catch well above the TAC.

Additionally, international pressure from the fishing industry frequently results in a TAC higher than scientists recommend. In 2009, for example, having reviewed the current biomass statistics, which showed the current stock to be at less than 15 percent of its original stock, ICCAT scientists recommended a total suspension of fishing. Ignoring their scientists' recommendation, ICCAT proceeded to set a quota of 13,500 tons. It did, however, also agree to establish new management measures for future years that would allow the stock to rebuild with an estimated 60 percent degree of confidence. While that sounds good, it turns out that if enforcement is less than perfect, and the resulting catch is above 13,500 tons, the probability that the stock would recover could not reach the 60 percent level by 2022. At the time, estimated illegal catches were 60,000 tonnes! This extraordinary amount of IUU (illegal, unreported, and unregulated) fishing for bluefin tuna was a large part of the problem. High prices were incentivizing illegal catches.

In 2011, the quota hit its lowest level, 12,900 metric tons; this quota was combined with stricter enforcement and bans on fishing for Atlantic tuna below spawning age. Locating schools of fish by aircraft was also banned. There was also a restriction on purse seine fleets to one month and added rules on bycatch and monitoring. These measures combined with a few years of warmer waters (leading to better survival rates of eggs and larvae) led to a surprisingly quick recovery of the fish stock!

The Atlantic bluefin story has gone from one of tragedy (of the commons) to a well-managed fishery. Time will tell if it remains so.

Sources: International Commission for the Conservation of Atlantic Tunas 2009 annual ICCAT meeting press release (November 16, 2009); ICCAT, www. iccat.org; Gronewold, G. (October 14, 2009). Is the bluefin tuna an endangered species? *Scientific American*. www.scientificamerican.com/article. cfm?id=bluefin-tuna-stocks-threatened-cites-japan-monaco; Draft amendment 7 to the Consolidated Atlantic Highly Migratory Species Fishery Management Plan, *National Marine Fisheries Service*. (August 2013). www. scribd.com/doc/161801821/NOAA-Draft-Bluefin-Tuna-Amendment; Porch, C. E., Bonhommeau, S., Diaz, G. A., Arrizabalaga, H., & Melvin, G. (2019). The journey from overfishing to sustainability for Atlantic Bluefin Tuna, Thunnus thynnus. The future of bluefin tunas. *Ecology, Fisheries Management, and Conservation*, 3.

Summary

Unrestricted access to commercially valuable species will generally result in overexploitation. This overexploitation, in turn, results in overcapitalization, depressed incomes for harvesters, and depleted stocks. Even extinction of the species is possible, particularly for populations characterized by easy, low-cost extraction. Where extraction costs are higher, extinction is unlikely, even with unrestricted access.

Both the private and public sectors have moved to ameliorate the problems associated with past mismanagement of commercial fisheries. By reasserting private property rights, many countries have stimulated the development of aquaculture. Governments in Canada and the United States have moved to limit overexploitation of the Pacific salmon. International agreements have been instituted to place limits on whaling. It is doubtful that these programs fully satisfy the efficiency criterion, although it does seem clear that more sustainable catches will result.

Using data from 4713 fisheries worldwide, representing 78 percent of global reported fish catch, Costello et al. (2016) estimate the global maximum sustained yield to be 98 million metric tons (not including illegal fishing). They forecast that business-as-usual fisheries management will result in the continued collapse of many of the world's fisheries. They suggest that commonsense reforms could increase both fish abundance (and hence food security) and profits.

Creative strategies for sharing the gains from moving to an efficient level of harvest could prove to be a significant weapon in the arsenal of techniques designed to protect a broad class of biological resources from overexploitation. An increasing reliance on individual transferable quotas (ITQs) and TURFs offers the possibility of preserving stocks without jeopardizing the incomes of those men and women currently harvesting those stocks. Strengthening property rights is a key component in generating both efficient and sustainable harvests. Approximately 20 percent of developing countries have implemented space-based (mostly in Asia and Pacific regions) or quota-based (mostly found in African nations) allocation systems.

It would be folly to ignore barriers to further action, such as the reluctance of individual harvesters to submit to many forms of regulation, the lack of a firm policy governing open-ocean waters, and the difficulties of enforcing various approaches. Whether these barriers will fall before the pressing need for effective management remains to be seen. Climate change is already affecting the marine environment, so looming challenges remain.

In this chapter we have focused on fisheries as an example of a renewable biological resource, but the models and the insights that flow from them can be used to think about managing other wildlife populations as well.

Discussion Questions

1. Is the establishment of the 200-mile limit a sufficient form of government intervention to ensure that the tragedy of the commons does not occur for fisheries within the 200-mile limit? Why or why not?
2. With discounting it is possible for the efficient fish population to fall below the level required to produce the maximum sustained yield. Does this violate the sustainability criterion? Why or why not?

Self-Test Exercises

1. Assume that the relationship between the growth of a fish population and the population size can be expressed as $g = 4P - 0.1P^2$, where g is the growth in tons and P is the size of the population (in thousands of tons). Given a price of $100 a ton, the marginal benefit of smaller population sizes (and hence larger catches) can be computed as $20P - 400$.
   a. Compute the population size that is compatible with the maximum sustainable yield. What would be the size of the annual catch if the population were to be sustained at this level?
   b. If the marginal cost of additional catches (expressed in terms of the population size) is $MC = 2(160 - P)$, what is the population size that is compatible with the efficient sustainable yield?
2. Assume that a local fisheries council imposes an enforceable quota of 100 tons of fish on a particular fishing ground for one year. Assume further that 100 tons per year is the efficient sustained yield. When 100 tons have been caught, the fishery would be closed for the remainder of the year.
   a. Is this an efficient solution to the common-property problem? Why or why not?
   b. Would your answer be different if the 100-ton quota were divided into 100 transferable quotas, each entitling the holder to catch 1 ton of fish, and distributed among the fishers in proportion to their historical catch? Why or why not?
3. In the economic model of the fishery developed in this chapter, compare the effect on fishing effort of an increase in cost of a fishing license with an increase in a per-unit tax on fishing effort that raises the same amount of revenue. Assume the fishery is private property. Repeat the analysis assuming that the fishery is a free-access common-property resource.
4. When trying to reduce the degree of inefficiency from an open-access fishery, would a regulation that increases the marginal cost of fishing effort by banning certain types of gear or a tax on effort be equally efficient? Why or why not?

   a.   In the typical economic model of an efficient fishery, would a fall in the price of fish generally result in a larger or a smaller sustainable harvest? Why?

   b.   Suppose the fishery allowed free access. Would a fall in the price of fish generally result in a larger or a smaller harvest? Why?

5. Suppose that a particular fishery experiences a technological change such that the fixed cost of fishing increases, but the marginal cost of fishing decreases. The change is such that the before and after total cost curves cross at an effort level higher than that associated with the before efficient sustained yield, but lower than the free-access level of effort.

   a.   What would the effect of this technological change be on the static efficient level of effort and the size of the static efficient level of harvest? Would they increase or decrease or are the effects ambiguous?

   b.   What would the effect of this technological change be on the level of effort and the size of the harvest in a free-access fishery? Would they increase or decrease or are the effects ambiguous?

Appendix: The Harvesting Decision: Fisheries

Defining the efficient sustainable yield for a fishery begins with a characterization of the biological relationship between the growth of the biomass and the size of the biomass. The standard representation of this relationship is

$$g = rS\left(1 - \frac{S}{k}\right), \tag{A.1}$$

where

      g = the growth rate of the biomass,
      r = the intrinsic growth rate for this species,
      S = the size of the biomass, and
      k = the carrying capacity of the habitat.

Since we want to choose the most efficient *sustained* yield, we must limit the possible outcomes we shall consider to those that are sustainable. Here we define a sustainable harvest level, h_s, as one that equals the growth of the population. Hence:

$$h_s = rS\left(1 - \frac{S}{k}\right). \tag{A.2}$$

    The next step is to define the size of the harvest as a function of the amount of effort expended. This is traditionally modeled as

$$h = qES, \tag{A.3}$$

where

      q = a constant (known as the "catchability coefficient"), and
      E = the level of effort.

The next step is to solve for sustained yields as a function of effort. This can be derived using a two-step procedure. First, we express S in terms of E. Then we use this newly derived expression for S along with the relationship in Equation (A.3) to derive the sustained yield expressed in terms of effort.

To define S in terms of E, we can substitute Equation (A.3) into Equation (A.2):

$$qES = rS\left(1 - \frac{S}{k}\right). \tag{A.4}$$

Rearranging terms yields

$$S = k\left(1 - \frac{qE}{r}\right). \tag{A.5}$$

Using $S = h/qE$ from Equation (A.3) and rearranging terms to solve for h yields

$$h_s = qEk - \frac{q^2 kE^2}{r}. \tag{A.6}$$

It is now possible to find the maximum sustainable effort level by taking the derivative of the right-hand side of Equation (A.6) with respect to effort (E) and setting the result equal to zero.

The maximum condition is

$$qk - 2\frac{q^2 kE}{r} = 0. \tag{A.7}$$

So

$$E_{msy} = \frac{r}{2q}, \tag{A.8}$$

where

E_{msy} = the level of effort that is consistent with the maximum sustained yield.

Can you see how to solve for the maximum sustainable yield, h_{msy}? (*Hint*: remember how the maximum sustained yield was defined in terms of effort in Equation (A.6)?)

To conduct the economic analysis, we need to convert this biological information to a net benefits formulation. The benefit function can be defined by multiplying Equation (A.6) by P, the price received for a unit of harvest. Assuming a constant marginal cost of effort, a, allows us to define total cost as equal to aE. Subtracting the total cost of effort from the revenue function produces the net benefits function:

$$\text{Net benefits} = PqEk - \frac{Pq^2 kE^2}{r} - aE. \tag{A.9}$$

Since the efficient sustained effort level is the level that maximizes Equation (A.9), we can derive it by taking the derivative of Equation (A.9) with respect to effort (E) and setting the derivative equal to zero:

$$Pqk - \frac{2Pkq^2 E}{r} - a = 0. \tag{A.10}$$

Rearranging terms yields

$$E = \frac{r}{2q}\left(1 - \frac{a}{Pqk}\right).$$

(A.11)

Note that this effort level is smaller than that needed to produce the maximum sustainable yield. Can you see how to find the efficient sustainable harvest level? Finally, we can derive the free-access equilibrium by setting the net benefits function in Equation (A.9) equal to zero and solving for the effort level.

Rearranging terms yields

$$E = \frac{r}{q}\left(1 - \frac{a}{Pqk}\right).$$

(A.12)

Note that this is larger than the efficient sustained level of effort. It may or may not be larger than the level of effort needed to produce the maximum sustained yield. That comparison depends on the specific values of the parameters.

Notes

1 https://www.fao.org/state-of-fisheries-aquaculture.
2 Hardin, Garrett. (1968). The tragedy of the commons. *Science*, *162*, 1243–1247.
3 This is not difficult to demonstrate mathematically. In our model, the yield (h) can be expressed as $h = qES$, where q is the proportion of the population harvested with one unit of effort, S is the size of the population, and E is the level of effort. One of the conditions a dynamic efficient allocation has to satisfy with an infinite discount rate is $P = a/qS$, where P is the constant price, a is the constant marginal cost per unit of effort, and qS is the number of fish harvested per unit of effort. By multiplying both sides of this equation by h and collecting terms, we obtain $Ph = aE$. The left-hand side is total benefits, while the right is total cost, implying net benefits are zero.
4 Note that we are ruling out monopoly behavior via our assumption that the price is not affected by effort level.
5 This will result in fewer fish for future generations as well as smaller profits if the resulting effort level exceeds that associated with the maximum sustainable yield. If the open-access effort level is lower than the maximum sustainable yield effort level (when extraction costs are very high), then reductions in stock would increase the growth in the stock, thus supplying more fish (albeit lower net benefits) to future generations.
6 This type of analysis was first used in Gordon (1954).
7 As one extreme example, Tillion (1985) reported that the 1982 herring season in Prince William Sound lasted only four hours and the catch still exceeded the area quota.
8 OECD. (2019). https://www.oecd.org/agriculture/government-subsidies-overfishing/#:~:text=Governments%20spend%20an%20estimated%20USD,sea%20and%20brought%20to%20port.
9 NOAA Catch Share Policy, www.nmfs.noaa.gov/sfa/management/catch_shares/about/documents/noaa_cs_policy.pdf (Accessed June 2017).
10 NOAA keeps a thorough catch share bibliography on its website. www.nmfs.noaa.gov/sfa/management/catch_shares/resources/references.html.
11 This occurs because the maximum bid from any potential entrant would be the value to be derived from owning that permit. This value is equal to the present value of future rents (the difference between price and marginal cost for each unit of fish sold). Competition will force the purchaser to bid near that maximum value, lest they lose the quota.
12 Ministry of Fisheries, New Zealand, www.fish.govt.nz/en-nz/default.htm.
13 European Commission. (2017). https://ec.europa.eu/fisheries/cfp_en.

14 https://ec.europa.eu/fisheries/sites/fisheries/files/docs/body/poster_tac2015_en.pdf.

15 For information and maps of marine protected areas of the United States, see http://marineprotectedareas.noaa.gov. For a worldwide atlas, see www.mpatlas.org.

16 The distribution of benefits and costs among current fishers also matters. Using a case study on the Northeast Atlantic Cod fishery, Sumaila and Armstrong (2006) find that the distributional effects of MPAs depend significantly on the management regime that was in place at the time of the development of the MPA and the level of cooperation in the fishery.

17 www.federalregister.gov/documents/2014/12/02/2014-28064/atlantic-highly-migratory-species-2006-consolidated-atlantic-highly-migratory-species-hms-fishery.

Further Reading

Acheson, J. M. (2003). *Capturing the Commons: Devising Institutions to Manage the Maine Lobster Industry*. Hanover, NH: University Press of New England. An impressive synthesis of theory and empirical work, combined with an insider's knowledge of the institutions and the people who run them, makes this a compelling examination of the history of one of America's most important fisheries.

Adler, J. H., & Stewart, N. (2013). Learning how to fish: Catch shares and the future of fisheries conservation. *UCLA Journal of Environmental Law & Policy*, 31(1), 150–197. A useful summary of the history, law, and economics of catch shares.

Clark, C. W. (1990). *Mathematical Bioeconomics: The Optimal Management of Renewable Resources*, 2nd ed. New York: Wiley-Interscience. Careful development of the mathematical models that underlie current understanding of the exploitation of renewable resources under a variety of property rights regimes.

N.O.A.A. Catch Share Policy: Executive Summary. (2013). www.nmfs.noaa.gov/sfa/domes_fish/catchshare/docs/noaa_cs_policy.pdf. A useful review of U.S. Fisheries Policy.

Review of Environmental Economics and Policy. (Summer 2012). 6(2). Contains several summary articles from the Symposium: Rights-Based Fisheries Management.

Schlager, E., & Ostrom, E. (1992). Property right regimes and natural resources: A conceptual analysis. *Land Economics*, 68, 249–262. A conceptual framework for analyzing a number of property rights regimes; the authors use this framework to interpret findings from a number of empirical studies.

Chapter 9

Forests

Storable, Renewable Resources

Introduction

Forests provide a variety of products and services. The raw materials for housing, wood products, and paper are extracted from the forest. In many parts of the world, wood is an important fuel. Trees cleanse the air by absorbing carbon dioxide and adding oxygen. Forests provide shelter and sanctuary for wildlife and they play an important role in maintaining the watersheds that supply much of our drinking water. The results of a vast amount of research also show that forest visits promote both physical and mental health.[1]

Although the contributions that trees make to our everyday life are easy to overlook, even the most rudimentary calculations indicate their significance. Almost one-third of the land in the United States is covered by forests, the largest category of land use, with the exception of pasture and grazing land. The comparable figure for the world is roughly 31 percent.

Managing commercial forests is no easy task. In contrast to crops such as cereal grains, which are planted and harvested on an annual cycle, trees mature very slowly. The commercial manager must decide not only how to maximize yields on a given amount of land but also when to harvest and whether to replant. In addition, a delicate balance must be established among the various possible uses of forests. Since harvesting the resource diminishes other values (such as protecting the aesthetic value of forested vistas or providing habitat for shade-loving species), establishing the proper balance requires some means of comparing the value of potentially conflicting uses. The efficiency criterion is one obvious possibility.

One serious societal problem, deforestation, has intensified climate change, decreased biodiversity, caused agricultural productivity to decline, increased soil erosion and desertification, and precipitated the decline of traditional cultures of people indigenous to the forests. Instead of forests being used on a sustainable basis to

DOI: 10.4324/9781032689111-10

provide for the needs of both current and subsequent generations, some forests are being "cashed in." Current forestry practices may be violating both the sustainability and efficiency criteria.[2] How serious is the problem and what can be done about it?

In the remainder of this chapter, we shall explore how economics can be combined with forest ecology to assist in efficiently managing this important resource. We begin by characterizing what is meant by an efficient allocation of the forest resource when the value of the harvested timber is the only concern. Starting simply, we first model the efficient decision to cut a single stand or cluster of trees with a common age by superimposing economic considerations on a biological model of tree growth. This model is then refined to demonstrate how the multiple values of the forest resource should influence the harvesting decision and how the problem is altered if planning takes place over an infinite horizon, with forests being harvested and replanted in a continual sequence. Turning to matters of institutional adequacy, we shall then examine the inefficiencies that have resulted or can be expected to result from both public and private management decisions and consider strategies for restoring efficiency.

Characterizing Forest Harvesting Decisions

Special Attributes of the Timber Resource

While timber shares many characteristics with other living resources, it also has some unique aspects. Timber shares with many other animate resources the characteristic that it is both an output and a capital good. Trees, when harvested, provide a salable commodity, but left standing they are a capital good, providing for increased growth the following year. Each year, the forest manager must decide whether to harvest a particular stand of trees or to wait for the additional growth. In contrast to many other living resources, however, the time between initial investment (planting) and recovery of that investment (harvesting) is especially long. Intervals of 25 years or more are common in forestry. Finally, forestry is subject to an unusually large variety of externalities, which are associated with either the standing timber or the act of harvesting timber. These externalities not only make it difficult to define the efficient allocation, but they also play havoc with incentives, making efficient management harder for institutions to achieve.

The Biological Dimension

Tree growth is conventionally measured on a volume basis, typically cubic feet, on a particular site. This measurement is taken of the stems, exclusive of bark and limbs, between the stump and a 4-inch top. For larger trees, the stump is 24 inches from the ground. Only standing trees are measured; those toppled by wind or age are not included. In this sense, the volume is measured in net, rather than gross, terms.

Based on this measurement of volume, the data reveal that tree stands go through distinct growth phases. Initially, when the trees are very young, growth is rather slow in volume terms, though the tree may experience a considerable increase in height. A period of sustained, rapid growth follows, with volume increasing considerably. Finally, slower growth sets in as the stand fully matures, until growth stops or decline sets in.

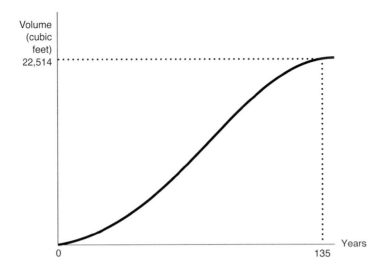

Figure 9.1 Model of Tree Growth in a Stand of Douglas Fir.

The actual growth of a stand of trees depends on many factors, including the weather, the fertility of the soil, susceptibility to insects or disease, the type of tree, the amount of care devoted to the trees, and vulnerability to forest fire or air pollution. Thus, tree growth can vary considerably from stand to stand. Some of these growth-enhancing or growth-retarding factors are under the influence of foresters; others are not.

Abstracting from these differences, it is possible to develop a hypothetical but realistic biological model of the growth of a stand of trees. Our model, as shown in Figure 9.1, is based on the growth of a stand of Douglas fir trees in the Pacific Northwest.[3] Notice that the figure is consistent with the growth phases listed previously, following an early period of limited growth with quicker growth in its middle ages, with growth ceasing after 135 years.

The Economics of Forest Harvesting

When should this stand be harvested? To start, assume that the only value of this forest is the timber harvested from it. From the definition of efficiency, in this circumstance the optimal harvest time (age) would maximize the present value of the net benefits from the wood. The size of the net benefits from the wood depends on whether the land will be perpetually committed to forestry or left to natural processes after harvest. For our first model, we shall assume that the stand will be harvested once and the land will be left as is following the harvest. We also shall assume that neither the price (assumed to be $1 per cubic meter) nor the harvesting costs ($0.30 per cubic meter) vary with time. The cost of planting or replanting this forest is assumed to be $1,000. This model illustrates how the economic principles of forestry can be applied to the simplest case, while providing the background necessary to move to a more complicated and more realistic example.

Planting costs and harvesting costs differ in one significant way—the time at which they are incurred. Planting costs are incurred immediately, while harvesting costs are incurred at the time of harvest. In a present-value calculation, harvesting costs are discounted because they are paid in the future, whereas planting costs are not discounted because they are paid immediately.

Having specified these aspects of the model, it is now possible to calculate the present value of net benefits that would be derived from harvesting this stand at various ages (see Table 9.1). The net benefits are calculated by subtracting the present value of costs from the present value of the timber at the chosen age of harvest. Three different discount rates are used to illustrate the influence of discounting on the harvesting decision. The undiscounted calculations ($r = 0.0$) simply indicate the actual values that would prevail at each age, while the positive discount rate takes the time value of money into account.

Some interesting conclusions can be gleaned from Table 9.1. First, higher discounting rates shorten the timing of the efficient harvest. Notice that the maximum undiscounted net benefits occur at an age of 135 years, when the volume is maximized. However, when a discount rate of only 0.02 is used, the maximum net benefits occur at an age of 68 years, roughly half the age of the undiscounted case.

Second, under these specific assumptions, the optimal harvest age is insensitive to changing the magnitude of the planting and harvesting costs. You can see this by comparing the age that yields the maximum value in the "value of timber" row and the age that yields the maximum value in the "net benefit" row. Notice that, for all discount rates, these two maxima occur at the same age. Even if both types of costs were zero, the optimal harvesting age would not be affected. The age that maximizes the value of the timber remains the same.

Third, with high enough discount rates, replanting may not be efficient. Note that with $r = 0.04$, the present value of net benefits is uniformly negative due to the assumed $1,000 planting cost. The harvest age that maximizes the present value of net benefits from a standing forest in this case would occur when the trees were about 40 years old, but the present value of costs of replanting would exceed the present value of the benefits so it would not be efficient to replant the harvested forest.

Higher discount rates imply younger harvesting ages because they are less tolerant of the slow timber growth that occurs as the stand reaches maturity. The use of a positive discount rate implies a direct comparison between the increase in the value of non-harvested timber (the opportunity cost of harvest) and the increase in value that would occur if the forest were harvested and the money from the sale invested at rate r. In the undiscounted case, using an r of zero implies that the opportunity cost of capital is zero, so it pays to leave the money invested in trees as long as some growth is occurring. If r is positive, however, the trees will be harvested as soon as the growth rate declines sufficiently that more will be earned by harvesting the trees and putting the proceeds in higher-yielding financial investments (in other words, when g, the growth rate in the volume of wood, becomes less than r (the interest earned on the invested revenue received from the harvest)).

The fact that neither harvesting nor planting costs affect the harvesting period in this model is easy to explain. Because they are paid immediately, the present value of planting costs is equal to the actual expenditure; it does not vary with the age at which the stand is harvested. Essentially, a constant is being subtracted from the value of timber at every age so it does not change the age at which the maximum occurs; it only affects the present value received from that harvest.

Table 9.1 Economic Harvesting Decision: Douglas Fir

Age (years)	10	20	30	40	50	60	68	70	80	90	100	110	120	130	135
Volume (cubic ft)	694	1,912	3,558	5,536	7,750	10,104	12,023	12,502	14,848	17,046	19,000	20,614	21,792	22,438	22,514
Undiscounted (r = 0.0)															
Value of Timber ($)	694	1,912	3,558	5,536	7,750	10,104	12,023	12,502	14,848	17,046	19,000	20,614	21,792	22,438	22,514
Cost ($)	1,208	1,574	2,067	2,661	3,325	4,031	4,607	4,751	5,454	6,114	6,700	7,184	7,538	7,731	7,754
Net Benefits ($)	−514	338	1,491	2,875	4,425	6,073	7,416	7,751	9,394	10,932	12,300	13,430	14,254	14,707	14,760
Discounted (r = 0.01)															
Value of Timber ($)	628	1,567	2,640	3,718	4,712	5,562	6,112	6,230	6,698	6,961	7,025	6,899	6,603	6,155	5,876
Cost ($)	1,188	1,470	1,792	2,115	2,414	2,669	2,833	2,869	3,009	3,088	3,107	3,070	2,981	2,846	2,763
Net Benefits ($)	−560	97	848	1,603	2,299	2,893	3,278	3,361	3,689	3,873	3,917	3,830	3,622	3,308	3,113
Discounted (r = 0.02)															
Value of Timber ($)	567	1,288	1,964	2,507	2,879	3,080	3,128	3,126	3,046	2,868	2,623	2,334	2,024	1,710	1,449
Cost ($)	1,170	1,386	1,589	1,752	1,864	1,924	1,938	1,938	1,914	1,860	1,787	1,700	1,607	1,513	1,435
Net Benefits ($)	−603	−98	375	755	1,015	1,156	1,190	1,188	1,132	1,008	836	634	417	197	14
Discounted (r = 0.04)															
Value of Timber ($)	469	873	1,097	1,153	1,091	960	835	803	644	500	376	276	197	137	113
Cost ($)	1,141	1,262	1,329	1,346	1,327	1,288	1,251	1,241	1,193	1,150	1,113	1,083	1,059	1,041	1,034
Net Benefits ($)	−672	−389	−232	−193	−237	−328	−415	−438	−549	−650	−737	−807	−862	−904	−921

Value of timber = price × volume/$(1 + r)^t$
Cost = $1,000 + ($0.30 × volume)/$(1 + r)^t$
Net benefits = value of timber − cost
Price = $1

Harvesting costs do not affect the age of harvest for a different reason. Since total harvesting costs are proportional to the amount of timber harvested ($0.30 for each cubic foot), neither the price nor the marginal cost of a cubic foot of wood varies with age; they are also constants. In the case of our numerical example, this constant net value before discounting is $0.70 (the $1 price minus the $0.30 marginal harvest cost). Regardless of the numerical value assigned to the marginal cost of harvesting, this net value before discounting is a constant that is multiplied by the volume of timber at each age divided by $(1 + r)^t$. It merely raises or lowers the net benefits curve; it does not change its shape, including the location of the maximum point. Therefore, net benefits will be maximized at the same age of the stand, regardless of the value of the marginal harvesting cost, as long as marginal harvesting cost is less than the price received; a rise in the marginal cost of harvesting will not affect the optimal age of harvest. (What is the optimal harvesting strategy if the marginal cost of harvesting is larger than the price?)

What effect could policy have on the harvesting age? Consider the effect of a $0.20 tax levied on each cubic foot of wood harvested in this simple model. Since this tax would raise the after-tax marginal cost of harvesting from $0.30 per cubic foot to $0.50 per cubic foot, it would have the same effect as a rise in harvesting cost. As we have already demonstrated, this implies that the tax would leave the optimal harvesting age unchanged, but it would lower the after-tax revenue received from that harvest.

The final conclusion from this numerical example relates to the interaction between discount rates and planting costs on the decision to replant. When high discount rates combine with high replanting costs, planting trees for commercial harvest would be less likely to yield positive net benefits than would be the case with lower discount rates. (Notice, for example, in Table 9.1, that replanting would be economically desirable only for discount rates lower than $r = 0.04$.) With high discount rates, tree growth is simply too slow to justify the planting expense; profit-maximizing harvesters would favor cutting down an existing forest, but not replanting it.

Extending the Basic Model

This basic model is somewhat unrealistic in several respects. For one, it considers the harvest as a single event rather than a part of an infinite sequence of harvesting and replanting. Typically, in the infinite planning horizon model, harvested lands are re-harvested and the sequence starts over again in a never-ending cycle.

At first glance, it may appear that this is no different from the case just considered. After all, can't one merely use this model to characterize the efficient interval between planting and harvesting for each period? The mathematics tells us (Bowes & Krutilla, 1985) that this is *not* the correct way to think about the problem, and with a bit of reflection it is not difficult to see why.

The single-harvest model we developed would be appropriate for an infinite planning period if and only if all periods were independent (meaning that decisions in any period would be unaffected by anything that went on in the other periods). If interdependencies exist among time periods, however, the harvesting decision must reflect those interdependencies.

Interdependencies do exist. The decision to delay this year's harvest imposes an additional cost in an infinite planning model that has no counterpart in our single-harvest model—the impact of this year's delay on the onset of the next harvesting cycle. In our single-harvest model, the optimum age to harvest occurs when the marginal benefit of an additional year's growth equals the marginal opportunity cost of capital. In other words, when the capital gains from letting the trees grow another year become equal to the return that could be obtained from harvesting the trees and investing the gains, the stand is harvested. In the infinite-planning horizon case, the opportunity cost of delaying the next cycle, which has no counterpart in the single-stand model, must also be covered by the gain in tree growth.

The effect of including the opportunity cost of delay in an infinite-horizon model can be rather profound. Holding all other aspects of the problems (such as planting and harvesting costs, discount rate, growth function, and price) the same, the optimal time to harvest (called the *optimal rotation* in the infinite-planning case) is *shorter* in the infinite-planning case than in the single-harvest case. This follows directly from the existence of the opportunity cost of delaying the next harvest. The efficient forester would harvest at an earlier age when they are planning to replant the same area than they would when the plot will be left inactive after the harvest.

This more complicated model also yields some other conclusions different from those in our original model, a valuable reminder of a point made earlier in this book—conclusions flow from a specific view of the world and are valid only to the extent that specific view captures the essence of a problem.

Consider, for example, the effect of a rise in planting costs. In our single-harvest model, this rise would have no effect on the optimal harvest age. In the infinite-horizon case, the optimal rotation is affected because higher planting costs reduce the marginal opportunity cost of delaying the cycle; fewer net benefits are lost by delaying the cycle, compared to the case with lower planting costs. As a result, the optimal rotation (the time between planting and harvesting that crop) would increase as planting costs increase. A similar result would be obtained when harvesting costs are increased. The optimal rotation period would be lengthened in that case as well. (Can you see why?)

Since increased harvesting costs in the infinite-horizon model lengthen the optimal rotation period, a per-unit tax on harvested timber would also lengthen the optimal rotation period in this model. Furthermore, lengthening the rotation period implies that the harvested trees would be somewhat older and, therefore, each harvest would involve a somewhat larger volume of wood.

Another limitation of our basic model lies in its assumption of a constant relative price for the wood over time. In fact, the relative prices of timber have been rising over time. Introducing relative prices for timber that rise at a constant rate in the infinite-horizon model causes the optimal rotation period to increase relative to the fixed-price case—, in essence, prices that are rising at a fixed rate act to offset (i.e., diminish) the effect of discounting. Since we have already established that lower discount rates imply longer rotation periods, it immediately follows that rising prices also lead to longer efficient rotation periods.

A final issue with the models as elaborated so far is that they all are concerned solely with the sale of timber as the only product. In fact, forests provide many other services such as habitat for wildlife, storing carbon, supplying recreational opportunities, and stabilizing watersheds. For these uses, additional benefits accrue to the standing timber that are lost or diminished when the stand is harvested.

It is possible to incorporate these benefits into our model to demonstrate the effect they would have on the efficient rotation. Suppose that the amenity benefits conveyed by a standing forest are positively related to the age of the forest. In the infinite-horizon case, the optimal rotation would once again occur when the marginal benefit of delay equaled the marginal cost of delay. When amenity values are considered, the marginal benefit of delay (which includes having these amenity values for another year) would be higher than in the models where amenity benefits are not considered. For this reason, considering amenity benefits would lengthen the optimal rotation. Further, if the amenity benefits are sufficiently large, it may be efficient to leave the forest as a wilderness area and never harvest it.

Sources of Inefficiency

The previous section considered the nature of the harvesting decision. In this section, we shall discover sources of inefficiency in that decision. These inefficiencies have the effect of biasing profit-maximizing decisions toward excessive rates of deforestation.

Perverse Incentives for the Landowner

Profit maximization does not produce efficient outcomes when the pattern of incentives facing decision makers is perverse. Forestry provides an unfortunately large number of situations in which perverse incentives produce very inefficient and unsustainable outcomes.

Privately owned forests are a significant force all over the world, but in some countries, such as the United States, they are the dominant force. Providing a sustainable flow of wood fiber is not the sole *social* purpose of the forest. When the act of harvesting timber imposes costs on other valued aspects of the forest (e.g., watershed maintenance, prevention of soil erosion, sequestering carbon, and protection of biodiversity), these costs are not borne by the decision maker; these amenity costs normally will not be adequately considered in profit-maximizing decisions.

This part of the benefits of the standing forest becomes an *external* cost of harvesting. Failure to recognize all of the social values of the standing forest provides an incentive not only to harvest an inefficiently large amount of timber in working forests, but also raises the specter of harvesting the forest even when preservation is the efficient alternative. For example, the historical controversy that erupted in the Pacific Northwest of the United States between environmentalists concerned with protecting the habitat of the northern spotted owl and loggers can, in part, be explained by externalities. To loggers the loss of the northern spotted owl is an external cost; environmentalists treat the loss of spotted owl habitat as a cost to all who value it. The logger's calculation concludes that harvesting makes sense, and the environmentalist's calculations conclude that the added benefit from protecting the habitat makes preserving the forest the desired outcome.

Government policies can also create perverse incentives for landowners. Historically, the rapid rate of deforestation in the Amazon, for example, was promoted in part by the Brazilian government. When the Brazilian government reduced taxes on income derived from cattle ranching, this change made it profitable to cut down forests and convert the land to ranching. This system of taxation encouraged higher-than-efficient rates of conversion of land from forests to pasture and subsidized an activity that, in the absence of the tax change, would not normally have been economically viable. In essence, Brazilian taxpayers were unknowingly subsidizing deforestation and thereby depreciating the value of their natural capital stock.

The Brazilian system of property rights over land also played a role in the early history of deforestation. Acquiring the rights to unallocated land simply by occupying it had been formally recognized since 1850. A "squatter" acquired a usufruct right (the right to continue using the land) by (1) living on a plot of unclaimed public land and (2) using it "effectively" for the required period. If these two conditions were met for 5 years, the squatter acquired ownership of the land, including the right to transfer it to others. A successful claimant received a title for an amount of land up to three times the amount cleared of forest. Notice the incentives that this system of property rights created. The more deforestation accomplished by the squatter, the larger the amount of land acquired. In effect, landless peasants could only acquire land by engaging in deforestation; due to this policy, the marginal benefits from clearing land were artificially high.

In recognition of their consequences, these perverse incentives were abandoned. However, resettlement programs have also promoted the expansion of paved roads, ports, waterways, railways, and hydroelectric power plants into the heavily forested central Amazonia region. These government policies radically changed the value of land uses that were competing with preserved forest and the result has been deforestation.

As a result of the resettlement program, many migrants engage in agriculture. Studying the decisions made by these farmers, Caviglia-Harris (2004) found that, as the land conversion model would suggest, the degree to which these farmers contribute to deforestation is impacted by market conditions as well as government policies. Market forces not only affect incentives to expand the scale of operation on deforested lands, but also affect incentives to choose particular forms of agriculture. For example, her empirical results show that cattle ownership by migrants significantly increases the percentage of deforestation. Therefore, as the market for cattle and its related products—milk and meat—advanced, deforestation levels also increased. A report published by Brazil's National Institute for Space Research (INPE) in 2021 estimated that 13,235 square kilometers (8224 square miles) of forest was lost between August 2020 and July 2021. That was an increase of 22 percent from the previous year.

Another source of inefficiency can be found in concession agreements, which define the terms under which public forests can be harvested. To loggers, harvesting existing forests has a substantial advantage over planting new forests: old growth can be harvested immediately for profit. By virtue of the commercial value of larger, older trees, considerable economic rent (called *stumpage value* in the industry) is associated with a standing forest.

In principle, governments have a variety of policy instruments at their disposal to capture this rent from the concessionaires, but they have typically given out the concessions to harvest this timber without capturing a fair share of the rent for the government.[4] As a result, the cost of harvesting is artificially reduced and loggers can afford to harvest much more forest than is efficient. The failure of government to capture this rent means that the wealth tied up in these forests has typically gone to a few, now-wealthy individuals and corporations rather than to the government to be used for the alleviation of poverty or other worthy national objectives.

The failure to capture the rent is not the only problem with concession agreements. Other contractual terms in these concession agreements have a role to play as well. Because forest concessions are typically awarded for limited terms, concession holders have little incentive to replant, to exercise care in their logging procedures, or even to conserve younger trees until they reach the efficient harvest age. The future value of the forest will not be theirs to capture. The resulting logging practices can destroy much of the younger stock by (1) the construction of access roads, (2) the felling and dragging of the trees, and (3) the elimination of the protective canopy. Although sustainable forestry would be possible for many of these nations, limited-term concession agreements make it unlikely.[5]

Finally, deforestation can result from illegal activities. Illegal harvesters have no incentive to protect future values and act as if their discount rate were infinite!

The list of losers from inefficient forestry practices frequently includes indigenous peoples who have lived in and derived their livelihood from these forests for a very long time. As loggers and squatters push deeper and deeper into forests, the indigenous people, who lack the power to stem the tide, are forced to relocate further away from their traditional lands.[6]

Perverse Incentives for Nations

Another source of deforestation involves external costs that transcend national borders. While it is reasonable to expect individual nations to take action to correct externalities that lie entirely within their borders, it is less likely to expect national policy to solve the transborder problem. Some international action would normally be necessary to restore efficiency in these cases.

Biodiversity. Due to species extinction, the diversity of the forms of life that inhabit the planet is diminishing at an unprecedented rate. And the extinction of species is, of course, an irreversible process. Deforestation, particularly the destruction of the tropical rainforests, is a major source of species extinction because it destroys the most biologically active habitats. Amazonia has been characterized by Norman Myers, the British environmentalist, as the "single richest region of the tropical biome." The quantity of bird, fish, plant, and insect life that is unique to that region is unmatched anywhere else on the planet.

One of the tragic ironies of the situation is that these extinctions are occurring at precisely the moment in history when we would be most able to take advantage of the gene pool this biodiversity represents. Modern techniques now make it possible to transplant desirable genes from one species into another, creating species with new characteristics, such as enhanced disease resistance or pest resistance. But the gene pool must be diverse to serve as a source of donor genes. Tropical forests have already contributed genetic material to increase disease resistance of cash crops, such as coffee and cocoa, and have been the source of some entirely new foods. Approximately one-quarter of all prescription drugs have been derived from substances found in tropical plants. Future discoveries, however, are threatened by deforestation.

Climate Change. Deforestation also contributes to climate change. Trees absorb and sequester carbon. Therefore burning trees, either as part of the substitution of this renewable source for fossil fuels or as part of the land clearing that is commonly associated with conversion of forests to agricultural land, adds CO_2 to the air by liberating the carbon sequestered within the trees. Wood is a renewable fuel, but is it a carbon-neutral fuel? As Debate 9.1 points out, opinions differ on the answer to that question.

Forests not only affect the climate, but they are also affected by the changing climate. As recent history has shown, climate has increased the number of intense forest fires around the globe. These fires are incredibly destructive not only to forests and the wildlife that depend on them, but also to the homes and businesses built near them. Further, the particulate pollution resulting from the fires has also had lasting effects on human health.

DEBATE 9.1

Is Firewood a Carbon-Neutral Fuel?

The role of wood in reaching climate goals is an important issue since the E.U.'s Renewable Energy Directive (REDII) counts biomass as a carbon-neutral fuel. At present, 60 percent of the E.U.'s renewable energy mix comes from burning wood pellets.

When wood is burned, it has two carbon dioxide effects on the atmosphere: first, trees harvested for burning are no longer absorbing carbon dioxide. The carbon dioxide that would have been absorbed is now added to the atmosphere (the harvesting effect). Second, wood combustion creates more carbon dioxide emissions per unit of electricity generated than coal (the combustion effect). So how can it be considered carbon-neutral?

Proponents of carbon neutrality argue that while fossil fuel use increases the total amount of carbon in the atmosphere, biomass combustion simply returns to the atmosphere the carbon that was absorbed as the plants grew. Therefore, they conclude, there is no net increase.

Proponents also argue that burning wood is better for the environment than burning coal and that logging natural forests is good for them because newly planted trees sequester more carbon than mature trees. Further, they argue that using wood by-products and residues for energy creates fewer emissions because they would have emitted carbon dioxide as they degraded anyway.

Opponents argue that in practice most wood pellets are not created from by-products or residues, but from standing trees. Further, while a sustainably managed forestry could ultimately make up the emissions from wood combustion, far more carbon dioxide is emitted into the air immediately than is removed by the sustainable managed forest. Even if the wood displaces coal, the most carbon-intensive fossil fuel, it would take a very long time to make up the deficit and that is time we don't have.

What do you think?

Sources: Duffy, P., Moomaw, W., Sterman, J., & Rooney-Varga, J. N. (2020). Burning wood is not a solution to climate change. *The Hill*. https://thehill.com/opinion/energy-environment/496021-burning-wood-is-not-a-solution-to-climate-change; Catanoso, J. (2021). The science of forest biomass: Conflicting studies map the controversy. https://news.mongabay.com/2021/07/the-science-of-forest-biomass-conflicting-studies-map-the-controversy

Sustainable Forestry

We have examined three types of decisions by landowners that affect the rate of deforestation—the harvesting decision, the replanting decision, and the conversion decision. In all three cases, profit-maximizing decisions may not be efficient, and these inefficiencies tend to create a bias toward higher rates of deforestation. These cases present both a challenge and an opportunity. The current level of deforestation is the challenge. The opportunity arises from the realization that correcting these inefficiencies can promote both efficiency and sustainability.

Does the restoration of efficiency guarantee sustainable outcomes? One common definition in forestry suggests that sustainable forestry can be realized only when the forests are maintained perpetually. Sustainable forestry would require harvests to be limited to the growth of the forest, leaving the volume of wood unaffected (or increasing) over time.

Efficiency is not necessarily compatible with this definition of sustainable forestry. Maximizing the present value involves an implicit comparison between the increase in value from delaying harvest (largely because of the growth in volume) and the increase in value from harvesting the timber and investing the earnings (largely a function of r, the rate of return earned on invested savings). With slow-growing species, the growth rate in volume is small. Choosing the harvest age that maximizes the present value of net benefits in slow-growing forests may well imply harvest volumes higher than the net growth of the forest.

The search for sustainable forestry practices that are also economically sustainable has led to consideration of new models of forestry. One involves a focus on planting rapidly growing tree species in plantations. Rapidly growing species raise the economic attractiveness of replanting because the invested funds are tied up for a shorter time. Species raised in plantations can be harvested and replanted at a low cost. Forest plantations have been established for such varied purposes as supplying fuelwood in developing countries and supplying pulp for paper mills in both industrialized and developing countries.

Plantation forestry is controversial, however, because of what it might mean for the amenity values of forests. Not only do plantation forests typically involve a single species of tree, which commonly results in a poor wildlife habitat, they also tend to require large inputs of fertilizer and pesticides to maintain peak growth.

In some parts of the world, the natural resilience of the forest ecosystem is sufficiently high that sustainability is ultimately achieved, despite decades of earlier unsustainable levels of harvest. In the United States, for example, sometime during the 1940s the net growth of the nation's timberlands exceeded timber removals. Subsequent surveys have confirmed that net growth has continued to exceed harvests, despite a rather large and growing demand for timber. The total volume of forest biomass in the United States has been growing since at least World War II; for the country, harvests during that period have been sustainable, although the harvests of some specific species in some specific areas have not.

Public Policy

One opportunity involves assuring that policies do not add to the inefficient incentives. For example, concessionaires should pay the full cost for their rights to harvest publicly controlled lands, including compensating for damage to the forests surrounding the trees of interest, and the magnitude of land transferred to squatters should not be a multiple of the amount of cleared forest.

Another approach involves enlisting the power of consumers in the cause of sustainable forestry. This process typically involves the establishment of standards for sustainable forestry, employing independent certifiers to verify compliance with these standards, and allowing certified suppliers to display a label designating compliance.

For this system to work well, several preconditions need to be met. The certification process must be reliable and consumers must trust it. Additionally, consumers must be sufficiently concerned about sustainable forestry to pay a price premium (over prices for otherwise comparable, but uncertified, products) that is large enough to make certification an attractive option for forestry companies. This means that the revenue should be sufficient to at least cover the higher costs associated with producing certified wood. Nothing guarantees that these conditions would be met in general. Example 9.1 examines how certification works in practice, including how effective it has been in a country that has experienced a lot of certification activity.

EXAMPLE 9.1

Producing Sustainable Forestry through Certification: Is It Working?

The Forest Stewardship Council (FSC) is an international, not-for-profit organization originally headquartered in Oaxaca, Mexico, with the FSC Secretariat relocating to Bonn, Germany, in 2003. The FSC was conceived in large part by environmental groups, most notably the World Wide Fund for Nature (WWF). The goal of the FSC is to foster "environmentally appropriate, socially beneficial, and economically viable management of the world's forests." It pursues this goal by being an independent third-party certifier of well-managed forests.

The FSC has developed standards to assess the performance of forestry operations. These standards address environmental, social, and economic issues. Forest assessments require one or more field visits by a team of specialists representing a variety of disciplines, typically including forestry, ecology/wildlife management/biology, and sociology/anthropology. Additionally, the FSC requires that forest assessment reports be subject to independent peer review. Any FSC assessment may be challenged through a formal complaints procedure. FSC–certified products are identified by an on-product label and/or off-product publicity materials. As of 2019, the FSC had certified 199 million hectares (a hectare equals 2.47105 acres).

Is FSC certification effective? The evidence is limited and mixed. A meta-analysis of scientific studies (Buriyalova et al., 2017) found that FSC certification in the tropics has reduced degradation and improved labor and environmental conditions in the affected forest—no small accomplishment. But Blackman et al. (2015), using a variety of techniques, found that the statistical analysis could not rule out the possibility that it had little effect on *deforestation* in Mexico. The author, Allen Blackman, suggested that small-scale, poorly performing logging operations are common in the tropics, and they aren't the ones likely to get certified. Another investigative report (Conniff, 2018) reviews some evidence of "blatant illegality" on the part of the FSC. We await other studies.

Sources: The Forest Stewardship Council website, www.fsc.org (Accessed January 13, 2022); Burivalova, Z., Hua, F., Koh, L. P., Garcia, C., & Putz, F. (2017). A critical comparison of conventional, certified, and community management of tropical forests for timber in terms of environmental, economic, and social variables. *Conservation Letters*, 10(1), 4–14. https://doi.org/10.1111/conl.12244; Blackman, A., Goff, L., & Rivera, M. (August 2015). Does eco-certification stem tropical deforestation? Forest Stewardship Council certification in Mexico. Environment for Development Discussion Paper Series DP 15-19; Conniff, R. (February 20, 2018). Greenwashed timber: How sustainable forest certification has failed. *Yale Environment 360*. https://e360.yale.edu/features/greenwashed-timber-how-sustainable-forest-certification-has-failed

Most of these changes could be implemented by individual nations to protect their own forests. And to do so would be in their interests as well as the interests of the international communities. By definition, inefficient practices cost more than the benefits received. The move to a more efficient set of policies would necessarily generate more net benefits, which could be shared in ways that build political support for the change. But what about the global inefficiencies—those that transcend national boundaries? How can they be resolved?

Several economic strategies exist. They share the characteristic that they all involve compensating the nations conferring external benefits to encourage conservation actions consistent with global efficiency.

Forestry Offsets (Credits)

How big a role might forests play in managing the threats posed by climate change? Austin et al. (2020) find that considerable mitigation benefits could be obtained not only from avoiding deforestation, but also from afforestation and reforestation. What policies are available to protect or enhance forestry's complementary absorption role in this crucial international effort?

One option involves forestry offsets.[7] In carbon offset markets, the creation and sale of forest offsets are one mechanism for compensating forest landowners for increasing the amount of carbon absorption from their land. Currently, three different project types are eligible to produce carbon offsets: afforestation or reforestation, avoided conversion, and improved forest management. Denominated in "metric tons of carbon-dioxide equivalent," these offsets could in principle help to counter the disincentives discussed earlier while providing another pathway for mitigating climate change. In practice, however, offsets have been controversial. The effectiveness of these systems is only as good as the emission accounting and certification processes that underlie them, and those systems have had mixed results.

Several strategies exist and some have already been discussed. Recall, for example, the discussion of Extractive Reserves and the World Heritage Convention in Chapter 5. Others, discussed in the following, include royalty payments and conservation easements.

Summary

Forests represent an example of a storable, renewable source. Typically, tree stands have three distinct growth phases—slow growth in volume in the early stage, followed by rapid growth in the middle years, and slower growth as the stand reaches full maturity. The owner who harvests the timber receives the income from its sale, but the owner who delays harvest will receive additional growth. The amount of growth depends on the part of the growth cycle the stand is in.

The efficient time to harvest a stand of timber is when the present value of social net benefits is maximized—that is, when the marginal gain from delaying the harvest one more year is equal to the marginal cost of the delay. For longer-than-efficient delays, the additional costs outweigh the increased benefits, while for earlier-than-efficient harvests, more benefits (in terms of the increased value of the timber) are given up than costs saved. For many species, the efficient age at harvest is 25 years or older.

The profit-maximizing harvest age depends on the circumstances the decision maker faces. When the plot is to be left fallow after the harvest, the efficient harvest occurs later than when the land is immediately replanted to initiate another cycle. With immediate replanting, delaying the current harvest imposes an additional cost— the resulting cost of subsequently delaying the next harvest—which, when factored into the analysis, makes it more desirable to harvest earlier.

Other factors affect the size of the efficient rotation as well. In general, the larger the discount rate, the earlier the harvest. With an infinite planning horizon model, increases in planting and harvesting costs tend to lengthen the optimal rotation, while in a single-harvest model they have no effect on the length of the efficient rotation. If the relative price of timber grows at a constant rate over time, the efficient rotation is longer than if prices remain constant over time. Finally, if standing timber provides amenity services (such as for recreation or wildlife management) in proportion to the volume of the standing timber, the efficient rotation will be longer in an infinite planning model than it would be in the absence of any amenity services. Furthermore, if the amenity value is large enough, efficiency would preclude any harvest of that forest.

Profit maximization can be compatible with efficient forest management under the right circumstances. In particular, in the absence of externalities, distortions caused by government policy or illegal harvests, profit-maximizing private owners have an incentive to adopt the efficient rotation and to undertake investments that increase the yield of the forest because that strategy maximizes their net benefits.

Additionally, not all private firms will follow efficient forest-management practices because they may choose not to maximize profits, they may be operating at too small a scale of operation, or externalities or public policy may create inefficient incentives. Finally, when amenity values are large and not captured by the forest owner, the private rotation period may fail to consider these values, leading to an inefficiently short rotation period or even harvesting forests that should be preserved.

Inefficient deforestation has also been encouraged by a failure to incorporate global benefits from standing forests: concession agreements can provide incentives to harvest too much too soon and may fail to provide adequate incentives to protect the interests of future generations. Property rights systems can make the amount of land acquired by squatters a multiple of cleared forestland and tax systems can discriminate against standing forests.

Substantial strides toward restoring efficiency as well as sustainability can be achieved simply by recognizing and correcting the perverse incentives, actions that can be and should be taken by the tropical-forest nations. But these actions will not, by themselves, provide adequate protection for the global interests in the tropical forests. Four schemes designed to internalize some of these transboundary benefits—extractive reserves, the World Heritage List, royalty payments, and forest certification—have already begun to be implemented.

However, even achieving an efficient rotation may not be sufficient to achieve a sustainable outcome. If the biological growth rate of the forest is sufficiently low, maximizing the present value of net benefits from harvesting may result in a harvest level that exceeds the growth of the forest. In this case the proceeds increase the present value more if they are invested in financial assets rather than forest assets. Finally, whether sustainable forest management is sufficient to assure that woody biomass combustion is a carbon-neutral fuel remains a debatable point.

Discussion Questions

1. Should U.S. national forests become "privatized" (sold to private owners)? Why or why not?
2. In his book *The Federal Land Revisited*, Marion Clawson proposed what he called the "pullback concept":

   Under the pullback concept any person or group could apply, under applicable law, for a tract of federal land, for any use they chose; but any other person or group would have a limited time between the filing of the initial application and granting of a lease or the making of the sale in which to "pull back" a part of the area applied for. … The user of the pullback provision would become the applicant for the area pulled back, required to meet the same terms applicable to the original application, … but the use could be what the applicant chose, not necessarily the use proposed by the original applicant. (216)

   Evaluate the pullback concept as a means for conservationists to prevent some mineral extraction or timber harvesting on federal lands.

Self-Test Exercises

1. Suppose there are two identical forest plots except that one will be harvested and left to regrow while the second will be cleared after the harvest and turned into a housing development. In terms of efficiency, which one should have the oldest harvest age? Why?
2. In Table 9.1, when $r = 0.02$, the present value of the cost rises for 68 years and then subsequently declines. Why?
3. As our energy structure transitions toward renewable fuels, forest-based biomass fuels have benefited from this transition. What are the likely effects of this transition on consumers, producers, and the states that host these resources?
4. Would a private forest owner normally be expected to reach an efficient balance between using their forest for recreation and for harvesting wood? Why or why not?
5. Compare forest certification and the certification of organic produce in terms of the relative degree to which each type of certification could, by itself, be expected to produce an efficient outcome.
6. Would a rise in the price of timber make sustainable forest practices more or less likely? Why?

Appendix: The Harvesting Decision: Forests

Suppose that an even-aged stand of trees is to be harvested at an age that maximizes the present value of the harvested timber. That age can be found by (1) defining the present value of the harvested timber as a function of the age of the stand, and (2) maximizing the function with respect to age.

$$\text{Present Value} = \left[PV(t) - C_b V(t) \right] e^{-rt} - C_p$$

where:

P = the price received per unit of harvested volume
$V(t)$ = the volume of timber harvested at age t
C_b = the per-unit cost of harvesting the timber
t = the age of the timber
C_p = the fixed cost of planting

Taking the derivative of the function with respect to age and setting it equal to zero yields[8]

$$(P - C_b)\frac{dV(t)}{dt} = (P - C_b)V(t)r$$

or rewriting yields

$$\frac{\dfrac{dV(t)}{dt}}{V(t)} = r$$

Translated into English, this condition implies that the rate of return from letting the stand grow over the last increment of age should be equal to the market rate of return.

Notes

1 Karjalainen, E., Sarjala, T., & Raitio, H. (2010). Promoting human health through forests: Overview and major challenges. *Environmental Health and Preventive Medicine, 15*(1), 1–8.
2 In this context, sustainability refers to harvesting no more than would be replaced by growth; sustainable harvest would preserve the interests of future generations by assuring that the volume of remaining timber was not declining over time.
3 The numerical model in the text is based loosely on the data presented in Clawson, M. (1977). *Decision Making in Timber Production, Harvest, and Marketing.* Research Paper R-4. Washington, D.C.: Resources for the Future, 13, Table 1. The mathematical function relating volume to age stand in Figure 9.1 is a third-degree polynomial of the form $v = a + bt + ct^2 + dt^3$, where v = volume in cubic feet, t = the age of the stand in years, and a, b, c, and d are parameters that take on the values 0, 40, 3.1, and –0.016, respectively.
4 One way for the government to capture this rent would be to put timber concessions up for bid. Bidders would have an incentive to pay up to the stumpage value for these concessions. The more competitive the bidding was, the higher the likelihood that the

government would capture all of the rent. In practice, many of the concessions have been given to those with influence in the government at far-below market rates. See Vincent, J. R. (May 1990). Rent capture and the feasibility of tropical forest management. *Land Economics, 66*(2), 212–223.

5 Currently, many foresters believe that the sustainable yield for closed tropical rainforests is zero, because they have not yet learned how to regenerate the species in a harvested area once the canopy has been destroyed. Destroying the thick canopy allows the light to penetrate and changes the growing conditions and the nutrient levels of the soil sufficiently that even replanting is unlikely to regenerate the types of trees included in the harvest.

6 For a contemporary example see Lanlois, J. (July 22, 2021). Land grabbers: The growing assault on Brazil's indigenous areas. *Yale Environment 360*. https://e360.yale.edu/features/land-grabbers-the-growing-assault-on-brazils-indigenous-areas.

7 We have previously discussed offsets in Chapter 13. For more information on the details of forestry offsets see Freedberg, W., & Smith, S. (2021). *Forest Carbon Market Solutions: A Guide for Massachusetts Municipalities*. Massachusetts Audubon Society, Inc. https://ag.umass.edu/sites/ag.umass.edu/files/land-conservation-tools/resources/forest_carbon_market_solutions.pdf.

8 If we had used a discrete time framework (i.e., $(1 + r)^t$ were used for discounting instead of e^{-rt}), then the optimal condition would be the same, except r would be replaced by $\ln(1 + r)$. You can verify that for the values of r we are using, these two expressions are approximately equal.

Further Reading

Amacher, G. S., Ollikainen, M., & Koskela, E. A. (2009). *Economics of Forest Resources*. Cambridge, MA: MIT Press. This book provides an introduction to forest economics and an overview of the development of the field.

Araujo, C., Bonjean, C. A., Combes, J. -L., Motel, P. C., & Reis, E. J. (2009). Property rights and deforestation in the Brazilian Amazon. *Ecological Economics, 68*(8–9), 2461–2468. This paper focuses on the impact of property rights insecurity on deforestation in the Brazilian Amazon.

Austin, K. G., Baker, J. S., Sohngen, B. L. et al. (2020). The economic costs of planting, preserving, and managing the world's forests to mitigate climate change. *Nature Communications, 11*, 5946. https://doi.org/10.1038/s41467-020-19578-z. The Intergovernmental Panel on Climate Change (IPCC) had reported that such forestry mitigation strategies, which include afforestation, reforestation, improved forest management, and avoided forest conversion, can play a critical role in the global abatement portfolio. The crucial question is at what cost? This article investigates the cost of reducing global GHG emissions via forest sector abatement.

FAO & UNEP. (2020). *The State of the World's Forests 2020: Forests, Biodiversity and People*. Rome: FAO & UNEP. https://doi.org/10.4060/ca8642en. This volume assesses progress to date in meeting global targets and goals related to forest biodiversity and examines the effectiveness of policies, actions, and approaches, in terms of both conservation and sustainable development outcomes.

Zhang, Daowei. (2016). Payments for forest-based environmental services: A close look. *Forest Policy and Economics, 72*, 78–84. This paper compares payments for environmental services with other policy and market mechanisms to encourage the efficient provision of environmental services on forested land.

Chapter 10

Land

A Locationally Fixed, Multipurpose Resource

Introduction

Land occupies a special niche not only in the marketplace, but also deep in the human soul. In its role as a resource, land has special characteristics that affect its allocation by markets. Topography matters, of course, but so does location, especially since, in contrast to many other resources, land's location is fixed. It matters not only *absolutely* in the sense that the land's location directly affects its value, but also *relatively* in the sense that the value of any particular piece of land is also affected by the uses of the land around it. In addition, land supplies many services, including providing habitats for all terrestrial creatures, not merely humans.

Some contiguous uses of land are compatible with each other, but others are not. In the case of incompatibility, conflicts must be resolved. Whenever the prevailing legal system treats land as private property, as in the United States, the market is one arena within which those conflicts are resolved.

How well does the market do? Are the land-use outcomes and transactions efficient and sustainable? Do they adequately reflect the deeper values people hold for land? Why or why not?

In this chapter, we shall begin to investigate these questions. How does the market allocate land? How well do market allocations fulfill our social criteria? Where divergences between market and socially desirable outcomes occur, what policy instruments are available to address the problems? How effective are they? Can they restore conformance between goals and outcomes?

DOI: 10.4324/9781032689111-11

The Economics of Land Allocation

Land Use

In general, as with other resources, markets tend to allocate land to its highest-valued use, as reflected by the users' willingness to pay. Consider Figure 10.1, which graphs three hypothetical land uses for a particular plot—residential development, agriculture, and wilderness.[1]

The left-hand side of the horizontal axis represents the central marketplace where agricultural produce is sold. Moving to the right on that axis reflects an increasing distance away from the market.

The vertical axis represents net benefits per acre. Each of the three functions, known in the literature as *bid rent functions*, records the relationship between distance to the center of the town or urban area and the net benefits per acre received from each type of land use. A bid rent function expresses the maximum net benefit per acre that could be achieved by that land use as a function of the distance from the center. All three functions are downward sloping because the cost of transporting both goods and people to the center lowers net benefits per acre for more distant locations.

According to Figure 10.1, a market process that allocates land to its highest-valued use would allocate the land closest to the center to residential development (a distance of *A*), agriculture would claim the land with the next best access (*A* to *B*), and the land farthest away from the market would remain wilderness (from *B* to *C*). This allocation maximizes the net benefits society receives from the land.

Although very simple, this model also helps to clarify both the processes by which land uses change over time and the extent to which market processes are efficient, subjects we explore in the next two sections.

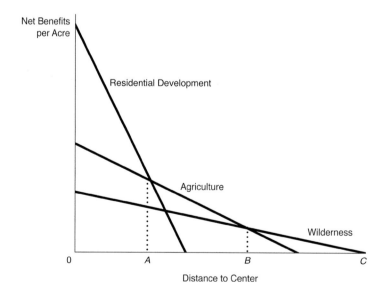

Figure 10.1 The Allocation of Land.

Land-Use Conversion

Conversion from one land use to another can occur whenever the underlying bid rent functions shift, and apparently in the United States they have shifted a great deal. The Economic Research Service of the U.S. Department of Agriculture found that urban land acreage more than quadrupled from 1945 to 2012 (Bigelow & Borchers, 2017, Table 2). This increase was about twice the rate of population growth over this period.

Conversion of nonurban land to urban development could occur when the bid rent function for urban development shifts up, the bid rent function for nonurban land uses shifts down, or any combination of the two. Two sources of the conversion of land to urban uses in the United States stand out: (1) increasing migration of both people and productive facilities to urban centers rapidly shifted the bid rent functions upward for urban land, including residential, commercial, industrial, and even associated transportation (airports, highways, etc.) and recreational (parks, etc.) uses; (2) rising productivity of the agricultural land allowed a smaller amount of land to produce a lot more food. Less agricultural land was needed to meet the rising food demand than would otherwise have been the case. While the amount of total land in the United States dedicated to farming has dropped considerably over time since 1920, irrigated acreage has been rising.

It seems unlikely that a straight-line extrapolation of the decline in agricultural land of the magnitude since 1920 into the future would be accurate. Since the middle of the 1970s, the urbanization process in the United States has diminished to the point that some urban areas are experiencing declining population. This shift is not merely explained by suburbia spilling beyond the boundaries of what was formerly considered urban.

Furthermore, as increases in food demand are accompanied by increasing food prices, the value of agricultural land should increase. Higher food prices would tend to slow the conversion of agricultural land to other uses.

What about agricultural land that is still used for agriculture, but not used for growing food? Its allocation is affected by the same kinds of factors. For example, the amount of land used to grow corn to produce ethanol has increased due to a policy that shifted out the demand curve for ethanol.

The Ethanol Story

In late 2007, Congress passed a new energy bill that included, among other things, a mandate for renewable fuels, including 5 billion gallons of ethanol made from grains, primarily corn, by 2022. Under that legislation ethanol carried a sizable subsidy, inducing more farmers to grow corn for ethanol rather than for food or livestock feed.

While some 14 percent of corn use went to ethanol production in the 2005–2006 crop year, according to the U.S. Department of Agriculture's Economic Research Service (ERS), that share rose to 36.5 percent by 2016. Even though ethanol represents a very small share of the overall gasoline market, its impacts on the agricultural sector were large.

The Role of Irrigation

Irrigated acreage is on the rise, both domestically and worldwide, although the rate of increase has been falling. Irrigation can increase yields of most crops by 100–400 percent and hence increase the value of the land on which these crops are grown. The FAO estimates that, over the next 30 years, 70 percent of the gains in cereal production will come from irrigated land, and by 2030 irrigated land in developing countries will increase by 27 percent.

However, irrigation, a traditional source of productivity growth, is also running into limits, particularly in the western United States. Some traditionally important underground sources used to supply water are not being replenished at a rate sufficient to offset the withdrawals. Encouraged by subsidies that transfer the cost to the taxpayers, consumption levels are sufficiently high that these water supplies are being exhausted. And climate change is intensifying the problem.

Contamination of the remaining water is also an issue. Irrigation of soils with water containing naturally occurring salts causes the salts to concentrate near the surface. This salty soil is less productive and, in extreme cases, kills the crops.

The Rise of Organic Food

Food markets have not only been affected by shifts in agricultural land use; they have also been affected by agriculture practices. The organic foods industry is the fastest-growing U.S. food segment. Between 2005 and 2011, certified organic pasture and rangeland fluctuated up and down, but certified organic cropland expanded nearly 80 percent, to 3.1 million acres.

Aided by the price premiums that buyers of organic food are willing to pay, U.S. sales of organic food and beverages have grown from $1 billion in 1990 to $69.9 billion in 2020.

Sources of Inefficient Use and Conversion

In the absence of any government regulation, are market allocations of land efficient? In some circumstances they are, but certainly not in all, or even most.

We begin by considering several sets of problems associated with land-use inefficiencies that commonly arise in industrialized countries: sprawl and leapfrogging, incompatible land uses, undervaluation of environmental amenities, the effects of taxes on land-use conversion, and market power. While some of these also plague developing countries, we follow with a section that looks specifically at some of the special problems developing countries face.

Sprawl and Leapfrogging

Two problems associated with land use that are receiving a lot of current attention are *sprawl* and *leapfrogging*. From an economic point of view, sprawl occurs when land uses in a particular area are inefficiently dispersed, rather than efficiently concentrated. The related problem of leapfrogging refers to a situation in which new development continues not as an extension of current development, but farther out. Thus, developers "leapfrog" over contiguous, perhaps even vacant, land in favor of land that is farther from the center of economic activity.

Several environmental problems are intensified with dispersed development. Trips to town to work, shop, or play become longer. Longer trips not only mean more energy consumed, but also frequently imply a change from the least polluting modes of travel (such as biking or walking) to automobiles, a much more polluting source. When the cars used for commuting have gasoline engines, dispersal drives up the demand for oil, results in higher air-pollutant emissions levels (including greenhouse gases), and increases the need for more steel, glass, and other raw materials to supply the increase in the number of vehicles demanded.

The Public Infrastructure Problem

To understand why inefficient levels of sprawl and leapfrogging might be occurring, we must examine the incentives faced by developers and how those incentives affect location choices.

One set of inefficient incentives can be found in the pricing of public services. New development beyond the reach of existing public sewer and water systems may necessitate extending those facilities if the new development is to be served. The question is, "who pays for this extension and how does that choice affect location decisions?"

If the developer is forced to pay for the extension as a means of internalizing the cost, they will automatically consider this as part of the cost of locating farther out. When those costs are passed on to the buyers of the newly developed properties, they will face a higher marginal cost of living farther out and are likely to be willing to pay less for a distant property.

Suppose, however, as is commonly the case, that the extensions of these services are financed by metropolitan-wide taxes. When the development costs are subsidized by all taxpayers in the metropolitan area, both the developers and potential buyers of the newly developed property find building and living farther out to be artificially cheap. A substantial part of the cost has been shifted to taxpayers, most of whom will not benefit from the new development. This bias prevents developers from efficiently considering the trade-off between developing the land more densely in currently served areas and building upon the less developed, but typically cheaper, land outside those areas. This bias promotes inefficient levels of sprawl.

Development farther from the center of economic activity can also be promoted either by transportation subsidies or by negative externalities. As potential residential buyers choose where to live, transportation costs matter. Living farther out may mean a longer commute or longer shopping trips. Implicitly, when living farther out means more and/or longer trips, these transport costs should figure into the decision of where to live: higher transportation costs increase the relative net benefits of living closer to the center so buyers are willing to pay a higher price for land that offers a shorter commute.

Subsidies can also inefficiently affect development choices. Many employers provide free employee parking even though providing that parking is certainly not free to the employer. Free parking represents a subsidy to the auto user and lowers the cost of driving to work. Since commuting costs (including parking) are typically an important portion of total local transportation costs, free parking is a subsidy that creates a bias toward more remote residential developments and encourages sprawl.

The conclusion is that if transportation costs are inefficiently low due to subsidies or uninternalized negative travel externalities, the resulting bias will inefficiently favor more distant locations.

While these factors can promote sprawl, they don't completely explain why developers skip over land that is closer in. Economic analysis (Irwin & Bockstael, 2007) has identified some other factors found to promote leapfrogging. These include features of the terrain (including its suitability for development), land-use external benefits (such as access to scenic bodies of water), and government policy (such as road building and urban large-lot zoning). Note that not all of these involve an inefficiency.

Incompatible Land Uses

As mentioned earlier, the value of a parcel of land will be affected not only by its location, but also by the character of the nearby land. This interdependence can be another source of inefficiency. When any land use confers external costs on another parcel of land, the allocation that maximizes net benefits for one landowner may not be the allocation that maximizes net benefits for society.

Interdependencies are rather common in land transactions. Houses near an airport are affected by the noise and neighborhoods near a toxic-waste facility may face higher health risks. Both situations negatively affect the desirability of that development and lower the prices a developer can expect to receive.

One current controversial example involves an ongoing battle over the location of large industrial farms where hogs are raised for slaughter. Some of the negative attributes of these farms (e.g., odors and water pollution from animal waste) fall on the neighbors. Since these costs are externalized, they tend to be ignored or undervalued by unregulated hog farm owners, creating a bias. In terms of Figure 10.1, the private net benefit curve for hog farms would lie above the social net benefit curve, resulting in an inefficiently high allocation of land to hog farms.

One traditional remedy for the problem of incompatible land uses involves a legal approach known as *zoning*. Enacted via an ordinance, zoning creates districts or zones with allowable land uses specified for each of those zones. Land uses in each district are commonly regulated according to such characteristics as type of use (such as residential, commercial, and industrial), density, structure height, lot size, structure placement, and activities allowed, among others. One aspect of the theory behind zoning is that locating similar land uses together can reduce the magnitude of the negative effects.

One major limitation of zoning is that it can promote urban sprawl. By setting stringent standards for all property (such as requiring a large lot for each residence and prohibiting multifamily dwellings), zoning can mandate a lower density. By reducing the allowed residential density, it can create or intensify house shortages, particularly for lower-income households.[2]

Undervaluing Environmental Amenities

Positive externalities, benefits that cannot be claimed by the owner, represent the mirror image of the negative externalities described previously. Many of the beneficial ecosystem goods and services associated with a particular land use may also not accrue exclusively to the landowner. Hence, that particular use may be undervalued by the landowner.

Consider, for example, a large tract of land that provides habitat for wildlife, possibly even endangered species, in its forests, streams, and rangelands. The owner would be unlikely to reap the benefits from providing this habitat. Typically, the owners do not receive the total benefits, thereby creating a bias in their decisions. Specifically, in this case, land uses that involve more of the undervalued activities will lose out to activities that convey more benefits to the landowner even when, from society's perspective, that choice is clearly inefficient.

Consider the implication of these insights in terms of Figure 10.1. The owner's decision whether to preserve the tract or develop it is biased toward development. Developed land would inefficiently expand and the habitat could be lost.

One remedy for environmental amenities that are subject to inefficient conversion due to the presence of positive externalities involves direct protection of those assets by regulation or statute. Endangered species' habitat could be put off limits for development.

Another common example involves the protection of wetlands. Wetlands help protect water quality in lakes, rivers, streams, and wells by filtering out pollutants and sediments. They also reduce flood damage by storing runoff from heavy rains and snow melts and provide essential habitat for wildlife. Regulations help to preserve the benefits from those functions by restricting activities that are likely to damage them. For example, draining, dredging, filling, and flooding are frequently prohibited in shoreland wetlands.

As Debate 10.1 points out, however, regulations designed to protect social values may diminish the value of the affected landowner's property and that creates controversy about their use.

DEBATE 10.1

Should Landowners Be Compensated for "Regulatory Takings"?

When environmental regulations, such as those protecting wetlands, are imposed, they tend to restrict the ability of the landowner to fully develop the land subject to the regulation. This loss of development potential frequently diminishes the value of the property and is known in the U.S. common law as a "regulatory taking." Should the landowner be compensated for that loss in value?

Those who support compensation say that it would make the government more likely to regulate only when it was efficient to do so. According to this argument, requiring governments to pay the costs of the regulation would force them to balance those costs against the societal benefits, making them more likely to implement the regulation only where the benefits exceeded the costs. Proponents also argue that it is unfair to ask private landowners to bear the costs of producing benefits for the whole society; those costs should be funded via broad-based taxes on the beneficiaries.

Opponents argue that forcing the government to pay compensation in the face of the severe budget constraints which most of them face would result in many (if not most) of these regulations not being implemented despite their efficiency. They also argue that fairness does not dictate compensation when the loss of property value is due to simply preventing a landowner from causing societal damage (such as destroying a wetland). Landowners should not have an unlimited right to inflict social damage. Furthermore, landowners are typically not expected to compensate the government when regulation increases the value of their land.

Current judicial decisions tend to award compensation only when the decline of value due to a regulatory taking is so severe as to represent a virtual confiscation of the property (100 percent loss in value). Lesser declines are typically not compensated.

Disagreeing with this set of rulings, voters in Oregon in 2004 approved Measure 37, which allowed individual landowners to claim compensation from the local community for any decrease in property value due to planning, environmental, or other government regulations. After witnessing the less-than-desirable effects of that measure, voters passed Measure 49 in 2007, which had the effect of narrowing the impact of Measure 37.

Which sets of arguments do you find most compelling? Why?

The Influence of Taxes on Land-Use Conversion

Many governments use taxes on land (and facilities on that land) as a significant source of revenue. For example, many governments tax estates (including the value of land) at the time of death and governments use taxes to fund education and other public services. In addition to raising revenue, however, certain taxes also can create incentives to convert land from one use to another, even when such conversions would not be efficient.

The Real Estate Tax Problem

In the United States, a *real estate tax*—a tax imposed on land and facilities on that land—is typically the primary source of funding for local governments. A real estate tax has two components: the tax rate and the tax base. The tax base (the taxable value of the land) is usually determined either by market value, as reflected in a recent sale, or as estimated by a professional estimator called an assessor.

An interesting aspect of this system is that, because land may be sold infrequently, the assessment is normally based upon estimated market value. This valuation estimate can be quite different from the value of the land in its current use. Therefore, when a land-intensive activity, such as farming, is located in an area under significant development pressure, the tax assessment may reflect the development potential of the land, whether or not the land is likely to be sold. Since the value of developable land is typically higher, potentially much higher, the tax payments required by this system may raise farming costs (and lower net income) sufficiently to result in a conversion of farmland to development, a conversion that would not occur if land were taxed solely on its current use.

Market Power

For all practical purposes, the total supply of land is fixed. Furthermore, since the location of each parcel is unique, an absence of good substitutes can sometimes give rise to market power problems. Because market power allows the seller to charge inefficiently high prices, market power can frustrate the ability of the market to achieve efficiency by preventing transfers that would increase social value. One example of this problem is when market power inhibits government acquisitions to advance some public purpose.

The "Frustration of Public Purpose" Problem

One of the functions of government is to provide certain services, such as parks, potable drinking water, sanitation services, public safety, and education. To provide these services, it may be necessary to convert land that is being used for a private purpose to a public use, such as creating a new public park or building a new road.

Efficiency dictates that this conversion should take place only if the benefits from the conversion exceed its costs. The public sector could simply buy the land from its current owner, of course, and that approach has much to recommend it. Not only would the owner be adequately compensated for giving up ownership, but an outright purchase would make sure that the opportunity cost of the land (represented by the inability of the previous owner to continue its current use) would be reflected in the decision to convert the land to public purpose. If the benefits from the conversion were lower than the cost (including the loss of benefits from the previous use as a result of the conversion), the conversion would not (and from an efficiency point of view should not) take place.

Suppose, however, the owners of the private land recognize that their ownership of the specific parcel of land most suited for this public purpose creates an opportunity to become a monopolist seller. To capitalize on this opportunity, they could hold out until such time as the public sector paid a monopoly price for the land. When this occurs, it could represent an inefficient frustration of the public purpose by raising the cost to an inefficiently high level.[3] Sellers with market power could inefficiently limit the amount of land acquired by the public sector to provide community access to such amenities as parks, bike paths, and nature trails.

In the United States the traditional device for controlling the "frustration of public purpose" problem is the legal doctrine known as *eminent domain*. Under eminent domain, the government can legally acquire private property for a "public purpose" by condemnation (forced transfer), as long as the landowner is paid "just compensation."

Two characteristics differentiate an eminent domain condemnation from a market transaction. First, while the market transfer would be voluntary, the transfer under eminent domain is mandatory—the landowner cannot refuse. Second, the compensation to the landowner in an eminent domain proceeding is determined not by agreement of both parties, but by a judicial determination of a fair price.

Notice that while this approach can effectively eliminate the "holdout" problem and force the public sector to pay for (and, hence, recognize) the opportunity cost of the land, it will only be efficient if the conversion is designed to fulfill a legitimate public purpose and the payment does, in fact, reflect the true opportunity cost of the land. Not surprisingly, both aspects have come under considerable legal scrutiny.

The eminent domain determination of just compensation typically involves one or more appraisals of the property provided by disinterested experts who specialize in valuing property. In the case of residential property, appraisals are commonly based on recent sales of comparable properties in the area, suitably adjusted to consider the unique characteristics of the parcel being transferred. Since in reasonable circumstances (e.g., a farm in the family for generations), this inferred value may not reflect a specific owner's true valuation,[4] it is not surprising that landowners frequently do not agree that the compensation ultimately awarded by this process is "fair"; appeals are common.

Controversy also is associated with the issue of determining what conversions satisfy the "public purpose" condition (see Debate 10.2).

DEBATE 10.2

What Is a "Public Purpose"?

The U.S. Constitution only allows the eminent domain power to be used to accomplish a "public purpose." What exactly is a public purpose?

Although acquiring land for typical facilities, such as parks and jails, is settled legal terrain, decisions that justify the use of eminent domain to condemn private neighborhoods to facilitate urban renewal by private developers are much more controversial.

For example, in *Kelo v. City of New London, Conn. 125 S.Ct. 2655* (2005), the court upheld the government development authority's right to use eminent domain to acquire parcels of land that it plans to lease to private developers in exchange for a developer agreement to develop the land according to the terms of a development plan that is approved by the government.

Those who support this decision point out that large-scale private developments face many of the same market power obstacles (such as "holdouts") faced by the public sector. Furthermore, since large-scale private developments of this type provide such societal benefits as jobs and increased taxes to the community, eminent domain is seen as justified to prevent inefficient barriers that inhibit development.

Opponents suggest that this is merely using governmental power to favor one set of private landowners (the developers) over others (the current owners of the land). And in many cases this land acquisition raises fairness concerns because it results in many displaced minority and/or lower-income residents.

From an economic point of view, should publicly regulated private development such as this be allowed to fulfill the "public purpose" test? When it is allowed, should the developers be under any special requirements to assure that public benefits are forthcoming or displaced parties are treated fairly?

Special Problems in Developing Countries

Insecure Property Rights

In many developing countries, property rights to land are either informal or nonexistent. Land uses may be determined on a first-come, first-served basis and the occupiers do not actually hold title to the land. Rather, taking advantage of poorly defined and/or poorly enforced property rights, they acquire the land simply by occupying it, not by buying or leasing it. Although the land is acquired for free, the holders run the risk of being evicted by someone else with an enforceable claim for the land. The displaced party could well be indigenous people who have occupied the land for a very long time.

The lack of clear property rights can introduce both efficiency and equity problems. The efficiency aspect is caused by the fact that a first-come, first-served system of allocating land affects both the nature of the land use and incentives to preserve its value. Early occupiers of the land determine the use and, since the land cost them nothing to acquire, the opportunity cost associated with other potentially more socially valuable uses is never considered. Hence, low-valued uses could dominate high-valued uses by default. This means, for example, extremely valuable forests or biologically diverse land could be converted to housing or agriculture even when other locations might be much better.

How about value preservation? Does a first-come, first-served allocation provide incentives to preserve the value of the land or to degrade it? Because occupiers with firm property rights could sell the land to others, the ability to resell provides an incentive to preserve its value to achieve the best possible price. If, on the other hand, any movement off the land causes a loss of all rights to the land, as would be the case with an occupier who does not hold a land title, those incentives to preserve the property's value are diminished.

This conflict also has an important equity dimension. The absence of property rights gives occupiers no legal defense against competing claims. Even if some indigenous people have sustainably used a piece of land for a very long period of time, without the protection of legal title any implicit property rights they hold are simply unenforceable. If marketable natural resources are discovered on "their" land, enormous political pressure will be exerted to evict the occupants, with few protections afforded to their interests.

Efficiency mandates that land-use conversion should take place only if the net benefits of the new use are larger than the net benefits of the old. The traditional means of determining when that test has been satisfied is to require that the current owners be sufficiently compensated such that they would voluntarily give up their land. If their rights are not enforceable and, hence, can simply be ignored, the land can be converted and they can be involuntarily displaced even when it is efficient to preserve the land in its current use. With formal enforceable property rights, current users could legally defend their interests. The questionable enforceability of informal rights would make current users holding those rights much more vulnerable.

The Poverty Problem

In many developing countries, poverty may constrain choices to the extent that degradation of the land can dominate sustainable use, simply as a matter of survival. Even when the present value of sustainable choices is higher, a lack of income or other assets may preclude taking advantage of the opportunity.

As one early article (Barbier, 1997) pointed out, poor rural households in developing countries generally only have land and unskilled labor as their principal assets. They have few human, financial, or physical capital assets. The unfortunate consequence of this situation is that poor households with limited holdings often face important labor, land, and cash constraints on their ability to invest in land improvements. Barbier relates the results of a study he conducted with Burgess in Malawi:

> In Malawi female-headed households make up a large percentage (42 percent) of the "core-poor" households. They typically cultivate very small plots of land (<0.5 ha) and are often marginalized onto the less fertile soils and steeper slopes.... They are often unable to finance agricultural inputs such as fertilizer, to rotate annual crops, to use "green manure" crops or to undertake soil and water conservation. As a result, poorer female headed households generally face declining soil fertility and crop yields, further exacerbating their poverty and increasing their dependence upon the land.

This degradation of land, due to inadequate investment in maintaining it, can cause farmers to migrate from that degraded land to other marginal land, only to have that land suffer the same fate. For similar reasons, poverty can exacerbate tropical deforestation, promote overgrazing, and hasten the inefficient conversion of land to agriculture.

Innovative Market-Based Policy Remedies

The previous sections identify several sources of market and public sector failure in the allocation of land to its various uses. One way to deal with those failures is to establish a complementary role between the economy and the government. If the policy remedies are to be efficient, however, they must be able to rectify the failures without introducing a new set of inefficiencies—no small task, as we shall see.

Establishing Property Rights

In areas where they do not already exist, merely establishing enforceable property rights can rectify some market inefficiencies, but the circumstances must be right for the outcome to be efficient. In an early, highly influential article, Harold Demsetz (1967) pointed out that the efficient system of property rights tends to evolve over time in the face of changing circumstances.

The establishment of formal property rights systems can mitigate or avoid the problems of overexploitation that can occur when land is merely allocated on a first-come, first-served basis. However, establishing a legally enforceable system of private property rights is a costly venture. In cases where land uses are relatively homogeneous and the land is abundant relative to the demand for it, any inefficiency associated with the absence of property rights could well be smaller than the significant cost associated with establishing a property rights system. As the demand for and value of land increase, however, a point will normally be reached when the inefficiencies associated with the absence of a property rights system become so large that bearing the additional administrative costs of establishing it becomes justified. Enforceable, transferable claims can encourage both efficient transfer and efficient maintenance of the value of the property, since in both cases the seller would benefit directly. In the absence of the specific circumstances giving rise to the inefficiencies noted in this chapter, establishing secure property rights can cause private and social incentives to coincide.

Transferable Development Rights

Owners of land that efficiency suggests should be preserved are typically opposed to zoning ordinances designed to promote preservation. As noted in Debate 10.1 they bear the costs of preservation while society as a whole reaps the benefits. One policy approach, *transferable development rights* (TDR), changes that dynamic.

TDR programs offer a method for shifting residential development from one portion of a community to another without putting all of the costs on the owner of the land designated for preservation. Local units of government identify *sending areas* (areas where development is to be prohibited or discouraged) and *receiving areas* (areas where development is to be encouraged).

Landowners in sending areas are allocated *development rights* based on criteria identified in adopted plans. Generally, the allocation depends upon the number and quality of developable sites available on their property.

Landowners seeking to develop in a receiving area must first buy a prespecified amount of development rights from landowners in a sending area. In principle, the revenue from selling these rights compensates the sending area owners for their inability to develop their land and, hence, makes them more likely to support the restrictions.[5] It seeks to preserve land without burdening either the public budget or the owners of the preserved land (see Example 10.1).

EXAMPLE 10.1

Controlling Land Development with TDRs in Practice

The New Jersey Pinelands is a largely undeveloped, marshy area in the southeastern part of the state encompassing approximately 1 million acres. This area provides habitat for several endangered species. In order to direct development to the least environmentally sensitive areas, the Pinelands Development Commission created Pineland Development Credits (PDCs), a form of transferable development rights.

Landowners in environmentally sensitive areas received 1 PDC in exchange for every 39 acres of existing preserved farmland, 1 PDC for every 39 acres of preserved upland, and 0.2 PDC for every 39 acres of wetlands. To create a demand for these credits, developers seeking to increase the standard density on land in the receiving area, which is specifically zoned for development, were required to acquire 1 PDC for every 4 units of density increase. The price of credits was set by the market.

To assure that the market would be vigorous enough, the commission also established a Pinelands Development Credit Bank to act as a purchaser of last resort for PDCs at the statutory price of $10,000 per credit. In 1990, the bank auctioned its inventory at the price of $20,200 per PDC. By 1997 developers had used well over 100 PDCs. In fiscal year 2020 total sales of transferable development rights were $555,100.00 with an average sale price per right of $9,739.00. One transferable development right equals one-quarter Pinelands Development Credit (PDC).

Sources: Anderson, R. C., & Lohof, A. Q. (1997). *The United States Experience with Economic Incentives in Environmental Pollution Control Policy*. Washington, D.C.: Environmental Law Institute; New Jersey Pinelands Development Commission website, www.state.nj.us/pinelands/pdcbank (Accessed July 22, 2021).

Conservation Easements

One particularly popular approach to preserving land is known as a *conservation easement*. A conservation easement is a legal agreement between a landowner and private or public agency that limits uses of the land in perpetuity to protect its conservation values.

Once created, conservation easements can be either sold or donated. If a donation benefits the public by permanently preserving important resources and meets other tax code requirements, it can qualify as a charitable tax deduction. The tax-deductible amount is the difference between the land's value with or without the easement.

From an economic point of view, a conservation easement allows the bundle of rights associated with land ownership to be treated as separable, transferable units. Separating out the development rights and allowing them to flow to the highest-valued use (conservation in this case) may allow the value of the entire bundle of rights for the land to be increased, while simultaneously preserving the land. The value of the bundle of unseparated entitlements would only be maximized if the owner of the property happened to be the one who placed the highest value on each and every entitlement—an unlikely possibility.

Suppose, for example, a landowner wants to continue to harvest timber from their land but does not want to convert it to housing. In the absence of a conservation easement, the owner is likely to face property taxes on the land that are based on highest-valued use (development) rather than its current use (timber harvest). If, however, the owner executes an agreement with a public or private entity that can legally administer a conservation easement, property taxes will fall (since the assessed value is now lower), and the owner will either get a substantial income tax break (in the case of a charitable donation of the easement to a qualified recipient) or the revenue (if the easement is sold). Meanwhile, the land is protected in perpetuity from any restricted uses that are specified in the easement and the current owner can use the land for all other legal purposes.

Conservation easements have much to recommend them. Since they are voluntary transactions, no one is forced to part with the development rights; consent is required for any transfer. This approach also allows land to be protected from unwanted uses much more cheaply than would be possible if the only option for protection were to purchase the land itself, rather than just specific rights contained in the easement.

Easements, however, can also introduce problems. Land uses affected by the conservation easement must be monitored to ensure that the terms of the agreement continue to be upheld and, if they are not, to bear the costs of a legal action to enforce compliance with the agreement. These legal actions are not cheap. In addition, the perpetual nature of conservation easements could become a problem if and when, in the far distant future, development becomes the efficient use.

Land Trusts

What kinds of entities can take on the monitoring and enforcement burdens associated with assuring compliance with the easement agreement, keeping in mind that these duties may last forever? Sometimes a government entity performs this role but, increasingly, legal entities, known as conservation *land trusts*, have been created for this purpose. A conservation land trust is a nonprofit organization that, as all or part of its mission, actively works to conserve land using a variety of means. It can purchase land for permanent protection or accept donations or bequests of either land or conservation easements. Because they are organized as charitable organizations under tax laws, donations of easements or land to a land trust can entitle the donor to a charitable deduction on his/her income tax.

Development Impact Fees

Development impact fees are charges imposed on a developer to offset the additional public-service costs of new development. Normally applied at the time a developer receives a building permit, the revenues are dedicated to funding the additional services, such as water and sewer systems, roads, schools, libraries, and parks and recreation facilities, made necessary by the presence of new residents in the area. Since the costs arising from those fees are presumably passed on to those buying houses in the development, in principle they protect against the public infrastructure problem by internalizing the costs of extending services beyond the current service area. Internalizing that externality restores the incentives associated with choosing the location of residential development and reduces one distortion that could otherwise promote inefficient leapfrogging and sprawl.

Real Estate Tax Adjustments

Several governments offer programs to discount real estate taxes as a means to protect a socially desired current use, particularly when undiscounted taxes are providing an inefficient bias against that use. Recall that when real estate taxes are based upon market value, rather than current use, the tax structure can put pressure on the owner to inefficiently convert the land. This would be particularly true if the current activities are land-intensive (farming or a preserved forest, for example) and the land could be sold profitably for a new residential development. This pressure can be inefficient to the extent that it understates external social benefits.

Under schemes to try to counteract this tax bias, eligible property owners seen as conferring uncompensated external benefits on the community are offered specified reductions in their assessed value. Programs are typically available to the property owner through an application process run by the relevant government body. Certain criteria must be met for each program for a parcel of land to be eligible and any future changes in the eligibility of the land enrolled in this tax relief program are subject to disqualification and a penalty.[6]

Summary

Land is an important environmental resource not only in its own right, but also as a complement to many related ecosystems. By providing habitat for wildlife, recharge areas for aquifers, and the foundation for such land-intensive activities as forestry and agriculture, the allocation of land lies at the core of a harmonious relationship between humans and the environment.

The market, which tends to allocate land to the use that maximizes its value, supports land conversion as the relative values of the various land uses change. For example, in the United States the amount of land allocated to agriculture has declined over time, while the allocations within types of agriculture have changed as well. In particular, relatively more agricultural land has been dedicated to the production of fuel (ethanol), due to a policy mandate, and more has been allocated to certified organic farms due to the price premium their produce can command.

While in principle the market allocates land to its highest and best use, in practice several attributes of land and the allocation process can result in inefficient, unsustainable, and/or unjust outcomes. Sources of these problems include not only market problems such as poorly specified property rights, market power, and externalities, but also public sector problems associated with tax and user fee structures that produce inefficient incentives. Furthermore, by constraining choices, poverty can also lead to both inefficient and unfair allocations of land.

Several policy instruments, some quite novel, are available to counteract socially undesirable outcomes. They include the formalization of property rights to protect users from intrusion, transferable development rights, and conservation easements to both reduce the cost and increase the likelihood that efficient preservation can take place. In terms of the public sector, policy options include changes to real estate tax structures and development impact fees to eliminate inefficient incentives, thereby promoting efficient land-use decisions. While this collection of policy options can correct some of the imbalances in the land-allocation system, most represent, at best, a movement in the right direction, not the full restoration of efficiency, fairness, or sustainability.

Discussion Question

1. Air pollution officials in California's Central Valley have opened a new front in the war against urban sprawl, and regulators and environmental advocates throughout the state are watching closely. Starting in March 2006, the San Joaquin Valley Air Pollution Control District in California became the first regulatory body in the country to impose fees on new residential and commercial

development specifically focused on reducing air pollution. Critics argue that this is an ineffective way to control pollution and will mainly drive up housing prices, making housing less affordable for the poor. Is this policy a good idea?

Self-Test Exercises

1. Suppose a city finds that its express highways into the city are congested and is considering two remedies: (1) imposing a congestion charge on all users of its expressways during the peak periods, and (2) adding a couple of lanes to the existing expressways. Would these remedies be expected to have the same effects on residential land use? Why or why not?
2. With respect to strategies used by land conservation groups to preserve land, conservation easements seem to be expanding more rapidly than buying land for preservation. In what respect might conservation easements be relatively more attractive to land conservation groups than simply purchasing the land? What is the economic incentive for landowners to donate land or conservation easements to the conservation organizations?
3. Suppose a government was trying to decide whether to fund primary and secondary education with either a property tax or an income tax. What implications might this choice have for land use in that area?
4. Changing demographics can also effect changes in land use. In the United States, the proportion of the population in the 65-and-older age bracket is growing. What effects might this have on the location and the nature of the residential housing stock?
5. In the United States, the production of ethanol fuel from corn is subsidized. Use bid rent function analysis to suggest what effects this subsidy might be expected to have on land use.
6. Increasingly sophisticated communications technology is allowing more people to work at home. What effect do you think this might have on land-use patterns, specifically the density of residential development?

Notes

1 For our purposes in this thought experiment, wilderness is a large, uncultivated tract of land that has been left in its natural state.
2 For evidence on the empirical relevance of this point, see McConnell et al. (2006a).
3 Although we are focusing here on a public-sector action, the same logic would apply to a developer trying to buy several pieces of land to build a new large development. One of the potential sellers could hold out for an inflated price, recognizing that their parcel was necessary for the development to go forward, but only the public sector is entitled to condemn property by eminent domain. For this reason private developers try to get local governments to act on their behalf. See Debate 10.2.
4 In this case, "true valuation" means a price that would have been accepted in a voluntary transaction in the absence of monopoly considerations.
5 For an analysis of how a program in Calvert County, Maryland, has worked, see McConnell et al. (2006b).
6 In the farmland program, for example, if the property no longer qualifies as a farmland tract, then the assessed penalty would be an amount equal to the taxes that would have been paid in the last 5 years if it had not been farmland, less the taxes that were originally assessed, plus any interest on that balance.

Further Reading

Bell, K. P., Boyle, K. J., & Rubin, J. (2006). *Economics of Rural Land-Use Change*. Aldershot: Ashgate. Presents an overview of the economics of rural land-use change; includes theoretical and empirical work on both the determinants and consequences of this change.

Hascic, I., & Wu, J. (2012). The cost of land use regulation versus the value of individual exemption: Oregon ballot measures 37 and 49. *Contemporary Economic Policy, 30*(2), 195–214. Examines the effects on land values of the zoning regulations that gave rise to Measure 37, the Oregon program mentioned in Debate 10.1.

Irwin, E. G., Bell, K. P., Bockstael, N. E., Newburn, D. A., Partridge, M. D., & Wu, J. J. (2009). The economics of urban–rural space. *Annual Review of Resource Economics, 1*, 435–459. Changing economic conditions, including waning transportation and communication costs, technological change, rising real incomes, and changing tastes for natural amenities, have led to new forms of urban–rural interdependence. This paper reviews the literature on urban land-use patterns, highlighting research on environmental impacts and the efficacy of growth controls and land conservation programs that seek to manage this growth.

Johnston, R. J., & Swallow, S. K. (Eds.). (2006). *Economics and Contemporary Land Use Policy*. Washington, DC: Resources for the Future. Explores the causes and consequences of rapidly accelerating land conversions in urban-fringe areas, as well as implications for effective policy responses.

Magliocca, N., McConnell, V., Walls, M., & Safirova, E. (2012). Zoning on the urban fringe: Results from a new approach to modeling land and housing markets. *Regional Science and Urban Economics, 42*(1–2), 198–210. This paper examines the effects of large-lot zoning on land conversion, land prices, and the spatial configuration and density of new development over a 20-year period.

McConnell, V., & Walls, M. (2009). US experience with transferable development rights. *Review of Environmental Economics and Policy, 3*(2), 288–303. This article summarizes the key elements in the design of TDR programs and reviews some existing markets to identify which have performed well and which have not.

Additional references and historically significant references are available on this book's Companion Website: www.routledge.com/cw/Tietenberg

PART II

Natural Resource Economics and Climate Change

Chapter 11

Climate Change
The Role of Energy Policy

Introduction

Energy is one of our most critical resources; without it life would cease. We derive energy from the food we eat. Through photosynthesis, the plants we consume—both directly and indirectly when we eat meat—depend on energy from the sun. The materials we use to build our houses and produce the goods we consume are extracted from the earth's bounty and then transformed into finished products with expenditures of energy.

Currently, many countries depend on oil and natural gas for most of their energy needs. According to the International Energy Agency (IEA), these resources together supply 60 percent of all primary energy consumed worldwide. (Adding coal, another fossil fuel resource, increases the share to 87 percent of the total.) Fossil fuels are depletable, nonrecyclable sources of energy and when they are burned, they contribute CO_2 to the atmosphere, thereby contributing to climate change.

Domestic natural gas and oil production in the United States remained relatively stable from the mid-1970s until the middle of the first decade of the twenty-first century. Then a new technology dramatically changed the cost of accessing new sources in shale, a type of sedimentary rock. Hydraulic fracturing, or "fracking" as it is popularly known, combines horizontal drilling with an ability to fracture deep shale deposits using a mixture of high-pressure water, sand, and chemicals. Not only does the fractured shale release large quantities of oil and gas, but this extraction process also costs less than accessing more conventional sources.

If there ever were an example of the profound effect a technical change can have, this was it! This new form of production has dramatically changed the energy situation in the United States. The change came with controversy due mainly to detrimental effects on drinking water, on wildlife habitat, and the fact that the benefits and the costs are received by different populations.

DOI: 10.4324/9781032689111-13

Since energy plays, and is expected to continue to play, such a large role in contributing to both the productivity of the economy and changing the climate, it is not surprising that a focus on energy is high on the policy agenda. How can we continue to use energy productively, while lowering energy's impact on the climate?

Future Pathways

Three main paths forward have emerged: (1) improving energy efficiency, (2) fuel switching, and (3) increasing beneficial electrification.

Energy Efficiency

Energy efficiency is defined as the amount of input energy required to provide a given service or output. Improving energy efficiency therefore involves lowering the amount of input energy to provide that service or product. For example, an energy *inefficient* heating system in a home would require more fuel to keep the home at a comfortable temperature than an energy-efficient heating system. Insulating a home, thereby retaining energy that would otherwise escape through air leaks, can also improve a home's energy efficiency. Energy efficiency investments help to meet the climate challenge by lowering emissions. As the world grapples with creating the right energy portfolio for the future, energy-efficiency policy is playing an increasingly complementary role. In recent years the amount of both private and public money being dedicated to promoting energy efficiency has increased a great deal, in no small part due to its ability to reduce emissions and lower energy costs at the same time.

Estimating the remaining opportunities for energy efficiency is not a precise science, but the conclusion that significant opportunities remain seems inescapable. The existence of these opportunities can be thought of as a necessary, but not sufficient, condition for government intervention. Although depending upon the level of energy prices and the discount rate, the economic return on these investments could in principle be too low to justify intervention, in most current circumstances that is not the case.

The strongest case for government intervention flows from the existence of externalities in energy choices. Markets are not likely to internalize these external costs on their own. Since the people making those energy-efficiency investments can capture only a portion of the total benefits, their decisions can be expected to undervalue its importance in their energy choices.

National security considerations, such as when Ukraine was attacked by Russia, and climate change externalities are two important examples. Another category involves external co-benefits (such as community health effects resulting from the reductions in health-impairing air pollution that accompany substituting to cleaner fuels).

The analysis provided by economic research in this area, however, makes it clear that the case for policy intervention extends well beyond externalities. Internalizing externalities is a very important, but incomplete, motivator for a policy response.

Consider just a few of the other foundations for policy intervention. Inadequately informed consumers can impede rational choice. One study (Sussman et al., 2022) found that renters are more likely to choose energy-efficient homes and less likely to choose inefficient homes when energy information labels are included in rental listings (something that is almost never done in today's rental market).[1] Further, limited access to capital can impede energy-saving investments even when they are efficient and could lower homeowner cost. Example 11.1 points out, however, that new billing practices are being developed that may help to diminish this affordability constraint.

EXAMPLE 11.1

On-Bill Financing in Hawaii: Solving the Up-Front Cost Problem

On April 8, 2019, Hawaii announced its Green Energy Money $aver (GEM$) on-bill financing program, a statewide initiative to make clean energy more affordable for homes and small businesses. This program provides easy-access financing for cost-effective energy efficiency upgrades as well as for rooftop solar panels and other renewable distributed energy systems. Most importantly, on-bill financing can save participants money immediately by approving only cash-flow-positive projects—those that provide average cost savings that exceed the cost of the monthly repayments including financing costs.

This system avoids the need for up-front costs. The investment in clean energy is conveniently repaid through a line item on the participant's monthly electric bill. Since a good history of utility bill payment is sufficient for participation, credit checks are unnecessary. Because the investment is tied to the utility meter (rather than to an individual), both the financing and the energy savings can easily be transferred from one participant to another as homes are sold. This enables longer repayment periods, which, along with cost-effective investments, facilitates a positive cash-flow outcome.

Source: https://www.eesi.org/articles/view/a-closer-look-at-hawaiis-innovative-financing-model-for-green-energy-investments.

Do policies to increase energy efficiency (such as subsidizing the cost of weatherizing a home) always lower emissions? Or can they trigger offsetting responses that end up undermining their effectiveness as a climate control measure? Example 11.2 explores the evidence.

EXAMPLE 11.2

Energy Efficiency: Rebound and Backfire Effects

Energy efficiency policies can trigger offsetting feedbacks that lower their effectiveness. The literature distinguishes two possible outcomes—the rebound effect and the backfire effect.

Consider an example. A weatherization subsidy could incentivize a homeowner to invest in insulating their home, thereby lowering both the amount and cost of energy needed to heat and/or cool the living space. If temperatures in the home were unaffected by this investment, no rebound effect would occur. However, a homeowner could respond to that lower cost by changing the thermostat setting to provide a more comfortable ambiance than before. Adding either a lower temperature in the summer or a higher temperature in the winter would trigger an offsetting increase in energy use. Any *increased* energy consumed in response to its lower cost is known as a rebound effect. Its counterpart, the backfire effect, occurs when the rebound effect is so large that a weatherization subsidy causes the post-subsidy energy use to increase. In this case the increase in energy from the change in temperature would be larger than the savings from lowering the amount of energy needed to maintain the same temperature.

These are possibilities, but what is the evidence on the existence, frequency, and magnitude of these effects? A review of the studies seeking to answer this question finds "that the existing literature does not support claims that energy efficiency gains will be reversed by the rebound effect" (Gillingham et al., 2016, p. 85). In other words, the existing literature provides little, if any, support for a backfire effect. It does, however, find some evidence of rebound effects that can, depending upon the context, range as high as 60 percent.

What does this imply for the effectiveness of energy efficiency policy? Since rebound effects can offset to some degree the direct energy-reducing effects of the policy, the authors conclude energy efficiency policies may be less effective in reducing energy (and reducing carbon emissions) than generally thought.

They also, however, note that the welfare effects of the rebound effects are ambiguous. Rebound effects result in an offsetting increase in damaging climate change impacts, but also raise the consumer net benefits of having a more comfortable home. The existing literature does not provide answers as to which is larger.

Source: Gillingham, K., Rapson, D., & Wagner, G. (Winter 2016). The rebound effect and energy efficiency policy. *Review of Environmental Economics and Policy, 10*(1), 68–88.

Fuel Switching

The second major pathway for mitigating emissions, fuel switching, starts from a recognition that some fuels contribute more to climate change risk than others. The most obvious way is when they are combusted to produce some specific type of useful energy (say producing electricity or powering a vehicle). How much of a risk of climate change is posed by combustion of a particular fuel depends on the amount of carbon contained within that fuel. As can be seen from Table 11.1, among the fossil fuels, coal contains the most carbon per unit of energy produced and natural gas contains the least.

Combusting higher-carbon fuels contributes more greenhouse gas emissions per unit of input energy than low-carbon fuels. It follows therefore that switching from high-carbon fuels to low-carbon or zero-carbon fuels, all other things being equal, can lower emissions.

Table 11.1 Pounds of CO_2 emitted per million British thermal units (Btu) of energy for various fuels

Coal (anthracite)	228.6
Coal (bituminous)	205.7
Coal (lignite)	215.4
Coal (subbituminous)	214.3
Diesel fuel and heating oil	161.3
Gasoline (without ethanol)	157.2
Propane	139.0
Natural gas	117.0

Source: Energy Information Administration. https://www.eia.gov/tools/faqs/faq.php?id=73&t=11 (Accessed August 27, 2021).

Beneficial Electrification

Beneficial electrification refers to electrifying energy end uses usually powered by fossil fuels in a way that reduces overall emissions and energy costs to such an extent that the end user and the environment both benefit. Examples include switching from gasoline to electric vehicles and/or electric heating/cooling systems when they are powered by clean electricity.

This new emphasis on beneficial electrification will require an expansion of generation capacity, while assuring that system reliability can be maintained or enhanced in the future. This has triggered some novel approaches designed to facilitate this transition.

One policy innovation, known as the forward capacity market, uses market forces to facilitate capacity planning. ISO-New England is the independent, not-for-profit corporation responsible for keeping electricity flowing across the six New England states and ensuring that the region has reliable, competitively priced wholesale electricity today and into the future.

The Forward Capacity Market (FCM) in New England is designed to assure that system will have sufficient cost-effective capacity resources to meet the future demands both where and when they are needed. Forward Capacity Auctions (FCAs) are held annually, three years in advance of the operating period. Potential capacity suppliers compete in auctions to obtain a commitment to supply capacity in exchange for a market-priced capacity payment.

The objective of the FCM is to assure that sufficient peak generating capacity for future reliable system operation will be available. Since ISO-NE does not itself generate electricity, to assure this future capacity, it solicits bids in a competitive auction for additional generating capacity. It also solicits bids for legally enforceable future reductions in peak demand from energy efficiency. Soliciting both types of bids allows ISO-NE to compare the cost of generating the electric capacity with the cost of reducing the need for that capacity, choosing whichever is cheapest. This system allows strategies for reducing peak demand to compete on a level playing field with strategies to expand capacity.

The FCM was designed in an earlier period for an earlier type of grid. How well it will provide cost-effective reliability for a very different mix of types of generators operating within a very different type of grid is a work in progress (Aagaard & Kleit, 2022). Specifically it needs to work out how to integrate lots of new evolving aspects in the search for optimal, cost-effective reliability. The options include demand response strategies such as time-of-use pricing, intermittent dispersed sources, and electricity storage.

The Potential Role for Nuclear Energy

Although other contenders do exist, the fuel receiving the most controversial attention as a possible carbon-free energy source is nuclear energy. Aside from the fact that it is not a renewable fuel, nuclear has two main limitations—safety and economics.

With respect to safety, two sources of concern stand out: (1) nuclear accidents or sabotage and (2) the storage of radioactive waste. Is the market able to make efficient decisions about the role of nuclear power in the energy mix? In both cases, the answer is no, given the current decision-making environment. Let's consider these issues one by one.

The production of electricity by nuclear reactors involves radioactive elements. If these elements escape into the atmosphere and expose humans to sufficient concentrations, they can induce birth defects, cancer, or death. Although some radioactive elements may escape during the normal operation of a plant, the greatest risk of nuclear power is posed by the threat of nuclear accidents or deliberate sabotage.

As an accident in Fukushima, Japan, in 2011 made clear, nuclear accidents could inject large doses of radioactivity into the environment. Unlike other types of electrical generation, nuclear processes continue to generate heat long after the reactor is turned off. The nuclear fuel must be continuously cooled, or the heat levels will escalate beyond the design capacity of the reactor shield. If the high heat causes the reactor vessel to fracture, clouds of dangerous radioactive gases and particulates can be released into the atmosphere.

Storing nuclear waste raises another concern. The waste-storage issue relates to both ends of the nuclear fuel cycle—the disposal of uranium tailings from the mining process and spent fuel from the reactors—although the latter receives most of the publicity. Uranium tailings contain several elements, the most prominent being thorium-230, which decays with a half-life of 78,000 years to a radioactive, chemically inert gas, radon-222. Once formed, this gas has a very short half-life (38 days).

The spent fuel from nuclear reactors contains a variety of radioactive elements with quite different half-lives. In the first few centuries, the dominant contributors to radioactivity are fission products, principally strontium-90 and cesium-137. After approximately 1000 years, most of these elements will have decayed, leaving the transuranic elements, which have substantially longer half-lives. These remaining elements would remain a risk for up to 240,000 years. Thus, decisions made today affect the level of future risk for a considerable period.

Another consideration is that nuclear power plant construction has become much more expensive over time, in part due to the increasing regulatory requirements designed to provide a safer system.

The transition to lower-carbon fuels has created some renewed interest in the nuclear option. The first new nuclear generator in the United States in 20 years entered commercial operation in Tennessee in 2016. During that year nuclear power plants provided a bit over 11 percent of the world's electricity and reactors were operating in 31 countries. The World Nuclear Association announced that some 440 nuclear power reactors were operating in 31 countries and over 60 power reactors were currently being constructed in 13 countries. China was constructing eight new reactors a year at the time.

Different nations have come to different conclusions about the role for nuclear energy. In 1980, the Swedish government decided to phase out nuclear power. In June 2010, the Swedish parliament voted to repeal this phase-out. While Germany and Belgium are phasing out their existing nuclear power, in 2022 President Macron of France announced an ambitious plan to build up to 14 new-generation reactors and a fleet of smaller nuclear plants.

The Role of Policy in Transitioning to Renewables

On the surface the role of energy policy in managing the climate threat sounds simple enough—combine more energy efficiency with a transition to low-carbon fuels and a growing role for beneficial electrification. Like many problems, however, the devil is in the details and the transition gets more complicated as the details emerge. Fortunately, economics can be helpful in resolving some of these complications.

Renewable energy comes in many different forms. Different sources will have different comparative advantages so, ultimately, a mix of sources will likely be necessary. The extent to which these sources will penetrate the market will depend upon their relative cost and consumer acceptance. New systems are usually initially less reliable and more expensive than old systems. Once they mature, reliability typically increases and cost declines; experience is a good teacher. Without policies to encourage early adopters, however, wait-and-see reactions may inefficiently lower the adoption rate.

Policy Design Issues

One strategy involves establishing specific renewable resource goals with transparent deadlines. For example, the E.U. Renewable Energy Directive establishes an overall policy for the production and promotion of energy from renewable sources. In July 2021, as part of the *European Green Deal* package, the European Commission proposed to align its renewable energy targets with its new climate ambition. The Commission increased its binding target of renewable sources in the E.U.'s energy mix to 40 percent by 2030 and proposed setting additional targets for increasing the uptake of renewable fuels, such as hydrogen in industry and transport.

Another strategy subsidizes pioneer investments via production or investment tax credits. Since early producers and consumers—the pioneers—typically experience both lower reliability and higher costs, procrastination can be an attractive individual strategy. From an individual point of view, waiting until all the bugs have been worked out and costs come down reduces the risk of making the investment. From a social point of view, however, if producers and consumers procrastinate about switching, the industry will not be able to reach a sufficient scale of operation. With targeted incentives for pioneers the market can become large enough to take advantage of economies of scale and achieve reliable performance. Once that happens the subsidies could be eliminated.

Another common policy approach for overcoming these obstacles involves combining renewable portfolio standards (RPS) for electricity generation with renewable energy credits (RECs). Renewable portfolio standards stipulate a minimum percentage of the total electricity generated that must come from specified renewable sources such as wind, hydro, or solar. The generating entity can either meet that standard directly by generating the requisite proportion from the specified renewable sources, or indirectly by purchasing renewable energy credits from other independent generators that have built specified qualifying sources in areas not subject to an RPS.

An independent generator producing electricity from a specified renewable source produces two salable commodities. The first is the electricity itself, which can be sold to the grid, while the second is the renewable energy credit that turns the environmental attributes (most importantly, the fact that it was created by a qualifying renewable source) into a legally recognized form of property that can be sold separately and used to demonstrate compliance with an RPS. Generally, renewable generators create one REC for every 1000 kilowatt-hours (or, equivalently, 1 megawatt-hour) of electricity placed on the grid.

Providing this form of flexibility in how compliance with the RPS is achieved lowers the compliance cost, not only in the short run (by allowing the RECs to flow to the areas of highest need) but also in the long run (by making renewable source generation more profitable than it would otherwise be in areas not under an RPS mandate).

By 2021, in the United States, some 30 states, Washington, D.C., and two territories had active renewable or clean energy requirements, while an additional three states and one territory have set voluntary renewable energy goals. Globally, as of April 2017, 173 countries had some form of RPS in place.

How cost effective have these policies been? Example 11.3 discusses a study that looks specifically at that question.

EXAMPLE 11.3

The Relative Cost Effectiveness of Renewable Energy Policies in the United States

The United States depends on both renewable portfolio standards and a suite of production and investment tax credits to promote renewable resources that reduce carbon emissions. A completely different approach, carbon pricing, puts a price directly on carbon emissions.[2] How cost effective are policies targeted exclusively at promoting renewable resources relative to policies that focus on carbon pricing?

Using a highly detailed model of regional and interregional electricity markets Palmer et al. (2011) examine this question over the period from 2010 to 2035. The analysis evaluates each of these policies in terms of their estimated relative effectiveness and cost effectiveness in reducing carbon emissions, as well as their effects on electricity prices.

Between the two renewable resource policies the tax credit was found to be the least cost-effective, with the renewable portfolio somewhat better. Because a tax credit involves a subsidy and the other policies do not, the tax credit leads to relatively lower electricity prices. These lower prices promote greater electricity consumption and hence relatively larger emissions. This offsetting increase in emissions diminishes the tax credit's cost effectiveness.

However, the best policy turned out to be the third, a particular form of carbon pricing. Carbon pricing creates very cost-effective incentives for emissions reduction. Additionally, it was the only policy considered in this study that increases the relative cost of using *nonrenewable* higher-carbon sources. Neither the tax credit nor the renewable portfolio standard directly discourages the use of high-carbon nonrenewable technologies at all; they apply only to renewable sources.

Source: Palmer, K., Paul, A., Woerman, M., & Steinberg. D. C. (2011). Federal policies for renewable electricity: Impacts and interactions. *Energy Policy*, 39(7), 3975–3991.

Other types of pricing play support roles in shaping the transition as well. One pricing strategy that promotes the use of renewable energy resources in the generation of electric power is known as a *feed-in tariff*. Used more commonly in Europe than in the United States, a feed-in tariff specifies in advance the prices received by anyone who installs qualified renewable generation capacity. The magnitude of the tariff is based upon the costs of supplying the power. Specifically, it is set high enough to assure installers a reasonable rate of return on their investment. In Germany this incentive payment is guaranteed for 20 years for each installed facility. Each year the magnitude of the payment for each cohort of newly constructed generators is reduced (typically in the neighborhood of 1–2 percent per year) in order to reflect expected technological improvements and economies of scale.

A feed-in tariff offers two different incentives: (1) it provides a price high enough to promote the desired investment, and (2) it guarantees the stability of that price over time rather than forcing investors to face the market uncertainties associated with fluctuating prices or subsidies that come and go.

Of course, when higher prices are paid to renewable investors, these costs must be borne by someone. In Germany the higher costs associated with the feed-in tariffs were typically passed along to electricity ratepayers. As a result, German electricity rates were relatively high. These higher costs were expected to be temporary, since rising fossil fuel costs were anticipated to rise above the relatively stable prices dictated by feed-in tariffs.

Spain took a different approach that produced different results. It refused to allow its electric utilities to pass on the increased cost of electricity resulting from the feed-in tariffs to consumers. As a result, its electricity system's financial deficit became unsustainable, and in 2013 Spain halted new feed-in tariff contracts for renewable energy. As we have seen so often in other policy circumstances, the implementation details matter.

Anther pricing strategy in the United States, *community solar*, is designed to allow homeowners to acquire solar energy, even if it is not possible for them to install panels on their property. Under this program homeowners can acquire a specific share of the kilowatt-hour production of a large solar farm. Depending on the option they choose, participants can either be owners (literally purchasing their share of panels as if they were built on their roof) or subscribers (paying a stipulated fee for each kwh produced by their share of panels).

Under a program called *Net Energy Billing (NEB)*, the electricity sold by a community solar farm (CSF) is sold to the local utility and all community solar shareholders receive a credit on their normal utility bill for the produced electricity from their share.

Transition Complexities

Let's just take a moment to reflect on one aspect of this transition—its effect on the nature of the electric grid. The grid will have to change dramatically in response to the new energy mix. This is a new ball game and the industry is still in learning mode, not only on how all these pieces fit together, but also the sequencing of that integration. Given all the uncertainty involved in optimizing over all these moving parts, some surprises are inevitable. To illustrate the point Example 11.4 tells the story of why, in 2020, oil prices went negative in some locations.

EXAMPLE 11.4

Negative Prices in the Energy Industry

In 2020, COVID-19 caused the demand for oil to drop sharply while production plans and contracts, made earlier in anticipation of higher demand, continued. This created an unexpected excess supply of oil. Storage was possible, but expensive. For example, hiring a series of tankers to onload and store any excess oil would be very costly. On April 20, 2020, a forward market benchmark price for a barrel of oil for May delivery fell to –$37.63 (Reed & Krause, 2020).

Why did this happen and what does a negative price mean? May 2020 futures contracts required buyers to take delivery of the physical oil after April 21, 2020. Now in a corner, traders were willing to pay buyers to take oil rather than pay for storage. Just like it sounds, negative prices mean that consumers were actually paid to consume more during the negative price periods.

Electricity markets also experienced negative prices in Germany, Belgium, Britain, France, the Netherlands, and Switzerland. Germany has the most experience with them (Reed, 2017). Germany's experiences of negative prices are often longer, and deeper, than they are in other countries (IDEA, 2020).

Prices in Germany's market dropped below zero when excess wind and solar generation occurred in the market. Since a complete shutdown of conventional generation plants, followed by a restart, would cost operators more than continuing production, fossil and nuclear power plants failed to reduce a compensating amount. Meanwhile battery storage capacity was not yet advanced enough to take in the excess generation. At times Germany was able to export some of its surplus electricity to its neighbors, helping to balance the market.

Sources: Reed, S., & Clifford, K. (April 20, updated April 27, 2020). Too much oil: How a barrel came to be worth less than nothing. *New York Times*. https://www.nytimes.com/2020/04/20/business/oil-prices.html; Reed, S. (December 25, 2017). Power prices go negative in Germany, a positive for energy users. *New York Times*. https://www.nytimes.com/2017/12/25/business/energy-environment/germany-electricity-negative-prices.html; International District Energy Association (IDEA). (May 1, 2020). Germany's negative price rules bring negative consequences. https://www.districtenergy.org/blogs/district-energy/2020/05/01/germanys-negative-price-rules-bring-negative-conse.

In the old regime the electricity market consisted of a series of large investor-owned utilities that built large generating plants at centralized locations to produce and sell electricity to customers. The electricity got to the users via a series of larger transmission lines and smaller distribution lines. The cost to the customers was based on the actual costs of supplying that electricity. This process was typically overseen by state public utilities commissions to assure that each supplier charged a reasonable price and supplied reliable service.

What is envisioned for the future is quite different. Electricity will be produced from a multifaceted portfolio of generators, not only by utilities, but also by independent companies generating electricity from large solar farms or collections of wind turbines. Further, these sources will be more geographically distributed (not centralized) and supply electricity more intermittently (producing when the sun shines and the wind blows) than large plants, which directly controlled supply, both geographically and over time.

Dealing with Intermittent Sources

Supply intermittency requires not only that the new grid must be able to integrate all these renewable sources into a smoothly functioning supply, but supply must also be synchronized with demand to assure that the demands can be met at all locations at all times.

At its core the main concern involves resolving a timing mismatch. The demand for electricity normally follows several temporal patterns. Although varying somewhat from region to region, the electricity consumed in a given period (referred to as electricity load) varies throughout the year in somewhat predictable patterns. In the United States, hourly electricity load is generally highest in the summer months when demand peaks in the afternoon as households and businesses are using air-conditioning on hot days. During the winter months, the hourly electricity load is less variable, but it peaks in both the morning and the evening. Load is generally lowest in the spring and autumn, when homes and businesses have less need for space heating or cooling. During a 24-hour cycle, electricity usage in a typical home follows the daily habits of its residents. Accordingly, the least amount of electricity is consumed at night when most people sleep.

The supply of solar and wind power does not follow these same patterns. It is produced when the sun shines and the wind blows, a pattern that creates some periods when supply exceeds demand and other times when demand exceeds supply. Yet the electrical system is required to provide the electricity when and where it is needed.

The key to synchronization involves structuring incentives so that both suppliers and consumers have incentives to tailor their choices to be consistent with the overall needs of the system. Two main ingredients are having means of storing electricity from surplus supply periods for subsequent use in deficit periods and time-varying pricing (TVP) that is designed to provide incentives compatible with that synchronization. TVP generally sets the highest prices when demand would otherwise exceed supply and the lowest prices when supply would otherwise exceed demand. How does this help?

On the demand side, TVP provides incentives to shift the timing of electric usage, such as washing clothes or charging electric vehicles, when grid electricity prices are lower. Many of these temporal patterns of demand and supply are known in advance so prices can be set in advance. Fortunately, new smart technologies are emerging that allow more sophisticated types of pricing systems with more detailed and faster responses to current situations on the grid by electricity grid managers as well as electricity buyers and sellers. This combination of pricing and enabling technology is the key to scaling up this timing synchronization, which in turn provides the means for fewer emissions, lower costs, and a more smoothly running electric grid.

It also provides more incentive for investing in the capability to store electricity (through large batteries, for example) for both homeowners and the utility. Stored power from the batteries can be sold to the grid or used directly by the generating households when prices are high and stored for later sale or use when grid prices are low. Fortunately, the cost of batteries has decreased considerably.

Storage possibilities are not exhausted by batteries. Another form, pumped storage, is now also in common use. Pumped hydroelectric storage facilities store water in an upper reservoir that was pumped from another reservoir at a lower elevation. During periods of high electricity demand, power is generated by releasing the stored water through turbines in the same manner as a conventional hydropower station. During periods of low demand (usually nights or weekends when electricity is also lower cost), the upper reservoir is resupplied by using lower-cost electricity from the grid to pump the water back to it. Pumped storage hydroelectric projects have been providing energy storage capacity and transmission grid ancillary benefits in the United States and Europe since the 1920s.

This combination of enhanced storage complemented by pricing incentives provides means for dealing with the intermittency timing mismatch (the "when" problem), but as explored next, the "where" problem is handled differently.

Integrating Distributed Energy Sources

One desirable characteristic of "distributed energy sources," including solar, wind, or even energy efficiency, is that, unlike large power plants that are centrally located, they can be located near users. By locating close to users, distributed energy sources can lower the distance (and hence the cost) of transporting electricity to remote users.

Could targeting these distributed sources at areas facing transmission constraints reduce the expense of building new transmission lines and hence be a cost-effective component in the energy mix needed by that region? As Example 11.5 points out, in the right circumstances, it can.

EXAMPLE 11.5

Thinking Outside of the Box: The Boothbay Pilot Project

The Boothbay Harbor region, a popular summer tourist destination on the Maine coast at the end of a peninsula, had a problem. The existing electricity transmission line serving the area no longer had the capacity to handle its large and growing summer electrical demand. The traditional response, upgrading the transmission line, would be very expensive. Could the problem be solved using another, cheaper way?

The Maine Public Utilities Commission decided to discover whether non-transmission alternatives (NTAs)—such as distributed generation, efficiency, storage, and new smart grid technologies—could solve electric grid reliability needs at lower cost and with less pollution than new transmission lines or transmission system upgrades. In 2012, the Commission established the Boothbay Smart Grid Reliability Pilot project to test the feasibility of NTAs as a cost-effective solution for this area. In its first 3-year initial phase, the Boothbay Pilot sought to provide experience-based evidence on whether a portfolio of NTAs could reduce electricity load under peak conditions on specific transmission assets by 2 megawatts, thereby avoiding an estimated $18 million transmission line rebuild.

Based upon the results for the initial phase of this project, the evidence suggests that the net cost of the accepted NTAs, together with administrative and operational expenses, would be less than 33 percent of the cost of building a new transmission line and would save ratepayers approximately $18.7 million (including energy savings) over the 10-year project life through 2025.

These results suggest that targeting an integrated package of distributed solutions at those geographic areas facing spatially isolated transmission constraints can, in the right circumstances, produce grid benefits well beyond the direct services they provide to individual customers.

Source: Grid Solar LLC. (January 19, 2016).
Final report: Boothbay Sub-Region Smart Grid Reliability Pilot Project.

Another new productive niche for distributed energy sources is to supply remote areas (in developing countries, for example) that previously have never had access to the electrical grid. As Example 11.6 points out, townships in Africa are creating solar microgrids using novel, technology-based financing models to supply these remote areas.

EXAMPLE 11.6

The Economics of Solar Microgrids in Kenya

Entrepreneurs are constructing solar photovoltaic microgrids in remote rural areas of Kenya. Microgrids in Kenya are small electricity generation and distribution systems that can operate independently of larger grids. Due to their small scale, they typically cannot supply electricity as cheaply as the larger grid. However, for remote areas that do not have access to the larger grid, the electricity from solar microgrids is typically cheaper than the other local energy alternative, producing electricity via diesel generators.

Installing these microgrids requires capital investment and these villages are typically poor and do not have access to this capital. How do they get around this significant barrier? Entrepreneurs supply the capital, own the solar panels, and sell the electricity to local homes and businesses. The product is electricity, not panel installation.

In one financial model, cloud-based software keeps track of consumption and payments via smart meters. The smart meters measure and control power to each customer in town by communicating remotely with payment software. Although power is cut off when the prepaid credit is exhausted, customers can top up their credit whenever they wish, in amounts as small as a few cents.

One problem is that the greatest demand for power is at night when the sun is not shining, but that problem is overcome with battery storage units that typically hold up to 24 hours of electrical consumption. Storage adds to the cost, but the cost increase apparently is not enough to eliminate the economic advantages of the microgrid to residents or the profitability to the entrepreneurs. Other studies (Lawrence Berkeley National Laboratory, 2017 and Kirubi et al., 2009) suggest that wind and solar electricity can now be economically and environmentally competitive for a large portion of Africa that previously did not have access to it.

Sources: Pearce, F. (October 27, 2015). African lights: Solar microgrids bring power to Kenyan villages. *Yale Environment 360*. http://e360.yale.edu/features/african_lights_microgrids_are_bringing_power_to_rural_kenya; Lawrence Berkeley National Laboratory. (March 27, 2017). The economic case for wind, solar energy in Africa. *ScienceDaily*. www.sciencedaily.com/releases/2017/03/170327172829.htm; Kirubi, C., Jacobson, A., Kammen, D. M., & Mills, A. (2009). Community-based electric micro-grids can contribute to rural development: Evidence from Kenya. *World Development, 37*(7), 1208–1221. doi: 10.1016/j.worlddev.2008.11.005.

Access to Critical Resources

One additional complicating element in energy policy arises when energy choices depend on the availability of "critical and strategic" inputs from foreign sources. Many nations are becoming increasingly dependent upon potentially hostile foreign sources for these critical materials.

A special concern arises when foreign suppliers have the power to limit supply of a critical resource that the importing country depends upon. The motives to limit supply include raising prices to increase profits or forcing one or more buyers to change some action that the sellers oppose.

In a normal competitive market suppliers typically would not have this power. Circumstances like materials imported through a dedicated pipeline or electrical transmission line create a dependence that is difficult to overcome in any reasonable amount of time, should those pathways be blocked. Vulnerability can also be created when a group of suppliers who collectively control a large part of the market form a cartel to coordinate their decisions.

This is not merely a hypothetical threat. Historically during the 1973 Arab–Israeli War, Arab members of the Organization of Petroleum Exporting Countries (OPEC), a cartel, imposed an embargo against the United States in retaliation for the U.S. decision to resupply the Israeli military.

In addition, in 2010, the Chinese government blocked exports to Japan of a crucial category of minerals used in products like electric vehicles, wind turbines, and guided missiles. This action was triggered by a dispute over Japan's detention of a Chinese fishing trawler captain.

Further, in 2021, when Europe was dependent on Russia for about 50 percent of its natural gas supply, natural gas prices rose dramatically, causing some European lawmakers to express concern that this dependency made them vulnerable. Subsequently in 2022, when Russia attacked Ukraine, this concern became very real. Their dependency severely limited, at least initially, their ability to join other nations in supporting Ukraine by sanctioning Russia's natural gas sales.

Looking forward to the transition to renewable non-carbon fuels, many strategic minerals are currently key ingredients in the production of both electric vehicles (EVs) and the expansion of the electrical grid. Lithium, nickel, cobalt, manganese, and graphite are crucial to battery performance, longevity, and energy density in the current generation of batteries. Rare earth elements are also essential for permanent magnets that are vital for wind turbines and EV motors.

And where are these minerals located? For lithium, cobalt, and rare earth elements, the world's top three producing nations control well over three-quarters of current global output. The Democratic Republic of the Congo (DRC) and People's Republic of China (China) were responsible for 70 percent and 60 percent respectively of global production of cobalt and rare earth elements in 2019. The level of concentration is even higher for operations processing the ore.

What can nations do if confronted with issues like this? What options do they have? If potential domestic supplies are sufficient, one possibility is for the importing country to become self-sufficient in the strategic material (eliminating the need for potentially vulnerable imports). Most countries do not have sufficient domestic supplies, so that is not actually much of an option. Even if they did have this capacity, self-sufficiency might not be the efficient choice if the environmental damages arising from mining the materials are large enough. Why would nations want any imports at all when national security is at stake?

The simple answer involves three critical elements: (1) seller-initiated supply restrictions are not certain events—they may never occur; (2) steps can be taken to reduce vulnerability by switching fuels or becoming more efficient in the use of the critical material, which would lower the demand curve for the critical material; or (3) steps can be taken to reduce the vulnerability of the remaining imports.

The expected damage caused by one or more seller-imposed supply restrictions depends on the likelihood, intensity, and duration of an occurrence. This means that expected damages from a supply restriction will be lower for imports having a lower likelihood of being embargoed. Importing, when possible, from sources that are less likely to restrict supply poses less risk. Those imports are more secure so their vulnerability is less.

Investing in lowering the amount of the critical input per unit of output is another possible approach to the problem. In terms of energy imports, reducing the amount of energy needed to produce a given set of services (heating buildings, driving cars, etc.) would lower demand and ultimately lower the necessary level of imports.

While most nations could not become self-sufficient, those who have domestic resources may seek to expand domestic supply. In the United States, for example, this has happened for both oil and gas due to fracking. The introduction of hydraulic fracturing technology has reduced imports.

A third approach, a strategic reserve, would tailor the response more closely to the national security problem. A strategic reserve is a stockpile of some of the critical material that is held to reduce the impact of a temporary supply restriction if it should occur. Not only would this lessen the damage that could be caused, but it would also be likely to reduce the likelihood that the supply will be restricted, since that would now be a less effective strategy. The Strategic Petroleum Reserve is a U.S. government complex of four sites with deep underground storage caverns created in salt domes along the Texas and Louisiana Gulf Coasts. The first oil was delivered to the newly constructed SPR in 1977.

Does the transition to renewable low- or no-carbon fuels reduce or intensify the national security concerns associated with the U.S. energy situation? The transition has two benefits. Unlike fossil fuels, wind and solar sources do not have highly geographically concentrated sources. Further, they are much more widely available domestically. Less dependence on energy imports means less vulnerability.

However, the heavy dependence on rare mineral sources in a few countries remains a concern. The United States has some domestic sources of some of these minerals, but new mineral mines usually have local detrimental effects and are heavily regulated. The industry is gearing up to recycle the minerals from end-of-use products and scientists are trying to discover cost-effective ways to extract lithium from sea water and/or processed water such as the brine in geothermal power systems. However, little actual experience provides definitive evidence on whether this can be done in a way that is not environmentally destructive but is financially feasible. Hope is also being placed in innovation that will find new economically feasible production possibilities for making the necessary components of the transition from more common, available materials.

Summary

How can we continue to use energy productively, while lowering energy's impact on the environment? Three main paths forward suggest themselves: (1) improving energy efficiency, (2) fuel switching to low- or non-carbon fuels, and (3) increasing the role for beneficial electrification powered by clean electricity. Energy efficiency investments can lower both energy costs and GHG emissions by eliminating energy waste. The second major pathway—fuel switching—starts from a recognition that not only do some fuels contribute more to climate change risk than others, but some sources are renewable rather than depletable. It follows therefore that switching from high-carbon depletable fuels to low-carbon or zero-carbon renewable fuels in electricity generation can not only reduce emissions, but this clean electricity can also support products like electric vehicles and efficient home heating and cooling, which further reduce emissions. This combination of pathways offers the opportunity not only to meet climate goals, but to do so cost-effectively.

Markets have played an important role in lowering prices of solar, wind, and batteries so the transition can be managed with lower costs than would have otherwise been possible. Markets have also taken advantage of the fact that renewable energy sources such as wind and solar are distributed technologies, a characteristic that offers some opportunities for reducing distribution and transmission cost. Further new microgrid strategies are now allowing affordable access to low-income households in developing countries that have not previously been served by an electrical grid.

Markets, however, are not a sufficient solution to achieve the climate goals in the timely manner required by efficiency. To overcome barriers created by market failures including externalities and the public good nature of the climate problem, markets must be complemented by government policies.

The transition also involves complexities where policies can help. These include such aspects as creating a new type of management system to harmonize demand and supply for an electric grid with a new mix of distributed, intermittent sources. It also includes the current dependency on a few countries for key minerals that currently are crucial for such components as battery storage, electric vehicles, and the expansion of the grid in terms of both its overall capacity and geographic coverage.

Many policies have been rolled out to fill in the gaps, including renewable portfolio standards complemented by renewable energy credits, as well as production and investment tax credits. Various economic strategies such as feed-in tariffs, net energy billing, on-bill financing, and time-varying pricing all play a role. These economic policy instruments provide incentives to facilitate the smooth integration of the various pieces of the transition.

In particular pricing strategies can stimulate new innovations. These innovations can hasten the transition by encouraging the development of new cost-effective technologies and speeding up the adoption of those technologies. It is far from clear what the ultimate mix will turn out to be, but it is not only very clear that government policy is a necessary ingredient in any smooth transition to a sustainable-energy future, but also that pricing policies can play an important role.

Economic studies provide guidance on the cost-effectiveness of a wide range of energy policies. Typically, they find that carbon pricing can, in principle, be the most comprehensive, cost-effective, efficient, and fair approach to resolving the climate crisis. In the next chapter we shall take a close look at that strategy in principle and in practice.

Discussion Questions

1. Should benefit-cost analysis play the dominant role, a complementary role, or no role in deciding the proportion of electric energy to be supplied by nuclear power? Why or why not?
2. Economist Abba Lerner once proposed a tariff on oil imports equal to 100 percent of the import price. This tariff would be designed to reduce dependence on foreign sources as well as to discourage OPEC from raising prices (since, due to the tariff, the delivered price would rise twice as much as the OPEC increase). Should this proposal become public policy? Why or why not?
3. Does the fact that the U.S. Strategic Petroleum Reserve has never been used to offset shortfalls caused by an embargo mean that the money spent in creating the reserve has been wasted? Why or why not?

Self-Test Exercises

1. Some time ago, a conflict between a paper company and a coalition of environmental groups arose over the potential use of a Maine river for hydroelectric power generation. As one aspect of its case for developing the dam, the paper company argued that without hydroelectric power the energy cost of operating some specific paper machines would be so high that they would have to be shut down. Environmental groups countered that the energy cost was estimated to be

too high by the paper company because it was assigning all of the high-cost (oil-fired) power to these particular machines. That was seen as inappropriate because all machines were connected to the same electrical grid and therefore drew power from all sources, not merely the high-cost sources. They suggested, therefore, that the appropriate cost to assign to the machines was the much lower average cost. Revenue from these machines was expected to be sufficient to cover this average cost. Who was right?

2. Explain why the existence of a renewable energy credit market would lower the compliance costs for utilities forced to meet a renewable portfolio standard.

3. a. Some new technologies, such as LED light bulbs, have the characteristic that they cost more to purchase than more conventional incandescent alternatives, but they save energy. How could you use the present value criterion to decide how cost-effective these new technologies are? What information would you need to do the calculations? How would the calculations be structured? How would you use the results of these calculations to decide on their cost-effectiveness?

   b. Some typical monthly electrical bills have two components: (1) a fixed monthly change (e.g., $10 a month) and (2) a usage component (e.g., $0.14 per kilowatt-hour consumed). If a utility is planning to raise the amount they charge customers for electricity, would you expect that increase to discourage, encourage, or have no effect on the demand for LED light bulbs? Does it depend on which component they change? Why or why not?

4. Electric heat pumps are technologies that in the right circumstances can be cost-effective sources of heating. In a cold climate they frequently complement more typical energy sources such as oil or natural gas boilers in order to reduce total energy costs. To be cost-effective, however, the savings on oil and natural gas from using the heat pumps must be large enough to justify both their initial costs and the subsequent cost of the additional electricity to run them. Would you expect the number of heat pump sales to be affected by the magnitude of local interest rates? Why or why not?

Notes

1 Sussman, R., Bastian, H., Conrad, S., Cooper, E., Tong, E., Sherpa, A., & Pourfalatoun, S. (2022). Energy labels affect behavior on rental listing websites: A controlled experiment. Washington, D.C.: American Council for an Energy-Efficient Economy. www.aceee.org/research-report/b2204.
2 Carbon pricing is explored in some detail in the companion to this book: Essentials of Environmental Economics.

Further Reading

Aagaard, T., & Kleit, A. (2022). *Electricity Capacity Markets*. Cambridge: Cambridge University Press. doi: 10.1017/9781108779159. This book examines the rationales for creating capacity markets, how capacity markets work, and how well these markets are meeting their objectives.

Anthoff, D., & Hahn, R. (2010). Government failure and market failure: On the inefficiency of environmental and energy policy. *Oxford Review of Economic Policy*, 26(2), 197–224. A selective survey of the literature to highlight what is known about the efficiency of particular kinds of policies, laws, and regulations in managing energy and environmental risk.

Fowlie, M., & Meeks, R. (2021). The economics of energy efficiency in developing countries. *Review of Environmental Economics and Policy*, 15(22), 238–260. This paper reviews the empirical evidence on both the private and social benefits of energy efficiency improvements in low- and medium-income countries.

Gillingham, K., Newell, R. G., & Palmer, K. (2009). Energy efficiency economics and policy. *Annual Review of Resource Economics*, 1, 597–620. Reviews economic concepts underlying decision making in energy efficiency and conservation and the related empirical literature.

Gillingham, K., Rapsony, D., & Wagner, G. (2016). The rebound effect and energy efficiency policy. *Review of Environmental Economics and Policy*, 10(1), 68–88. One argument against energy efficiency, called the rebound effect, occurs when the actual energy savings are lower than initially expected due to offsetting consumption increases. This article reviews the outstanding literature on the magnitude and policy implications of the rebound effect.

Schmalensee, R. (2009). Evaluating policies to increase electricity generation from renewable energy. *Review of Environmental Economics and Policy*, 6, 45–64. Evaluates policies aimed at increasing the generation of electricity from renewable sources based upon on a review of experience in the United States and the European Union.

Shenot, J., Prause, E., & Shipley, J. (November, 2022). Using Benefit-Cost Analysis to Improve Distribution System Investment Decisions: Regulatory Assistance Project Reference Report. https://www.raponline.org/wp-content/uploads/2022/11/rap-shenot-prause-shipley-using-benefit-cost-analysis-reference-report-2022-november.pdf. Electric utility regulators are paying closer attention than ever before to individual distribution system investment decisions, in part because of the rapid growth in distributed energy resources and the need for new grid modernization investments. This guide was developed to explore how benefit-cost analysis could inform and improve those decisions.

Additional references and historically significant references are available on this book's Companion Website: www.routledge.com/cw/Tietenberg

Chapter 12

Climate Change

Adaptation: Floods, Wildfires, and Water Scarcity

Introduction—The Role of Adaptation Policy

Mitigation policies are important tools for reducing emissions.[1] Mitigation of emissions is absolutely necessary, but not sufficient. As we reach tipping points, certain impacts of climate change are becoming unavoidable. While the degree of damage associated with those impacts can, in part, be mitigated with carbon pricing, not all impacts are preventable. Climate adaptation, the subject of this chapter, is an inevitable component of the mix of policies needed to manage the risks from climate modification.

The Intergovernmental Panel on Climate Change (IPCC) defines climate adaptation as

> In human systems, the process of adjustment to actual or expected climate and its effects, in order to moderate harm or exploit beneficial opportunities. In natural systems, the process of adjustment to actual climate and its effects; human intervention may facilitate adjustment to expected climate and its effects.
>
> (IPCC, 2018)

The IPCC outlines two types of adaptation policies: (1) *proactive* policies, which involve taking action in anticipation of a climate change impact; or (2) *reactive* policies, which are taken in response to a climate change impact that has already occurred.

Reactive adaptation policies have been the most common practices in many places—responding to damages from hazards such as wind, floods, and fires. As the intensity and frequency of these events are expected to grow, reactive policies become very expensive. How do individuals, towns, cities, and countries prioritize among the many possible proactive policies?

DOI: 10.4324/9781032689111-14

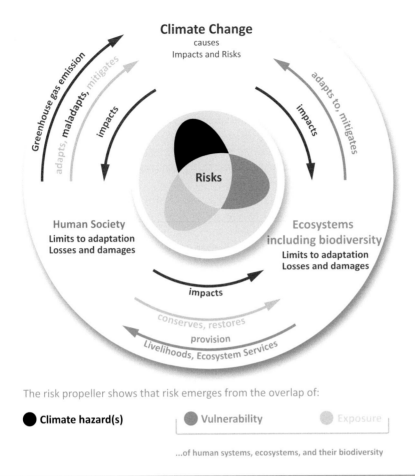

The risk propeller shows that risk emerges from the overlap of:

● **Climate hazard(s)**   ● **Vulnerability**   ● Exposure

...of human systems, ecosystems, and their biodiversity

Figure 12.1 Perspectives on Climate Vulnerability and Risk.

Source: Figure SPM.1 in IPCC, 2022: Summary for Policymakers [H.-O. Pörtner, D.C. Roberts, E.S. Poloczanska, K. Mintenbeck, M. Tignor, A. Alegría, M. Craig, S. Langsdorf, S. Löschke, V. Möller, A. Okem (eds.)]. In: *Climate Change 2022: Impacts, Adaptation, and Vulnerability. Contribution of Working Group II to the Sixth Assessment Report of the Intergovernmental Panel on Climate Change* [H.-O. Pörtner, D.C. Roberts, M. Tignor, E.S. Poloczanska, K. Mintenbeck, A. Alegría, M. Craig, S. Langsdorf, S. Löschke, V. Möller, A. Okem, B. Rama (eds.)]. Cambridge University Press, Cambridge, UK and New York, NY, USA, pp. 3-33, doi:10.1017/9781009325844.001.

Adaptation planning first involves conducting a vulnerability assessment to determine who and what is at risk and to what extent. The IPCC outlines this process in the schematic in Figure 12.1. The IPCC (2022) has stated with certainty that human society causes climate change. The report further stipulates,

Climate change, through hazards, exposure and vulnerability generates impacts and risks that can surpass limits to adaptation and result in losses and damages. Human society can adapt to, maladapt and mitigate climate change, ecosystems can adapt and mitigate within limits. Ecosystems and their biodiversity provision livelihoods and ecosystem services. Human society impacts ecosystems and can restore and conserve them.[2]

The vulnerability of a particular location is determined by examining the level of exposure to the risks and the number and types of hazards faced. While hazards are driven by changes in the climate, vulnerability and exposure are influenced to a large extent by socio-economic conditions and, as such, adaptation policies are very context- and location-specific. For example, rising sea levels is a hazard faced by many locations, but some have a higher capacity to adapt.

The Netherlands, with its considerable experience managing the risks from an encroaching ocean and the resources at its disposal, is well positioned to cope effectively. On the other hand, other places, such as some poor island nations have much lower capacity to adapt and thus have higher vulnerability.

Adaptation and Mitigation—Complements or Substitutes?

Whereas mitigation strategies try to limit damage by limiting the emissions that cause the impacts, adaptation tends to limit damage by reducing the damage caused by the impacts that do occur. The two strategies are complements in the sense that the optimal policy response contains both adaptation and mitigation. Since the marginal cost function for each strategy is upward sloping, this normally means that an optimal strategy would employ both mitigation and adaptation. Deviating from this optimum necessarily means that costs would be higher than necessary.

In another, equally meaningful sense the two strategies are also substitutes: more of one typically means less is needed of the other. To understand how they can be substitutes remember that the optimal level of either strategy would be to invest up to the point where the marginal cost of an additional unit of that strategy is equal to the marginal damages reduced by that unit. So, for either strategy, higher marginal damages imply a higher demand for investing more in that strategy.

If the strategies are substitutes, a reduction in the marginal cost of mitigation, for example, should lower the demand for adaptation. Why? Let's think this through. In an optimal policy, a lower marginal cost of mitigation with an unchanged marginal damage would imply a higher optimal level of mitigation. This increased level of mitigation would lower the resulting marginal damage not only for additional units of mitigation, but for additional units of adaptation as well. The lower resulting marginal damages for adaptation would lower the demand for it. In this sense mitigation and adaptation are substitutes: increase the amount of one and the efficient amount of the other decreases.

If you search the internet you will discover that some pundits think about mitigation and adaptation as an either/or choice. They further suggest that policymakers should choose the one that is cheaper. Economic analysis points out that this is a false choice.

- First of all, as noted previously, upward-sloping marginal cost functions for each strategy normally mean that an optimal approach would employ both strategies. Deviating from this optimum causes the costs to be higher than necessary.
- Second, to the extent that adaptation and mitigation are substitutes, they are not perfect substitutes. Adaptation strategies are necessarily targeted at specific problems in specific geographic areas, whereas mitigation strategies have broader, global damage-reduction effects.
- Third, to some extent their timing may differ. Mitigation is necessarily done early to prevent emissions from building up in the atmosphere. Some adaptation can be done early as well, but some can also be delayed until a better understanding of the intensity and location of damages emerges.

As one World Bank study put it:

> There is a need for an integrated portfolio of actions ranging from avoiding emissions (mitigation) to coping with impacts (adaptation) and to consciously accepting residual damages.... However, some irreversible losses cannot be compensated for. Thus, mitigation might be in many cases the cheapest long-term solution to climate change problems and the most important to avoid thresholds that may trigger truly catastrophic consequences.[3]

While mitigation strategies can be regional, national, or international, adaptation strategies are very localized. Adaptation, by necessity, is location- and context-specific. Unlike mitigation strategies, it is frequently less obvious which adaptation strategies might be best. The decision-making tools of economics can be very helpful in these situations. Measuring costs and benefits of adaptation strategies, considering *who* benefits and why, and acknowledging the time-sensitivity make benefit-cost analysis and cost-effectiveness analysis powerful tools for decision making (recall Chapter 3). Efficient adaptation is the minimization of the sum of damage costs from climate change plus the cost of adaptive actions.

What forms can adaptation strategies take? They can involve a mix of public and private strategies. They range from large-scale infrastructure changes—such as building sea walls to protect against sea level rise—to behavioral shifts such as when individuals waste less water, farmers plant different crops, and households relocate their dwellings to higher land for flood protection.

In the rest of this chapter, we examine examples of policies and strategies used to enhance adaptation. Although the range of possibilities is large and to some extent location-specific, to illustrate the role economics can play we focus on three areas: flooding caused by increased storm frequency and intensity as well as from sea level rise; wildfires caused by extreme drought and development in fire-prone areas; and water scarcity from increased frequency of drought. The number and cost of climate and weather disasters are increasing. Climate change is increasing the frequency and intensity of climate disasters, while at the same time increased exposure (more people living in floodplains or encroaching on fire-prone areas) and vulnerability combine to exacerbate the damages. Figure 12.2 shows that the number and magnitude of damages are on the rise.

2020 was a record-shattering year of billion-dollar events; 4th-highest annual costs ($95.0 billion)

	Annual average cost	Average events per year
• 1980–2020	$45.7 billion	7.0
• 2011–2020	$89.0 billion	13.5
• 2016–2020	$121.3 billion	16.2

Figure 12.2 Number and Cost of Billion-Dollar Disasters.

Source: NOAA. (2021). https://www.climate.gov/media/11833.

Climate Adaptation: Flood Risks—Storms, Sea Level Rise, and Storm Surges

One threat to sustainability comes from natural disasters such as hurricanes, floods, and wildfires, which are intensified by climate change. In 2021, there were a record 47 weather disasters causing over $1 billion in damages; the top three of those were flooding events in the United States, Central Europe, and China, which caused in total over $150 billion in damages. The year 2021 was the third costliest on record for weather-related disasters, coming in at US$329 billion in damages. The costliest year was 2017, reaching a record $519 billion in damages. Flooding causes more damage and impacts more people worldwide than any other natural disaster. Germany experienced $20 billion in flood damages in 2021 and Belgian floods caused $1.7 billion in damages.[4] Flooding in China caused $30 billion in damages. The costliest disaster in the United States in 2021 was Hurricane Ida, estimated at $75 billion. The following year (2022), Hurricane Ian topped that, causing $113 billion in damages (National Hurricane Center).

Building a culture of resilience could reduce nations' vulnerability to disasters as well as the costs they impose.

What exactly is resilience? In the ecology literature *resilience* refers to an ecosystem's ability to bounce back (recover) from a shock. According to the IPCC, resilience is the "capacity of social, economic, and environmental systems to cope with a hazardous event or trend or disturbance, responding or reorganizing in ways that maintain their essential function, identity, and structure, while also maintaining the capacity for adaptation, learning, and transformation."[5]

According to the National Research Council (2012), "Resilience is the ability to prepare and plan for, absorb, recover from, and more successfully adapt to adverse events."

How much difference could an increase in resilience make? A study conducted by the Multihazard Mitigation Council found that for every dollar spent on pre-disaster investments in resilience to prepare for earthquakes, wind, and flooding, about $4 were saved in post-disaster damages.

Readers of this book will recognize some of the strategies that could promote resilience. One involves providing better information to homeowners, businesses, and governments to apprise them of both the risks being faced and cost-effective ways of mitigating those risks. Another is to implement policies that provide incentives for private risk reduction investments.

Flood Insurance in the United States

Floods are one of the most prevalent and most costly types of natural disasters. One instrument that can be used to promote resilience in the face of flood risk is flood insurance.

The National Flood Insurance Program (NFIP) was established in 1968 with the passage of The National Flood Insurance Act. Frequent flooding of the Mississippi River in the early 1960s led to the perception that floods were uninsurable risks and, as such, there was a lack of availability of private insurance. One of the reasons for this was that private insurance companies rely on pooled risk. In any population of people, not all of them are expected to use their insurance, so those people subsidize those who need to file a claim. People are willing to pay annual premiums to ensure that they do not lose larger amounts of money at one point in time. With floods, the entire community is typically affected and as such the insurance company must pay out a significant amount of money, typically more than they took in in premiums.

The NFIP is managed by the Federal Emergency Management Administration (FEMA). The goals are:

1 To provide flood insurance.
2 To improve floodplain management.
3 To develop floodplain maps.

In principle, a well-designed flood insurance program could both reduce the economic damages caused and provide funds to lower the recovery time following a flood. With climate change intensifying flood risks, enhanced insurance-financed resilience could be especially cost-effective.

As Example 12.1 points out, however, the insurance program has to be both well designed and appropriately implemented if it is to be effective; otherwise, it can end up increasing the damages. The devil really is in the details.

EXAMPLE 12.1

Enhancing Resilience against Natural Disasters with Flood Insurance

Among other characteristics an efficient flood insurance design requires (1) premium levels high enough to cover the claims and (2) a structure of premiums that reflects the actual severity of the risk faced by the individual premium payers.

In the United States, NFIP flood insurance isn't mandatory, but homes and businesses in designated flood-prone areas must carry flood insurance to qualify for federally backed mortgages. Maps are used not only to designate areas that are flood prone, but also to characterize their degree of risk.

In practice does this program meet the two efficiency tests? In a nutshell ... it does not.

Premium levels have historically been too low to cover the claims. In 2018, the NFIP debt resulting from claims exceeding premium revenue was $20.5

billion. Furthermore, attempts by Congress to raise premiums produced a backlash, resulting in a political inability to raise premiums to the efficient level.

An added factor involves the maps that are used to characterize the risk. Since climate change is intensifying flood risk, older maps necessarily underestimate the risk. Unfortunately, the process of updating the maps has not kept pace, so underestimates are common.

Some problems with the structure of premiums have emerged as well. In efficient policy designs, policyholders who undertake measures that lower the risk to their structures should face lower premiums to reflect the lower risk. These premium discounts would provide the motivation for homeowners and businesses to reduce risks. As Kousky and Shabman (2016) report, the NFIP has been offering substantial premium reductions for elevating the structures, but not for other effective flood mitigation measures. As a result, those other measures are underutilized, and damages are higher than necessary. As a practical matter the program mainly enables people to rebuild in the same areas without doing enough to mitigate future risks.

One would expect that these incentives would lead to higher future claims.

A study by the Natural Resources Defense Council found that some 2109 NFIP–covered properties across the United States have flooded more than ten times, and the NFIP paid to rebuild them after each flood. One covered home has flooded 40 times and received a total of $428,379 in flood insurance payments.

Kousky et al. (2021) further note that the grandfathering of insurance premiums does not reflect changing risk conditions. Grandfathering, a policy that NFIP has continued, prevents premiums from increasing. Keeping rates constant sends incorrect signals about the real risk of flooding. In a study for Queens, N.Y., they found that maintaining 2020 premiums through 2050 would result in a huge financial shortfall for the NFIP.

The mere existence of a flood insurance program is not, by itself, evidence of efficient resilience.

Sources: National Research Council. (2012). *Disaster Resilience: A National Imperative*. Washington, D.C.: The National Academies Press; Kousky, C., & Shabman, L. A. (July 29, 2016). The role of insurance in promoting resilience. www.rff.org/blog/2016/role-insurance-promoting-resilience; Moore, R. (August 11, 2016). Flood, rebuild, repeat: The need for flood insurance reforms. www.nrdc.org; Kousky, C., Kunreuther, H., Xian, S., & Lin, N. (2021). Adapting our flood risk policies to changing conditions. *Risk Analysis, 41*(10), 1739–1743.

Increased frequency and intensity of storms and flooding have challenged the financial viability of the NFIP. Hurricane Katrina in 2005, followed closely in the same year by Rita and Wilma, created a huge debt burden for the NFIP.

The year 2017 was the second highest for flood damages claims in NFIP's 50-year history. Hurricanes Harvey, Irma, and Maria saw claim payouts and projected payouts totaling over $10 billion, well over revenues from that same year. The following year, 2018, was similar with Hurricane Matthew and the impacts of the Louisiana floods causing millions of dollars in damages. The NFIP borrows money from the U.S. Treasury to cover shortfalls, but since 2005, the program has been in financial distress (Figure 12.3).

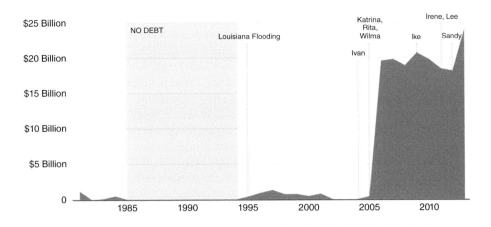

With increased frequency and intensity of large storm events, programs such as the NFIP are starting to move from reactive policies to those that are more proactive.

Proactive versus Reactive Adaptation Strategies

Rebuilding after a flood or hurricane is a reactive strategy. The way it currently works subsidized flood insurance actually provides *a perverse incentive*, meaning it incentivizes an inefficient behavior.

If the government pays, people will rebuild. Current rules that require funds to be used to rebuild in the same place exacerbate what is already a *moral hazard*. Recall from introductory economics, a moral hazard is a situation in which there is a lack of incentive to protect against risk. In this case, that lack of incentive follows from the fact that subsidized insurance protects policyholders from its consequences. The extra risks of living in a high-risk area are passed along to taxpayers.

These types of perverse incentives can intensify the risks in the long run. The NFIP has hit its borrowing ceiling several times and some debt has been forgiven, but the amount of debt the program is carrying is not sustainable. Several policies and programs have been put into place to try to remedy those perverse incentives, some more proactive than others.

Recent reforms have been aimed at strengthening the program. The Biggert–Waters Flood Insurance Reform Act of 2012 attempted to make the program more financially and structurally sound by raising flood insurance rates and by no longer subsidizing second homes and repeat-loss homes (those that had been flooded more than once). The Homeowner Flood Insurance Affordability Act of 2014 capped rate increases at 18 percent annually and repealed certain rate increases in order to keep flood insurance affordable. It also allowed properties that are in newly mapped flood zones to buy flood insurance at a preferred risk rate for one year. As of 2018 there were nearly 3.6 million flood insurance policies in approximately 1450 communities.[6]

None of these policies prevent building in the flood zones, but there are some other programs aimed at making communities less prone to high flood damages. The National Flood Insurance Program and the Federal Emergency Management Agency take some measures aimed at encouraging adaptation. Federal hazard mitigation grants provide funds for communities to invest in adaptation infrastructure. As we will see later in this chapter, these programs pass a benefit-cost test by wide margins.

Another program is the Community Rating System (CRS).[7] CRS communities receive flood insurance premium discounts for actions that reduce the damages from flood events. Communities that join the CRS program receive a score of 1 to 10. A community at high risk with no protections in place would receive a score of 10 and residents and businesses pay full premiums for flood insurance. Communities that undertake adaptation measures[8] receive points that can reduce their score. For every point a score drops, communities receive a 5 percent discount in flood insurance, for a possible discount of 45 percent for a score of 1 (FEMA, 2018).

Finally, in the most proactive reform, the Disaster Recovery Reform Act (DRRA) was signed into law October 5, 2018, as part of the Federal Aviation Administration Reauthorization Act of 2018. The Hazards Mitigation Grants Program provides funds to communities to mitigate future disaster risks. The DRRA modifies the Hazards Mitigation Grants Program with a focus on increasing mitigation and improving resilience to hurricanes, floods, and wildfires. This program funds public infrastructure projects that increase community resilience before a disaster occurs. It allows applicants for flood claims to pursue other resilience options rather than simply rebuilding the same structure in the same place. One key feature is that under the DRRA 6 percent of the post-disaster assistance FEMA provides each year will be set aside for FEMA's Pre-Disaster Mitigation fund. By providing more funding for pre-disaster mitigation, damage claims will be lower.

In 2021, FEMA announced "Risk Rating 2.0," an update to its pricing methodology meant to better communicate flood risks and create more equitable pricing. The new pricing structure will be based on the value of the home and the unique flood risk of each property. Previously, homeowners with high-valued homes were paying too little and those with low-valued homes, too much, and this policy is meant to remedy that inequity.

Flood Insurance around the World

Flood insurance can differ by who "backs" the insurance (the government or the private sector) as well as whether the flood risk is bundled together with other risks. The possible combinations result in four types of insurance: bundled flood insurance backed by private markets; bundled flood insurance backed by the government; optional flood insurance backed by private markets; and optional flood insurance backed by the government.

The United States follows the model in the last category; the NFIP is backed by the federal government. The flood risk is not bundled with any other risks (such as fire). As discussed previously, because of the numbers of policies in high-risk areas, this program struggles to be financially viable.

Germany, Austria, and South Africa follow a similar model of unbundled flood insurance, but in these cases the insurance is backed by private markets. The opt-in (or optional) model suffers from the same issue as the NFIP, with high numbers of policies in high-risk areas. With private backers, however, prices fluctuate more and it is hard to keep prices low.

Insurance companies use the idea of pooled risk in order to pay out claims for those experiencing damage from flooding events. Optional/non-bundled insurance frequently causes a situation in which most policy-holders experience damage, since low-risk policies are not bundled with high-risk.

One solution to this problem is to bundle different risks together under one insurance policy, thus spreading out the risk. If fewer policyholders are likely to make claims, financial viability is more likely. Maximizing the risk pool helps keep costs low, especially if the insurance is backed by private markets, which is the case in the United Kingdom, Hungary, and China.

France and Spain also bundle risks for insurance but use a model that is backed by the government. In France, for example, home and building insurance contracts are required by law to protect against natural disasters including floods. Private insurers are responsible for a certain amount and after that the government pays the remainder.

In many developing countries in Asia where flooding is a huge problem, most residents are unable to afford to pay for flood insurance. According to the Geneva Association, in 2014, "only 10 percent of losses from all types of natural disasters in Asia were insured compared with 60 percent in North America."[9]

Rethinking Flood Insurance

In the United States, take-up rates[10] are surprisingly low, despite mandates to purchase flood insurance for those that live in the mapped flood zones. Take-up rates are only about 49 percent (Kunreuther, 2018). Why is this the case? Kunreuther (2018) and Meyer and Kunreuther (2017) suggest that individuals tend to underprepare for disasters and other risks for six reasons.

1. **Myopia**—the tendency to focus on overly short future time horizons when appraising immediate costs and the potential benefits of protective investments.
2. **Amnesia**—the tendency to forget too quickly the lessons of past disasters.
3. **Optimism**—the tendency to underestimate the likelihood that losses will occur from future hazards.
4. **Inertia**—the tendency to maintain the status quo or adopt a default option when there is uncertainty about the potential benefits of investing in alternative protective measures.
5. **Simplification**—the tendency to selectively attend to only a subset of the relevant facts to consider when making choices involving risk.
6. **Herding**—the tendency to base choices on the observed actions of others.

Myopia refers to the idea that while a safer home might be appealing, the up-front costs can be large and tend to overshadow the potential for reduced losses in the future. Homeowner *amnesia* arises, for example, when many homeowners who have voluntarily purchased flood insurance tend not to renew that policy once they have experienced a few subsequent periods with no storms. People also tend to be *optimistic* and believe they will be immune from threats, especially those with a low probability of occurrence. *Inertia* or simple procrastination is easier than large changes and impacts the purchase of flood insurance. Flood probabilities are not easy to interpret and the tendency to *simplify* the risks may lead homeowners to underestimate them. Finally, many homeowners simply do what their neighbors do, succumbing to *herding*. Flood insurance purchases have been found to be less correlated with flood risk than with whether residents believed their neighbors purchased flood insurance! Can you think of other examples that fit these categories when you or others you know have underprepared or ignored risks? It isn't hard to find examples.

Flood insurance is one mechanism that can help individuals and communities be more resilient to flood risks, but there are certainly others. The NFIP typically requires that funds paid out in damage claims be used to rebuild a house in the same location. If that location is subject to frequent or increased flooding, homeowners are likely to be rebuilding again and again. Is there a better way? Preventing flood damages in the form of zoning changes and new building codes can save significant amounts of money. Is it worth the cost? What about for other disasters?

Given the rising frequency of disaster events and the increasing costs of recovery from those disasters across the United States, strategies aimed at reducing those damages can be very beneficial. The strategies or mitigation actions prevent property loss and loss of life. As we saw in Chapter 3, benefit-cost analysis is a powerful tool that can aid in decision making. The National Institute of Building Sciences produces an annual report that details the costs and benefits of meeting and exceeding building codes for flood, wind, fire, and earthquake hazards. It also reports the costs and benefits of select utility and transportation infrastructure mitigation and for federal hazard mitigation grants. The original study (2005) showed that every $1 spent on mitigation saves an average of $4 in future disaster costs. The most recent reports, due to the inclusion of additional data and analyses, show that the returns are actually higher.

Table 12.1 details the results by type of risk and adaptation strategy.

Table 12.1 Benefit-Cost Ratios for Each of the Four Adaptation Strategies for Each of Five Different Types of Hazards

National Benefit-Cost Ratio Per Peril*BCR numbers in this study have been rounded	Exceed common code requirements	Meet common code requirements	Utilities and transportation	Federally funded
Overall Hazard Benefit-Cost Ratio	4:1	11:1	4:1	6:1
Riverine Flood	5:1	6:1	8:1	7:1
Hurricane Surge	7:1	Not applicable	Not applicable	Too few grants
Wind	5:1	10:1	7:1	5:1
Earthquake	4:1	12:1	3:1	3:1
Wildland-Urban Interface Fire	4:1	Not applicable	Not applicable	3:1

These results find that on average, for every $1 spent on federal grants, $6 in future disaster costs are prevented (a benefit-cost ratio of 6:1!). Assuring that current model building codes are met returns $11 for every $1 invested, while upgraded (stronger than current) codes would result in a 4:1 benefit-cost ratio. Finally, upgrading the nation's utilities and transportation infrastructure would return $4 for every $1 spent on making them more resilient.

Notice that the highest payoffs vary by the type of risk. For riverine floods the biggest bang for the buck can be obtained from improving utilities and transportation infrastructure. For wind and hurricanes, it is meeting the 2018 International Building Codes for new buildings. For hurricane surges and wildland-urban interface fires, it involves enacting new, stronger codes.

What do these benefits include? The 2018 report quantifies benefits including future deaths, nonfatal injuries, repair costs for damaged buildings and contents, sheltering costs for displaced persons, loss of revenue to businesses due to interruption, loss of economic activity in the community, loss of services such as those from hospitals and schools that are damaged, insurance costs, and search and rescue costs. In particular, they find that just implementing the adoption of model codes and mitigating infrastructure would prevent 600 deaths, 1 million nonfatal injuries, and 4000 cases of post-traumatic stress disorder (PTSD). They also find that designing buildings to exceed 2015 building codes would result in 87,000 new long-term jobs.

Clearly, these adaptation investment strategies that are designed to increase resilience also increase efficiency. As the frequency (and intensity) of natural disasters increases and the cost of disaster recovery increases, pre-event adaptation planning is key. Moving from reactive strategies (insurance and rebuilding) to more proactive strategies can pay off.

Sea Level Rise and the Role for Adaptation

Flooding from increased intensity of storms is just one of the impacts of climate change. Sea level rise is another. Projections for sea level rise vary by location and emissions scenario, but sea levels are rising and will continue to rise, likely at increasing rates.[11]

Sea level rise visualization tools provide some insight into what is at risk. For example, the NOAA Sea Level Rise Viewer[12] allows users to input different sea level rise scenarios and examine vulnerability and who and what is at risk. Billions of dollars of buildings and critical infrastructure are at risk. Critical infrastructure includes things like bridges, roads, wastewater treatment plants, levees, and so on.

Exposure to the risks of sea level rise is high, both globally and in the United States. Presently, about 40 percent of the world's population (2.4 billion people) lives within 100 kilometers of the coast.[13] In the United States, approximately 128 million people live on the coast. Forty percent of those live in areas with elevated coastal hazard risk as defined by the NOAA. Annually, coastal counties produce more than $8.3 trillion in goods and services, employ 58.3 million people, and pay $3.4 trillion in wages.[14]

Adaptation to higher sea levels and the increased flood risk that comes with those higher seas can take several forms: hard infrastructure, soft infrastructure, green infrastructure, and simply moving people and infrastructure away from the risks (managed retreat).

Does economics have anything to say about how best to protect that economic value? It turns out that the tools of economics can be very helpful in prioritizing among options.

Sea rise adaptation strategies include shoreline stabilization policies. Defensive structures harden the shoreline to prevent erosion from waves. These include bulkheads or seawalls. Offensive structures dissipate wave energy before it reaches the shoreline, like breakwaters. Living shorelines stabilize the shore through enhancement of natural habitat, including sills and marshes (Stafford, 2018). These adaptation strategies all have different benefits and costs.

Defensive or hard structural barriers like seawalls or bulkheads are extremely expensive. They can also reduce access to the water and cause flooding at neighboring properties by diverting the water to nearby shoreline. They also interrupt the natural shoreline ecosystems. On the benefits side, they are durable and will stabilize the shoreline.

Offensive structures like breakwaters are more permeable and do less damage to the shoreline ecosystem. They allow access to the water. They can also maintain water quality and they allow runoff from the land back to the sea. They are also relatively inexpensive.

Living shorelines are becoming popular stabilization tools because they are the most natural. A living shoreline is a protected coastal barrier made of natural materials such as plants, sand, or rock. Some living shorelines have been made of materials such as oyster bags. They serve to break waves and protect the marsh or land behind them. They are also the most inexpensive, but they do require maintenance. They take time to establish, but once established work well to prevent flooding.

Another alternative is beach renourishment, the subject of Example 12.2.

Adaptation can buy time, as with beach nourishment, or it can be a more permanent solution with strategies such as managed retreat.

EXAMPLE 12.2

Shoreline Stabilization and Beach Renourishment: Buying Time

Many cities and towns look to beach renourishment as a way to maintain the large economic value that beaches provide to recreationists, businesses, property owners, and the ecosystem by protecting the ecosystem services value that beaches provide as nesting habitat for shorebirds and sea turtles.

Beach renourishment typically involves the dredging of sand from offshore and moving that sand to the shoreline to increase the height and/or width of the beach.

In the United States, beach renourishment projects have been implemented on approximately 350 miles of coastline, mostly on the Atlantic and Gulf Coasts at a cost of approximately $3 billion between 1950 and 2006 (Qui & Gopalakrishnan, 2018). Sea level rise augmented by storm surges causes erosion on many beaches, but as sand costs have increased, beach renourishment becomes a more costly, but often necessary solution.

The northern barrier island that makes up part of the Outer Banks in North Carolina includes the towns of Duck, Kitty Hawk, Kill Devil Hills, and Nags Head. In an interesting (unplanned) experiment, the town of Nags Head chose to replenish the sand on their outer beaches in 2011. This project was financed locally through a fund that included monies from increased occupancy and property taxes. Neighboring Kitty Hawk was not part of the beach renourishment area and hence could be considered a control on this experiment.

When Hurricane Sandy hit in 2012, the difference in damages between the two towns was stark. South Nags Head, which had a history of damage from major storms, suffered no significant structural damage to buildings or infrastructure. Nags Head experienced only about $250,000 in damages, while the neighboring towns of Kill Devil Hills and Kitty Hawk recorded millions of dollars in damages.[15] The neighboring towns subsequently renourished their beaches.

Each time a beach is renourished it gets more expensive, as sand is harder to find and even what is found is further from the shore. There is not enough money, nor enough sand, for renourishment to be anything but a short-term adaptation strategy.

Beach renourishment also creates an interesting feedback loop. A renourished beach attracts development and raises property values. Higher property values (and the increased revenue from property taxes the municipalities earn) create pressure to continue renourishment. Qui and Gopalakrishnan (2018) find that beach renourishment does, as expected, improve property values, but not surprisingly, beachfront and nearshore property owners gain disproportionately more than others.

Short-term adaptations do buy time. As then Nags Head Mayor Bob Oakes suggested after Hurricane Sandy, this one was successful in increasing the resilience of Nags Head.

> The comparison between the flooding, standing water and massive quantities of sand left on the road in Kitty Hawk and the relatively minor overwash in South Nags Head could not be any starker, and there is growing evidence that the beach nourishment Nags Head completed last year has performed as advertised. It's a really dramatic comparison between South Nags Head and Kitty Hawk.
>
> (*North Beach Sun*, November 2012)

Sources: Qiu, Y., & Gopalakrishnan, S. (2018). Shoreline defense against climate change and capitalized impact of beach nourishment. SSRN 3117979; Tabb, K. (November 29, 2012). Thoughts on Hurricane Sandy. *North Beach Sun*. www.northbeachsun.com/outer-banks-thoughts-on-hurricane-sandy.

Managed Retreat: Buyouts

Another flood adaptation strategy involves not rebuilding on vulnerable land. After Hurricane Ike hit Texas, FEMA bought back 756 damaged or destroyed homes. Those homes were then removed and the land converted to parkland (Meyer & Kunreuther, 2017). The buyout cost $103 million.

Buyouts typically do two important things. First, they move people away from a flood hazard zone, by purchasing the home and mandating that homeowners use the money to buy or build on higher ground. Second, the damaged homes are typically either destroyed, with the transformation of the land into the park, or allowed to revert to some natural state. These open spaces serve as valuable flood control, as they can now store water during flood events. Further, if these open spaces revert to marshlands, which have valuable flood control properties, they can also serve to protect other nearby properties.

Between 1989 and 2017, more than 40,000 homes have been bought out by FEMA. The program bought homes from eligible homeowners who opted in after Hurricane Sandy, including several Staten Island neighborhoods. Residents used the funds to move elsewhere.

After Hurricane Harvey, approximately 4000 homeowners in the Houston area volunteered to have their homes purchased. Harris County, Texas, has a buyout program that relies on FEMA funds. The buyout program has moved slowly and only a few hundred homes had been purchased within the two years after Harvey hit.

Buying out homes after a disaster is partially reactive, in that the homes were damaged by the storm, but proactive in that homeowners cannot rebuild in the same high-risk location. Most proactive, however, would be moving people away from the flood risk prior to a major flood event. This is starting to happen in several locations.

Prioritizing among Adaptation Options in the Presence of Ethical Boundaries

The analytical tools that economists use to facilitate effective decision making are the primary tools used by agencies such as the World Bank to prioritize among the many adaptation policies available—benefit-cost analysis and cost-effectiveness analysis. As you may recall from Chapter 3, these decision-making tools can be very powerful for evaluating different choices. Benefit-cost analysis is widely known and frequently used but can be challenging when it confronts basic questions of fairness or gender equity.

One emerging question deals with who gets to participate in government programs.[16] Buyouts, for example, which many times rely on benefit-cost analysis to identify which homes are eligible, may only define homes in high-valued neighborhoods as eligible. (Can you see why that might be the typical outcome?) Environmental justice considerations could in principle be included with the use of distributional benefit-cost analysis that considers the weights of the benefits and costs (or *who* is benefiting and *who* is paying), but using that form of analysis requires a conscious political decision to do so.

Cost-effectiveness can be useful when the benefits, but not the costs, are expressed in physical terms rather than monetary terms.

A third option, multi-criteria analysis, uses qualitative and quantitative data to prioritize options and is useful when it is not possible to quantify the costs and benefits. Challenges arise when different experts use different criteria to weigh the options.

Economics tools are very powerful aids for decision making but need to be combined with location-specific criteria and knowledge if they are to produce equitable outcomes.

Information as an Adaptive Strategy

One strategy for dealing with risks of these sorts is to try to provide specific information to potential victims early enough for them to minimize their risks by taking such actions as leaving the area or fortifying the area where they will take refuge. You may immediately feel, as we did, that more information earlier is obviously better. As Example 12.3 points out, perhaps that intuition is less obvious than we thought.

EXAMPLE 12.3

What to Expect When You Are Expecting a Hurricane: Hurricane Exposure and Birth Outcomes

How many times have you watched with fascination or horror the forecasted path of a hurricane? The cone-shaped anticipated path of a hurricane is reported based upon necessarily uncertain current forecasts. Because hurricanes do change paths, the earlier a forecast is released, the more uncertainty there is in the expected (and ultimate actual) landfall location. Thinking a hurricane will make landfall in the location you live, whether it eventually does or does not, causes stress for those who live there. Urgent preparations, and in some cases evacuation, may lead to unnecessary stress for those ultimately not at risk.

Do the benefits of early warning outweigh the costs? Hochard et al. (2022) address this question. As it turns out, these stressors induce negative birth outcomes for pregnant women. A large and growing literature addresses the health impacts of high-stress events. In a recent paper by Almond et al. (2018), they note, "most economists now accept that disasters early in life are likely to have negative long-term effects on survivors, i.e., shocks that are extreme enough are likely to have persistent effects. Moreover, the fetal origins perspective will never be pivotal in a cost-benefit analysis of measures designed to forestall such disasters."

In statistical analysis, a Type I error is a false positive. Imagine if you receive a diagnosis for something you do not actually have, like being told by a doctor that you are pregnant when in reality, you are not. A Type II error, on the other hand, is a false negative. This would be the case of a doctor telling you that you are *not* pregnant when you actually are! A hurricane forecast center is set up to avoid Type II errors (the hurricane is coming, but you are told it is not), but not Type I errors.

The "cone of uncertainty" tracks the most likely hurricane path. It is likely you have watched the forecasts of the path of a hurricane and have noticed when it suddenly alters its path. Forecasts are getting better, but the data that get released very early and a week out—the data on which a forecast is based—are riddled with uncertainty.

When Hurricane Irene was headed for North Carolina (August 2011), nearly two-thirds of those who were preparing for direct impact ultimately received only mild wind and rain. In a study of over 700,000 births in the months surrounding Hurricane Irene, Hochard et al. find that birth outcomes were impaired in sites that did not end up in the path of the storm despite spending time in the "cone of uncertainty." In fact, for every additional 6 hours spent in the cone of uncertainty, birth weights drop by 4 grams. Low birth weights are linked to negative outcomes in adults such as increased susceptibility to diseases, lower aptitude, lower IQ, and lower productivity and wages later in life. They compare a control group (babies born in the five-year window before Hurricane Irene)[17] to a treatment group (babies exposed *in utero* during Hurricane Irene), using data from the North Carolina Department of Health and Human Services and National Oceanic and Atmospheric Administration's National Hurricane Center. Even though the western portion of the state was not hit by the hurricane, time spent in the cone of uncertainty led to impaired birth outcomes for women exposed, psychologically but not necessarily physically, to the storm. This is the cost of a Type I error. The authors conclude that actual storm damages depend on both predicted and actual storm paths. With the intensity and frequency of hurricanes expected to increase, forecasting agencies are likely to become increasingly risk-averse. Risk-aversion also comes at a cost, though. Ultimately this begs the question: when is the ideal time to release a forecast?

Sources: Hochard, J., Li, Y., & Abashidze, N. (2022). Associations of hurricane exposure and forecasting with impaired birth outcomes. *Nature Communications, 13*(6746); Almond, D., Currie, J., & Duque, V. (2018). Childhood circumstances and adult outcomes: Act II. *Journal of Economic Literature, 56*(4), 1360–1446.

Climate Adaptation: Wildfire Risk and Management

Another type of increasingly severe climate disaster with its own unique set of adaptation policies is wildfires. With climate change causing drought and drier conditions as well as longer fire seasons, wildfires have increased in size and frequency. Globally, the risk of large wildfires has increased even in areas previously considered low risk or unaffected by fire. In the western United States, the average annual area burned grew by about 1200 percent between the 1970s and the 2000s (Wibbenmeyer & Dunlap, RFF, 2021).

Climate change, combined with increases in the number of people living near high wildfire risk forested zones, has caused the damages from wildfires to rise significantly. In 2020, damages from wildfires in the United States totaled US$16.5 billion. Wildfire response expenditures reached $2 billion in 2020 (Bayham et al., 2022). The ten most destructive fires have all been within the last 15 years. The increased prevalence of woodsmoke now causes 25 percent of Americans' exposure to PM2.5, harmful fine particulate matter (RFF, 2021 and Burke et al., 2021), suggesting that the mortality and morbidity costs are not small. One study is telling: smoke from fires in the Brazilian Amazon from deforestation has been found to be responsible for the premature death of almost 3000 people (Reddington et al., 2015, as cited in UNEP, 2022). Moeltner et al. (2013) estimate that hospital admissions increase by 0.3 percent per unit of smoke. They value this cost at $2.2 million. Johnston et al. (2021) estimate that the 2019–2020 Australian fire season increased health care costs by AU$1.95 billion.

Other damages include runoff and erosion from post-wildfires that can cause water quality and infrastructure damage. Increased sediment can shorten reservoir lifespan and cause water utilities to move to alternate supplies. These damages all have large economic and social costs. In an early study, Loomis (2003) found that using prescribed burns to reduce the incidence of more severe fires could save $24 million per year in public infrastructure maintenance costs. Burn scars tend to erode quickly in storms and drinking water can be severely affected. Road closures and bridge collapses also occur. There have been very few economic analyses of the impacts (Bayham, 2022).

What policy options are in place to mitigate wildfires and wildfire damages? Policy options for adaptation to increased wildfire risk include fuel management (prescribed burns and forest thinning); response preparedness, including increasing firefighting personnel and better information coverage; policies that require power utilities to shut off power when fire danger is high; wildfire insurance; and building codes and restricting development in fire-prone areas.[18] As you can imagine, some of these policies are more politically feasible than others.

Thinking back to Figure 12.1, risk is the intersection of the hazard (the likelihood of a fire), the exposure (value of the property), and the vulnerability of that property. All of the policies listed above may be utilized together. The risk can be increased or decreased by where building occurs. But as Wibbenmeyer and Dunlap explain, "While mitigating risk should be a goal of policymakers, functioning insurance markets can help homeowners and businesses cope with the risk that remains." Example 12.4 considers the effectiveness of building codes.

EXAMPLE 12.4

Mandatory Adaptation Benefits Homeowners AND Their Neighbors?

Economists Patrick Baylis and Judson Boomhower consider the effectiveness of mandatory versus voluntary adaptation to wildfires. Using a unique data set that includes property-level data for U.S. homes exposed to wildfire between 2000 and 2020, they examine the effect of building codes on building survival and the spatial externalities (positive) on neighboring structures. As in flood insurance, many homes are only partially insured, and some are uninsured. This means the benefits of building codes also include reduction in the uninsured risk.

Focusing on California, they look at pre- and post-building code homes on the same street. They find that wildfire building codes in California reduced average structure loss by about 40 percent and to a close neighbor's home by 6 percent! Building codes help build resilience in residential communities. Even with these benefits, however, they find that building codes only pass a benefit-cost test for new homes, not existing homes.

As Platinga et al. (2022) note, however, fires are more likely to stop spreading as they approach homes that are of higher value than for those of lower value. Anderson et al. (2020) find something similar. Fuel management is more likely to occur near neighborhoods with higher socio-economic status, perhaps due to the more intense lobbying efforts of those communities. Fire suppression efforts with a more equitable distribution of benefits are clearly necessary. Universal building codes can help with this. However, if the codes are only for new homes, this begs the question of where the new homes are located.

Sources: Baylis, P. W., & Boomhower, J. (2022). *Mandated vs. Voluntary Adaptation to Natural Disasters: The Case of US Wildfires* (No. w29621). National Bureau of Economic Research; Plantinga, A. J., Walsh, R., & Wibbenmeyer, M. (2022). Priorities and effectiveness in wildfire management: Evidence from fire spread in the western United States. *Journal of the Association of Environmental and Resource Economics*, 9(4), 603–639; Anderson, S., Plantinga, A., & Wibbenmeyer, M. (2020). Inequality in agency responsiveness: Evidence from salient wildfire events. Washington, D.C.: Resources for the Future, 36.

Climate Adaptation: Managing Water Shortages

As discussed earlier in this chapter, climate change will increase the frequency and intensity of flooding at some times and in some areas. At the same time, other areas will experience increased climate-induced water shortages. Impending water shortages can be dealt with by increasing water supplies (desalination of ocean water in coastal areas, for example), by learning to use less, or by increasing prices. The increasing need to conserve water during times of drought is giving rise to some novel adaptation mechanisms in water pricing, particularly municipal water pricing.

Water scarcity is not a new topic by any means and economics has played a role in helping communities allocate water across multiple users. What we have learned from these experiences therefore may provide a foundation for developing particular strategies for dealing with increasing water scarcity in many regions. The task will not be easy. Many legal barriers inhibit the achievement of efficient water allocation, but municipalities have a variety of pricing structures to choose from that can be helpful for adaptation during either short-term or long-term water scarcity. Let's begin with the efficient allocation of freshwater.

The Efficient Allocation of Scarce Water

In defining the efficient allocation of water, distinguishing whether surface water or groundwater is being tapped is crucial. In the absence of storage, the allocation of surface water involves distributing a fixed renewable supply among competing users. Intergenerational effects are less important because future supplies depend on natural phenomena (such as precipitation) rather than on current withdrawal practices. For groundwater, on the other hand, withdrawing water now does affect the resources available to future generations. In this case, the allocation over time is a crucial aspect of the analysis. For the time being, we will focus on surface water.

An efficient allocation of surface water must (1) strike a balance among a host of competing users, and (2) supply an acceptable means of handling the year-to-year variability in water flow. The former issue is acute because so many different potential users have legitimate competing claims. Some (such as municipal drinking water suppliers or farmers) withdraw the water for consumptive use, while others (such as swimmers or boaters) use the water, but do not consume it. The variability challenge arises because surface water supplies are not constant from year to year or month to month. Since precipitation, runoff, and evaporation all change from year to year, in some years less water will be available for allocation than in others. Not only must a system be in place for allocating the average amount of water, but above-average and below-average flows must also be anticipated and allocated.

With respect to allocating among competing users, the dictates of efficiency are quite clear—the water should be allocated so that the marginal net benefit is equalized for all uses. (Remember that the marginal net benefit is the vertical distance between the demand curve for water and the marginal cost of extracting and distributing that water for the last unit of water consumed.)

To demonstrate why efficiency requires equal marginal net benefits, consider a situation in which the marginal net benefits are not equal. Suppose, for example, that at the current allocations the marginal net benefit to a municipal user is $2,000 per acre-foot, while the marginal net benefit to an agricultural user is $500 per acre-foot. If an acre-foot of water were transferred from the farm to the city, the farm would lose marginal net benefits of $500, but the city would gain $2,000 in marginal net benefits. Total net benefits from this transfer would rise by $1,500. Since marginal net benefits fall with use, the new marginal net benefit to the city after the transfer will be less than $2,000 per acre-foot and the marginal net benefit to the farmer will be greater than $500 (a smaller allocation means moving up the marginal net benefits curve), but until these two are equalized we can still increase net benefits by transferring water. Because net benefits are increased by this transfer, the initial allocation could not have maximized net benefits. Since an efficient allocation maximizes net benefits, any allocation that fails to equalize marginal net benefits cannot be efficient.

The bottom line is that if marginal net benefits have not been equalized it is always possible to increase net benefits by transferring water from those users with low net marginal benefits to those with higher net marginal benefits. By transferring the water to the users who value the marginal water more, the total net benefits of the water use are increased; those losing water are giving up less than those receiving the additional water are gaining. When the marginal net benefits are equalized, no such transfer is possible without lowering net benefits. This concept is depicted in Figure 12.4.

Consider a water supply represented by S_T, where the amount of water available is Q_T. Suppose there are two different users represented by marginal net benefit curve A and marginal net benefit curve B. These could be a municipality (A) and an irrigation district (B). In this figure the municipality has higher demand (higher willingness to pay). The total (aggregate) marginal net benefit is the horizontal sum of the two demand curves. What is the efficient allocation of water across these two users with different marginal values for water? The optimal allocation is where demand ($MNBA + MNB_B$) equals the total supply of water. At that price, the optimal allocation occurs where MNB = the price of Q^*_A and Q^*_B. Thus, the efficient allocation would give Q^*_A to user A (the municipality) and Q^*_B to user B. For the optimal allocation, notice that the marginal net benefit is equal for the two users. This allocation maximizes total net benefits or the area under the two demand curves up to their allocation of water.

Suppose instead, however, that the state or water authority decides, for equity or political reasons, to simply divide the available water equally between the two users,

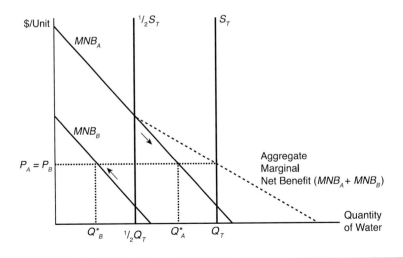

Figure 12.4 The Efficient Allocation of Surface Water.

giving each an amount $Q_A = Q_B = \frac{1}{2}Q_T$. Can you see how this is inefficient? This allocation would result in different marginal net benefits for each user. If marginal net benefit is not equalized, then we haven't maximized net benefits.

Notice also that the marginal net benefit for both users is positive in Figure 12.4. This implies that water sales should involve a positive marginal scarcity rent. Could we draw the diagram so that the marginal net benefit (and, hence, marginal scarcity rent) would be zero? How?

Marginal scarcity rent would be zero if water were not scarce. If the availability of water as presented by the supply curve was greater than the amount represented by the point where the aggregate marginal net benefit curve intersects the axis, water would not be scarce. Both users would get all they wanted; their demands would not be competing with one another. Their marginal net benefits would still be equal, but in this case they would both be zero.

Now let's consider the second problem—dealing with fluctuations in supply. As long as the supply level can be anticipated, the equal marginal net benefit rule still applies, but different supply levels may imply very different allocations among users. This is an important attribute of the problem because it implies that simple allocation rules, such as each user receiving a fixed proportion of the available flow or high-priority users receiving a guaranteed amount, are not likely to be efficient.

Suppose now that we use the same graph in a different way. Suppose in this case the total water supply is equal to $\frac{1}{2}S_T$. How should the lower water supply be efficiently allocated between the two users? The answer is that the first user would get it all. Do you see why? With $\frac{1}{2}S_T$, user B receives no water, while user A receives it all since A's willingness to pay is higher everywhere than B's. Why does the efficient allocation change so radically between S_T and $\frac{1}{2}S_T$? The answer lies in the shape of the two demand curves for water.

The marginal net benefit curve for water in use A lies above that for B, implying that as supplies diminish, the cost (the forgone net benefits) of doing without water is much higher for A than for B. To minimize this cost, more of the burden of the shortfall is allocated to B than A. In an efficient allocation, users who can most easily find substitutes or conserve water receive proportionately smaller allocations when supplies are diminished than those who have few alternatives. Of course, efficiency is not the only allocation criterion when it comes to a necessary resource like water.

In reality, however, a complex set of institutions and laws governing water inhibits water from moving to its highest-valued use. Interestingly, the preceding graph mimics the situation on the Colorado River in the Southwest United States. The Colorado River Compact of 1922 allocates river flows between the upper basin states of Colorado, Wyoming, Utah, and New Mexico and the lower basin states of Arizona, California, and Nevada. The Compact commits the upper basin states to deliver an average of 7.5 million acre-feet per year to the lower basin states. At the time of the signing, states thought they were splitting the flows equally while leaving plenty for Mexico. In reality, flows of the river were much lower than thought and more recently the mega drought has led to reservoirs dropping to precipitously low levels. Farmers in Arizona have already been called out, meaning they will receive massively reduced allocations of Colorado River water. Additionally, the legal doctrine of *prior appropriation*, for example, that governs water allocation in much of the western United States prevents the efficient allocation of water.

In the earliest days of settlement in the American Southwest and West, the government had a minimal presence. As water was always a significant factor in the development of an area, the first settlements were usually oriented near bodies of water. The property rights that evolved, called *riparian rights*, allocated the right to use the water to the owner of the land adjacent to the water. This was a practical solution because, by virtue of their location, these owners had easy access to the water. Furthermore, enough sites provided access to water that virtually all who sought water could be accommodated.

With population growth and the consequent rise in the demand for land, this allocation system became less appropriate. As demand increased, the amount of land adjacent to water became scarce, forcing some spillover onto land that was not adjacent to water. The owners of this land began to seek means of acquiring water to make their land more productive.

At about this time, with the discovery of gold in California, mining became an important source of employment. With the advent of mining came a need to divert water away from streams to other sites. Unfortunately, riparian property rights made no provision for water to be diverted to other locations. The rights to the water were tied to the land and could not be separately transferred.

As economic theory would predict, this situation created a demand for a change in the property rights structure from riparian rights to one that was more congenial to the need for transferability. The waste resulting from the lack of transferability became so great that it outweighed any transition costs of changing the system of property rights. The evolution that took place in the mining camps became the forerunner of what has become known as the *prior appropriation doctrine*.

The miners established the custom that the first person to arrive had the superior (or *senior*) claim on the water. Later claimants hold *junior* (or subordinate) claims. In practice, this severed the relationship that had existed under the riparian doctrine between the rights to land and the rights to water. As this new doctrine became adopted in legislation, court rulings, and seven state constitutions, widespread diversion of water based on prior appropriation became possible. This first-in-time-first-in-right doctrine paid no mind to economic principles.

This was only the beginning. The demand for land in the arid West and Southwest was still growing, creating a complementary demand for water to make the desert bloom. The tremendous profits to be made from large-scale water diversion created the political climate necessary for federal involvement.

The federal role in water resources originated in the early 1800s, largely out of concern for the nation's regional development and economic growth. Toward these ends, the federal government built a network of inland waterways to provide transportation. Since the Reclamation Act of 1902, the federal government has built almost 700 dams to provide water and power to help settle the West.

While the economics suggests allocating water until the marginal value is equal across users, reality has not reflected that. As water scarcity increases with climate change, the appropriate pricing of water will become more and more important.

What about municipal water that provides water to homes and businesses?

Municipal Water Pricing

Municipal water utilities must balance the competing goals of revenue stability, providing signals about water scarcity, reasonable prices for commercial users, and equitable prices for homeowners.

Water utilities are typically regulated because they have a monopoly in the local area. One typical requirement for the rate structure of a regulated monopoly is that it earns only a "fair" rate of return. Excess profits are not permitted.

The prices charged by water distribution utilities do not promote efficiency of use, either. Both the level of prices and the rate structure are at fault. In general, the price level is too low and the rate structure does not adequately reflect the costs of providing service to different types of customers.

Water utilities have a variety of options to choose from when charging their customers for water, knowing they need to balance pricing with revenue stability and water conservation during drought. In general, utilities can simply charge a fee or utilize a volumetric pricing method (Figure 12.5). Volume-based price structures require metering, but they send signals about water scarcity, by charging a marginal value per unit of consumption. The most effective of these during drought or in water-scarce regions is a rate that increases with consumption. Under these increasing block structures, the price per unit of water consumed rises as the amount consumed rises. Fifty-eight percent of utilities worldwide utilize a rate that increases with consumption.

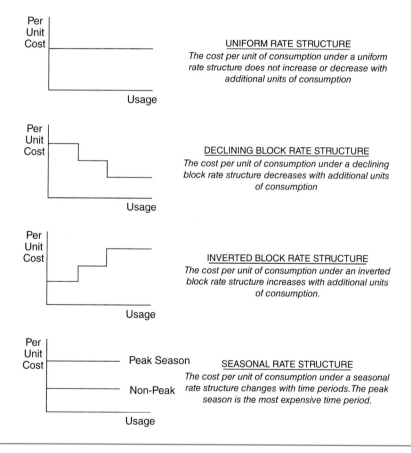

Figure 12.5 Water Pricing Rate Structures.

Source: Four examples of consumption charge models from water rate structures in Colorado: How Colorado cities compare in using this important water use efficiency tool, September 2004, p.8 by Colorado Environmental Coalition, Western Colorado Congress, and Western Resource Advocates.

How many U.S. utilities are using increasing block pricing? As Table 12.2 indicates, the number of water utilities using increasing block rates is on the rise, but the increase has been slow. However, decreasing block rates have declined dramatically, highlighting a move to pricing that better reflects the availability of water (Figure 12.6).

An increasing block structure encourages conservation by ensuring that the marginal cost of consuming additional water is high. This type of rate structure is also considered most equitable in that those who need some water but cannot afford the marginal price paid by more extravagant users can have access to water without placing their budget in as much jeopardy as would be the case with a uniform price.

Table 12.2 Pricing Structures of Public Water Systems in the United States (1982–2021)

	1982	1991	1998	2004	2008	2010	2013	2016	2018	2021
	%	%	%	%	%	%	%	%	%	%
Fixed	1	3	—	—	—	—	—	1	2	2
Linear	35	35	34	39	32	31	30	39	34	37
Decreasing Block	60	45	35	25	28	19	18	5	4	3
Increasing Block	4	17	31	36	40	49	52	55	60	58
Total	100	100	100	100	100	100	100	100	100	100

Source: Raftelis Rate Survey. (2021). Raftelis Financial Consulting and Global Water International 2021 Tariff Survey. https://www.globalwaterintel.com/products-and-services/market-research-reports/tariff-survey-2020.

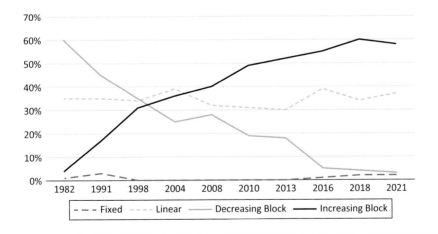

Figure 12.6 Pricing Structures for Public Water Systems in the United States (1982–2021).

> ### Table 12.3 World Cities and Rate Structures 2021

Rate Type	Number of Cities	Percentage
Fixed	9	2%
Flat Rate or Linear	207	37%
Increasing Block Rate	331	58%
Declining Block Rate	14	2%
Other	6	1%
Total	567	100%

What about internationally? Global Water International's 2021 tariff survey suggests that worldwide the trend is also moving toward increasing block rates (Table 12.3).

Since their survey in 2012, the number of increasing or inverted block rates increased (from 48 percent to about 58 percent in 2021). Increasing block rates are now the most frequently utilized pricing structures. Just about all the cities that reported have some sort of volumetric pricing, mostly flat and increasing block rates. Interestingly, nine of the 14 declining block rates are in U.S. cities.

Other aspects of the rate structure are important as well. Efficiency dictates that prices equal the marginal cost of provision (including marginal user cost when appropriate). Several practical corollaries follow from this theorem. First, prices during peak demand periods should exceed prices during off-peak periods. For water, peak demand is usually during the summer. It is peak use that strains the capacity of the system and therefore triggers the need for expansion. Therefore, seasonal users should pay the extra costs associated with the system expansion by being charged higher rates. Few current water pricing systems satisfy this condition in practice, though some cities in the southwest United States are beginning to use seasonal rates. For example, Tucson, Arizona, has a seasonal rate for the months of May through September. Also, for municipalities using increasing block rates with the first block equal to average winter consumption, one could argue that this is essentially a seasonal rate for the average user. The average user is unlikely to be in the second or third blocks, except during summer months.

In times of drought, seasonal pricing makes sense, but is rarely politically feasible. Under extreme circumstances, such as severe drought, however, cities are more likely to be successful in passing large rate changes that are specifically designed to facilitate coping with that drought. In one historical example, during the period from 1987 to 1992, Santa Barbara, California, experienced one of the most severe droughts of the last century. To deal with the crisis of excess demand, the city of Santa Barbara changed both its rates and rate structure ten times between 1987 and 1995 (Loaiciga & Renehan, 1997). In 1987, Santa Barbara utilized a flat rate of $0.89 per hundred cubic feet (ccf). By late 1989, they had moved to an increasing block rate consisting of four blocks with the lowest block at $1.09 per ccf and the highest at $3.01 per ccf. Between March and October of 1990, the rate rose to $29.43 per ccf (748 gallons) in the highest block! Rates were subsequently lowered, but the higher rates were successful in causing water use to drop almost 50 percent. It seems that when a community is faced with severe drought and community support for using pricing to cope is apparent, major changes in price are indeed possible. As droughts become more frequent or more intense, these adaptations in pricing can ensure water availability.

In response to the more recent severe drought in California, then-Governor Jerry Brown mandated a 25 percent reduction in water use for residential customers. From a utility perspective, however, large reductions in consumer use can risk revenue stability and utilities may have trouble covering their (large) fixed costs. Recall that water utilities are natural monopolies with very high fixed costs. Example 12.5 compares an alternative price structure focused on revenue stability with increasing block rates. In this case, revenue stability can be achieved, but at the expense of equitable pricing.

EXAMPLE 12.5

The Cost of Conservation: Revenue Stability versus Equitable Pricing

In January 2014, California Governor Jerry Brown proclaimed a drought state of emergency and asked all Californians to reduce water consumption by 20 percent. In April 2015, an executive order was issued that increased this to 25 percent. California was experiencing a severe drought and the state was running short of water. While these types of mandates do promote conservation of water, extreme reductions in water use can wreak havoc on water utility revenues since consumption-based rates help to cover utility costs.

As you have learned, natural monopolies, companies with very high fixed costs and hence declining average and marginal costs, must try to balance efficient pricing with covering their costs (including the fixed costs). Water utilities that charge consumption-based rates would suffer from revenue shortfalls when consumers conserve.

Spang et al. (2015) present a theoretical argument for a solution to the problem of revenue stability. They recommend a consumption-based fixed rate (CBFR) that divides a consumer's bill into three parts. Each part is based on a type of utility cost: fixed costs, fixed-variable costs (fixed costs that can rise with expansion, for example), and purely variable costs. Table 12.4 illustrates these types of costs.

The CBFR distributes fixed-fixed costs across all users while distributing the partial variable and variable costs more proportionally based on a percentage of total water consumed that month; that is, costs times (consumer's consumption/ total water consumed systemwide).

Curious about whether the CBFR would work in practice, Bates College senior Amy Schmidt decided to try to find out. For her undergraduate senior thesis, Schmidt collected water utility data for two towns, one in California and one in Colorado, and found that the CBFR does indeed stabilize revenues, but at the expense of the low water users.

In other words, the CBFR solves the revenue problem, but creates inequities across individual water users. Low water users (usually lower-income users) see large bill increases in some cases, while high water users benefit significantly with lower water bills.

Table 12.4 Cost Definitions and Categorization

Fixed-Fixed Costs: Constant regardless of system use	Compliance costs, safety checks, office personnel, treatment plant energy use, etc.
Fixed-Variable Costs: Exist regardless of system use, but change in magnitude based on system demand	Piping infrastructure, chemicals, repairs and maintenance, etc.
Variable Costs: Depend directly upon consumption levels	Water purchases, energy for water pumping, etc.

Table 12.5 Estimated Consumer Bills as a Percentage of Actual under Simulated CBFR System, FY 2013–2014

	Lomita (%)	Longmont (%)
High-use consumers (50 hcf) % IBR System	CA 30	CO 35
Average-use (35 hcf) % IBR System	40	171
Low-use (15 hcf) % IBR System	63	268

Source: Adapted from Schmidt and Lewis (2017).

Both towns—Lomita, California, and Longmont, Colorado—currently use increasing block rates. For both towns, the CBFR formula provides greater financial savings for high-use versus low-use consumers. This is due to the fact that high fixed costs are split evenly across all consumers. For Longmont, Colorado, medium and low users' bills actually increase significantly. For the low-use water consumers, water bills nearly triple (Table 12.5).

This result is due, in part, to how costs are categorized at this utility. For both towns, the CBFR clearly creates some inequities in pricing. While solving one problem, it creates another.

The results suggest caution with the CBFR method given the equity considerations. It could be useful, however, during times of severe drought on a temporary basis to mitigate threats of revenue shortfalls.

Given these equity implications Schmidt and Lewis (2017) simulated a modified CBFR price structure with prices partially weighted by household income. Using this proportional pricing method or "scaled consumption-based fixed rates," high-use consumers face increased water bills and low-use water consumers will pay approximately 30 percent less. They recommend consideration of such an alternative pricing model. The scaled consumption-based fixed rate (SCBFR) appears to be a better option for ensuring revenue stability for the utility without jeopardizing affordability for low-income households.

Sources: Schmidt, A., & Lewis, L. (2017). The cost of stability: Consumption-based fixed rate billing for water utilities. *Journal of Contemporary Water Research and Education, 160,* 5–24; Spang, E. S., Miller, S., Williams, M., & Loge, E. J. (2015). Consumption-based fixed rates: Harmonizing water conservation and revenue stability. *American Water Works Association, 107,* 164–173.

Cape Town, South Africa, nearly ran out of water in 2018. The City of Cape Town instituted extremely severe restrictions on water usage, both on volume and on type of use. High fines were used to enforce these restrictions. Water tariffs were also hiked significantly. The crisis was averted, but the combination of a changing climate and rising demand suggests there is more to be done.

Another corollary of the marginal-cost pricing theorem is that when it costs a water utility more to serve one class of customers than another, each class of customers should bear the costs associated with its respective service. Typically, this implies that those farther away from the source or at higher elevations (requiring more pumping) should pay higher rates. In practice, utility water rates make fewer distinctions among customer classes than would be efficient. As a result, higher-cost water users are in effect subsidized; they receive too little incentive to conserve and too little incentive to locate in parts of the city that can be served at lower cost.

Full Cost Recovery Pricing

Another available pricing mechanism is to allow water utilities to earn more than a normal rate of return by charging a full cost recovery (FCR) price for water services. Full cost recovery includes both environmental and resource costs. Since allocative efficiency cannot be achieved without users receiving a clear signal regarding the value of water, FCR is a potential solution.

Full cost recovery is one of the pillars of the European Union's Directive on Water Policy. This Water Framework Directive states, "Member States shall ensure that water-pricing policies provide adequate incentives for water users to use water resources efficiently, and thereby contribute to the environmental objectives of this objective." What would implementing FCR pricing mean for member states?

Reynaud (2016) assesses the impact of FCR pricing on European households in nine countries (Austria, Bulgaria, Czechia, Estonia, France, Greece, Italy, Portugal, and Spain). In particular, he was interested in the impacts of price changes on consumption and also on affordability and equity.

For the first measure, consumption, Reynaud estimates the required price increase resulting from implementing FCR pricing and estimates the price elasticity of demand (responsiveness to price). Not surprisingly, the results vary significantly by country. For Estonia and Italy, prices rise significantly and water consumption decreases by 21.2 percent and 33.8 percent respectively. For Italy, he measures the largest loss of consumer surplus at 81.2 euros per capita. This is likely due to the high price-responsiveness of Italian households. The results are more moderate for Bulgaria, Czechia, and Spain and there is very little effect for the others.

Water affordability is measured as the share of household income that is spent on water and a "water-poor" household is one that spends 3 percent or more of its income on water services. Of the nine countries examined, water affordability only becomes a problem in Bulgaria under FCR pricing since there households would then devote more than 3 percent of income on water services.

Clearly, FCR pricing must be evaluated on a case-by-case basis. Reynaud suggests that efficiency dictates that all households should pay the efficient price. Income redistribution schemes could then be utilized to address water affordability. In practice, however, such schemes might be difficult to implement. In the absence of such a scheme, subsidies or social pricing will be second best. Several European countries have implemented some form of social pricing.

Desalination and Wastewater Recycling

Changes in precipitation patterns due to climate change, combined with rising water demands, are exacerbating existing water scarcity issues in some areas and creating them in others. According to the United Nations, more than two billion people live in countries experiencing "high water stress" (UNWater, 2021).[19] That number is expected to grow.

Solving water scarcity issues will become increasingly challenging, but desalination technologies, water reuse, and capturing (and storing) rainwater are all helping to make water supplies more reliable. Desalination provides only about 1 percent of drinking water worldwide but is likely to see increased use.

Until recently, desalinized seawater has been prohibitively expensive and thus not a viable option outside of the Middle East. However, technological advances in reverse osmosis, nanofiltration, and ultrafiltration methods have reduced the price of desalinized water, making it a potential new source for water-scarce regions. Reverse osmosis works by pumping seawater at high pressure through permeable membranes. According to Global Water Intelligence approximately 21,000 desalting plants were in operation in 2021. Desalination operations can be found in over 150 countries, though nearly half are in the Middle East and North Africa. Large numbers of facilities are also located in the United States, China, and Australia. These plants produce about 25 billion gallons per day (Jones et al., 2019).

All of the current facilities are in wealthy countries. The current technology is energy-intensive and hence very expensive. Costs vary considerably, but even the lowest-cost projects ($750 per acre-foot) are more than double the cost of groundwater in most places (Katz, 2014).[20] Costs can be as high as $2,000 per acre-foot. Costs are expected to continue to fall by as much as 20 percent over the next five years. However, many projects are being built at extraordinary cost. Example 12.6 looks at the feasibility of desalination in northern China.

In the United States, Florida, California, Arizona, and Texas have the largest installed capacity. However, actual production has been mixed. In Tampa Bay, for example, a large desalination project was contracted in 1999 to provide drinking water. This project, while meant to be a low-cost ($0.45/m^3) state-of-the-art project, was hampered by difficulties. Although the plant became fully operational at the end of 2007, projected costs were $0.67/m^3 (Gleick, 2006). In 1991, Santa Barbara, California, commissioned a desalination plant in response to the previously described drought that would supply water at a cost expected to be $1.22/m^3. Shortly after construction was completed, however, the drought ended and the plant was never operated. In 2000, the city sold the plant to a company in Saudi Arabia. It has been decommissioned but remains available should current supplies run out.

In California, desalinated water from a desalination facility in San Diego costs approximately $2,000 per acre-foot, much more than the city currently pays for water diverted from the Colorado River and San Joaquin River Delta. The Carlsbad plant, however, provides more than 10 percent of the region's drinking water. There are currently ten desalination plants in California, with more in the planning stages. In China, the choices between moving water or desalting it both prove to be exceptionally expensive (Example 12.6).

EXAMPLE 12.6

Moving Rivers or Desalting the Sea? Costly Remedies for Water Shortages

In most of northern China, freshwater is extremely scarce. China has been pursuing immense engineering projects in order to bring new water sources to this desperately dry, yet rapidly growing region. One three-phase project involves the diversion of water from the Yangzi River basin through hundreds of kilometers of canals and pipelines at extraordinary cost ($34 billion so far). The project is only partially complete. The other is a $4.1 billion power and desalination plant in the port city of Tianjin. The Beijing Power and Desalination Plant began operating in 2009. The capacity of the desalination plant will satisfy only a small portion of China's demand for water.

As of 2013, water from the plant cost 8 yuan per cubic meter (about $1.30) to produce. Diverted water from the Yangzi is expected to cost about 10 yuan. Both of these are at least 60 percent higher than what households were paying, though water rates are rising. Even if higher water prices were imposed on consumers, prices would be unlikely to cover the true cost of either source. Desalination is very energy intensive. In China, that energy comes mainly from burning dirty coal. Diverting water is not without external costs, either. Diverting water deprives southern China of the water needed to combat drought. Developing scarcity in a crucial resource like water can force some tough choices!

Source: Economist. (February 9, 2013). Removing salt from seawater might help slake some of northern China's thirst, but it comes at a high price.

In early 2011, a large desalination project in Dubai and another in Israel were scrapped mid-construction due to lower-than-expected demand growth and cost, respectively. These two projects represented 10 percent of the desalination market. Increased water scarcity and the rising cost of alternative sources will eventually level the playing field for this technology-based adaptation strategy. In fact, the cost of desalination has been cut in half in the last 30 years (Robbins, 2019).

Desalination is not externality-free, however, and there are serious environmental concerns. Desalination is very energy-intensive, contributing to climate change, and the process also returns briny water to the sea, which depletes oxygen. Finally, the pumping of seawater can result in unintended losses of small organisms and fish larvae. To remedy this, some plants are starting to utilize brackish water rather than pull water directly from the sea. Texas now has 49 plants that are using brackish water. Clearly, desalination will not solve water scarcity issues, but is certainly a tool to cover some demand. Conservation and pricing are another.

Roles for Public and Private Institutions

Effective adaptation policies need to involve both the private and public sectors. One way to think about the optimal respective roles for the public and private sectors is to look closely at the role private decision makers—households and businesses—can be expected to play (and indeed have already played in response to climate threats that have already occurred). Will private agents adapt to a modified climate? Are those reactions likely to be both effective and sufficient or is there a role for the public sector to fill in gaps?

A review of economic research in this area by Fankhauser (2016) makes it clear that the answer to the first question is a resounding "yes!" Private agents do adapt. One of the most studied sectors, agriculture, reveals clear differences in agricultural practices, such as crop choices, under different climate conditions. In the longer term, farmers also respond to weather fluctuations by adjusting the size of their farm or moving into non-farm activities.

Although few studies examine business investments in adaptation, the fact that households adjust their energy consumption to climatic factors is well documented. Both energy demand and the demand for associated products like air-conditioning units are found (as expected) to vary both seasonally and across climate zones. Further, these private responses have been found to produce substantial social benefits in terms of reduced mortality and enhanced well-being.

While the literature does provide compelling evidence that private agents do adapt, it does not provide compelling evidence that these responses are either completely effective or sufficient. To start with, the number of adaptation investment situations that have been studied is very limited. Further, few of those that have been studied focus on adaptation to the kinds of major damages that are expected from a changing climate. More importantly, however, the literature documents a number of barriers that inhibit private actions, thereby reducing the effectiveness of a purely private adaptation strategy.

- Property rights matter. (Remember the earlier discussion about the differences in energy efficiency investment incentives between renters and owners?) Because they would incur the losses caused by property damages, owners have higher incentives to invest in adaptation than renters. In general, ambiguous or compromised property rights can be a barrier to effective private action.
- Effective private action depends on good information on both the nature of risks and options for adapting to them. Much of this information about future risks is a public good, which means that it will be undersupplied unless the government supplies it or participates in its supply.
- Adaptation choices can also be limited by affordability, including how a low income diminishes the ability to borrow.
- Finally, much of the adaptation would involve public capital like roads or public transportation systems, and the effectiveness of many private adaptation responses would be affected by those public adaptation responses.

Even this brief list suggests a multifaceted role for governments:

- They should identify circumstances that lead to adaptation market failures and adopt policies that correct or remove the distortions in incentives that lead to the failures.
- They should provide public information on the risks being posed by a changing climate.
- They should provide financial mechanisms for assisting populations facing affordability problems with adaptation.
- They should develop adaptation plans for publicly owned capital such as the transportation infrastructure.

Summary

Climate mitigation refers to interventions that reduce greenhouse gas emissions. Adaptation refers to actions that decrease vulnerability or increase resilience. Ultimately, we need both.

Climate change impacts from flooding, wildfires, and drought are already being felt in many places. Regardless of what mitigation policies we pursue, adaptation strategies are also and will continue to be necessary. Adaptation to climate change is appropriately considered the more difficult problem. Adaptation strategies are very context- and location-specific. What works in one place may not in another. Local considerations such as the amount of available financing are important. Distributional effects of costs and benefits must also be considered.

Fortunately, economic analysis of the climate change problem not only defines the need for action, but also sheds light on effective forms that action might take. Benefit-cost analysis and cost-effectiveness analysis are powerful analytical methods that can aid in decision making when multiple options and time frames are being considered. Distributional benefit-cost analysis can help ensure that benefits and costs are most equitably distributed.

Policies can be reactive to the damages that actually occur (providing emergency shelters after every flood) or proactive to reduce local vulnerability to the climate changes and, hence, reduce the resulting damages (managed retreat). Clearly the latter is likely to be more cost-effective in the long run. Managed climate retreat can prevent an urgent climate refugee crisis, for example.

Adaptation is ongoing and is very context- and location-specific. There is much work to be done in this rapidly growing area of environmental economics.

Discussion Questions

1. What is your national, regional, or state government doing about climate change? Has your community participated in the CRS program? If so, how is it working out? What about buyouts? Is anyone working on an adaptation plan in your area? Do the basics of those approaches seem consistent with some of the characteristics of an efficient strategy discussed in this chapter? Why or why not?

2. *An ounce of prevention* is a common phrase in health care. It also seems to hold true for mitigation of storm and flood damages. How does benefit-cost analysis help with decision making on mitigation strategies?

3. What pricing system is used to price the water you use at your college or university? Does this pricing system affect your behavior about water use (length of showers, etc.)? How? Could you recommend a better pricing system in this circumstance? What would it be?

Self-Test Exercises

1. a. This chapter makes the point that typically, a cost-effective climate change policy would involve both emissions mitigation and adaptation, rather than choosing one approach or the other. Why?
   b. Under what conditions, if any, might it be cost-effective to use only emissions mitigation or adaptation, but not both?

2. Suppose that in a particular area the consumption of water varies tremendously throughout the year, with average household summer use exceeding winter use by a great deal. What effect would this have on an efficient rate structure for water?

3. One major concern about the future is that water scarcity will grow, particularly in arid regions where precipitation levels may be reduced by climate change. Will our institutions provide for an efficient response to this problem?

4. To think about this issue, let's consider groundwater extraction over time using the two-period model as our lens.
   a. Suppose the groundwater comes from a well you have drilled upon your land that taps an aquifer that is not shared with anyone else. Would you have an incentive to extract the water efficiently over time? Why or why not?
   b. Suppose the groundwater is obtained from your private well, which is drilled into an aquifer that is shared with many other users who have also drilled private wells. Would you expect that the water from this common aquifer will be extracted at an efficient rate? Why or why not?

5. Water is an essential resource. For that reason moral considerations exert considerable pressure to assure that everyone has access to at least enough water to survive. Yet it appears that equity and efficiency considerations may conflict. Providing water at zero cost is unlikely to support efficient use (marginal cost is too low), while charging everyone the market price (especially as scarcity sets in) may result in some poor households not being able to afford the water they need. Discuss how block-rate pricing attempts to provide some resolution to this dilemma. How would it work?

Notes

1 Mitigation policies are explored in some detail in the companion to this book: *Essentials of Environmental Economics*.
2 IPCC AR6. (2022). Summary for Policymakers, 6.
3 Shalizi, Z., & Lecocq, F. (August 2010). To mitigate or to adapt: Is that the question? Observations on an appropriate response to the climate change challenge to development strategies. *The World Bank Research Observer*, 25(2), 295–321, 295.
4 Yale Climate Connections. (2022).

5 IPCC glossary of terms. (2018).
6 www.fema.gov/national-flood-insurance-program-community-rating-system
7 www.fema.gov/national-flood-insurance-program-community-rating-system
8 These adaptation activities are organized into four categories: provision of public information; mapping and regulations; flood damage reduction; and flood preparedness.
9 www.claimsjournal.com/news/international/2017/09/05/280336.htm
10 Take-up rates are the number of homeowners enrolled in the insurance program.
11 https://oceanservice.noaa.gov/hazards/sealevelrise/sealevelrise-tech-report.html
12 https://coast.noaa.gov/slr
13 www.un.org/sustainabledevelopment/wp-content/uploads/2017/05/Ocean-fact-sheet-package.pdf
14 https://coast.noaa.gov/states/fast-facts/economics-and-demographics.html
15 Personal communication, Andrew Keeler, Coastal Studies Institute, Eastern Carolina University, May 2019.
16 Have there been buyouts in your city or town? You can search the FEMA database at: https://apps.npr.org/fema-table (Accessed July 2022).
17 The control group consisted of approximately 620,000 observations from earlier years involving pregnant women who did not experience a hurricane.
18 Wibbenmeyer, M., & Dunlap, L. (2021). Wildfires in the United States 102: Policy and solutions. RFF Explainer.
19 www.unwater.org/water-facts/scarcity
20 An acre-foot of water is the amount of water it takes to cover 1 acre of land, 12 inches deep, or about the amount a family of five in the United States uses in a year.

Further Reading

Carleton, T., Jina, A., Delgado, M., Greenstone, M., Houser, T., Hsiang, S., Hultgren, A., Kopp, R. E., McCusker, K. E., Nath, I., Rising, J., Rode, A., Seo, H. K., Viaene, A., Yuan, J., & Zhang, A. T. (2022). Valuing the global mortality consequences of climate change accounting for adaptation costs and benefits. *The Quarterly Journal of Economics*, 137(4), 2037–2105. https://doi.org/10.1093/qje/qjac020. A globally comprehensive set of estimates of mortality risk due to temperature increases from climate change inclusive of adaptation costs.

Colgan, C. S. (2016). The economics of adaptation to climate change in coasts and oceans: Literature review, policy implications and research agenda. *Journal of Ocean and Coastal Economics*, 3(2), 1.

Fankhauser, S. (2016). Adaptation to climate change. *Grantham Research Institute on Climate Change and the Environment Working Paper No. 255*. www.lse.ac.uk/GranthamInstitute/publication/adaptation-to-climate-change. (Accessed April 1, 2017). *A survey of the economics of adaptation.*

Fourth National Climate Assessment: Volume II: Impacts, Risks, and Adaptation in the United States. (2018). https://nca2018.globalchange.gov.

Griffen, R. C. (2016). *Water Resource Economics: The Analysis of Scarcity, Policy and Projects*, 2nd ed. Cambridge, MA: MIT Press. Excellent coverage of the economics of resource allocation focusing on conservation, groundwater, water marketing, and demand and supply estimation for water.

IPCC AR6. (2022). *Climate Change 2022: Impacts, Adaptation and Vulnerability*. https://www.ipcc.ch/report/ar6/wg2.

Lago, M., Mysiak, J., Gómez, C. M., Delacámara, G., & Maziotis, A. (Eds.). (2015). *Use of Economic Instruments in Water Policy: Insights from International Experience*. Cham, Switzerland: Springer International. www.springer.com/us/book/9783319182865. An assessment of economic policy instruments (EPIs) with case studies from Cyprus, Denmark, France, Germany, Hungary, Italy, Spain, and the United Kingdom, as well as from Australia, Chile, Israel, and the United States.

Meyer, R., & Kunreuther, H. (2017). *The Ostrich Paradox: Why We Underprepare for Disasters*. Philadelphia, P.A.: Wharton Digital Press.

U.S. Environmental Protection Agency. (2016). Climate Change Indicators in the United States, 4th ed. *EPA 430-R-16-004*. www.epa.gov/climate-indicators. This report presents 37 indicators to help readers understand changes observed from long-term records related to the causes and effects of climate change, the significance of these changes, and their possible consequences for people, the environment, and society.

Chapter 13

Sustainable Development
Meeting the Challenge

Introduction

Delegations from 178 countries met in Rio de Janeiro during the first two weeks of June 1992 to begin the process of charting a sustainable development course for the future global economy. Billed by its organizers as the largest summit ever held, the United Nations Conference on Environment and Development (known popularly as the Earth Summit) sought to lay the groundwork for solving intergenerational global environmental problems. The central focus for this meeting was *sustainable development*.

What is sustainable development? According to the World Commission on Environment and Development, which is widely credited with initiating this concept, "Sustainable development is development that meets the needs of the present without compromising the ability of future generations to meet their own needs" (World Commission on Environment and Development, 1987).

What does sustainable development imply about changes in the way our system operates? How could the transition to sustainable development be managed? Where does the global community stand currently on our progress in achieving sustainable development? Will the global economic system automatically supply a smooth transition to sustainable development, or will policy changes be needed? If so, what policy changes?

The Basic Elements of Sustainable Development

At its core sustainable development began as an environmental justice concept. The initial version crafted in Rio focused on intergenerational justice—making sure future generations are protected from earlier-generation decisions that compromise their well-being.

DOI: 10.4324/9781032689111-15

In the early years of human existence our resource base was much larger relative to the population and our ability to negatively impact future generations was relatively small. If local resource stocks became depleted, we could move on to another untapped location.

Current generations can affect the sustainable welfare levels of future generations both positively and negatively. On the positive front we can use our resources to accumulate a larger capital stock, providing future generations with shelter, productivity, and transportation.

Another lasting positive contribution to future generations would come from what economists call human capital—investments in people. Though the people who receive education and training are mortal, the stream of innovative ideas they bring forth are not: human creativity can endure by serving as a foundation for subsequent new ideas.

Although current generations can lay the groundwork for a more hospitable future, they can also have the opposite impact. GHGs are altering the climate and intensifying droughts, storms, forest fires, heat waves, rising sea levels, etc. The imperfect storage of radioactive wastes could increase the likelihood of genetic damage in the future. Emissions of gases such as chlorofluorocarbons and hydrochlorofluorocarbons can, by depleting the atmosphere's ozone, raise the incidence of skin cancer. The ongoing reduction of genetic diversity in the stock of plants and animals could well jeopardize future biodiversity. We have learned that we no longer have the luxury of ignoring our impact on the future.

The concept of sustainable development asks us to replace our short-term thinking, which focuses mainly or exclusively on what is good for our generation, with a perspective that also considers how our actions affect the world our children, grandchildren, and great-grandchildren will inhabit.

In this chapter we examine how this concept has evolved over time and where we stand. How do we transition to a form of development that is both sustainable and just? What role do our institutions play? Can our economic system be counted upon to automatically choose a growth path that produces sustainable, fair welfare levels, or not?

The Sufficiency of Market Allocations in Attaining Just, Sustainable Outcomes

As we have seen in this book, some specific circumstances give rise to specific kinds of market imperfections, while in other circumstances markets can be quite efficient. We begin by considering some of the major market imperfections to assess how each affects the quest for sustainable development.

Market Imperfections

Market imperfections can arise in several different forms, including intertemporal externalities, open-access resources, and information deficiencies. In each of these cases improper incentives can be created that can interfere in important ways with the quest for sustainable, just development.

Normally we might think that merely assuring that we depend on renewable resources would guarantee sustainability since renewable resources, unlike depletable resources, are able to regenerate. That logic has two potential flaws: (1) even a stable flow of renewable resources might not be large enough to fill the needs of future generations, and (2) some types of renewable resources can be depleted. A governance system that allows completely open access to biological resources such as fisheries can promote, and commonly has promoted, unsustainable allocations. Diminished stocks are left for the future. In the extreme, some harvested species become extinct.

Intertemporal externalities are another source of market failure that can undermine the ability of the market to produce sustainable outcomes. Emissions of greenhouse gases impose a cost (climate-related damages) on future generations that is external to the current generation. Current actions to reduce the gases impose costs on this generation, but the bulk of the benefits would not be felt until later. Both economic theory and current experience clearly forecast that in the absence of additional corrective measures by governments too many greenhouse gas emissions would be forthcoming for the sustainability criterion to be satisfied; this could, if not corrected, even become an existential challenge.

Finally, even in specific circumstances when markets might produce sustainable outcomes if all decision makers had full information, full information is a very high bar. Market outcomes depend on the decisions of millions of consumers; when those decision makers are inadequately informed their decisions are unlikely to produce the best decisions for them, much less the best societal outcomes.

While market imperfections normally do exacerbate the problem of unsustainability, the more general conclusion that markets always promote unsustainability, however, is not correct. Even when market outcomes benefit current generations at the expense of future generations, the market can, in the right circumstances, limit the damage by promoting innovation that makes substitutes available. As we have seen with respect to the falling costs of solar panels, electric vehicles, and electrical storage batteries, market innovation can increase the speed and reduce the cost of the transition to an electrical system that is based upon renewable resources.

To be sure the flexibility and responsiveness of markets to scarcity can be an important component of the transition to sustainability, but the notion that markets would, if left to their own devices, automatically provide for a sustainable future is a false hope.

The Evolution of the Sustainable Development Concept

The original concept of sustainable development focused mainly on achieving a just intergenerational allocation of resources. It involved setting goals to assure that the resource base on which economic activity depends would be sustained, not exhausted, or degraded. It started with a recognition that would seem obvious—depletable resources can, in fact, be depleted. Supplies of resources that might be crucial for key sectors in the economy are not unlimited.

Renewable resources have the distinct advantage that in principle they regenerate. However, even renewable resources such as water from recharging aquifers are not immune from becoming scarce. Demand could run high enough to deplete aquifers, a traditional source of water, if the extraction rate exceeds the recharge rate.

The basic logic underlying the quest for sustainable development is that our planet, on which we all depend, has a limited capacity for life-sustaining services and our economy does not by itself prevent that capacity from being exceeded. A partnership between government and the economy would be essential.

To try to get countries on the same page about how to proceed, the United Nations Conference on Environment and Development (UNCED), known popularly as the Earth Summit, was convened in Rio de Janeiro in 1992. Among other topics, the Earth Summit addressed strategies for controlling toxic substances, for controlling climate risks by developing strategies for mitigating GHG emissions, for protecting biodiversity, and for dealing with anticipated shortages of water supplies.

With respect to climate policy, it initiated the United Nations Framework Convention on Climate Change (UNFCCC). Signed by 154 states, it laid the groundwork for periodic follow-up meetings of signatory countries known as the UNFCCC Conference of Parties.

With respect to protecting biodiversity the Convention on Biological Diversity was opened for signatures at the Earth Summit and received enough signatures to enter into force in 1993. This international treaty was designed to develop cooperative national strategies for the conservation and sustainable use of biological diversity.

Finally, the Earth Summit issued Agenda 21, a comprehensive plan of action to build a global partnership for sustainable development. It sought to improve human lives while protecting the planetary basis on which development depends.

In 2000, the United Nations enlarged the concept of sustainable development by establishing the Millennium Development Goals (MDGs), which focused on assuring that ALL citizens, including those in the developing world, would have access to the necessities of life. The MDGs established objectives for tackling extreme poverty and hunger, preventing deadly diseases, and expanding primary education to all children, among other development priorities.

Finally in 2015, the United Nations General Assembly established a more detailed and comprehensive collection of 17 interlinked global Sustainable Development Goals (SDGs) to "achieve a better and more sustainable future for all." These were designed to be a set of universal, measurable objectives that could motivate and track progress in meeting the urgent environmental, political, and economic social justice challenges facing the world. The international agreement on these goals made it clear that merely assuring that development produced economic growth was not enough. Justice would only be served when the fruits from sustainable development were shared in a just fashion, not only among generations, but also within generations. Everyone should have access to basic needs such as food and water and basic services such as education and medical care.

The Current Sustainable Development Vision in Practice

Having defined the objectives, what are the chief components of the mix of strategies to achieve that vision? We start with climate change, the major threat to future generations.

The climate goal seeks to reduce global greenhouse gas emissions to a net-zero level by 2050. This would be achieved mainly by decarbonizing the energy sector via a transition from high-carbon, depletable fossil fuels to zero-carbon renewable resources such as solar and wind, with possible complementary roles for hydrogen and nuclear power.

This transition would be accompanied by an expanded role for beneficial electrification in transportation (electric vehicles) and heating and cooling (heat pumps), as well as investments in energy efficiency to reduce energy waste. Due to its higher global warming potential, scientists believe that curbing methane emissions would be a priority near-term way to put the planet on a more sustainable temperature trajectory.

Focusing future decarbonization efforts primarily on substantially increasing electric generation from renewables like wind and solar presents some related challenges. Beneficial electrification will require more electricity to be generated and transmitted in the future, while maintaining system reliability. Further, electric utilities must provide reliable power whenever and wherever it is needed by their customers. Unlike fossil fuel plants, which can normally generate power as needed, solar and wind plants run only intermittently. Solar farms produce no power at night, little on cloudy days, and less during the winter than the summer.[1] Wind generators produce power only when the wind is blowing.

Studies that compare the demand for electric power over time with the amount supplied by solar and wind would reveal a gap of unfulfilled power needs during those times when wind and solar are not producing enough to meet demand. Therefore, enabling wind and solar to be the foundation of the future electrical power system requires some means to seamlessly fill the power gap when the renewables are not producing.

The two main current contenders are battery storage and nuclear.[2] Battery storage works by drawing and storing power from the grid at those times when current electricity generation exceeds demand and supplying it to the grid when demand would otherwise exceed supply. Nuclear is an alternative generation source that does not produce any carbon emissions. Establishing the proper role for nuclear, however, is controversial (Debate 13.1).

Different nations may well come to different conclusions. In 1980, the Swedish government decided to phase out nuclear power. In June 2010, its parliament voted to repeal this phase-out. Germany and Belgium are phasing out their existing nuclear power, while in 2022, President Macron of France announced an ambitious plan to build up to 14 new-generation reactors and a fleet of smaller nuclear plants.

DEBATE 13.1

What Role Should Nuclear Power Play in Our Energy Future?

Typical arguments (Jacobson, 2019) against reliance on nuclear energy in the future are:

1. **Long Time Lag between Planning and Operation**. Nuclear takes a lot longer to build than other zero-carbon sources of energy and we don't have the time.
2. **Cost**. The costs of nuclear energy are higher than other zero-carbon fuels and are growing.

3. **Weapons Proliferation Risk**. Processing uranium for nuclear plants makes it easier to produce nuclear weapons.
4. **Safety Risk**. Remember the Three Mile Island plant meltdown (1979), the explosion and burnout of the Chernobyl plant (1986), and the flooding accident in Fukushima (2011)?
5. **Mining Lung Cancer Risk**. Miners are exposed to natural radon gas, some of whose decay products are carcinogenic.
6. **Risk from Radioactive Waste**. Most spent radioactive fuel rods from nuclear plants are stored at the same site as the reactor that consumed them. The growing number of shuttered reactors has spawned a new decommissioning business model that promises to remediate sites quickly, but also raises new questions about safety, financial assurance, cleanup standards, and waste disposition.
7. **New Generation IV nuclear plants do have fewer problems and have a lower expected cost, but no commercial versions have yet been built**.

Arguments (Budinger, 2019; Rhodes, 2018) for a greater role for nuclear include:

1. **The scale of new battery construction that would be needed if we were to depend solely on batteries is impractical**. Even our best solar farms produce significant power only about 25 percent of the time, while even in the windiest locations; wind farms will almost surely need to use backup power more than half the time.
2. **Nuclear safety in historical perspective**. The three notable accidents, Three Mile Island, Chernobyl, and Fukushima, were rare exceptions to the safety record of more than a thousand reactors (on ships and land) that have been operating safely for as long as 60 years.
3. **The cost, safety, and timing of the newest (Generation IV) nuclear generators are promising**. Gen IV technologies are totally different from previous generators, and many have already been thoroughly tested in research labs. Most produce much less waste and some even use existing waste as fuel. Because of their design, they are of little value to terrorists or weapons-makers. Best of all, they are walk-away safe—the physics of Gen IV stops the reaction automatically if the reactor gets too hot. No operator or mechanical intervention is necessary.
4. **The outlook**. More than 50 entrepreneurial ventures in the United States are working on various Gen IV reactor designs. Some are getting close, but currently companies working on Gen IV designs haven't received permission to build them. Before any American Gen IV reactors can be built commercially and brought to market, major changes must be made to the regulatory system.

What is your view? Why?

Sources: Budinger, B. (August 9, 2019). Why wind and solar aren't enough: Both suffer from an intermittency problem. A plausible back-up source is needed—and there's only one. *Democracy: A Journal of Ideas*; Rhodes, R. (July 19, 2018). Why nuclear power must be part of the energy solution. *Yale Environment 360*. https://e360.yale.edu/features/why-nuclear-power-must-be-part-of-the-energy-solution-environmentalists-climate; Jacobson, M. Z. (June 20, 2019). The 7 reasons why nuclear energy is not the answer to solve climate change. https://eu.boell.org/en/2021/04/26/7-reasons-why-nuclear-energy-not-answer-solve-climate-change.

What about the biodiversity and ecosystem components of sustainable development? In 2021, an influential and comprehensive document (Dasgupta, 2021) argued that to close a significant gap between what we may demand from nature in the future and what it can supply to us, we must recognize that humanity is embedded in nature, not external to it. The implication that flows from that insight is that more attention and resources must be focused on protecting, enhancing, and maintaining the ecosystems on which we depend.

Renewable resources are not a panacea. As earlier chapters have pointed out, major renewable food sources such as fisheries and agriculture can be degraded and/or depleted if not managed carefully. Further, they can be limited by climate change as it intensifies droughts, floods, temperatures to inhospitable levels, and fires. It is far from obvious that the ecological systems will provide a sufficient foundation for meeting the Sustainable Development Goals without devoting more attention and resources to achieving that outcome.

In thinking about these issues it is useful to return to the two major economic forces that provide one key to answering this question—supply and demand. Economic forces are powerful and we have seen how they can either promote sustainability or degrade it, depending on the circumstances. Fortunately, well-designed policies can help to align those forces, when necessary, thereby facilitating the outcomes we seek.

A useful complementary framing vision, known as the *Circular Economy*, is still evolving, but is playing an increasing role, especially in Europe. It seeks to replace the old linear production cycle of make–use–discard with a more restorative and regenerative circular design for the economy. Some examples of key components[3] offer suggestive pathways for affecting both supply and demand. Many of the principles apply to all natural resources regardless of whether they are depletable or renewable.

Some examples involve reducing the demand for natural resources by limiting or eliminating waste in the production and use of new products, as well as by increasing the useful life of products so they have to be replaced less often. Others involve designing products so that when they reach the end of their useful life, they can easily become inputs in the production of new products rather than waste, thus completing the circle. Food supply can be enhanced by encouraging regenerative agriculture practices that retain, rather than deplete, valuable natural nutrients in the soil.

Finally, both intergenerational and intragenerational justice must be a part of not only generational outcomes, but the processes to reach them as well. A just process would assure meaningful involvement of all people regardless of race, color, national origin, or income, with respect to the development, implementation, and enforcement of sustainability laws, regulations, and policies. Sustainable development should also produce fair outcomes for all with respect to the consequences from the implementation and enforcement of sustainability laws, regulations, and policies. In particular, as the SDGs suggest, no one should be left behind.

The Evolution of Sustainable Development Metrics

A well-known saying in the business community is that you can't manage what you can't measure. How do we judge success over time in achieving a just balance between meeting the needs of present and future generations? What metrics can we use? Since the process of metric development has evolved over time, we will briefly describe that evolution to provide some temporal context for current metrics.

The initial attempts to devise informative metrics focused on revealing whether economic growth, as measured by national income accounts, was being maintained. The underlying logic was that if the economy was growing, well-being was surely increasing. The common saying "a rising tide lifts all boats" captures the underlying perception that economic growth benefits everyone. But does it?

Modifying Conventional National Income Metrics. The national income accounts were originally designed to be *output measures*, which attempt to indicate how many goods and services have been produced, not *well-being* measures, which seek to reveal how well off we are. A true measure of sustainable development would increase whenever we, as a nation or as a world, were better off and decrease whenever we were worse off. The original national income metric did not fulfill that role, so attempts were made to modify what we had to work with.

The measure of economic development with which most are familiar is based upon the GDP (gross domestic product) metric. This number represents the sum of the outputs of goods and services produced by the economy in any year. Prices are used to weight the importance of these goods and services in the GDP. Conceptually, this is accomplished by adding up the value added by each sector of the production process until the product is sold.

Why weight by prices? Some means of comparing the value of extremely dissimilar commodities is needed. Prices provide a readily available system of weights that considers the value of those commodities to consumers. Prices should reflect both the marginal benefit to the consumer and the marginal cost to the producer.

Since GDP is not a measure of well-being (and was never meant to be one), it should not be surprising that increases in this indicator may not reliably represent increases in development or well-being even in an aggregate sense. Consider a few of the deficiencies.

While this indicator (appropriately) includes the rise of the capital stock, it also includes the value of new machines that are merely replacing worn-out ones. To compensate for the fact that some investment merely replaces old machines and does not add to the size of capital stock, a new concept known as *net domestic product* (NDP) was introduced. NDP is defined as the gross domestic product minus depreciation.

NDP and GDP share the deficiency that they are both influenced by inflation. If the flow of all goods and services were to remain the same while prices doubled, both NDP and GDP would also double. Well-being, however, would not have doubled.

To resolve this problem, national income accounts now present data on *constant-dollar* GDP and *constant-dollar* NDP. These numbers are derived by "cleansing" the actual GDP and NDP data to take out the effects of price increases. Conceptually, this is accomplished by defining a market basket of goods that stays the same over time. Each year, this same basket is repriced. If the cost of the goods in the basket went up 10 percent, we know that prices (of this specific basket) went up by 10 percent, because the quantities were held constant. This information is used to remove the effects of prices on the indicators; remaining increases should be due to an increased production of goods and services.

Another correction that is commonly made to the existing accounts involves dividing real GDP or *constant-dollar* NDP by the population to get a *per capita* metric. This correction allows us to see whether goods and services over time are keeping pace with population growth. This is about as close as we can get to a welfare-oriented output measure using conventional accounting data. Yet it is a far cry from being an ideal welfare indicator.

In particular, changes in constant-dollar GDP per capita fail to distinguish between economic growth resulting from a true increase in income, and economic growth resulting from a depreciation in what economists have come to call "natural capital," the stock of environmentally provided assets, such as the soil, the atmosphere, the forests, wildlife, and water.

The traditional definition of income was articulated by Sir John Hicks (1939):

> The purpose of income calculations in practical affairs is to give people an indication of the amount they can consume without impoverishing themselves. Following out this idea, it would seem that we ought to define a man's income as the maximum value which he can consume during a week, and still expect to be as well off at the end of the week as he was at the beginning.
>
> (172)

Although human-created capital (such as buildings and bridges) is treated in a manner consistent with this definition, natural capital (a forest, for example) is not. As we noted earlier, no increase in economic activity is recorded as an increase in income until depreciation has been subtracted from gross returns. That portion of the gains that merely serves to replace worn-out capital is not appropriately considered income.

No such adjustment was made for natural capital in the standard national income accounting system. Depreciation of the stock of natural capital is by default therefore incorrectly counted as income.

Consider an analogy. Many educational institutions in the United States have large financial endowments. When considering their budgets for the year, these institutions take the revenue from tuition and other fees and add in some proportion of the interest and capital gains earned from the endowment. Except in extraordinary circumstances, standard financial practice does not allow the institution to treat the entire endowment principal as spendable income.

Yet that is precisely what the traditional national accounts allow us to do in terms of natural resources. If we degrade our soils, deplete our mines, and cut down our forests, the resulting economic returns are treated as income. The decline in the endowment of natural capital is not considered. Even worse is the fact that the expenditures to clean up a major oil spill are counted as an increase in economic activity that drives the GDP up.

Because the Hicksian definition is violated for natural capital, policymakers can be misled. By relying upon misleading information, policymakers are more likely to unintentionally undertake unsustainable development strategies. Motivated by a recognition of these serious flaws in the current system of accounts, some industrial countries have now proposed (or in a few cases have already set up) systems of modified accounts, including Norway, France, Canada, Japan, the Netherlands, and Germany.

Enter Donut Economics

Particularly missing, even among these adjusted accounts, is their failure to include specific consideration of protecting future generations from planetary threats such as climate change or biodiversity loss, among others, and assuring that all people enjoy access to basic human rights and services as called for in the SDGs.

Economist Kate Raworth, a senior research associate at Oxford University's Environmental Change Institute, has suggested that this more inclusive set of goals and associated metrics could be captured by a simple, but meaningful, visualization that integrates several sustainability goals and metrics. In her book *Donut Economics: 7 Ways to Think Like a 21st Century Economist*, she presents this visualization (Figure 13.1).

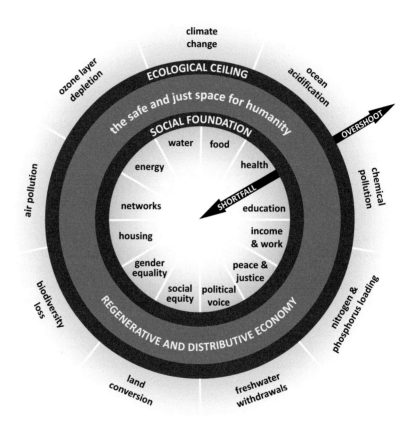

Figure 13.1 The "Donut Economics" Concept.

Source: "A Safe & Just Space for Humanity—Can We Live Within the Doughnut—Kate Raworth—13th February 2012 (figure 4: The 'Doughnut Economics' Concept developed by Oxford economist Kate Raworth)" is adapted by the publisher with the permission of Oxfam, Oxfam House, John Smith Drive, Cowley, Oxford OX4 2JY UK www.oxfam.org.uk. Oxfam does not necessarily endorse any text or activities that accompany the materials, nor has it approved the adapted text.

It has three main components: (1) a safe and just place in the middle, shaped like a donut; (2) the outer edge of the donut depicts the ecological ceiling, with nine categories of possible exceedances of the ceiling; and, finally, (3) the inside edge of the donut depicts possible shortfalls in meeting 12 social foundations that identify the basic rights and services that all of humanity should have. In this visualization the sustainable development goal is achieved when all the world's people attain their place in the donut "safe and just space" with no violations either of the planetary boundary or the social foundations boundary.

The categories that make up the 12 social foundations are based upon the 19 internationally agreed-upon United Nations SDGs. They represent the basic human rights and quality of life that it was felt all humans in the sustainable society should enjoy.[4] The actual metrics used to measure the current status of efforts to provide these basic human rights and services are commonly the percentage of the population that has yet to meet the goals. The deadline for meeting the 12 social foundation goals is 2030.[5] Annual progress on the SDGs is monitored by the United Nations, and the reports are posted on the web, making this aspect of the donut metric relatively easy to track.

The Donut Economic categories that make up the planetary boundaries came from an international team of scientists.[6] They used scientific evidence to propose nine specific categories of planetary boundaries that could be violated by human perturbations. Those nine categories are: climate change, ocean acidification, chemical pollution, nitrogen and phosphorus loading, freshwater withdrawals, land conversion, biodiversity loss, air pollution, and ozone layer depletion. For seven of the categories the study also proposes thresholds below which the risk of destabilization is likely to remain low enough to provide a "safe operating space" for global development. For the other two categories (air pollution and chemical pollution) no safe levels of perturbation were yet determined.

Figure 13.2 shows the donut economics graph when these progress measurements are applied. Each planetary ceiling category experiencing overshooting is depicted by a bar radiating out from the outer edge of that planetary ceiling category. Shortcomings in meeting the social foundation goals are depicted by an area radiating toward the center from the inner boundary of the donut. Success would be depicted as the absence of any violations of either boundary; the unencumbered donut would depict a situation in which the basic needs of all planetary inhabitants would be met without violating any planetary boundaries.

This figure makes clear that the current sustainable development process, as judged by these metrics, still has some work to do. Both boundaries are experiencing exceedances.

Of the nine planetary boundaries, four have been identified as experiencing overshooting—climate change, biodiversity loss, excessive land conversion, and nitrogen and phosphorus overfertilization. When the Raworth book was published, no boundary level had yet been determined for chemical pollution or atmospheric aerosol loading.

With respect to the social foundations, every single category has unmet goals. This characterization flows from the fact that millions of people around the world are still living below the specified social foundation thresholds. Behind these stark figures lie the human suffering of those who do not get enough to eat, do not have access to adequate health care, education, housing, and so on. Many of these are children. The COVID-19 pandemic intensified the shortfalls.

The donut economics concept not only identifies specific challenges the development process faces in achieving a just and safe outcome, but it also provides the basis

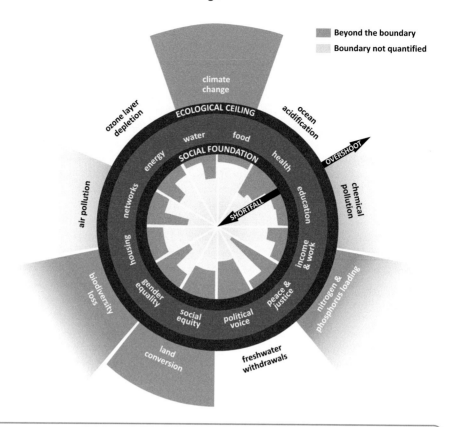

Beyond the boundary

Boundary not quantified

Figure 13.2 The Status of Current Sustainable Development Efforts from a Donut Economics Perspective.

Source: Raworth, K. (2017). *Doughnut Economics: Seven Ways to Think Like a 21st-Century Economist*. London: Random House Business Books, 2017, 258.

for a "one-glance" visual depiction of where we stand in terms of achievement of the internationally established goals. By identifying both where current actions have fallen short and the degree of the shortfall, it provides a more comprehensive and inclusive guidance for directing future efforts in a way that previous metrics could not.

Where does this leave the role for economic growth in sustainable development? Raworth suggests that everyone should become a growth agnostic. She points out that depending on the circumstances, growth can be helpful or harmful to the achievement of the goals. The key, she argues, is to focus rather on creating an economy that is regenerative and fair, letting economic growth's role be defined by how well it helps to achieve that goal.

Meeting the Challenges

To think about how the challenges posed by this more inclusive sustainable development vision can be met in general and the role economics can play in facilitating the transition, consider both its intergenerational and intragenerational components.

The Intergenerational Challenge

Starting with the climate challenge, the pathway envisioned to meet it involves a complete or near-complete transition to zero-carbon, renewable sources of energy from the current heavy reliance on fossil fuels. How can economics as a field of inquiry and markets as institutions facilitate this transition?

For a start, the economic evidence is clear that in the absence of action to mitigate the emissions of greenhouse gases, the increasing damages resulting from climate change will make future societies collectively worse off. Indeed, the leading edge of those damages has already arrived, with growing economic impact. Although taking the necessary actions to manage these threats will not be costless, the economic evidence is clear—the potential cost of inaction is much greater than the cost of taking action.

The Respective Roles for Government and Markets

By making clear both the strengths and weakness of both markets and governments, economics demonstrates that neither is sufficient to meet these challenges by itself, but they could usefully combine their roles to form an effective partnership.

Markets are not only good at providing innovation, but they are also good at achieving the necessary change cost effectively. Market-induced innovation has already helped by substantially lowering the costs of renewable energy sources like solar, wind, and energy storage. However, due to market imperfections such as fuel-choice externalities (where carbon damages are understated in fuel choices) and free-rider effects associated with research and development choices (where innovators receive only a portion of the benefits they create), by themselves markets are not likely to result in both sufficient emissions reductions and sufficient research and development investment by the time they are needed.

Governments can play a major role by correcting these imperfections, either by filling in the gaps or by redirecting the incentives. They can also help by incentivizing early adoptions by the pioneers to move the markets to scale more quickly and by assisting in financing where necessary to assure that affordability constraints don't inhibit fair treatment.

Economics can facilitate the partnership by providing insights on the likely consequences of various policy strategies that might be considered by it. Carbon pricing is the most obvious illustration of this point. When the government puts the appropriate price on emissions (via a carbon tax or an emissions trading system) that action prevents shifting the cost associated with those emissions onto others. Once those who cause the cost are forced to bear it, the necessary incentives to prevent the climate overshoot can be restored. Furthermore, economic studies make clear that this specific policy choice allows us in principle to manage the climate risk both comprehensively and cost-effectively, an advantage most alternative policies (or even policy packages) do not have.

It can also help to achieve a just pathway for this transition. Unlike other programs promoting emission mitigation, carbon pricing schemes provide revenue while they change incentives. This revenue can be used, and in some existing programs is being used, to assure that the most vulnerable people are not adversely affected by the transition.

It is important, however, not to get rigidly committed to a particular policy package based upon what it could achieve in principle. Enacting optimal policies requires specific government actions, including setting the right price on carbon. Economics can help to identify the required prices, but enacting legislation that produces the right prices is up to the government. Carbon pricing is spreading to new geographic areas and being applied to new types of applications (Example 13.1). Yet so far the global aggregate emissions reductions achieved or pledged by governments are not yet sufficient to meet the established climate goals in terms of the amount of emission reductions or their timing.

The current array of implemented carbon prices is too low to generate the necessary emissions reductions in time. Further, existing policies are not comprehensive enough in terms of the scope of their coverage, both geographically and across economic sectors. While basic economic principles and empirical studies can establish what the optimal price paths and coverage should be, that is little comfort if governments prove politically incapable of putting those components into effect.

EXAMPLE 13.1

Metropolitan Tokyo's Cap-and-Trade Program for Buildings

The Tokyo Cap-and-Trade Program (TCTP) implemented on April 1, 2010, was the first such scheme in Asia and Japan. In this program facilities that consume more than 1500 kiloliters of energy (crude oil equivalent) a year are required to reduce emissions below a facility-specific baseline. Other than reducing emissions through their own efforts, facilities falling under this program can achieve their reduction targets by procuring the excess emission reductions of other facilities through emissions trading. If the target is not achieved, the facility will be ordered to make a further reduction by the amount of their shortfall multiplied by 1.3. Facilities failing to carry out the order will be publicly named and subject to penalties. The facility will also have to pay the purchase price for offset credits procured by the governor of Tokyo to cover the shortage.

The program applies to about 1300 facilities: in the commercial sector, about 1000 office buildings, public buildings, and commercial facilities; in the industrial sector, about 300 factories and other facilities. The total emissions from targeted facilities account for 40 percent of all CO_2 emissions from the commercial and industrial sectors in the Tokyo area.

In March 2020, the Tokyo Metropolitan Government released emission data for fiscal year 2018. It reported that, compared to base-year emissions, aggregate emissions were reduced by 27 percent overall among covered entities, thereby exceeding the 15–17 percent target.

Significant reductions were made through proactive efforts to save energy, such as introducing LED lighting, and 90 percent of the facilities were able to meet their reduction targets through such internal initiatives. The remaining 10 percent of the facilities used emissions trading to reach their targets.

Sources: Tokyo Metropolitan Government. https://www.metro.tokyo.lg.jp/english/topics/2016/161116.html; The UN's Sustainable Development Goals website: https://sustainabledevelopment.un.org/index.php?page=view&type=99&nr=297&menu=1449

Economic research, however, may even be able to help to build the political will to enact the necessary actions. Studies have made clear, for example, that mitigating greenhouse gas emissions helps to achieve multiple planetary boundary goals, not merely the climate goal. For example, about 30 percent of the carbon dioxide emissions that are released into the atmosphere are absorbed by the oceans. As the absorbed carbon dissolves, it triggers a series of chemical reactions that increase ocean acidification. The important implication is that as policies reduce carbon dioxide emissions, they simultaneously reduce future ocean acidification.

Further, according to the Harvard T. H. Chan School of Public Health[7] reducing the burning of fossil fuels simultaneously reduces several associated pollutants that lead to early death, heart attacks, respiratory disorders, stroke, and the exacerbation of asthma, among others. These climate action co-benefits increase the net benefits from the transition away from fossil fuels without requiring additional air pollution control policies that would increase the costs. Note that since these pollutant concentrations are reduced in the areas where the emissions are reduced (not globally), they are not subject to free-rider barriers to political action. The more carbon emissions an area reduces, the more health co-benefits the residents of that area receive.

Additionally, carbon pricing programs can be designed to respond to unexpected outcomes as time passes, a characteristic that is rare among emissions mitigation strategies. If the emissions reductions fall below expectations, automatic price adjustment mechanisms would be triggered by these circumstances. Waiting for additional enabling legislation would not be necessary. When response timing is very important, as it is in this case, that is an important feature.

Finally, delay in action raises the ultimate cost and exposes younger generations to much higher risks. It is not surprising that the youth of today are increasingly becoming climate activists—their future is at stake.[8]

Government–market partnerships can also help in other ways. Beneficial electrification, a key component, will require more electricity to be generated and transmitted in the future, while maintaining system reliability. Assuring grid reliability not only depends upon the required additional capacity arriving at the right time, but also in the right places. Policies such as forward capacity markets and public funding for some research and development are evolving to fill this role. Connecting the Eastern and Western grids is also a possible component of the grid upgrade in the United States. Examining the benefits and cost of sharing generation resources and adding flexibility across regions, one study (Bloom et al., 2022) reports estimated benefit-to-cost ratios as high as 2.5, indicating significant value to increasing the transmission capacity between the interconnections, not only within each of the regional grids.

Interestingly, polls have shown that policy packages that could complement carbon pricing might politically be able to fill the gap between what is needed and what is currently being achieved. According to economic studies, if such a combination of policy types could be enacted globally, the mix could be aggressive enough, timely enough, and comprehensive enough to produce the necessary emissions reductions. Although economic studies also conclude that the complementary policies would not be as cost-effective as an exclusive reliance on the appropriate carbon pricing approaches, when governments cannot implement sufficiently aggressive carbon pricing programs that argument is less compelling.

Partnerships can also play a role in managing planetary overshoot risks in addition to climate change. In protecting biodiversity, for example, market-based policy instruments are increasingly being enlisted to allow the commonly understated social benefits of biodiversity to get their due (OECD, 2021b). By placing an additional cost on the use of the natural resource or the emission of a pollutant, to reflect the negative environmental externalities that they generate, they provide incentives for both producers and consumers to behave in a more environmentally sustainable way.

Public discussions have focused on the importance of a partnership of the market and "the government," but in truth, climate change is a global problem. Solving a global problem requires international cooperation among many governments—no mean feat. As economic game theory studies make clear, free-rider problems hinder the creation and durability of the requisite international agreements. However, that literature has also given rise to a growing literature focusing on strategies, such as forming an international climate club, activating climate border adjustment policies, exploiting co-benefits, and identifying issue linkage, to tame the free-rider barrier. Fortunately, these general concepts are now being explored in practice, especially in Europe.

The Intragenerational Challenge

The intragenerational sustainability dimension envisions a transition that is fair to all within each generation as well as among generations. Sustainability should assure not only an adequate and safe place for each generation, but also make sure that all individuals within each generation have access to the basic human rights and services that undergird that safe place.

The underlying premise expressed by the SDGs is that sustainable development should leave no one behind. As one of its monitoring steps, the UN calculates an SDG index for each country for which adequate data is available. The first step is to produce a score for each of its goals, using the arithmetic mean of indicators associated with that goal. These goal scores are then averaged across all 17 SDGs to obtain the country's SDG Index score. The score can be interpreted as a percentage of SDG achievement by that country.

In its *Sustainable Development Report 2021: The Decade of Action for the Sustainable Development Goals* the U.N. had enough data to calculate index scores for 165 countries. For those 165 countries the scores ranged from a high of 85.90 (Finland) to a low of 38.25 (Central African Republic). The highest scores were achieved in European countries and the lowest in Africa.[9]

Africa has emerged as the continent that would face the most difficulties in reaching its goals and be the most helped by the SDGs being globally achieved. For that reason, it has become the focus of additional attention. The *2020 Africa SDG Index and Dashboards Report* provides some context for that focus.

- Nine out of ten extremely poor people in the world are found in Africa. The consequences of COVID-19 have posed additional challenges for achieving SDG 1 (end poverty) in Africa by 2030.
- Evidence indicated that 135 million people globally were found to be food insecure in 2020 with the majority, about 73 million, living in Africa.
- Inadequate basic services and access to clean water have been a great challenge for the continent. In Sub-Saharan Africa, about 63 percent of people have difficulties in accessing basic water services.
- Extreme inequality persists within African countries and cities as well as between countries. Evidence from African countries shows that children in the poorest quintile of the population are up to three times more likely to die before their fifth birthday than children in the richest quintiles.

In 2009, the United Nations reiterated that "each country has primary responsibility for its own economic and social development and that the role of national policies, domestic resources and development strategies could not be overemphasized." However, it also noted that "national development efforts need to be supported by an enabling international economic environment ...."[10]

Significant barriers must be overcome. In her book *The Challenge for Africa*, Wangari Maathai, the first African woman to win the Nobel Peace Prize, points out that the modern African nation is a superficial creation—a loose collection of ethnic communities, or, in her term, "micro-nations" brought together in a single "macro-nation" by the colonial powers. Some countries include hundreds of micro-nations, others a few.

Dr. Maathai points out that political loyalties in these nations flow mainly to micro-nations rather than to the macro-nation. Conflicts among the micro-nations are common. This fractured structure, further complicated by the many different languages involved within the macro-nations, makes effective national governance difficult even in the best of times. And the recent past has not been the best of times.

In 2019, the International Monetary Fund (IMF) estimated that the low-income developing countries (LIDCs) would have to increase their SDG outlays by roughly 12 percent of GDP to achieve the 2030 targets. LIDCs are a group of 59 IMF member countries with income per capita below a threshold level. LIDCs contain one-fifth of the world's population—1.5 billion people—but account for only 4 percent of global output. This required level of incremental spending was estimated to be beyond the means of these countries, leading to an SDG financing gap on the order of $300 to $500 billion per year (Gaspar et al., 2019).[11]

In terms of filling that financing gap, the *2022 Financing for Sustainable Development Report: Bridging the Finance Divide*[12] finds that while rich countries were able to support their pandemic recovery with record sums borrowed at ultra-low interest rates, the poorest countries spent billions servicing their debt, money that could have supported investments in sustainable development. The pandemic shock plunged 77 million more people into extreme poverty in 2021, and by the end of the year many economies remained below pre-2019 levels. During this period the LIDCs fell even further behind. The negative effects from extreme poverty and the loss of basic empowering services such as health care, adequate nutrition, and education can even have intergenerational consequences.[13]

Low-income countries will need additional international funding in order to address the specific climate challenges they face. In response, several funding measures have been launched to address climate issues, including the UN's Green Climate Fund and Adaptation Fund. The Green Climate Fund, established under the framework of the UNFCCC, aims to assist developing countries in investing in low-emission and climate-resilient development. The Adaptation Fund supports financing projects and programs to help developing countries become more resilient to reduce the impacts of climate change that no longer can be avoided.

These international organizations also work closely with national development banks in the member countries, including low-income countries. These established relationships make cooperation easier, not only in setting up financing, but also in passing along examples of successful strategies in other, similar countries.

In the higher-income countries, carbon pricing revenue can become very useful in pursuing a just transition within those countries. Several of the current carbon pricing program designs offer the possibility of returning sufficient revenue back (dividends) to households to assure that low-income households would receive more money back than they paid in higher energy prices.

Some of these just transition designs have already made their way into operating programs. In the Canadian National Carbon Pricing System all carbon pricing proceeds are returned to the jurisdiction of origin. This program was designed to assure that most Canadian families receive more money back than they pay in carbon prices, with low-income Canadians benefiting the most. Currently 90 percent of fuel-charge proceeds directly support families through payments delivered through quarterly payments.

In California some of the revenue from their cap-and-trade program flows directly to California residents to offset the increased cost of electricity and natural gas caused by the state's climate initiatives. The rest of the money goes toward projects that further reduce greenhouse gas emissions or improve water quality. At least 35 percent of these investments are made in disadvantaged communities as well as in low-income communities and households. In disadvantaged neighborhoods, those investments could mean enhanced public transit, increasing access to renewable energy, or constructing energy-efficient, affordable housing.

Another method for easing the transition for lower-income households involves the use of progressive pricing and tax structures. Pricing water to households via an increasing block system is a common example. The first monthly block of water is available for a very reasonable price, but customers who consume larger and larger monthly amounts (say, to water large lawns) must pay an increasing price per unit for the overage. Since wealthier households generally consume more water, this pricing scheme can produce a more just cost-recovery system by assuring that all have access to a basic amount of water at a reasonable price.

Other strategies for assuring just outcomes exist. One traditional means is to involve both national and local governments in the financing of essential services such as education. Financing just transitions at least partially from taxation is usually much more progressive than asking each project to be completely self-financed or completely locally financed.

Government financing can also provide economic incentives to help low-income households make their homes more energy efficient. The up-front costs of some investment options can preclude lower-income households from investing due to their lack of access to the necessary loans. Since some governments already provide public funds to help low-income households pay for high heating costs in colder climates, investing in sealing energy leaks is frequently a cheaper way over the long run to help these households.

This point is generally applicable. Investments that achieve financial sustainability by providing the services needed to correct the problem (health, education, sanitation) can have a longer and deeper impact than simply helping to finance the resulting consequences of underinvestment in these services (sickness, skill deficits, etc.) year after year.

Other opportunities for government financial support involve helping displaced workers and the communities that are hard hit by the transition. In the United States, some states, such as Wyoming, North Dakota, Alaska, New Mexico, and West Virginia are heavily dependent on fossil fuel-related revenues to support public services. Using stylized scenarios of future energy use, one study[14] estimates that through 2050, nationwide revenues in these communities decline 16, 50, and 80 percent respectively under business-as-usual, 2°C temperature target, and 1.5°C temperature target scenarios.

Although more jobs are expected to be created during the energy transition, the new jobs will generally match neither the geographic location of displaced workers nor the existing skills they offer. Grants can help to support workers by helping them develop necessary skills for the job market of the future. Further, in Virginia, West Virginia, and Pennsylvania some abandoned U.S. coal mines are being transformed into solar farms, but that is not the norm.

The European Union has created a "Just Transition Fund" that will focus on the European regions and sectors that are most affected by the transition due to their dependence on fossil fuels. Support provided through the Just Transition Fund is focused on the economic diversification of the territories most affected by the climate transition as well as on the reskilling and active inclusion of their workers and jobseekers.

Fortunately, new kinds of financial institutions are also being developed to increase the flow of capital investments into green activities. For example, *green banks* have been established specifically to facilitate the flow of investment capital into low-carbon, climate-resilient infrastructure, as well as into other green sectors such as water and waste. These banks typically take the form of either a government-owned or quasi-public bank that receives a set amount of government money to launch and then leverage private money to fund eligible projects. Green banks help secure capital for clean energy projects, including solar, at favorable rates to otherwise difficult-to-serve market segments. Lowering these development costs, in turn, makes it possible for developers to sell their solar at lower prices. Green banks have been established at the national level (Australia, Japan, Malaysia, Switzerland, United Kingdom), state level (California, Connecticut, Hawaii, New Jersey, New York, and Rhode Island in the United States), county level (Montgomery County, Maryland, United States), and city level (United Arab Emirates).[15]

The Evolving Roles of Technology, the Business Community, and Nongovernmental Organizations

In some cases, sustainable development presents new business opportunities arising from new technologies. For example, many especially poor, rural parts of the world have previously not had access to electricity because extending the grid to these areas would not have been economically viable. With the transition to renewables, however, access to electricity in these communities is now not only possible but spreading. Studies (Lawrence Berkeley National Laboratory, 2017; Kirubi et al., 2009) suggest that since electricity from solar and wind no longer relies on extensive and expensive transmission lines to get it from distant centralized plants, it can now be economically and environmentally competitive for a large portion of Africa (recall Example 12.6).

Other opportunities have arisen from mobile phone technology. In developing countries, bank branches and fixed-line telecommunications are scarce, whereas mobile phones are plentiful. Typically, low-income users buy airtime by the minute. Due to its liquidity, airtime became a form of "mobile money." Cash can be used to purchase minutes, and unused minutes can then be converted back into money. Mobile phone entrepreneurs then simplified the process by skipping the airtime connection aspect of these transactions and they began directly selling fungible credits that customers could use as financial accounts.

The economic impact of making these low-cost financial services available to people who previously had no access goes well beyond convenience. Long trips are no longer necessary to pay out-of-town bills or to arrange financial transfers with remote family members. Small business owners can now use mobile money to pay bills for supplies more easily or to receive payments from customers.

Suri and Jack (2016) estimated that access to the Kenyan mobile money system M-Pesa increased per-capita consumption levels and lifted 194,000 households, or 2 percent of Kenyan households, out of extreme poverty. Women were especially benefited. Wieser et al. (2019) found somewhat similar impacts from another mobile money system in Uganda.

Providing low-cost financial access to previously unserved populations in developing countries through mobile money systems created an additional important opportunity as well. These mobile money systems provided the basis for some intriguing policy experiments that provided a means for the world to find out how well one much-discussed, but rarely used, option in development specialist circles, *unconditional cash transfers*, could work in practice.

GiveDirectly (GD) is an international NGO founded in 2009. Its mission is to make unconditional cash transfers (UCTs) to a group of poor households in developing countries for a prespecified amount of time to give them a "pump-priming" boost in breaking out of poverty. GD began operations in Kenya in 2011. It sent UCTs of at least twice the average monthly household consumption in the area, to randomly chosen poor households in western Kenya using the mobile money service M-Pesa. Transfers were sent between June 2011 and January 2013 (Example 13.2).

EXAMPLE 13.2

The Effects of an Unconditional Cash Transfer System in Kenya

Researchers (Haushofer & Shapiro, 2016) set up a controlled experiment to study the impacts of this program on recipients, as well as the spillover effects on both their nonrecipient neighbors and their towns. The study examined the economic effects of UCTs on consumption (including temptation goods—alcohol, tobacco, and gambling), asset holdings, and income, as well as broader welfare effects on health, food security, education, and female empowerment.

They found that households receiving the transfers increased both consumption and savings (in the form of durable good purchases and investment in their self-employment activities). Increases in food expenditures and food security were also observed, but, contrary to some expectations, spending on temptation goods did not increase. Households invested in livestock and durable assets (notably metal roofs), and these investments led to increases in revenue from agricultural and business activities, although no significant effects on profits were observed in this short time horizon. No evidence of conflict resulting from the transfers was uncovered. On the contrary, large increases in psychological well-being and an increase in female empowerment were observed, with a large positive spillover effect on nonrecipient households in treatment villages.

A subsequent follow-up study by the same team (Haushofer & Shapiro, 2018) examined the impacts of the transfers on economic and psychological outcomes three years after the beginning of the program. The effects were similar to those observed in their earlier study. Further, comparing recipient households to nonrecipients in distant villages, the study found that transfer recipients had accumulated 40 percent more assets than control households, equivalent to 60 percent of the initial transfer. Further, the study tested different treatment modes to find out whether the nature of the transfers mattered. These included whether transfers were made to men or women, or whether they were in monthly payments, a single lump-sum, or a large or small transfer. None of these treatment differences had a significant effect on the outcomes.

Sources: Haushofer, J., & Shapiro, J. (2016). The short-term impact of unconditional cash transfers to the poor: Experimental evidence from Kenya. *The Quarterly Journal of Economics*, 131(4), 1973–2042. doi: 10.1093/qje/qjw025; Bureau of Economic Research; Haushofer, J., & Shapiro, J. (2018). *The Long-Term Impact of Unconditional Cash Transfers: Experimental Evidence from Kenya.* https://jeremypshapiro.appspot.com/papers/Haushofer_Shapiro_UCT2_2018-01-30_paper_only.pdf

A worldwide system of NGOs is also playing a complementary role in assuring a just form of sustainable development can be achieved.[16] Many of these, including GiveDirectly, are funded by private donations from individuals or foundations who care. To provide some sense of the scale of activity by NGOs consider one example. According to the Worldwide NGO Directory some 449 NGOs are operating in southern Africa, with 157 of those focusing on education.

Efforts designed to enhance the effectiveness of the complementary roles of governments, markets, businesses, and nongovernmental organizations are under way. Specific sustainable development strategies that would offer pathways for meeting both the intergenerational and intragenerational components of sustainable development have been created and are evolving as new experience is gained. These strategies in turn are driving the emergence of complementary new technologies that are facilitating the transition by lowering costs, expanding the array of options, and hastening the transition to scale. New organizations are springing up to help with any remaining gaps that emerge.

Summary

The international sustainable development concept was featured initially at the Earth Summit, held in Rio de Janeiro in 1992. Ethically based, its focus was on making sure that development choices by the current generation did not reduce or impair development options for future generations. This was a period where concerns not only about the economy's impact on climate were rising, but also general concerns about the world's substantial dependence on a finite resource base. Not only could selected, crucial depletable resources be exhausted, but renewable biological resources could also be jeopardized to the detriment of both humans and other members of the biosphere. The premise behind the meeting was that our planet, on which we all depend, has a limited capacity for life-sustaining services and that capacity must not be degraded or exceeded by the development process. Development outcomes must be sustainable.

One important outcome of the Earth Summit was the establishment of new organizations, notably the Intergovernmental Panel on Climate Change and the Convention on Biological Diversity, to focus on specific aspects of the evolving sustainable development plan and to bring together international expertise to work collectively on each of these issues.

How can sustainable development be achieved and what roles do our institutions play? Would continuing the current path automatically result in a development path that produces sustainable welfare levels, or could it choose one that leads us onto an irreversible, unsustainable path?

History has taught that both governments and markets have strengths and weaknesses. For a challenge of this magnitude a complementary partnership between governments and markets would be essential. Neither would be sufficient by itself. A carefully assembled mix of government policies and market actions would be necessary.

To guide the evolving emergence of that mix, well-designed metrics to track the degree to which the initial outcomes are succeeding or not are necessary. The traditional metric involved monitoring economic growth as measured by the national income accounts. The logic was that if the economy was growing, well-being was surely increasing.

Over the years global inequality rose considerably and a greater share of the fruits of growth went to higher-income households. Lower-income households in lower-income countries were especially being left behind and negative intergenerational effects from those impacts would only intensify the problems over time.

Recognizing that a focus purely on economic growth, however measured, was not sufficient, in 2015 the U.N. General Assembly agreed on a set of Sustainable Development Goals (SDGs). International agreement on these goals represented a considerable broadening in the scope of sustainable development objectives and associated metrics. The SDGs laid out a set of universal, measurable objectives that could motivate and track progress in meeting the urgent environmental, political, and social justice global challenges facing the world. Sustainable development became the international community's overarching plan to ensure that all human beings from present to future generations could thrive and experience fulfilling lives while ensuring that all progress occurs in harmony with nature. Further, they set up a system for tracking periodic progress in meeting those goals to allow adjustments to be made to the process as needed.

The economic evidence is clear that in the absence of action to mitigate the emissions of greenhouse gases, the increasing damages resulting directly and indirectly from climate change would not only make future generations collectively worse off, but lower-income households would be especially vulnerable. The evidence also confirms that the leading edge of those damages has already arrived, causing a growing economic impact. Taking the necessary actions to manage these threats will not be costless, but the potential cost of inaction is much greater than the cost of acting.

Current sustainable development plans seek to reduce global greenhouse gas emissions to a net-zero level by 2050. This would be achieved mainly by decarbonizing the electricity sector via a transition from high-carbon, depletable fossil fuels to low-carbon or no-carbon renewable resources. This transition would be coupled with investments in energy efficiency and increased electrification of sectors that formerly depended on fossil fuels, such as transportation and the heating and cooling of buildings.

Given the large number of low-income households and low-income countries, this can only fully be accomplished if the transition is financed in a way that is both fair and affordable for all. An increasing network of international organizations, national governments, and nongovernmental organizations is gearing up to meet this need.

Sustainable development also has begun a transition to the circular economy. This transition focuses on lowering the dependence on all types of depletable natural resources, not just energy, by replacing the old production cycle of make–use–discard with more restorative and regenerative designs. Also included in this general concept is regenerative agriculture. By using principles and practices that build soil health, regenerative farmers and ranchers sequester carbon, clean waterways, and protect wildlife.[17]

The challenge is formidable. Currently the existing metrics reveal the world community has made progress but is not yet on track to meet either the climate change goals or the SDG social goals by the specified deadlines.

However, room for optimism exists. Investing in GHG emission mitigation helps to achieve multiple planetary boundary goals with a single policy, not merely the climate goal. In addition, reducing the burning of fossil fuels simultaneously reduces several associated health-damaging air pollutants. These climate action co-benefits not only increase the net benefits from the transition away from fossil fuels without requiring additional policies, but those benefits are received locally so they don't suffer from free-rider effects.

The war on Ukraine and the persistent pandemic have created several supply-chain problems. Specifically, higher prices and decreased availability of fossil fuels have raised concerns about their reliability. In this environment energy sources that can be accessed domestically, such as solar and wind, have become more attractive relative to imported fossil fuels.

Additionally, carbon pricing programs can be designed to respond to unexpected outcomes as time passes, a characteristic that is rare among emissions mitigation strategies. If the emissions reductions fall below expectations, carbon pricing policies can be designed with automatic price adjustment mechanisms that would be triggered by those circumstances. Waiting for additional enabling legislation would not be necessary. When response timing is very important, as it is in the quest for sustainable development, that is an important feature.

More good news flows from the unique, enormous business opportunities provided by this challenge that are very attractive to entrepreneurs. The transition will be truly disruptive to the old regime. Not only will the energy sector be radically transformed, but sectors that depend upon it will be transformed as well. This kind of disruptive change creates huge opportunities for new markets that can facilitate the transition.

Automakers, for example, are already committed to a relatively rapid transition to electrical vehicles of all types, and those new types will spawn new ventures such as autonomous vehicles for personal travel and commercial shipping. These vehicles are expected to cost less to maintain and less per mile to drive, making these opportunities the kind that entrepreneurs love to see.

One study focused on the nature of historic large market disruptions such as this one (Door & Seba, 2020)[18] found that adoptions of new technologies tend to follow an S-shaped curve—early slow growth in adoptions followed, after a tipping point is reached, by exponential growth. If this historical process is repeated in this transition, it could imply that the perceived slow start is quite compatible with ultimately achieving the established goals on time. The study concludes:

> We are on the cusp of the fastest, deepest, most profound disruption of the energy sector in over a century. Our analysis shows that 100% clean electricity from the combination of solar, wind, and batteries (SWB) is both physically possible and economically affordable across the entire continental United States as well as the overwhelming majority of other populated regions of the world by 2030.
>
> (7)

The road may be strewn with obstacles and current social institutions may deal with those obstacles with less finesse than might have been hoped, but the pathway is clear. The world community has met large challenges before and now has a new opportunity to prove those successes were only the beginning.

Discussion Questions

1. Consider a possible mechanism for controlling population. According to an idea first put forth by Kenneth Boulding in 1964, everyone would be given the right to produce one (and only one!) child, so a couple could produce two. Because this scheme over a generation allows each member of the current population to replace themselves, births would necessarily equal deaths and population stability would be achieved. This scheme would award each person a certificate, entitling the holder to have one child. Couples could pool their certificates to have two. Every time a child was born, a certificate would be surrendered. Failure to produce a certificate would cause the child to be put up for adoption. Certificates would be fully transferable. Is this a good idea? What are its advantages and disadvantages? Would it be appropriate to implement this policy now in the United States? For those who believe that it would, what are the crucial reasons? For those who believe it is not appropriate, are there any circumstances in any countries where it might be appropriate? Why or why not?
2. "Every molecule of a nonrenewable energy resource used today precludes its use by future generations. Therefore, the only morally defensible policy for any generation is to use only renewable resources." Discuss.
3. "Future generations can cast neither votes in current elections nor dollars in current market decisions. Therefore, it should not come as a surprise to anyone that the interests of future generations are ignored in a market economy." Discuss.

Self-Test Exercise

1. If a natural disaster, such as the the 2024 floods in East Africa or the 2023 Earthquake in Turkey and Syria, hits food production, use supply and demand analysis to figure out how this affects consumers and producers. Does everyone lose or are some groups better off? Why?

Notes

1 Shorter winter days, snow cover, clouds, and a lower angle of the sun all reduce the amount of sunlight solar panels can harvest.

2 Regions with large hydropower systems, such as Norway and Quebec, have a third choice—timing their hydropower production to coincide with the periods where solar and wind are not producing. While important in those regions, this option is not globally available.

3 For more details consult the Ellen MacArthur Foundation Circular Economy Website: https://ellenmacarthurfoundation.org/topics/circular-economy-introduction/overview.

4 The details on both the specific social foundation goals to be achieved in these categories and the metrics to identify the degree of progress can be found in Table 1 on page 255 in Raworth (2017). The latest updates to the goals can be found at: https://sdgs.un.org/goals.

5 A complete list of the interim targets and the indicators used to ascertain achievement can be found on the web at: https://sdgs.un.org/goals. To find the indicators, click on the goal of interest and on the new page click on the "Targets and Indicators" heading below the "Related Topics" heading.

6 Steffen, W., Richardson, K., Rockström, J. et al. (2015), Table 1, 1259855-4.

7 https://www.hsph.harvard.edu/c-change/subtopics/fossil-fuels-health.

8 IPCC. (2022). *Climate Change 2022: Mitigation of Climate Change. Contribution of Working Group III to the Sixth Assessment Report of the Intergovernmental Panel on Climate Change*. https://www.ipcc.ch/report/ar6/wg3.

9 *Sustainable Development Report 2021: The Decade of Action for the Sustainable Development Goals*. Cambridge, U.K.: Cambridge University Press. doi: 10.1017/9781009106559.

10 The official development assistance program is overseen by the United Nations' Inter-agency Task Force on Financing for Development, and its annual reports can be found at: https://developmentfinance.un.org.

11 Gaspar, V., Amaglobeli, D., Garcia-Escribano, M., Prady, D., & Soto, M. (2019). *Fiscal Policy and Development: Human, Social, and Physical Investment for the SDGs*. IMF Staff Discussion Note. www.imf.org/en/Publications/Staff-Discussion-Notes/Issues/2019/01/18/Fiscal-Policy-and-Development-Human-Social-and-Physical-Investments-for-the-SDGs-46444.

12 United Nations, Inter-agency Task Force on Financing for Development. (2022). *Financing for Sustainable Development Report 2022*. New York: United Nations. https://developmentfinance.un.org/fsdr2022.

13 Moore, K. (July 1, 2005). *Thinking about Youth Poverty through the Lenses of Chronic Poverty, Life-Course Poverty and Intergenerational Poverty*. Chronic Poverty Research Centre Working Paper No. 57. SSRN: https://ssrn.com/abstract=1753655 or http://dx.doi.org/10.2139/ssrn.1753655.

14 Raimi, D., Grubert, E., Higdon, J., Metcalf, G., Pesek, S., & Singh, D. (January 2022). *The Fiscal Implications of the US Transition away from Fossil Fuels*. Resources for the Future Working Paper 22-3. https://www.rff.org/publications/working-papers/the-fiscal-implications-of-the-us-transition-away-from-fossil-fuels.

15 The Green Bank Network. https://greenbanknetwork.org.

16 For a discussion of the economics of NGOs see Werker, E., & Ahmed, F. Z. (Spring 2008). What do nongovernmental organizations do? *Journal of Economic Perspectives, 22*(2), 73–92.

17 For examples of regenerative practices and policies that could support those practices see Sharma, A., Bryant, L., & Lee, E. (2022). *Regenerative Agriculture: Farm Policy for the 21st Century—Policy Recommendations to Advance Regenerative Agriculture*. NRDC Report: 22-02-A. https://www.nrdc.org/sites/default/files/regenerative-agriculture-farm-policy-21st-century-report.pdf.

18 Door, A., & Seba, T. (October 2020). *Rethinking Energy 2020–2030: 100% Solar, Wind, and Batteries Is Just the Beginning*. A RethinkX Sector Disruption Report. https://www.rethinkx.com/energy.

Further Reading

Aagaard, T., & Kleit, A. (2022). *Electricity Capacity Markets*. Cambridge: Cambridge University Press. doi: 10.1017/9781108779159. This book examines the rationales for creating capacity markets, how capacity markets work, and how well these markets are meeting their objectives.

Dasgupta, P. (2021). The Economics of Biodiversity: The Dasgupta Review. *London, U.K.: H.M. Treasury.* This influential and comprehensive document argues that in order to close a significant gap between what we demand from nature in the future and what it can supply to us, we must recognize that humanity is embedded in nature, not external to it. More attention and resources must be focused on protecting and maintaining the ecosystems on which we depend.

Ellen MacArthur Foundation Circular Economy Website: https://ellenma carthurfoundation.org/topics/circular-economy-introduction/overview. A comprehensive source for material on the circular economy in principle and practice.

Henry, C., Rockström, J., & Stern, N. (Eds.). (2020). *Standing up for a Sustainable World: Voices of Change*. Cheltenham, U.K.: Edward Elgar Publishing Ltd. This book showcases not only the need for urgent action, but also the necessary changes for a transition to a sustainable, resilient, and equitable world.

Johnson, J. A., Ruta, G., Baldos, U., Cervigni, R., Chonabayashi, S., Corong, E., Gavryliuk, O., Gerber, J., Hertel, T., Nootenboom, C., & Polasky, S. (2021). *The Economic Case for Nature: A Global Earth-Economy Model to Assess Development Policy Pathways*. Washington, D.C.: World Bank. https://openknowledge. worldbank.org/handle/10986/35882. License: CC BY 3.0 IGO. This report presents an integrated ecosystem-economy modeling exercise to assess economic policy responses to the global biodiversity crisis. Modeling the interaction between nature's services and the global economy to 2030, the report points to a range and combination of policy scenarios available to reduce the impact of nature's loss on economies.

Laubinger, F., Lanzi, E., & Chateau, J. (2020). *Labor Market Consequences of a Transition to a Circular Economy: A Review Paper. OECD Environment Working Papers, No. 162.* Paris: OECD Publishing. https://doi.org/10.1787/e57a300a-en. This paper is the first of its kind to review the state-of-the art literature on the labor market implications of a transition to a circular economy. The reviewed studies suggest that a transition to a circular economy can generate a positive net effect on employment, though the labor implications can differ widely across sectors and regions and some may experience significant losses.

OECD. (2021). Biodiversity, Natural Capital, and the Economy: A Policy Guide for Finance, Economic and Environment Ministers. *OECD Environment Policy Paper No. 26.* https://www.oecd.org/environment/biodiversity-natural-capital-and-the-economy-1a1ae114-en.htm. This paper includes better leveraging of fiscal policy and economic instruments to support the conservation and sustainable use of biodiversity and improving biodiversity outcomes linked to trade, including by reforming environmentally harmful and market-distorting government support.

Raworth, K. (2017). *Doughnut Economics: Seven Ways to Think Like a 21st-Century Economist*. White River Junction, V.T.: Chelsea Green Publishing. The originator of the idea of donut economics provides more details on the vision and the visualization of the concept.

Seba, T. (August 17, 2021). The Great Disruption—Rethinking Energy, Transportation, Food & Agriculture. This talk is available on the web at: https://www.youtube.com/watch?v=Kj96nxtHdTU. An optimistic outlook that suggests that the proposed energy transition will not only occur faster than many think, but it will have much wider positive implications for the future.

Steffen, W., Richardson, K., & Rockström, J. (February 13, 2015). Planetary boundaries: Guiding human development on a changing planet. *Science*, *347(6223)*. doi: 10.1126/science.1259855. The work that provides the basis for the planetary boundaries in the donut economics figure.

United Nations. Sustainable Development: The Seventeen Goals. https://sdgs.un.org/goals. (Accessed February 16, 2022). This is the official site for understanding the specific targets used to measure progress and the status on meeting the goals

Answers to Self-Test Exercises

Chapter 1

1. A shortage would promote higher prices, thereby lowering demand until it equaled the new smaller supply. Since this acts to reduce rather than intensify the shortage, it is a negative feedback loop. If consumers anticipate these higher prices, however, thereby buying and hoarding extra amounts before the prices rise, this is an example of a positive feedback loop because it intensifies the shortage.

Chapter 2

1. a. This is a public good, so add the 100 demand curves vertically. This yields $P = 1000 - 100q$. This demand curve would intersect the marginal-cost curve when $P = 500$, which occurs when $q = 5$ miles.

   b. The economic surplus is represented by a right triangle, where the height of the triangle is $500 ($1,000, the point where the demand curve crosses the vertical axis, minus $500, the marginal cost) and the base is 5 miles. The area of a right triangle is $1/2 \times$ base $\times$ height $= 1/2 \times $500 \times 5 = $1,250$.

2. a. Set $MC = P$, so $80 - 1q = 1q$. Solving for q finds that $q = 40$ and $P = 40$.

   b. Consumer surplus = $800. Producer surplus = $800. Consumer surplus plus producer surplus = $1,600 = economic surplus.

   c. The marginal revenue curve has twice the slope of the demand curve, so MR $= 80 - 2q$. Setting MR = MC yields $q = 80/3$ and $P = 160/3$. Using Figure 2.2, producer surplus is the area under the price line (FE) and over the marginal-cost line (DH). This can be computed as the sum of a rectangle (formed by FED and a horizontal line drawn from D to the vertical axis) and a triangle (formed by DH and the point created by the intersection of the horizontal line drawn from D with the vertical axis).

   d. The area of any rectangle is base $\times$ height. The base = 80/3 and the

$$\text{Height} = P - MC = \frac{160}{3} - \frac{80}{3} = \frac{80}{3}.$$

Therefore, the area of the rectangle is 6400/9. The area of the right triangle is

$$\frac{1}{2} \times \frac{80}{3} \times \frac{80}{3} = \frac{3200}{9}.$$

$$\text{Producer surplus} = \frac{3200}{9} + \frac{6400}{9}$$

$$= \frac{\$9,600}{9}.$$

$$\text{Consumer surplus} = \frac{1}{2} \times \frac{80}{3} \times \frac{80}{3}$$

$$= \frac{\$3,200}{9}.$$

$$\frac{\$9,600}{9} > \$800$$

$$\frac{\$3,200}{9} < \$800$$

$$\frac{\$12,800}{9} < \$1,600$$

3. The policy would not be consistent with efficiency. As the firm considers measures to reduce the magnitude of any spill, it would compare the marginal costs of those measures with the expected marginal reduction in its liability from reducing the magnitude of the spill. Yet the expected marginal reduction in liability from a smaller spill would be zero. Firms would pay $X regardless of the size of the spill. Since the amount paid cannot be reduced by controlling the size of the spill, the incentive to take precautions that reduce the size of the spill will be inefficiently low.

4. If "better" means efficient, this common belief is not necessarily true. Damage awards are efficient when they equal the damage caused. Ensuring that the award reflects the actual damage will appropriately internalize the external cost. Larger damage awards are more efficient only to the extent that they more closely approximate the actual damage. Whenever they promote an excessive level of precaution that cannot be justified by the damages, awards that exceed actual cost are inefficient. Bigger is not always better.

5. a. Descriptive. It is possible to estimate this linkage empirically.
   b. Normative. A descriptive analysis could estimate the impacts of expenditures on endangered species, but moving from that analysis to a conclusion that expenditures would be wasted requires injecting values into the analysis.
   c. Normative. A descriptive analysis could compare the effects of privatized and non-privatized fisheries, but moving from these results to a conclusion that the fisheries must be privatized to survive normally requires an injection of values. If the data revealed that all privatized fisheries survived and none of the others did, the move to "must" would have a very strong descriptive underpinning.

d. Descriptive. This linkage could be estimated empirically directly from the data.

e. Normative. This statement could be descriptive if it was stated as "birth control programs actually contribute to a rise in population" since this is an empirical relationship that could be investigated. However, as stated, it allows a much wider scope of aspects to enter the debate, and weighing the importance of those aspects will normally require value judgments.

6. a. A pod of whales is a common-pool resource to whale hunters. It is characterized by nonexclusivity and divisibility.

b. A pod of whales is a public good to whale watchers since it is characterized by both nondivisibility and nonexclusivity.

c. The benefits from reductions of greenhouse gas emissions are public goods because they are both nondivisible and nonexclusive.

d. For residents, a town water supply is a common-pool resource because it is both divisible and nonexclusive to town residents. It is not a common-pool resource for nonresidents since they can be excluded.

e. Bottled water is neither; it is both divisible and exclusive. In fact it is a private good.

Chapter 3

1. With risk neutrality, the policy should be pursued because the expected net benefits ($0.85 \times \$4,000,000 + 0.10 \times \$1,000,000 + 0.05 \times -\$10,000,000 = \$3,000,000$) are positive. Related Discussion Question: Looking at these numbers, do you think risk neutrality is how you would actually think about this situation? Or would you be more risk-averse and weigh the third outcome more heavily than its expected likelihood?

2. a. Cost-effectiveness in this case (according to the second equimarginal principle) requires that that target be met (ten fish removed) and the marginal costs of each method be equal. We know that $q_1 + q_2 + q_3 = 10$ and that $MC_1 = MC_2 = MC_3$. The key is to reduce this to one equation with one unknown. Since $MC_1 = MC_2$ we know that $\$10q_1$ will equal $\$5q_2$, or $q_1 = .5q_2$. Similarly, $MC_2 = MC_3$, so $\$5q_2 = \$2.5q_3$ or $q_3 = 2q_2$. Substituting these values into the first equation yields $.5q_2 + 1q_2 + 2q_2 = 10$. So $q_2 = 10/3.5 = 2.86$ (to two decimal places). That means $q_1 = 1.43$ and $q_3 = 5.72$. (The fact that this adds to 10.01 rather than 10.00 is due to rounding.)

b. All three of these methods have a marginal cost that increases with the amount removed. Thus, the cost of removing the first fish for each is cheaper than removing the second fish with that method, and so on. Consider the marginal cost of removing the last fish if all fish are removed by method 3. In that case the marginal cost would be $\$2.5 \times 10$ or $\$25$. Notice that the cost-effective allocation, the cost of removing the last fish when the marginal costs are equal (using q_1 for the calculation), is $\$10 \times 1.43 = \$14.30$. In the case of increasing marginal costs, using a combination is much cheaper.

c. In this case you would only use method 3 because the marginal cost of removing each fish would be $\$2.5$. This is lower than the MC for method 1 ($\$10$) and lower than the MC for method 2 ($\$5$). Note that the marginal costs only have to be equal for the methods that are actually used. The marginal costs for unused methods will be higher.

3. Since the benefit-cost test requires that the present value of benefits be greater than the present value of the costs, we can find the maximum allowable current cost by calculating the present value of the benefits. This can be calculated as $500,000,000,000/(1 + r)^{50}$ where r is either 0.10 or 0.02. Whereas with a 10 percent discount rate the present value is approximately $4.3 billion, with a 2 percent discount rate it is approximately $185.8 billion. Clearly the size of the discount rate matters a lot in determining efficient current expenditures to resolve a long-range problem.

Chapter 4

1. In order to maximize net benefits, Coast Guard oil-spill prevention enforcement activity should be increased until the marginal benefit of the last unit equals the marginal cost of providing that unit. Efficiency requires that the level of the activity be chosen so as to equate marginal benefit with marginal cost. When marginal benefits exceed marginal cost (as in this example), the activity should be expanded.

2. a. According to the figures given, the per-life cost of the standard for unvented space heaters lies well under the implied value of life estimates given in the chapter, while per-life cost implied by the proposed standard for formaldehyde lies well over those estimates. In benefit-cost terms, the allocation of resources to fixing unvented space heaters should be increased, while the formaldehyde standard should be relaxed somewhat to bring the costs back into line with the benefits.

   b. Efficiency requires that the marginal benefit of a life saved in government programs (as determined by the implied value of a human life in that context) should be equal to the marginal cost of saving that life. Marginal costs should be equal only if the marginal benefits are equal and, as we saw in the chapter, risk valuations (and hence the implied value of human life) depend on the risk context, so it is unlikely they are equal across all government programs.

3. a. The total willingness to pay for this risk reduction is $200 million ($50 per person × 4 million exposed people). The expected number of lives saved would be 40 (1/100,000 risk of premature death × 4,000,000 exposed population). The implied value of a statistical life would be $5,000,000 ($200,000,000 total willingness to pay/40 lives saved).

   b. The program is expected to save 160 lives ((6/100,000 − 2/100,000) × 4,000,000). According to the value of a statistical life (value of mortality risk reduction) in (a), the program will have more benefits than costs as long as it costs no more than $800,000,000 ($5,000,000 value per life × 160 lives saved).

Chapter 5

1. a. Carbon reduction credits are generally created in developing countries that do not have a cap on their emissions. Since their purpose is to be used as one means of complying with emissions limits imposed by a cap, they have no value in the country of origin. Making them transferable across national

boundaries allows them to be sold to the highest bidder. This transferability provides incentives for the credit supplier to create the credits and to sell them to the highest bidders. The buyers who acquire the credits are likely to have the most to gain from their acquisition. Efficiency is enhanced because both the buyer and the seller gain from the transaction and so net benefits are increased.

b. Conservation banking allows landowners to fulfill their conservation obligations on one site by acquiring the requisite conservation entitlements from a much larger project on another site. If these entitlements were not transferable from one site to another, the original owner would have to fulfill the obligation on their own land. Because that approach would likely be smaller in scale; typically would involve less-suitable, fragmented habitat; and would be more expensive, transferability allows the obligation to be met with lower cost and at a better (less fragmented) scale, while making more appropriate habitat available to the endangered species.

2. With a rise in demand in the recreational fishery its members are likely to want to increase their catch shares. In the absence of inter-sector transferability this is likely to occur only if an administrative process changes the historical catch shares to allocate more to the recreational fishery and less to the commercial fishery. Any such change is likely to be opposed by the commercial fishery members since each share transferred represents a monetary loss for them. With inter-sector transferability, however, the recreational fishery members would have to buy the additional shares. They would do this by offering a higher price for catch shares, resulting in a shift in some shares from the commercial to the recreational fishery. Transferability reduces conflict because the transactions are voluntary and in this case the sellers gain, not lose.

Chapter 6

1. a. Ten units would be allocated to each period.
   b. $P = \$8 - 0.4q = \$8 - \$4 = \$4$
   c. User cost $= P - MC = \$4 - \$2 = \$2$
2. Because in this example the static allocations to the two periods (those that ignore the effects on the other period) are feasible within the 20 units available, the marginal user cost would be zero. With a marginal cost of $4.00, the net benefits in each period would independently be maximized by allocating ten units to each period. In this example no intertemporal scarcity is present, so price would equal a $4.00 marginal cost.
3. Refer to Figure 6.2. In the second version of the model, the lower marginal extraction cost in the second period would raise the marginal net benefit curve in that period (since marginal net benefit is the difference between the unchanged demand curve and the lower MC curve). This would be reflected in Figure 6.2 as a parallel leftward shift out of the curve labeled "Present Value of Marginal Net Benefits in Period 2." This shift would immediately have two consequences: it would move the intersection to the left (implying relatively more would be extracted in the second period), and the intersection would take place at a higher vertical distance from the horizontal axis (implying that the marginal user cost would have risen).

a. The higher discount rate would lower the present value of the net benefit function in the second period. This would be reflected as a rotation of that function downward to the right. The new function would necessarily cross the $PVMNB_1$ function at a point further to the right and lower than before the discount rate change. The fact that the intersection is further to the right implies that more is being allocated to Period 1 and less to Period 2. The fact that the intersection is lower implies that the present value of the marginal user cost has declined.

b. Since a higher discount rate lowers the present value of allocations made to the second period, allocating relatively more of the resources to the first period will increase the present value derived from them. The present value of the marginal user cost is lower since the marginal opportunity cost of using the resources earlier has gone down.

c. Increasing the second-period demand is reflected in the two-period model by a shift (not a rotation) in the $PVMNB_2$ curve upward and to the left. After the shift, this new function will necessarily intersect the $PVMNB_1$ curve closer to the left-hand axis and higher up on the Y-axis. This implies an increase in the relative amount allocated to the second period (thereby reducing the amount allocated to the first period) and a higher present value of the marginal user cost.

d. When demand is increasing in the future (hence making the marginal resources relatively more valuable), it makes sense to save more for the future. This is accomplished by a rise in the marginal user cost, which results in higher prices. The higher prices provide the incentive to save more for the future. More is consumed in the second period despite the higher prices because the demand curve has shifted out.

Chapter 7

1. From the hint, $MNB_1/MNB_2 = (1 + k)/(1 + r)$. Notice that when $k = 0$, this reduces to $MNB_2 = MNB_1(1 + r)$, the case we have already considered. When $k = r$, then $MNB_1 = MNB_2$; the effect of stock growth exactly offsets the effect of discounting, and both periods extract the same amount. If $r > k$, then $MNB_2 > MNB_1$. If $r < k$, then $MNB_2 < MNB_1$.

2. a. With a demand curve shifting out over time, the marginal net benefits from a given future allocation increase over time. This raises the marginal user cost (since it is the opportunity cost of using the resource now) and, hence, the total marginal cost. Thus, the initial user cost would be higher.

   b. Less of the resource would be consumed in the present; more would be saved for the future.

3. a. This turns out to have the same effect as the environmental cost pictured in Figures 7.6a and 7.6b. The tax serves to raise the total marginal cost and, hence, the price. This tends to lower the amount consumed in all periods compared to a competitive allocation.

   b. The tax also serves to reduce the cumulative amount extracted because it raises the marginal cost of each unit extracted. Some resources that would have been extracted without the tax would not be extracted with the tax; their after-tax cost to the producer exceeds the cost of the substitute. The price would be higher with the tax in all periods prior to the without-tax switch point. After that time the price would be equal to the price of the substitute with or without the tax.

4. The cumulative amount ultimately taken out of the ground is determined by the point at which the marginal extraction cost equals the maximum price consumers will pay for the depletable resource. In this model the maximum price is the price of the substitute. Neither the monopoly nor the discount rate affects either the marginal extraction cost or the price of the substitute, so they will have no effect on the cumulative amount ultimately extracted. The subsidy, however, has the effect of lowering the net price (price minus subsidy) of the substitute. The intersection of marginal extraction cost and the net price will, therefore, occur when a smaller cumulative amount has been extracted than would be the case in the absence of the subsidy.

5. They would not produce the same switch point. The switch would be faster under the subsidy. While they would result in the same cumulative amount of the depletable resource being extracted, the speed with which it would be extracted would be faster with the subsidy. By raising the after-tax price the tax would reduce demand (and hence the speed with which the depletable resource would be used up), while the subsidy would, by lowering the marginal user cost, increase demand (and hence increase the rate at which the depletable resource was extracted).

6. a. The impending tax would lower the after-tax, per-unit revenue to the extractors of the depletable resource once it was enacted. In anticipation of this change suppliers would have an incentive to shift extraction to periods before the tax is imposed; relatively more would be extracted earlier. Because the cumulative amount extracted is determined by the price of the substitute, which is not changed by the act, the total amount extracted would remain unchanged. Only the timing would be affected.

   b. In this case the pending tax would have the same incentive to shift extraction earlier as in (a), but the cumulative amount extracted of the depletable resource would go down. The rising marginal cost, including the tax, would hit the marginal cost of the abundant resource at a lower level of cumulative extraction.

Chapter 8

1. a. The maximum sustainable yield is obtained when the marginal benefit of an additional reduction in the population size is zero: $20P - 400 = 0$ or $P = 20,000$ tons. The maximum sustainable yield can then be calculated using the g equation: $g = 4(20) - 0.1(20)^2 = 40$ tons.

   b. The efficient sustained yield can be found by setting marginal cost equal to marginal benefit: $20P - 400 - 2(160 - P)$; therefore, $P = 32.7$, which is a larger population than the one that would produce the maximum sustainable yield.

2. a. No, despite the fact that this approach yields the efficient sustainable yield, this would not be an efficient solution. Net benefits would not be maximized because costs would be too high. Everyone would have an incentive to capture as large a share of the quota for themself as possible as quickly as possible. This would lead to excessively large boats and would not guarantee that the fishers who could catch the fish most cheaply would do the harvesting. The net benefits would be smaller than possible.

b. Yes, this would be efficient. This quota system creates exclusive property rights and, therefore, eliminates the need to catch as much as possible and as soon as possible. Each fisher can proceed on the most individually appropriate schedule because their share of the catch is guaranteed. Since the need to rush harvesting is eliminated, the need for excessively large boats is also eliminated. Fishers with high harvesting costs would find it in their interest to sell their quotas to fishers with low harvesting costs in order to maximize their return from their quota. These transfers would guarantee that the fish are caught by those with the lowest harvesting costs, so net benefits are maximized.

3. The increase in the license fee is represented as a parallel upward shift of the total cost line, whereas the per-unit tax on effort is represented as a leftward rotation of the total cost curve around the zero-effort point. The latter increases the marginal cost of fishing effort, while the former has no effect on the marginal cost. In the private-property fishery, the license fee will have no effect on effort (unless it is so high as to make fishing unprofitable, in which case the effort will drop to zero), while the tax on effort will unambiguously reduce effort. In the free-access fishery, both will reduce effort by exactly the same amount. (Remember, in the free-access fishery the equilibrium occurs where total cost equals total benefit. Since these two policy instruments raise the same revenue, both affect total cost by the same amount.)

4. When trying to reduce the degree of inefficiency from an open-access fishery, a regulation that increases the marginal cost of fishing effort by banning certain types of gear would be less efficient than a tax on effort. Although they both rotate the total cost of effort upward, the tax imposes a transfer cost, which is compatible with efficiency because it does not waste net benefits, and the gear restriction is incompatible with efficiency because in this case the net benefits are simply lost, not merely transferred.

   a. In answering this question remember that the benefits are defined as price times the quantity of fish harvested. A fall in the price of fish would be reflected as a movement inward of that benefit curve. In the typical economic model of an efficient fishery, a fall in the price of fish would generally result in a smaller sustainable harvest. The efficient level of effort is determined where $MB = MC$. A fall in the price of fish lowers MB but leaves MC unchanged. The only way to reestablish $MB = MC$ is by increasing MB by lowering effort, which, because the efficient point is to the left of the maximum sustained yield, would lower the sustainable harvest.

   b. If the fishery allows free access, the effect is a bit more complex. Remember that for a free-access fishery the equilibrium level of effort occurs where $TB = TC$. In this case, because the TB curve has shifted downward, the effort level is reduced. That effect is the same as in (a). However, in this case, because the free-access equilibrium is normally to the right of the maximum sustained yield effort level, lowering the effort level means a higher sustained harvest. In essence, in this case, taking the pressure off the fish population allows that population to experience more sustained growth, which means that more fish can be caught with less effort.

5. a. This change is such that the after curve has a flatter slope but a higher intercept with the Y-axis. For the static efficient level of effort, where $MB = MC$, the MC would have fallen. Reestablishing $MB = MC$ would be accomplished by expanding effort (thereby, lowering MB—remember MB is the tangent to

[or slope of] the *TB* curve) until it once again equaled *MC*. Increasing effort on this side of the maximum sustained yield point would necessarily *increase* the size of the sustained harvest.

b. In a free-access fishery, since the total cost is lower after the change, effort would expand. However, since this level of effort is to the right of the maximum sustained yield point, this increased effort would result in a smaller sustained yield.

Chapter 9

1. The plot being turned into a housing development would have the shortest rotation period (youngest age) because the cost of delaying the harvest would be greatest in this case. It would include an additional cost—the cost of delaying the construction of the housing development—that would have to be factored in, causing net benefits to be maximized at an earlier harvest age.

2. The cost trend is the result of two offsetting trends. Harvesting cost is a function of the volume of wood, so it increases as the volume of wood increases. Since these costs are discounted, however, costs further in the future are discounted more. When the tree growth gets small enough, the discounting effect dominates the growth effect and the present values of the costs decline.

3. A relative increase in the demand for forest-base biomass fuels would increase the value of wood used for this purpose. To the extent that this added supply of fuel holds household energy costs lower than they would otherwise have been, consumers benefit, but they might lose if they use wood for other purposes (as its price would be likely to rise). The producers of this fuel will benefit, but producers of more traditional fuels would lose. Producers of products from wood other than fuels (say, paper mills using the wood for pulp) would lose as their costs would rise. To the extent that this domestic biomass fuel substitutes for imported fuel, the state can expect an income increase as the funds formerly sent abroad are now spent locally where they have a higher multiplier effect.

4. The market would be expected to reach an efficient balance if the owner was actively engaged in selling both recreation and harvested wood. In this case the forest owner compares the marginal net benefits (reflected in their respective revenue streams) of various combinations of harvesting and recreation and chooses the combination that yields the highest net benefit. If, however, as is common, the private owner sells only harvested wood, recreational uses would be undervalued.

5. Certification is especially effective when the benefits being protected by the certification process are directly received by the purchaser. It is less effective when conveying benefits that do not directly affect the purchaser. Both certification systems convey a considerable amount of information that is about externalities. For forests, for example, they can convey whether the wood is sustainably harvested, but sustainably harvested wood is apparently indistinguishable from unsustainably harvested wood in terms of its ability to be used to build a house, construct furniture, and so on. The real benefits are indirect and psychological—knowing that the harvesting process is not degrading the environment. Organic-produce certification produces many of those same indirect psychological benefits, but in addition this form of certification conveys some

information (the absence of pesticide residues, for example) that directly can affect the consumer. For this reason, organic-produce certification is probably a bit more likely to produce a more efficient outcome, all other things being equal.

6. A rise in the price of timber would make it more likely that harvested forests would be replanted and would make land conversion to another use less likely. Both of these reinforce components of sustainable forestry. On the other hand, it would also make the rewards from illegal harvesting higher, which is incompatible with sustainable forestry. Hence the answer depends upon the likelihood of illegal activity.

Chapter 10

1. The congestion charge would raise the cost of transportation for commuters, while the increased number of lanes would reduce it (considering travel time). According to the bid rent function analysis, the congestion charge would make the residential bid rent function steeper and encourage more density in the urban area and less expansion into the suburban areas served by those expressways. Conversely, the new lanes would make the bid rent function less steep and encourage more people to move into the suburbs.

2. Land confers a bundle of entitlements to the owner. Conservation easements allow the transfer of only the specific entitlements of interest (typically the development rights). For land conservation organizations, buying only the entitlements of interest is considerably cheaper than buying the land itself. Therefore, conservation groups could stretch a given budget over many more pieces of land with conservation easements than by buying the land outright. Donors may value some specific entitlements more than any market price they could get for them (and hence want to retain them, an option afforded by conservation easements), but for other entitlements the market price (or the value of the tax deduction) may be higher, making sale or donation the best option. An owner of a forest, for example, may wish to continue to harvest wood from that land, while being willing to donate the development rights when they have little or no interest in selling the forest to a developer anyway.

3. The simplest difference is that relative to an income tax, property tax funding would make land and the improvements on that land more expensive to own. This, in turn, would raise the cost of all land-intensive activities such as forestry or farming relative to activities requiring much less land. It might also cause all firms engaging in land-intensive activities to consider if they could get away with using less land. It might cause some residents, for example, to downsize to smaller units.

4. Many answers, of course, are possible for this question, but here are a few possibilities:
   a. In this age group we could expect to have a smaller household size (as any children are grown and gone), thereby lowering the need for housing space. We might expect some of these households to downsize to smaller dwelling units.
   b. We might expect some movement back into urban areas as the need for space declines and difficulties with mobility arise.
   c. Access to schools could become less important and access to medical facilities more important.

d. In the face of diminishing human energy to do landscaping and mainte-nance, condominiums could become relatively more attractive, since all their landscaping and maintenance is handled by the association in return for a monthly fee. Since most condominium units are smaller than owners' previous housing, this is also a way to downsize.

e. As health problems commonly rise with age, assisted living facilities should become more common and some retirees will move to be closer to their children.

f. As older households are likely to be less constrained by either work or parenting schedules, they are freer to move to locales offering especially high-quality, age-appropriate leisure-time activities.

g. Since household net worth is probably higher after a lifetime of earning, this wealth might well also promote more seasonal second-home sales.

Notice that many of these hypotheses are testable by examining the appropriate data. Are condos becoming a greater percent of the residential housing stock? Are older households moving back into urban areas? Has second-home buying become more prevalent? Sounds like a good research project.

5. Because the ethanol subsidy raises the profitability of growing corn as a fuel, it should (1) increase the amount of domestic land allocated to agriculture (since more per acre is now earned), (2) increase the amount of domestic agricultural land allocated to fuel corn (since the net benefits per acre of that specific land use have increased), and (3) lower the amount of domestic land allocated to producing food crops as farmers, in response to these net benefit per-acre changes, allocate more land to fuel and less to food crops (most obviously, but not only, corn).

6. Working at home reduces the amount of commuting and hence the cost of commuting. One implication is a lower incentive to locate close to work. If workplaces are densely located, working at home should make more remote locations relatively more attractive. Hence, according to this effect, the density of development might be expected to decline.

Chapter 11

1. The paper company. The high-cost energy is appropriately assigned to the five paper machines because that is the energy cost that would be eliminated if the machines were shut down. The company would not shut down all energy sources in proportion; it would shut down the most expensive sources. In making a shutdown decision, therefore, it is essential that the machines in question cover the cost of the energy that would be saved if the machines were shut down; otherwise, the company is losing money.

2. The existence of a renewable energy credit market would lower the compliance costs associated with meeting a renewable portfolio standard by providing more flexibility to compliance units. For example, without such a market utilities would have to ensure that they supplied the requisite amount of renewable power within their market area regardless of whether that market area was suitable for that renewable power. With a renewable energy credit market, producers can create the renewable power in those areas that are most suitable (e.g., have the requisite wind flow, water flow, or solar flux) and sell any excess

to jurisdictions that could only generate their own renewable power at a much higher cost. Substituting this more efficiently produced (and hence lower-cost) power for the more inefficiently produced (and hence higher-cost) power allows the standard to be met at a lower cost.

3. a. When comparing two bulbs that give the same amount of light, you would need to specify: (1) the planning horizon (how many years will be covered by the analysis), (2) the cost of each type of bulb, (3) how much the bulbs can be expected to be used on average per year, (4) how long the bulbs will last before they need to be replaced, (5) how much electricity is used by each type of bulb, and (6) the per-kilowatt-hour cost of the electricity. The planning horizon would be no longer than the useful life of an LED bulb. Each year in the planning horizon would be a column and each row would be either one of the data items used in the calculation or the results of the calculations for that year—two rows would contain the amount spent on the purchase of bulbs each year for each type of bulb, another two rows would contain the amount spent on electricity to run each bulb during the periods of use, and the two primary rows would contain the present value of the cost of each bulb for that year. The present value of the cost of each bulb would be found by summing the individual year present value results over all the years of the planning horizon. The most cost-effective bulb would be the one that has the lowest present value of cost over that planning horizon.

    b. It depends crucially on which component is changed. Changing the monthly charge would affect both bulb calculations the same and hence not change the difference between them. Changing the kilowatt-hour charge, however, would hit the incandescent bulb much harder since that type of bulb consumes more electricity. Therefore an increase in the kilowatt-hour charge would relatively discourage incandescent bulbs and encourage LED bulbs.

4. Yes, you would expect the magnitude of interest rates to affect the decision, especially for those who borrow the money to finance the purchase. Not only does it increase the financing cost of purchasing the heat pump, but this interest rate would typically be used as the discount rate in calculating the cost-effectiveness of the purchase. A higher discount rate lowers the relative importance of the energy savings in the decision (since they are spread out over the future years, whereas the cost of the purchase occurs in the first year).

Chapter 12

1. a. This chapter notes that both approaches involve upward-sloping supply curves. The cost-effective mix requires marginal control costs to be equal. Note that the cost-effective allocation (where marginal cost is equalized) is the point at which marginal cost two curves cross. This point normally would involve some of both activities. Can you draw an example?

    b. The only time the curves would not cross is when the marginal cost of one of these approaches is uniformly lower for all levels of an activity than the marginal cost of any activity of the other approach. In that admittedly unusual case, it would make sense to only use the activity that has the uniformly lower marginal costs. Depending on the accounting stance, however, it is not hard to understand why a local community might prefer to focus on adaptation since the benefits would be local rather than global.

2. Since the amount of capacity needed would depend on the maximum flow during the year, the extra cost of expanding capacity during this high-flow period should be reflected in higher prices charged to users during these periods.

3. a. For the case in which the groundwater comes from a private well that taps a private aquifer, with perfect information the owner would have an incentive to extract the water at an efficient rate. The private owner would face all costs, both present and future, and be able to balance them accordingly. The *social* present value of marginal net benefit curves for both periods would be identical to the *private* present value of marginal net benefit curves for both periods. Note, however, the very important "perfect information" caveat. If the owner doesn't know what is there, they can't very well allocate it efficiently, regardless of how good the incentives are.

   b. For the case in which the groundwater is obtained from your private well that is drilled into an aquifer that is shared with many other users who have also drilled private wells, an efficient allocation would not be expected. Perverse incentives would arise both within any particular time period and over time. Because this is a divisible resource, within a time period, each user would know that any unit not extracted by them could well be extracted by a neighbor. The incentive is to take more than the efficient amount to avoid losing it. Over time, the users would act as if the marginal user cost is zero since the trade-off between the present and the future that characterizes the situation in part (a) is lost. Whereas in a private well whatever I don't use now I can simply use later, that is not true in a shared aquifer. Water not used by me now may well be used by someone else and be gone forever. This particular institutional arrangement encourages the overuse of water and thereby serves to intensify any problems of scarcity.

4. The key to using the tiered system for this purpose is to distinguish water needs by monthly volume. Specifically, the first block could contain a basic amount of water that fulfills essential purposes, while the second block contains all other water above that amount. The first block would be priced at a low level, while the second block price would reflect all of the scarcity rent generated by the marginal user cost as well as the marginal cost of extraction and distribution. Since the positive marginal user cost means that the marginal revenue for that block would be above the marginal extraction plus distribution cost, the utility could still cover its expenses despite the low cost of the first units. Meanwhile, because most households would consume at least some more water than allowed in the first block, the price they would face for the additional water would be the efficient (marginal cost) price in the second block. The fact that the price for the additional water would be the efficient price would preserve incentives to conserve an efficient amount.

Chapter 13

1. A natural disaster 2024 floods in East Africa, would shift the supply curve to the left and raise prices. Consumers would be unambiguously worse off as their net benefits would be reduced. Suppliers who lost their entire crop would be

unambiguously worse off, but the effects on other suppliers could be positive. All suppliers (foreign suppliers, for example) whose crops were completely unaffected would be better off as the higher prices for their crops would raise their producer surplus. For suppliers that lost some, but not all, of their crops, it would depend on how the magnitude of the losses from the destroyed crops compared to the magnitude of the gain from selling the remainder at a higher price.

Glossary

Absorptive Capacity The ability of the environment to absorb pollutants without incurring damage.

Acid Rain The atmospheric deposition of acidic substances.

Acute Toxicity The degree of harm caused to living organisms as a result of short-term exposure to a substance.

Additionality A traditional requirement for carbon credits to be certified; they are additional only if they would not have occurred in the absence of a market for credits.

Adjusted Net Savings An indicator that attempts to measure whether an economy is acting sustainably when judged by the weak sustainability criterion. (Formerly called genuine savings.)

Aerobic Water containing sufficient dissolved oxygen concentrations to sustain organisms requiring oxygen.

Age Structure Effect Changes in the age distribution induced by the rate of population growth.

Agglomeration Bonus A voluntary incentive mechanism that is designed to protect endangered species and biodiversity by reuniting fragmented habitat across private land in a manner that minimizes landowner resistance.

Alternative Fuels Unconventional fuels such as ethanol and methanol.

Ambient Allowance System A type of transferable permit system in which allowances are defined in terms of the right to affect the concentration at a receptor site by a given amount. This design can achieve a cost-effective allocation of control responsibility when the objective is to achieve a prespecified concentration objective at a specific number of receptor locations.

Ambient Standards Legal ceilings placed on the concentration level of specific pollutants in the air, soil, or water.

Anaerobic Water containing insufficient dissolved oxygen concentrations to sustain life.

Anthropocentric Human-centered.

Aquaculture The controlled raising and harvesting of fish. (Called "mariculture" when, as is the case with some salmon fisheries, the facilities are in the ocean.) Aquaculture can provide the opportunity to create a private-property regime for affected fisheries.

Asset   An entity that has value and forms part of the wealth of the owner.

Assigned Amount Obligations   The level of greenhouse gas emissions that ratifying nations are permitted under the Kyoto Protocol.

Asymmetric Information   A source of market failure that can arise when all of the economic agents involved in a transaction do not have the same level of information.

Automobile Certification Program   The testing of automobiles at the factory for conformity to federal emissions standards.

Average-Cost Pricing   When prices charged for resource use are based on average costs. (Sometimes used by regulatory agencies to ensure that regulated firms make zero economic profits, but it is not normally efficient.)

Base-Load Plants   Electric generators that produce virtually all the time. (They generally have high fixed costs, but low variable costs.)

Beneficial Electrification   Electrifying energy end uses usually powered by fossil fuels in a way that reduces overall emissions and energy costs.

Benefit-Cost Analysis   An analysis of the quantified gains (benefits) and losses (costs) of an action.

Benefits Transfer   Transferring benefits estimates developed in one context to another context as a substitute for developing entirely new estimates.

Best Available Technology Economically Achievable   A more stringent effluent standard than best practicable control technology, which has been defined by the EPA as "the very best control and treatment measures that have been or are capable of being achieved."

Bid Rent Function   This function relates the maximum price per unit of land as a function of distance from the urban center that would be offered for a type of land use such as residential or agricultural.

Biochemical Oxygen Demand   The measure of the oxygen demand placed on a stream by any particular volume of effluent.

Block Pricing   A form of pricing in which the charge per unit of consumption is held fixed until a threshold is reached where a new per-unit charge is imposed for all consumption beyond the threshold. For increasing block pricing, the per-unit charge after the threshold is higher.

Bycatch   Untargeted fish that are unintentionally caught as part of the harvest of targeted species.

Cap-and-Trade System   A form of emissions trading where the government specifies a cap on emissions and allocates allowances to emission sources, either by gifting or auctioning, based upon this cap. These allowances are freely transferable among sources. Distinguished from the earlier credit form of emissions trading.

Carbon Club   An international arrangement designed specifically to encourage sufficient cooperation among member nations to produce the emission reductions necessary to achieve the internationally established goals. This idea envisions two main policy parameters: (1) a stipulated international carbon price that all club members would have to enact, and (2) a uniform tariff that all nonmembers (those who have failed to enact that carbon price) would face on all goods exported from non-club members into the club member states.

Carbon Neutrality   Achieving annual zero net anthropogenic (human caused or influenced) CO_2 emissions by a certain date.

Carbon Tax   A policy that would control climate modification by placing a per-unit emissions tax on the carbon content of carbon-emitting sources.

Carbon Tax Adjustment Mechanisms (CTAMs)   CTAMs are designed to adjust predefined carbon prices over time if evidence indicates they would be insufficient to produce the desired levels of emissions reduction achieved by the specific dates. The two versions include (1) a version where both the triggering condition and the adjusting responses are prespecified and occur automatically once the condition is triggered, and (2) a version where the triggering condition and the process that will craft the response are prespecified, but the exact adjustments that will flow from that process are discretionary and determined only when the emissions trigger reduction is breached.

Cartel A collusive agreement among producers to restrict production and raise prices. In this case the group tends to act like a monopolist and to share the gains from collusive behavior.

Chapter 11 A provision in the North American Free Trade Agreement that protects investors from government regulations that decrease the value of their investments.

Choke Price The maximum price anyone would be willing to pay for a unit of the resource. At prices higher than the choke price, the demand for that resource would be zero.

Chronic Toxicity The degree of harm caused to living organisms as a result of continued or prolonged exposure to a substance.

Circular Economy An economy that is restorative or regenerative by intention and design. It replaces the traditional "use it then throw it away" concept with restoration, shifts toward the use of renewable energy, eliminates the use of toxic chemicals, and aims for the elimination of waste through the superior design of materials, products, systems, and business models.

Clean Development Mechanism An emissions trading mechanism set up under the Kyoto Protocol that allows industrialized countries to invest in greenhouse-gas–reducing strategies in developing countries and to use the resulting certified reductions to meet their assigned amount obligations.

Climate Neutrality Achieving annual zero net anthropogenic (human caused or influenced) greenhouse gas (GHG) emissions by a certain date. By definition, climate neutrality means every ton of anthropogenic GHG emitted is compensated with an equivalent amount of GHG removed.

Closed System No inputs enter the system, and no outputs leave the system.

Coase Theorem A remarkable proposition, named after Nobel Laureate Ronald Coase, that suggests that in the absence of transaction costs, an efficient allocation will result regardless of the property rule chosen by the court.

Co-Benefits (and co-costs) Co-benefits (or co-costs) arise when compliance with a regulation leads to additional benefits (or costs) that are not directly related to that regulation's intended target.

Cobweb Model A theory in which long lags between planting decisions and harvest can influence farmers' production decisions in such a way as to intensify or dampen price fluctuations.

Command and Control Controlling pollution via a system of government-mandated legal restrictions. Under this approach the government has the responsibility not only for setting the environmental targets, but also for allocating the source-specific responsibilities for meeting those targets.

Common-Pool Resource A resource that is shared among several users.

Common-Property Regime A property rights system in which resources are managed collectively by a group.

Community Land Trust An organization set up to acquire and hold land for the benefit of a community. Frequently used to provide affordable access to land for members of the community.

Comparative Advantage In trade theory a comparative advantage prevails for products that have the lowest opportunity cost of production.

Compensating Variation A method for evaluating the welfare effects of a price increase. It is the increase in income it would take to make the consumer as well off as they were before the price increase.

Competitive Equilibrium The resource allocation at which supply and demand are equal when all agents are price takers.

Composite Asset An asset made up of many interrelated parts.

Composition of Demand Effect Shifts in demand brought about by changes in the relative cost of inputs. (For example, rising costs of ores coupled with stable prices for recycled inputs could make the products of firms relying more heavily on recycled inputs relatively less expensive and hence more attractive to consumers.)

Compound Risks Two or more risks occurring simultaneously or sequentially one after another.

Compounding Risks Compound risks where the potential collective effect can be greater than the sum of its parts.

Congestion Externalities Higher costs imposed on others resulting from an attempt to use resources at a higher-than-optimal capacity. Commonly used with reference to traffic flows.

Congestion Pricing Charging higher tolls during peak hours to discourage vehicle traffic (and the resulting air pollution) and encourage public transit ridership.

Conjoint Analysis A survey-based technique that derives willingness to pay by having respondents choose between alternate states of the world where each state of the world has a specified set of attributes and a price.

Conjunctive Use The combined management of surface and groundwater to optimize their joint use and to minimize the adverse effects of excessive reliance on a single source.

Conservation Easements Legal agreements between landowners and land trusts or government agencies that permanently limit uses of land in specifically defined ways in order to protect its conservation value.

Constant Dollar Output measures that have been purged of increases due to price rises.

Consumer Surplus The value of a good or service to consumers above the price they have to pay for it. Calculated as the area under the demand curve that lies above the price.

Consumption The amount of goods and services consumed by households.

Consumptive Use In water law this refers to water that is removed from the source without any return.

Contingent Ranking A valuation technique that asks respondents to rank alternative situations involving different levels of environmental amenity (or risk). These rankings can then be used to establish trade-offs between more of the environmental amenity (or risk) and less (or more) of other goods that can be expressed in monetary terms.

Contingent Valuation A survey method used to ascertain willingness to pay for services or environmental amenities.

Conventional Pollutants Relatively common substances found in most parts of the country and presumed to be dangerous only in high concentrations.

Corporate Average Fuel Economy (CAFE) Standards Minimum average miles-per-gallon standards imposed on each auto manufacturer for new vehicles sold in a specific vehicle class. Autos are in one class and SUVs and light trucks in another.

Cost Containment Reserve (CCR) The CCR is an emissions trading method for dealing with situations where prices might rise to politically unacceptable levels. It consists of a quantity of allowances in addition to the cap which are held in reserve. These are sold if and when allowance prices would otherwise exceed predefined price levels.

Criteria Pollutants Conventional air pollutants with ambient standards set by the Environmental Protection Agency (includes sulfur oxides, particulate matter, carbon monoxide, ozone, nitrogen dioxide, and lead).

Current Reserves Known resources that can profitably be extracted at current prices.

Damped Oscillation In the absence of further supply shocks, the amplitude of price and quantity fluctuations decreases to the point of equilibrium.

Debt–Nature Swap The purchase and cancellation of developing-country debt in exchange for environmentally related action on the part of the debtor nation.

Deep Ecology The view that the environment has an intrinsic value, a value that is independent of human interests.

Degradable Pollutants that are capable of being decomposed chemically or biologically.

Demand Curve A function that relates the quantity of a commodity or service consumers wish to purchase to the price of that commodity.

Deposition Pollution that transfers from the air to the earth's surface (land or water).

Development Impact Fees One-time charges designed to cover the additional public service costs of new development.

Differentiated Regulation Imposing more stringent regulations on one class of sources (such as new vehicles) than on others (such as used vehicles).

Discount Rate The rate used to convert a stream of benefits and/or costs into its present value.

Dissolved Oxygen Oxygen that naturally occurs in water and is usable by living organisms.

Divisible Consumption One person's consumption of a good diminishes the amount available for others. (For example, if I use some timber to build my house, you receive no benefits from that timber.)

Donut Economics A visual presentation of the progress of sustainable development in meeting a specific set of goals that are achieved when all the world's people are in a "safe and just space." This implies that all people have basic human rights and quality of life without overshooting any of the nine planetary boundaries. The name is derived from the fact that the "safe and just place" is shaped like a donut.

Double Dividend A second welfare advantage that accrues to revenue-raising pollution-control policy instruments (over and above the welfare gain due to pollution reduction) when the revenue is used to reduce distortionary taxes (thereby reducing the welfare losses associated with those taxes).

Downward Spiral Hypothesis A positive feedback loop in which increasing population triggers a cycle of sustained, reinforced environmental degradation.

Dry Deposition Occurs when air pollutants get heavy and fall to the earth's surface (land or water) as dry particles.

Dynamic Efficiency The chief normative economic criterion for choosing among various allocations occurring at different points in time. An allocation satisfies the dynamic efficiency criterion if it maximizes the present value of net benefits that could be received from all possible ways of allocating those resources over time.

Dynamic Efficient Sustained Yield The sustained yield that produces the highest present value of net benefits.

Economies of Scale The percentage increase in output exceeds the percentage increase in all inputs. Equivalently, average cost falls as output expands.

Ecosystem Services Services supplied by nature that directly benefit at least one person.

Ecotourism A form of tourism that appeals to ecologically minded travelers. It can serve as a source of revenue to protect the local ecosystem.

Efficient Pricing A system of prices that supports an efficient allocation of resources. Generally, efficient pricing is achieved when prices are equal to total marginal cost.

Emission Charge A charge levied on emitters for each unit of a pollutant emitted into the air or water.

Emission Standard A legal limit placed on the amount of a pollutant an individual source may emit.

Emissions Allowance System A type of transferable permit system in which the permits are defined in terms of the right to emit a stipulated amount of emissions. This design can be used to achieve a cost-effective allocation of control responsibility for uniformly mixed pollutants.

Emissions Banking Firms are allowed to store emissions reduction credits or allowances for subsequent use or sale.

Emissions Containment Reserve (ECR) An ECR is used to complement minimum auction prices in emissions trading programs by reducing the number of allowances that are available to be sold at low prices. This mechanism consists of two key components: (1) a prespecified trigger price, to determine whether an ECR program is activated in a particular auction; and (2) if activated, a prespecified number of allowances up for bid that would be transferred to the ECR and would not be sold.

Emissions Reduction Credit (ERC) Part of a transferable permits system. Any source reducing emissions beyond required levels can receive a credit for excess reductions. These can be banked for future use or sold to other sources.

Emissions Trading An economic incentive-based alternative to the command-and-control approach to pollution control. Under emissions trading, a regulatory agency specifies an allowable level of pollution that will be tolerated and allocates emission allowances. Total emissions authorized by these allowances cannot exceed the allowable level. Pollution sources are free to buy, sell, or otherwise trade allowances to be sure they have enough to cover their emissions.

Energy-Efficiency Investment An investment that is designed to reduce the amount of energy input required to supply a given amount of useful energy services such as lighting or heating.

Enforceability Property rights should be secure from involuntary seizure or encroachment from others.

Entropy Amount of energy not available for work.

Environmental Justice The fair treatment and meaningful involvement of all people regardless of race, color, national origin, or income, with respect to the development, implementation, and enforcement of environmental laws, regulations, and policies. It is achieved when everyone enjoys the same degree of protection from environmental and health hazards.

Environmental Kuznets Curve An empirical relationship that shows environmental degradation first increasing, then decreasing, as per-capita income increases.

Environmental Sustainability This definition of sustainability is fulfilled if the physical stocks of designated resources do not decline over time.

Equivalent Variation A method for evaluating the welfare effects of a price increase. It is the reduction in income that would leave a consumer indifferent between accepting the income reduction or accepting the price increase.

Estate Tax A tax paid on the fair market value of property after the owner's death.

Eutrophic A body of water containing an excess of nutrients.

E-Waste Waste involving used electronics such as TVs, tablets, or mobile phones.

Ex ante **Analysis** Studies designed to predict the outcomes from a proposed policy based upon present and past data.

Exclusivity All benefits and costs accrued as a result of owning and using the resources should accrue to the owner, and only the owner, either directly or indirectly by sale to others.

Expected Present Value of Net Benefits The sum over possible outcomes of the present value of net benefits for a policy, where each future outcome is weighted by its probability of occurrence.

Expected Value In situations where the value of a resource depends on which of several outcomes might prevail, the expected value of a resource is the sum over all outcomes of the likelihood of each outcome multiplied by the value that would prevail in that outcome.

Experimental Economics Using controlled, scientific experiments for testing what choices people make in specific circumstances.

Ex-post **Analysis** Studies designed to identify the outcomes that occurred from a policy action using actual outcome data after it was implemented.

Extended Producer Responsibility The belief that manufacturers of products should have the responsibility to take the packaging and the products back at the end of their useful lives in order to promote efficient packaging and recycling. (Also called the "take-back" principle.)

External Diseconomy The affected party is damaged by an externality. (For example, my well is polluted by chemicals from a factory next door.)

External Economy The affected party is benefited by an externality. (For example, my neighbor decides not to develop a wetland that serves as a recharge area for my water supply.)

Externality The welfare of some agent, either a firm or household, depends on the activities of some other agent. The externality can take the form of either an external economy or external diseconomy.

Feebates A system that combines taxes on purchases of new high-emitting vehicles with subsidies for new purchases of low-emitting vehicles. The revenue from the taxes is supposed to serve as the primary source of funding for the subsidies.

Feedback Loop A closed path that connects an action to its effect on the surrounding conditions that, in turn, can influence further action.

Fixed Cost Costs that do not vary with output.

Fleet Average Standard Used in the Corporate Average Fuel Economy standards, this standard is imposed on the sales weighted average of vehicles sold rather than forcing every vehicle to meet it.

Forward Capacity Market A component of the long-term wholesale electricity market that seeks to ensure resource adequacy and grid reliability, locally and system-wide. The market is designed to promote sufficient economic investment in supply and demand capacity resources where and when they will be needed.

Free-Rider Effect When a good exhibits both the consumptive indivisibility and non-excludability properties, consumers may enjoy the benefits of goods purchased by others without paying anything themselves. (For example, countries that decide not to take any steps to control global warming can "free ride" on the steps taken by others.)

Fuel-Economy Standards   A government program that mandates how many miles per gallon a manufacturer's new cars must achieve by specific deadlines.

Full Cost Pricing   In water management this pricing system seeks to recover not only all of the costs of providing water and sewer services but also the cost of replacing the depreciated capital in older water systems.

Fund Pollutants   Pollutants for which the environment has some absorptive capacity; if the rate of emission exceeds this capacity, then fund pollutants accumulate.

Gaia Hypothesis   An example of a negative feedback loop suggesting that, within limits, the world is a living organism with a complex feedback system that seeks an optimal physical and chemical environment.

Genetically Modified Organisms   A term that designates crops that carry new traits that have been inserted through advanced genetic engineering methods involving the manipulation of DNA.

Genuine Progress Indicator   A sustainability indicator that attempts to establish the trend of well-being over time by taking into account the effects of development on resource depletion, pollution damage, and distribution of income.

Global Environmental Facility   An international organization, loosely connected to the World Bank, that provides loans and grants to developing countries to facilitate projects that contribute to solving such global problems as protecting the oceans, preserving biodiversity, protecting the ozone layer, and controlling climate modification. The fund uses the "marginal external cost" rule to allocate funds.

Government Failure   An inefficiency produced by some government action.

Greenhouse Gases   Global pollutants that contribute to climate modification by absorbing the long-wave (infrared) radiation, thereby trapping heat that would otherwise radiate into space. (Includes carbon dioxide, methane, and chlorofluorocarbons, among others.)

Green Paradox   An effect that occurs when a program that is designed to reduce emissions paradoxically either speeds up the flow of emissions or increases the total amount of emissions.

Groundwater   Subsurface water that occurs beneath a water table in soils, rocks, or fully saturated geological formations.

Groundwater Contamination   Pollution that leaches into a water-saturated region.

Hartwick Rule   The weak sustainability criterion can be fulfilled if all scarcity rent from depletable resources is invested in capital.

Health Threshold   A standard to be defined with a margin of safety sufficiently high that no adverse health effects would be suffered by any member of the population as long as the pollutant concentration is no higher than the standard.

Hedonic Property Values   The values of environmental amenities (or risks) that are determined from differences in the values of property exposed to different levels of the amenities (or risks).

Hedonic Wage Studies   A valuation technique that allows the value of an environmental amenity (or risk) to be determined from differences in the values of wages paid to workers exposed to different levels of the amenity (or risk).

High-Grading   Discarding low-value fish such as juveniles in favor of high-value fish in order to increase the income derived from a harvest quota.

Host Fees   Fees collected from disposers that are used to compensate a community hosting a regional landfill. Designed to increase the willingness of communities to host these facilities.

Hypothetical Bias   Ill-considered responses that may arise in surveys based on contrived rather than actual situations or choices.

Impact Analysis   An analysis that attempts to make explicit, to the extent possible, the consequences of proposed actions. May mix quantitative with qualitative information and monetized with nonmonetized information.

Income Elasticity   Measures the percentage change in demand for commodities or services in response to a 1 percent change in income.

Individual Transferable Quotas (ITQs)   A means of protecting a fishery and the income derived from it by limiting the number of fish caught. Individual fishers are allocated quotas that entitle them to portions of the authorized total allowable catch. These quotas can be transferred to other fishers or used to legalize their harvest.

Indivisible Consumption   One person's consumption of a good does not diminish the amount available for others. (For example, the benefits I receive from controlling greenhouse gases do not diminish the benefits you receive.)

Information Bias   Arises when contingent valuation survey respondents are forced to value attributes with which they have little or no experience.

Intangible Benefits   Benefits that cannot be easily assigned a monetary value.

Interactive Resources   The size of the resource stock is determined jointly by biological considerations and actions taken by humans.

Isoquant   A curve showing possible combinations of two inputs that produce the same output level.

Joint Implementation   A project-based emission trading mechanism set up under the Kyoto Protocol in which an investor from one industrialized country can get emission reduction credits for certified greenhouse gas reductions resulting from investments in a project in another industrialized country.

Junior Claims   Used in water management, this class of rights for specified amounts of water is subordinate to senior claims. In times of water scarcity, these rights become valid once the senior claims have been fulfilled.

Just Transition   A sustainable development transition that seeks to ensure that its benefits are shared widely, while also supporting those who stand to lose economically, be they countries, regions, industries, communities, workers, or consumers.

Kyoto Protocol   An international agreement to control greenhouse gases that went into effect in February 2005.

Land Trust   An organization specifically established to hold conservation easements and to ensure that the use of land conforms to the terms of the easements.

Latency   The period between exposure to a toxic substance and the detection of harm caused by that substance.

Law of Comparative Advantage   A country or region should specialize in the production of those commodities for which it has a comparative advantage.

Law of Diminishing Marginal Productivity   In the presence of a fixed factor, successively larger additions of variable factors will eventually lead to a decline in the marginal productivity of the variable factors.

Law of Diminishing Returns   The relationship between inputs and outputs when some inputs are increased and others are fixed, eventually leading to the decreased productivity of the variable inputs.

Lead Phase-Out Program   A transferable permit program designed to lower the costs of phasing out lead in gasoline as well as to eliminate lead earlier than otherwise would have been possible. It allocated transferable rights to use lead in refining gasoline to refiners. The number of rights declined over time until they expired at the end of the program.

Leapfrogging   Refers to a situation where new development takes place not at the edge of current development, but further out, skipping over tracts of land that are closer in.

Liability Rules   Rules used in courts that award monetary compensation from an injurer to an injured party after damage has occurred.

Low-Emission Vehicles   A class of vehicles that emit fewer emissions per mile driven than conventional vehicles.

Marginal Cost of Exploration   The marginal cost of finding additional units of the resource.

Marginal-Cost Pricing   Basing the prices charged for resource use upon marginal costs. (This pricing scheme is generally consistent with efficiency.)

Marginal External Cost Rule   Used by the Global Environmental Facility to disperse funds. According to this rule, the facility will fund additional expenses associated with investments that contribute to the global environment (produce positive global net benefits) but cannot be justified domestically (since the domestic marginal costs exceed domestic marginal benefits). Countries are expected to pick up that portion of the expenses that can be justified domestically (where the domestic marginal benefits exceed domestic marginal costs).

Marginal Extraction Cost   The cost of mining an additional unit of resource.

Marginal Opportunity Cost   The additional cost of providing the last unit of a good as measured by what is given up.

Marginal User Cost   Present value of forgone future opportunity costs at the margin.

Marginal Willingness to Pay   The amount of money an individual is willing to pay for the last unit of a good or service.

Marine Reserve   A specific geographic area that prohibits harvesting of fish and enjoys a high level of protection from other threats such as pollution.

Market Economy   An economic system in which resource allocation decisions are guided by prices that result from the voluntary production and purchasing decisions by private consumers and producers.

Market Failure   An inefficient allocation produced by a market economy.

Maximum Sustainable Yield   The maximum harvest that could be sustained forever.

Microgrid   A group of interconnected electrical loads and distributed energy resources with clearly defined boundaries that acts as a single controllable entity. Depending on the situation, microgrids may be either connected to a larger electrical grid or operate completely independently.

Minimum Viable Population   The level of population below which regeneration is negative, leading ultimately to extinction.

Model   Formal or informal framework for analysis that highlights some areas of the problem in order to better understand complex relationships.

Monopoly   A situation in which the seller side of the market is dominated by a single producer.

Montreal Protocol   An international agreement to control ozone-depleting gases.

Multilateral Fund   A fund set up by the parties to the Montreal Protocol to help developing countries meet the phase-out requirements for ozone-depleting gases.

Myopia   Nearsightedness; excessive concern for the present.

Natural Capital   The endowment of environmental and natural resources.

Natural Equilibrium   Stock levels of biological populations that persist in the absence of outside influences.

Natural Resource Curse Hypothesis   Suggests that countries with abundant natural resources are likely to grow more slowly than their lesser-endowed counterparts.

Negative Feedback Loop   A closed path of action and reaction that is self-limiting rather than self-reinforcing.

Negligence   A doctrine in tort law suggesting that the party responsible for a tortious act owes a duty to the affected party to exercise due care. Failure to fulfill that duty can lead to a requirement for the injurer to pay compensation to the victim.

Net Benefit   The excess of benefits over costs resulting from some allocation.

New Scrap   Waste composed of the residual materials generated during production. (Also called preconsumer scrap.)

New Source Review Process   All large new or expanding sources are subject to pre-construction review and permitting. These firms are typically subjected to more stringent requirements. The specific requirements depend on whether the source is attempting to locate in an attainment or a nonattainment area.

Nonattainment Region   A region in which the pollution concentrations exceed the ambient standards, so more stringent environmental regulations are in effect.

Noncompliance Penalty   A charge used to reduce the profitability of noncompliance with pollution control requirements. It is designed to eliminate all the economic advantage gained from noncompliance.

Nonconsumptive Use   In water law this refers to a use that does not involve diverting the water from the source or that does not diminish its availability. (Swimming, for example.)

Nonexcludability   No individual or group can be excluded from enjoying the benefits a resource may confer, whether they contribute to its provision or not.

Nongovernmental Organization (NGO)   A nonprofit, voluntary citizens' group, which is organized on a local, national, or international level to address issues in support of the public good.

Nonpoint Sources   Diffuse sources such as runoff from agricultural or developed land.

Nonrenewable Resources   Resources that cannot be reproduced during a human timescale, so their supply is considered finite and limited.

Nonuniformly Mixed Pollutants   For these pollutants, the damage they cause is a function not only of the amount of emissions but also of the location of the emissions sources. (Examples include particulates and lead.)

Nonuse (Passive-Use) Values   Resource values that arise from motivations other than personal use.

Normative Economics   The branch of economics that is concerned with evaluating the desirability of alternative resource allocations. It is concerned with "what ought to be."

Nutrient Sensitive Waters   Water bodies that have excessive levels of nutrients causing algal blooms, low oxygen levels, and increased fish kills.

Occupational Hazards   Risks undertaken during the course of a job.

Old Scrap   Waste recovered from products used by consumers. (Also called postconsumer scrap.)

Open-Access Resources   Common-pool resources with unrestricted access.

Open System   A system that imports and exports matter or energy.

Opportunity Cost   The net benefit forgone because the resource providing the service can no longer be used in its next-most-beneficial use.

Optimal   Best or most favorable option.

Optimization Procedure   A systematic method for finding the optimal means of accomplishing an objective.

Option Value   The value people place on having the option to use a resource in the future.

Output Measure   A measure currently used in national income accounting to indicate how many goods and services have been produced.

Overallocation   More than the optimal level of a resource is dedicated to a given use or time period.

Overshoot and Collapse   A forecast that involves exceeding the natural carrying capacity of the environment, with the consequence that society collapses.

Oxygen Sag   A point of low dissolved oxygen concentration generally located around effluent injection points.

Ozone-Depleting Gases   Global pollutants that destroy the stratospheric ozone layer. (Includes chlorofluorocarbons and halons, among others.)

Pareto Optimality   An allocation such that no reallocation of resources could benefit any person without lowering the net benefits for at least one other person. (Named after economist Vilfredo Pareto.)

Pay-as-You-Drive (PAYD) Insurance   A system in which an individual's annual premium for automobile insurance is calculated by multiplying a rating factor times the number of miles driven. It is designed to reduce inefficiency by internalizing those costs of accidents that are related to the amount of driving.

Peaking Units   Those electricity-producing facilities used only during peak periods. (They generally have low fixed costs, but high variable costs.)

Peak-Load Pricing   Charging resource users during the peak period the higher cost of supplying resources during that period. The surcharge during the peak period is designed to cover the cost of expansion since the need to expand is triggered by increased demands during the peak period.

Peak Periods   Times of especially high resource demand. (For example, the demand for electricity during the hottest part of the summer when air conditioning is in heavy use.)

Pecuniary Externalities   External effects that are transmitted through higher prices. (For example, the value of my land increases because surrounding employers expand their operations, thereby creating a scarcity of housing in the immediate area.) Unlike most externalities, pecuniary externalities do not generally result in inefficient allocations.

Performance Bond   An amount of money required to be placed into a trust fund by those initiating risky projects to cover the costs of any anticipated damages.

Persistent Pollutants   Inorganic synthetic pollutants with complex molecular structures that are not effectively broken down in water.

Planning Horizon   The time period over which the benefits and costs are considered in time-related decisions. For a specific investment such as a power plant, for example, the planning horizon might correspond to the useful life of the project. For forestry, it could either correspond to the age of the stand of trees when harvested (the finite planning horizon) or extend forever (the infinite planning horizon).

Point Sources   Sources of pollution that discharge effluent through a readily identifiable emission point such as an outfall or discharge pipe. (Most industrial and municipal sources are point sources.)

Pollution Havens Hypothesis   Stricter environmental regulations in one country either encourage domestic production facilities to locate in countries with less-stringent regulations or encourage increased imports from those countries.

Porter Induced Hypothesis   Firms facing stringent environmental regulations derive a competitive advantage because they are forced to innovate. Innovation typically increases productivity.

Positive Economics   The branch of economics that is concerned with describing alternative resource allocations without forming a judgment as to their desirability. Concerned with "what is."

Positive Feedback Loop   A closed path of action and reaction that is self-reinforcing rather than self-limiting.

Potential Reserves   The amount of resource reserves potentially available at different price levels.

Present Value   The current discounted value of a stream of benefits and/or costs over time.

Present Value Criterion   Resources should be allocated to those uses that maximize the present value of the net benefits received from all possible uses of those resources.

Price Controls   The establishment of maximum or minimum prices by the government.

Primary Effects   The direct, measurable effects of an action.

Primary Standard   An ambient air pollution standard designed to protect human health.

Prior Appropriation Doctrine   Entitlements for water are allocated to the agent who diverts and first puts water to a beneficial use.

Private Marginal Cost   The cost of producing an additional unit of the resource that is borne by the producer.

Producer Surplus   The value of a good or service to producers above the cost to them of producing it. Calculated as the area below the demand curve that is above marginal cost.

Product Charges   A charge imposed on a product that is associated with emissions (such as a gasoline tax). This indirect form of controlling emissions is used when placing the charge directly on emissions proves difficult.

Property Rights   A bundle of entitlements defining the owner's rights, privileges, and limitations for use of the resource.

Property Rules   Legal rules that govern the initial allocation of entitlements. Valuation of the entitlement is left to the market.

Property Tax   A tax on the value of land and the improvements on it.

Proposition 65   A California law that requires companies producing, using, or transporting one or more of the specified substances in amounts over the "safe harbor" threshold to notify those who are potentially impacted.

Public Good   A resource characterized by non-exclusivity and indivisibility.

Real Consumption Per Capita   Constant-dollar consumption divided by population.

Real Resource Costs   As opposed to transfer costs, these are costs borne by both private parties and society as a whole because they involve the loss of net benefits, not merely their transfer.

Rebound Effect   An increase in consumption that results from an energy-efficiency investment (i.e., lowers the amount of input energy necessary to produce a given level of useful energy services). Examples including driving more miles after acquiring a fuel-efficient car or turning up the target temperature after making your house more energy efficient.

Receiving Areas   Those areas under a transferable development rights system where rights acquired from owners in the sending area can be used.

Recycling Surcharge   Imposed at the time of commodity purchase, this charge attempts to recover from the consumer the cost of recycling and/or disposal of the commodity after its useful life.

Regional Pollutants Pollutants that can cause damage some distance from the emission source. (Examples include the precursors for acid rain and tropospheric ozone.)

Regressive Distribution Net benefits from a policy received by various income groups represent a larger portion of the income of the rich than of the poor.

Renewable Energy Credit An official record granted to producers of qualified renewable energy that can be sold separately from the energy to allow the recovery of the extra costs associated with renewable power. It can be used to prove compliance with a renewable portfolio standard.

Renewable Portfolio Standards These standards specify enforceable targets and deadlines for producing specific proportions of electricity from renewable resources.

Renewable Resources Resources that can be naturally regenerated over time on a human timescale.

Rent Seeking The use of resources in lobbying and other activities directed at securing increased profits through protective regulation or legislation.

Resilience The ability of a system or community, exposed to hazards, to resist, and/or recover in a timely and efficient manner, including through the preservation and restoration of its essential basic services and functions.

Res Nullius Regime A property rights system in which no one owns or exercises control over resources. Resources covered by this regime can usually be exploited on a first-come, first-served basis.

Resource Endowment The natural occurrence of resources in the earth's crust and atmosphere.

Resource Taxonomy A classification system used to characterize the nature of natural resource stocks in terms of the certainty of the stock estimates and the economic likelihood of their recovery.

Return Flow A term used in water management that refers to the unconsumed portion from an upstream user's water allocation that will eventually return to the watercourse (and, hence, be available to a downstream user).

Revenue-Neutral Tax or Fee A government charge that does not add to the total government revenue. This can be achieved by such means as rebating the revenue back to households or lowering the rates on existing charges such that the decrease in revenue from those sources equals the increase in revenue from the revenue-neutral source, leaving total revenue unchanged.

Riparian Rights Allocates the right to use water to the owner of the land adjacent to the water, as long as no adverse effects are imposed on other rights holders.

Risk-Free Cost of Capital Rate of return earned on an investment when the risk of earning more or less than expected returns is zero.

Risk-Neutrality Options that produce the same expected value are equally valued.

Risk Premium Additional rate of return required to compensate the owners of the capital when the expected and actual returns may differ. It represents compensation for a willingness to undertake some risk.

Scale Effects How the size of an operation affects average costs.

Scarcity Rent Producer's surplus that persists in long-run equilibrium due to fixed supply or increasing costs.

Secondary Effects Indirect consequences of an action; beyond primary effects.

Secondary Standard An ambient standard designed to protect those aspects of human welfare other than health.

Sending Areas Areas where the owners of land can sell rights in a transferable development rights system that can be used in receiving areas, but not the sending areas.

Senior Claims   Used in water management, this class of claims entitles the holder to a priority for specified amounts of water. These rights have a higher priority in times of low water availability than junior claims.

Social Cost of Carbon   The additional economic damage that would accrue from emitting one more ton of CO2 or CO2–equivalent into the atmosphere.

Socialist Economy   A centrally planned economy where the means of production are controlled by the government.

Social Marginal Cost   The cost of producing an additional unit of the resource that is borne by society at large. Generally includes private marginal costs plus external marginal costs.

Sprawl   An inefficient land use pattern where the uses are excessively dispersed.

Stable Equilibrium   A level of stock that will be restored following temporary shocks.

Starting-Point Bias   Arises when a contingent valuation survey respondent is asked to check off their answer from a predetermined range of possibilities and the answers depend on the range specified by the survey instrument.

Static Efficiency   The chief normative economic criterion for choosing among various allocations when time is not an important consideration. An allocation satisfies the static efficiency criterion if it maximizes the net benefits from all possible uses of the resource.

Static Efficient Sustained Yield   The sustained catch level in a fishery that produces the largest annual recurring net benefit.

Stationary Source   An immobile pollution source. (Factories, for example, as opposed to automobiles.)

Statistically Significant   Observed differences are unlikely to result from pure chance.

Stock Pollutants   Pollutants that accumulate in the environment because the environment has little or no absorptive capacity for them.

Strategic Bias   A respondent provides a biased answer to a contingent valuation survey in order to influence a particular outcome.

Strategic Petroleum Reserve   A petroleum stockpile established by an importing nation to minimize the damage that could be done by an embargo imposed by a foreign supplier. It would serve as an alternative source of supply for a short period.

Stratosphere   The atmosphere that lies above the troposphere. It extends to about 31 miles above the earth's surface.

Strict Liability   A tort law doctrine requiring that the party responsible for pollution contamination compensate victims for damage caused. Differs from negligence in that the victim does not have to prove that the injurer was negligent.

Suboptimal Allocation   An allocation that could be rearranged so that one or more people could be made better off while no one was made worse off. (Also called an inefficient allocation.)

Subsidies   Payments or tax breaks from the government that make the cost to the buyer lower than the marginal cost of production.

Substitution   Replacing one resource with another. May occur, for example, when the original resource is no longer cost effective or is diminishing in quantity or quality.

Sulfur Allowance Program   A transferable permit program targeted at electric utilities that was designed to reduce sulfur emissions from 1980 levels by 10 million tons. Involves an auction and an emissions cap.

Surface Water   The freshwater in rivers, lakes, and reservoirs that collects and flows on the earth's surface.

Sustainable Forestry   Forestry practices that are consistent with one of the definitions of sustainability, though most commonly this term refers to compatibility with the environmental sustainability criterion.

Sustainable Yield   Harvest levels that can be maintained indefinitely, achieved by setting the annual harvest equal to the annual net growth of the population.

Synergistic   The dose-response relationship is dependent upon several interrelated factors.

Systemic Risk   A risk posed when an event causes economic damages to part of the economy that results in secondary damages that spread throughout the entire economic system. First identified in finance, it is also called a non-diversifiable risk because it affects the entire portfolio.

"Take-Back" Principle   The belief that manufacturers of products should have the responsibility to take the packaging and the products back at the end of their useful lives in order to promote efficient packaging and recycling. (Also called extended producer responsibility.)

Tangible Benefits   Benefits that can reasonably be assigned a monetary value.

Technological Progress   An innovation in process or technique that allows more output or services to be derived from a given set of inputs.

Thermal Pollution   Pollution caused by the injection of heat into a watercourse.

Third Parties   Victims who have no contractual relationship to a pollution source. (They are neither consumers of the product produced by the source nor employed by the source.)

Total Cost   The sum of fixed and variable costs.

Toxicity   The degree of harm caused to living organisms as a result of exposure to the substance.

Toxic Release Inventory   A system for reporting toxic emissions releases from individual facilities in the United States. By making the data public, it was designed to warn communities of the risks they face and to encourage reductions prior to regulation.

Transaction Costs   Costs incurred in attempting to complete transactions. (For example, in buying a home, these might include payments to the broker for arranging the sale, to the bank for one-time special fees, and to the government for the required forms. The value of the time expended in negotiating would also be a transaction cost.)

Transferability   Property rights can be exchanged among owners on a voluntary basis.

Transfer Coefficient   A coefficient used in simulating pollutant flows. It relates the degree to which pollution concentrations at a specific receptor site are increased by a one-unit increase in emissions from a specific source.

Transfer Cost   A cost to a private party that is not a cost to society as a whole because it involves a transfer of net benefits from one private party to another.

Troposphere   The atmosphere that is closest to the earth. Its depth ranges from about 10 miles over the equator to about 5 miles over the poles.

Two-Part Charge   As used in water management, this type of charge combines volume pricing with a monthly fee that doesn't vary with the amount used. The monthly fee is designed to help cover fixed costs.

Underallocation   Less-than-optimal levels of a resource are dedicated to a given use or time period.

Uniform Emission Charge   A charge on effluent that applies the same per-unit rate to all sources regardless of their size or location.

Uniform Treatment A strategy to reduce effluent levels by the same specified percentage at each emissions level.

Uniformly Mixed Pollutants For these pollutants, the damage done to the environment depends on the amount of emissions that enters the atmosphere. The location of emissions is not a matter of policy concern. (Examples include ozone-depleting gases and greenhouse gases.)

User Cost Opportunity cost created by scarcity. It represents the value of an opportunity forgone when the resource can no longer be used in its next best use. (For example, for a unit of a depletable resource used now, the user cost is the net benefits that would have been received by saving it and using it during the next time period.)

Usufruct Right Holders of this right may use a resource (normally subject to restrictions), but do not have full ownership rights, such as the privilege of being able to sell it to someone else.

Variable Cost Production costs that vary with output.

Volume Pricing Making the cost of the service a function of the volume used. Used in both trash disposal and water distribution.

Welfare Measure A measure that reflects whether economic activity increases or decreases society's well-being.

Wet Deposition Occurs when air pollutants fall to land or water during rain or snow events.

Zero Discharge No emissions of the targeted pollutant are allowed.

Zero-Emission Vehicle Automobiles that directly emit no air pollutants. (Examples include vehicles powered by solar energy or fuel cells.)

Zoned Effluent Charge A charge on effluent that applies different per-unit rates to sources depending on their location. Generally sources closer to, and upstream from, locations with more serious pollution problems face higher rates.

Index

Pages in *italics* refer to figures, pages in **bold** refer to tables, and pages followed by "n" refer to notes.

Printed in the United States
by Baker & Taylor Publisher Services